Annual Editions: Physical Anthropology, 28/e

Elvio Angeloni

http://create.mheducation.com

ISBN-10: 1260180328   ISBN-13: 9781260180329

Contents

Unit 5 147

Unit 6 195

Unit 7 217

Detailed Table of Contents

Unit 2: Primates

No Alpha Males Allowed, Steve Kemper, *Smithsonian*, 2013
Karen Strier's research on the muriquis monkeys of Brazil has underscored the fact that primates are a varied group with diverse social structures and more complex behavior than ever thought before. They may even provide us with insights as to how our own ancestors came to the ground and became who we are today.

Love in the Time of Monkeys, Eduardo Fernandez-Duque and Benjamin Finkel, *Natural History*, 2014
Since monogamy is the standard among humans, but rare in the rest of the animal kingdom, it is instructive to examine why it exists in a species of monkey where it is apparently related to ecological resource distribution.

Becoming Jane, Tony Gerber, *National Geographic*, 2017
As a young Englishwoman with no formal scientific background, Jane Goodall managed to conduct chimpanzee research in Africa. Faced with the resistance of a primarily male science establishment, she revolutionized primate fieldwork and made significant, surprising discoveries. She went on to author dozens of books, mentor new generations of scientists, and promote wildlife conservation around the world.

The Gorillas Dian Fossey Saved, Elizabeth Royte, *National Geographic*, 2017
To some in Rwanda, she was a menacing intruder, but her fight against poachers kept mountain gorillas from being wiped out. Today, even with an uptick in population, the great apes face new challenges: the potential for disease spillover from human and livestock waste, a restricted range, climate change, and a loss of genetic diversity due to inbreeding.

The 2% Difference, Robert Sapolsky, *Discover*, 2006
Now that scientists have decoded the chimpanzee genome, we know that we share 98% of our DNA with chimps. So how can we be so different? The answer lies in the fact that a very few mutations make for some very big differences.

Dim Forest, Bright Chimps, Christophe Boesch and Hedwige Boesch-Achermann, *Natural History*, 1991
Contrary to expectations, forest-dwelling chimpanzees seem to be more committed to cooperative hunting and tool use than are savanna chimpanzees. Such findings may have implications for the understanding of the course of human evolution.

One for All, Frans de Waal, *Scientific American*, 2014
Although caring tendencies are common in primates, they seem to have become an absolute survival necessity in our human ancestors who came to cooperate with each other on a much more extensive level, shared in a reciprocal manner and identified with others in need, pain or distress.

Unit 3: Sex and Gender

Powers of Two, Blake Edgar, *Scientific American*, 2014
Theories abound as to why humans are primarily monogamous since most mammals are not, but pair-bonding does seems to have something to do with the way in which our ancestors cooperated in food-getting and sharing and what would seem to have been the most effective way to raise large-brained offspring in need of prolonged care.

When Do Girls Rule the Womb? Jennifer Abbasi, *Discover*, 2013
While demographers have pointed to cultural factors to explain the sex ratio imbalance which favors the birth of boys over girls in such societies as China, India and South Korea, they have not been able to explain why the same trends in sex ratio at birth exist in societies that do not value sons more than daughters and, furthermore, why in certain situations, regardless of cultural preferences, more girls may be born than boys. Perhaps an evolutionary model is in order.

Brains Are Not Male or Female, Jessica Hamzelou, *New Scientist*, 2015
Although there are hormonal differences between men and women that have to do with sexual and reproductive functions, the superficial differences in their brains have nothing to do with intellectual skills.

Promiscuous Men, Chaste Women, and Other Gender Myths, Cordelia Fine and Elgar Marka, *Scientific American*, 2017
Expanding upon Charles Darwin's theory of sexual selection, some evolutionary biologists have proposed that the males of many species (humans included) have evolved purely aesthetic traits, such as the peacock's tail, that appeal to females. The short

answer for this has to do with risk-taking males on the one hand and highly selective females on the other. There is much evidence to the contrary, however. In many cases, females are the greater risk-taker while males are being highly selective.

Preface

This edition of *Annual Editions: Physical Anthropology* contains a variety of articles relating to human evolution. The writings were selected for their timeliness, relevance to issues not easily treated in the standard physical anthropology textbooks, and clarity of presentation.

Whereas textbooks tend to reflect the consensus within the field, *Annual Editions: Physical Anthropology* provides a forum for the controversial. We do this in order to convey to the student that the study of human development is an evolving entity in which each discovery encourages further research and each added piece of the puzzle raises new questions about the total picture.

Our final criterion for selecting articles is readability. All too often, the excitement of a new discovery or a fresh idea is deadened by the weight of a ponderous presentation. We seek to avoid that by incorporating essays written with enthusiasm and with the desire to communicate some very special ideas to the general public.

Included in this volume are a number of features that are designed to make it useful for students, researchers, and professionals in the field of anthropology. Each unit is preceded by an overview, which provides a background for informed reading of the articles and emphasizes critical issues. *Learning Outcomes* accompany each article and outline the key concepts that students should focus on as they are reading the material. *Critical Thinking* questions, found at the end of each article, allow students to test their understanding of the key points of the article. The *Internet References* section can be used to further explore the topics online.

Those involved in producing this volume wish to make the next one as useful and effective as possible. Your criticism and advice are always welcome. Any anthology can be improved. This continues to be—annually.

Editor

Elvio Angeloni received his BA from UCLA in 1963, MA in anthropology from UCLA in 1965, and MA in communication arts from Loyola Marymount University in 1976. He received the Pasadena City College Outstanding Teacher Award in 2006 and has since retired from teaching. He has produced several films, including *Little Warrior,* winner of the Cinemedia VI Best Bicentennial Theme, and *Broken Bottles,* shown on PBS. He served as an academic adviser on the instructional television series *Faces of Culture.* He is also the academic editor of *Annual Editions: Anthropology* and co-editor of *Annual Editions: Archaeology.* His primary area of interest has been indigenous peoples of the American Southwest. Contact: evangeloni@gmail.com

Academic Advisory Board

Members of the Academic Advisory Board are instrumental in the final selection of articles for the *Annual Editions* series. Their review of the articles for content, level, and appropriateness provides critical direction to the editor(s) and staff. We think that you will find their careful consideration reflected in this book.

Unit 1

UNIT

Prepared by: Elvio Angeloni

Evolutionary Perspectives

As we reflect upon where the biological sciences have taken us over the past 300 years, we can see that we have been swept along a path of insight into the human condition, as well as into a heightened controversy on how to handle this potentially dangerous and/or unwanted knowledge of ourselves.

Certainly, Gregor Mendel, in the late nineteenth century, could not have anticipated that his study of pea plants would ultimately lead to the better understanding of over 3,000 genetically caused diseases, such as sickle-cell anemia, Huntington's chorea, Tay-Sachs, and hemophilia. Nor could he have foreseen the present-day controversies over matters such as cloning and genetic engineering. The significance of Mendel's work, of course, was his discovery that hereditary traits are conveyed by particular units that we now call "genes," a then-revolutionary notion that was later followed by a better understanding of how and why such units change. It is the knowledge of the process of "mutation," or alteration of the chemical structure of the gene, that is now providing us with the potential to control the genetic fate of individuals. This does not mean, however, that we should not continue to look at the role the environment plays in the development of what might be better termed as "genetically influenced conditions," such as alcoholism.

The other side of the evolutionary coin is natural selection, a concept provided by Charles Darwin and Alfred Wallace. Natural selection refers to the "weeding out" of unfavorable mutations and the perpetuation of favorable ones.

As our understanding of evolutionary processes becomes more refined, the theory of natural selection, unfortunately, continues to be poorly understood by the general public. Ever since Darwin published *On the Origin of Species* in 1859, for instance, there have been those who have embraced it as supportive of everything from communism to laissez-faire capitalism. But these interpretations say more about the theorists and their socioeconomic agenda than they do about the actual facts of human nature or even the social context in which human beings evolved. If the battle with "Social Darwinism" isn't enough, scientists throughout the same period of history have had to confront creationists with fallacies in their thinking as well as remind the rest of us why this battle is so important. There is something to be learned from these conflicts. Consider the claim of the "intelligent design theory" that nature is too orderly to have come about by a random process. What is missing from this view is the fact that natural selection is not a theory of chance, but is instead a process that results in the *appearance* of intentional design. In fact, what we see in nature is not the absolute perfection that one might expect from a purposeful god, but, rather, the somewhat orderly but less than ideal adaptation on the part of creatures that must make do with what they have. We must keep in mind that science is not simply an established and agreed-upon body of knowledge. Rather, it is a way of thinking and a method of investigation in which we seek understanding for its own sake and not for some comforting, preconceived ideas.

Article   Prepared by: Elvio Angeloni

The Facts of Evolution

Michael Shermer

Learning Outcomes

After reading this article, you will be able to:

- Discuss evolution as a *historical* science.
- Summarize the evidence for evolution.

> *The affinities of all the beings of the same class have sometimes been represented by a great tree. I believe this simile largely speaks the truth. As buds give rise by growth to fresh buds, and these, if vigorous, branch out and overtop on all sides many a feebler branch, so by generation I believe it has been with the great Tree of Life, which fills with its dead and broken branches the crust of the earth, and covers the surface with its ever branching and beautiful ramifications.*
>
> —Charles Darwin,
> On the Origin of Species, 1859

The theory of evolution has been under attack since Charles Darwin first published *On the Origin of Species* in 1859. From the start, its critics have seized on the *theory* of evolution to try to undermine its facts. But all great works of science are written in support of some particular view. In 1861, shortly after he published his new theory, Darwin wrote a letter to his colleague, Henry Fawcett, who had just attended a special meeting of the British Association for the Advancement of Science during which Darwin's book was debated. One of the naturalists had argued that *On the Origin of Species* was too theoretical, that Darwin should have just "put his facts before us and let them rest." In response, Darwin reflected that science, to be of any service, required more than list-making; it needed larger ideas that could make sense of piles of data. Otherwise, Darwin said, a geologist "might as well go into a gravelpit and count the pebbles and describe the colours." Data without generalizations are useless; facts without explanatory principles are meaningless. A "theory" is not just someone's opinion or a wild guess made by some scientist. A theory is a well-supported and well-tested generalization that explains a set of observations. Science without theory is useless.

The process of science is fueled by what I call *Darwin's Dictum*, defined by Darwin himself in his letter to Fawcett: "all observation must be for or against some view if it is to be of any service."

Darwin's casual comment nearly a hundred and fifty years ago encapsulates a serious debate about the relative roles of data and theory, or observations and conclusions, in science. In a science like evolution, in which inferences about the past must be made from scant data in the present, this debate has been exploded to encompass a fight between religion and science.

Prediction and Observation

Most essentially, *evolution is a historical science*. Darwin valued above all else prediction and verification by subsequent observation. In an act of brilliant historical science, for example, Darwin correctly developed a theory of coral reef evolution years before he developed his theory of biological evolution. He had never seen a coral reef, but during the *Beagle*'s famous voyage to the Galápagos, he had studied the types of coral reefs Charles Lyell described in *Principles of Geology*. Darwin reasoned that the different examples of coral reefs did not represent different types, each of which needed a different causal explanation; rather, the different examples represented different stages of development of coral reefs, for which only a single cause was needed. Darwin considered this a triumph of theory in driving scientific investigation: Theoretical prediction was followed by observational verification, whereby "I had therefore only to verify and extend my views by a careful examination of coral reefs." In this case, the theory came first, then the data.

The publication of the *Origin of Species* triggered a roaring debate about the relative roles of data and theory in science. Darwin's "bulldog" defender, Thomas Henry Huxley, erupted in a paroxysm against those who pontificated on science but had never practiced it themselves: "There cannot be a doubt that the method of inquiry which Mr. Darwin has adopted is not only rigorously in accord with the canons of scientific logic, but that it is the only adequate method," Huxley wrote. Those "critics exclusively trained in classics or in mathematics, who have never determined a scientific fact in their lives by induction from experiment or observation, prate learnedly about Mr. Darwin's method," he bellowed, "which is not inductive enough, not Baconian enough, forsooth for them."

Darwin insisted that theory comes to and from the facts, not from political or philosophical beliefs, whether from God or the godfather of scientific empiricism. It is a point he voiced succinctly in his cautions to a young scientist. The facts speak for themselves, he said, advising "the advantage, at present, of being very sparing in introducing theory in your papers; let theory guide your observations, but till your reputation is well established, be sparing of publishing theory. It makes persons doubt your observations." Once Darwin's reputation was well established, he published his book that so well demonstrated the power of theory. As he noted in his autobiography, "some of my critics have said, 'Oh, he is a good observer, but has no power of reasoning.' I do not think that this can be true, for the *Origin of Species* is one long argument from the beginning to the end, and it has convinced not a few able men."

Against Some View

Darwin's "one long argument" was with the theologian William Paley and the theory Paley posited in his 1802 book, *Natural Theology: or, Evidences of the Existence and Attributes of the Deity, Collected from the Appearances of Nature.* Sound eerily familiar? The scholarly agenda of this first brand of Intelligent Design was to correlate the works of God (nature) with the words of God (the Bible). Natural theology kicked off with John Ray's 1691 *Wisdom of God Manifested in Works of the Creation,* which itself was inspired by Psalms 19:11: "The Heavens declare the Glory of the Lord and the Firmament sheweth his handy work." John Ray, in what still stands as a playbook for creationism, explains the analogy between human and divine creations: If a "curious Edifice or machine" leads us to "infer the being and operation of some intelligent Architect or Engineer," shouldn't the same be said of "the Works of nature, that Grandeur and magnificence, that excellent contrivance for Beauty, Order, use, &c. which is observable in them, wherein they do as much transcend the Efforts of human Art and infinite Power and Wisdom exceeds finite" to make us

"infer the existence and efficiency of an Omnipotent and All-wise Creator"?

Paley advanced Ray's work through the accumulated knowledge of a century of scientific exploration. The opening passage of Paley's *Natural Theology* has become annealed into our culture as the winningly accessible and thus appealing "watchmaker" argument:

> In crossing a heath, suppose I pitched my foot against a stone, and were asked how the stone came to be there. I might possibly answer, that, for any thing I knew to the contrary, it had lain there forever. But suppose I had found a watch upon the ground, and it should be enquired how the watch happened to be in that place. The inference, we think, is inevitable; that the watch must have had a maker; that there must have existed, at some time and in some place or other, an artificer or artificers who formed it for the purpose which we find it actually to answer; who comprehended its construction, and designed its use.

But life is far more complex than a watch—so the design inference is even stronger!

> There cannot be design without a designer; contrivance without a contriver . . . The marks of design are too strong to be got over. Design must have had a designer. That designer must have been a person. That person is GOD.

For longer than we have had the theory of evolution, we have had theologians arguing for Intelligent Design.

From Natural Theology to Natural Selection

After abandoning medical studies at Edinburgh University, Charles Darwin entered the University of Cambridge to study theology with the goal of becoming a Church of England cleric. Natural theology provided him with a socially acceptable excuse to study natural history, his true passion. It also educated Darwin in the arguments on design popularized by Paley and others. His intimacy with their ideas was respectful, not combative. For example, in November 1859, the same month that the *Origin of Species* was published, Darwin wrote his friend John Lubbock, "I do not think I hardly ever admired a book more than Paley's 'Natural Theology.' I could almost formerly have said it by heart." Both Paley and Darwin addressed a problem in nature: the origin of the design of life. Paley's answer was to posit a top-down designer—God. Darwin's answer was to posit a bottom-up designer—natural selection. Natural theologians took this to mean that evolution was an attack on God, without giving much thought to what evolution is.

Ever since Darwin, much has been written about what, exactly, evolution is. Ernst Mayr, arguably the greatest evolutionary theorist since Darwin, offers a subtly technical definition: "evolution is change in the adaptation and in the diversity of populations of organisms." He notes that evolution has a dual nature, a "'vertical' phenomenon of adaptive change," which describes how a species responds to its environment over time, and a "'horizontal' phenomenon of populations, incipient species, and new species," which describes adaptations that break through the genetic divide. And I'll never forget Mayr's definition of a species, because I had to memorize it in my first course on evolutionary biology: "A species is a group of actually or potentially interbreeding natural populations reproductively isolated from other such populations."

Mayr outlines five general tenets of evolutionary theory that have been discovered in the years since Darwin published his revolutionary book:

1. *Evolution:* Organisms change through time. Both the fossil record of life's history and nature today document and reveal this change.
2. *Descent with modification:* Evolution proceeds through the branching of common descent. As every parent and child knows, offspring are similar to but not exact replicas of their parents, producing the necessary variation that allows adaptation to the ever-changing environment.
3. *Gradualism:* All this change is slow, steady, and stately. Given enough time, small changes within a species can accumulate into large changes that create new species; that is, macro-evolution is the cumulative effect of microevolution.
4. *Multiplication:* Evolution does not just produce new species; it produces an increasing number of new species.

And, of course,

5. *Natural selection:* Evolutionary change is not haphazard and random; it follows a selective process. Codiscovered by Darwin and the naturalist Alfred Russel Wallace, natural selection operates under five rules:

   A. Populations tend to increase indefinitely in a geometric ratio: 2, 4, 8, 16, 32, 64, 128, 256, 512, 1024 . . .
   B. In a natural environment, however, population numbers must stabilize at a certain level. The population cannot increase to infinity—the earth is just not big enough.
   C. Therefore, there must be a "struggle for existence." Not all of the organisms produced can survive.
   D. There is variation in every species.
   E. Therefore, in the struggle for existence, those individuals with variations that are better adapted to the

environment leave behind more offspring than individuals that are less well adapted. This is known as *differential reproductive success.*

As Darwin said, "as more individuals are produced than can possibly survive, there must in every case be a struggle for existence, either one individual with another of the same species, or with the individuals of distinct species, or with the physical conditions of life."

The process of natural selection, when carried out over countless generations, gradually leads varieties of species to develop into new species. Darwin explained:

It may be said that natural selection is daily and hourly scrutinising, throughout the world, every variation, even the slightest; rejecting that which is bad, preserving and adding up all that is good; silently and insensibly working, whenever and wherever opportunity offers, at the improvement of each organic being in relation to its organic and inorganic conditions of life. We see nothing of these slow changes in progress, until the hand of time has marked the long lapses of ages, and then so imperfect is our view into long past geological ages, that we only see that the forms of life are now different from what they formerly were.

The time frame is long and the changes from generation to generation are subtle. This may be one of the most important and difficult points to grasp about the theory of evolution. It is tempting to see species as they exist today as a living monument to evolution, to condense evolution into the incorrect but provocative shorthand that humans descended from chimpanzees—a shorthand that undercuts the facts of evolution.

Natural selection is the process of organisms struggling to survive and reproduce, with the result of propagating their genes into the next generation. As such, it operates primarily at the local level. The Oxford evolutionary biologist Richard Dawkins elegantly described the process as "random mutation plus non-random cumulative selection," emphasizing the non-random. Evolution is not the equivalent of a warehouse full of parts randomly assorting themselves into a jumbo jet, as the creationists like to argue. If evolution were truly random there would be no biological jumbo jets. Genetic mutations and the mixing of parental genes in offspring may be random, but the selection of genes through the survival of their hosts is anything but random. Out of this process of self-organized directional selection emerge complexity and diversity.

Natural selection is a description of a process, not a force. No one is "selecting" organisms for survival or extinction, in the benign sense of dog breeders selecting for desirable traits in show breeds, or in the malignant sense of Nazis selecting prisoners at Auschwitz-Birkenau. Natural selection, and thus evolution, is unconscious and nonprescient—it cannot look forward to anticipate what changes are going to be needed for survival. The evolutionary watchmaker is blind, says Dawkins, *pace* Paley.

By way of example, once when my young daughter asked how evolution works, I used the polar bear as an example of a "transitional species" between land mammals and marine mammals, because although they are land mammals they spend so much time in the water that they have acquired many adaptations to an aquatic life. But this is not correct. It implies that polar bears are *on their way* (in transition) to becoming marine mammals. They aren't. Polar bears are not "becoming" anything. Polar bears are well adapted for their lifestyle. That's all. If global warming continues, perhaps polar bears will adapt to a full-time aquatic existence, or perhaps they will move south and become smaller brown bears, or perhaps they will go extinct. Who knows? No one.

Where Are All the Fossils?

Evolution is a historical science, and historical data—fossils— are often the evidence most cited for and against it. In the creationist textbook, *Of Pandas and People*—one of the bones of contention in the 2005 Intelligent Design trial of *Kitzmiller et al. v. Dover Area School District*, in Dover, Pennsylvania—the authors state: "Design theories suggest that various forms of life began with their distinctive features already intact: fish with fins and scales, birds with feathers and wings, mammals with fur and mammary glands . . . Might not gaps exist . . . not because large numbers of transitional forms mysteriously failed to fossilize, but because they never existed?"

Darwin himself commented on this lack of transitional fossils, asking, "Why then is not every geological formation and every stratum full of such intermediate links?" In contemplating the answer, he turned to the data and noted that "geology assuredly does not reveal any such finely graduated organic chain; and this, perhaps, is the gravest objection which can be urged against my theory." So where *are* all the fossils?

One answer to Darwin's dilemma is the exceptionally low probability of any dead animal's escaping the jaws and stomachs of predators, scavengers, and detritus feeders, reaching the stage of fossilization, and then somehow finding its way back to the surface through geological forces and unpredictable events to be discovered millions of years later by the handful of paleontologists looking for its traces. Given this reality, it is remarkable that we have as many fossils as we do.

There is another explanation for the missing fossils. Ernst Mayr outlines the most common way that a species gives rise to a new species: when a small group (the "founder" population) breaks away and becomes geographically—and thus reproductively— isolated from its ancestral group. As long as it remains small

and detached, the founder group can experience fairly rapid genetic changes, especially relative to large populations, which tend to sustain their genetic homogeneity through diverse interbreeding. Mayr's theory, called *allopatric speciation,* helps to explain why so few fossils would exist for these animals.

The evolutionary theorists Niles Eldredge and Stephen Jay Gould took Mayr's observations about how new species emerge and applied them to the fossil record, finding that gaps in the fossil record are not missing evidence of gradual changes; they are extant evidence of punctuated changes. They called this theory *punctuated equilibrium.* Species are so static and enduring that they leave plenty of fossils in the strata while they are in their stable state (equilibrium). The change from one species to another, however, happens relatively quickly on a geological time scale, and in these smaller, geographically isolated population groups (punctuated). In fact, species change happens so rapidly that few "transitional" carcasses create fossils to record the change. Eldredge and Gould conclude that "breaks in the fossil record are real; they express the way in which evolution occurs, not the fragments of an imperfect record." Of course, the small group will also be reproducing, following the geometric increases that are observed in all species, and will eventually form a relatively large population of individuals that retain their phenotype for a considerable time—and leave behind many well-preserved fossils. Millions of years later this process results in a fossil record that records mostly the equilibrium. The punctuation is in the blanks.

The Evidence of Evolution

In August 1996, NASA announced that it discovered life on Mars. The evidence was the Allan Hills 84001 rock, believed to have been ejected out of Mars by a meteor impact millions of years ago, which then fell into an orbit that brought it to Earth. On the panel of NASA experts was paleobiologist William Schopf, a specialist in ancient microbial life. Schopf was skeptical of NASA's claim because, he said, the four "lines of evidence" claimed to support the find did not converge toward a single conclusion. Instead, they pointed to several possible conclusions.

Schopf's analysis of "lines of evidence" reflects a method of science first described by the nineteenth-century philosopher of science William Whewell. To prove a theory, Whewell believed, one must have more than one induction, more than a single generalization drawn from specific facts. One must have multiple inductions that converge upon one another, independently but in conjunction. Whewell said that if these inductions "jump together" it strengthens the plausibility of a theory: "Accordingly the cases in which inductions from classes of facts altogether different have thus jumped together, belong only to the best established theories which the history of science contains. And, as I shall have occasion to refer to this particular feature in their evidence, I will take the liberty of describing it by a particular phrase; and will term it the Consilience of Inductions." I call it a *convergence of evidence.*

Just as detectives employ the convergence of evidence technique to deduce who most likely committed a crime, scientists employ the method to deduce the likeliest explanation for a particular phenomenon. Cosmologists reconstruct the history of the universe through a convergence of evidence from astronomy, planetary geology, and physics. Geologists reconstruct the history of the planet through a convergence of evidence from geology, physics, and chemistry. Archaeologists piece together the history of civilization through a convergence of evidence from biology (pollen grains), chemistry (kitchen middens), physics (potsherds, tools), history (works of art, written sources), and other site-specific artifacts.

As a historical science, evolution is confirmed by the fact that so many independent lines of evidence converge to its single conclusion. Independent sets of data from geology, paleontology, botany, zoology, herpetology, entomology, biogeography, comparative anatomy and physiology, genetics and population genetics, and many other sciences each point to the conclusion that life evolved. This is a convergence of evidence. Creationists can demand "just one fossil transitional form" that shows evolution. But evolution is not proved through a single fossil. It is proved through a convergence of fossils, along with a convergence of genetic comparisons between species, and a convergence of anatomical and physiological comparisons between species, and many other lines of inquiry. For creationists to disprove evolution, they need to unravel all these independent lines of evidence, as well as construct a rival theory that can explain them better than the theory of evolution. They have yet to do so.

The Tests of Evolution

Creationists like to argue that evolution is not a science because no one was there to observe it and there are no experiments to run today to test it. The inability to observe past events or set up controlled experiments is no obstacle to a sound science of cosmology, geology, or archaeology, so why should it be for a sound science of evolution? The key is the ability to test one's hypothesis. There are a number of ways to do so, starting with the broadest method of how we know evolution happened.

Consider the evolution of our best friend, the dog. With so many breeds of dogs popular for so many thousands of years, one would think that there would be an abundance of transitional fossils providing paleontologists with copious data from which to reconstruct their evolutionary ancestry. Not

so. In fact, according to Jennifer A. Leonard of the National Museum of Natural History in Washington, D.C., "the fossil record from wolves to dogs is pretty sparse." Then how do we know the origin of dogs? In a 2002 issue of *Science,* Leonard and her colleagues report that mitochrondrial DNA (mtDNA) data from early dog remains "strongly support the hypothesis that ancient American and Eurasian domestic dogs share a common origin from Old World gray wolves." In the same issue of *Science,* Peter Savolainen from the Royal Institute of Technology in Stockholm and his colleagues note that the fossil record is problematic "because of the difficulty in discriminating between small wolves and domestic dogs," but their study of mtDNA sequence variation among 654 domestic dogs from around the world "points to an origin of the domestic dog in East Asia ~15,000 yr B.P." from a single gene pool of wolves. Finally, Brian Hare from Harvard and his colleagues describe the results of their study in which they found that domestic dogs are more skillful than wolves at using human communicative signals indicating the location of hidden food, but that "dogs and wolves do not perform differently in a nonsocial memory task, ruling out the possibility that dogs outperform wolves in all human-guided tasks." Therefore, "dogs' social-communicative skills with humans were acquired during the process of domestication." Although no single fossil proves that dogs came from wolves, the convergence of evidence from archaeological, morphological, genetic, and behavioral "fossils"reveals the ancestor of all dogs to be the East Asian wolf.

The tale of human evolution is revealed in a similar manner (although here we do have an abundance of transitional fossil riches), as it is for all ancestors in the history of life. One of the finest compilations of evolutionary convergence is Richard Dawkins's magnum opus, *The Ancestor's Tale,* 673 pages of convergent science recounted with literary elegance. Dawkins traces innumerable "transitional fossils" (what he calls "concestors"—the "point of rendezvous" of the last common ancestor shared by a set of species) from *Homo sapiens* back four billion years to the origin of replicating molecules and the emergence of evolution. No one concestor proves that evolution happened, but together they reveal a majestic story of a process over time. We know human evolution happened because innumerable bits of data from myriad fields of science conjoin to paint a rich portrait of life's pilgrimage.

But the convergence of evidence is just the start. The *comparative method* allows us to infer evolutionary relationships using data from a wide variety of fields. Luigi Luca Cavalli-Sforza and his colleagues, for example, compared fifty years of data from population genetics, geography, ecology, archaeology, physical anthropology, and linguistics to trace the evolution of the human races. Using both the convergence and comparative methods led them to conclude that "the major stereotypes, all based on skin color, hair color and form, and facial traits, reflect superficial differences that are not confirmed by deeper analysis with more reliable genetic traits." By comparing surface (physical) traits—the phenotype of individuals—with genetic traits—the genotype—they teased out the relationship between different groups of people. Most interesting, they found that the genetic traits disclosed "recent evolution mostly under the effect of climate and perhaps sexual selection." For example, they discovered that Australian aborigines are genetically more closely related to southeast Asians than they are to African blacks, which makes sense from the perspective of the evolutionary timeline: The migration pattern of humans out of Africa would have led them first to Asia and then to Australia.

Dating techniques provide evidence of the timeline of evolution. The dating of fossils, along with the earth, moon, sun, solar system, and universe, are all tests of evolutionary theory, and so far they have passed all the tests. We know that the earth is approximately 4.6 billion years old because of the convergence of evidence from several methods of dating rocks: Uranium Lead, Rubidium Strontium, and Carbon-14. Further, the age of the earth, the age of the moon, the age of the sun, the age of the solar system, and the age of the universe are consistent, maintaining yet another consilience. If, say, the earth was dated at 4.6 billion years old but the solar system was dated at one million years old, the theory of evolution would be in trouble. But Uranium Lead, Rubidium Strontium, and Carbon-14 have not provided any good news for the so-called Young Earth creationists.

Better yet, the fossils and organisms speak for themselves. *Fossils do show intermediate stages,* despite their rarity. For example, there are now at least eight intermediate fossil stages identified in the evolution of whales. In human evolution, there are at least a dozen known intermediate fossil stages since hominids branched off from the great apes six million years ago. *And geological strata consistently reveal the same sequence of fossils.* A quick and simple way to debunk the theory of evolution would be to find a fossil horse in the same geological stratum as a trilobite. According to evolutionary theory, trilobites and mammals are separated by hundreds of millions of years. If such a fossil juxtaposition occurred, and it was not the product of some geological anomaly (such as uplifted, broken, bent, or even flipped strata—all of which occur but are traceable), it would mean that there was something seriously wrong with the theory of evolution.

Evolution also posits that *modern organisms should show a variety of structures from simple to complex, reflecting an evolutionary history rather than an instantaneous creation.* The human eye, for example, is the result of a long and complex pathway that goes back hundreds of millions of years.

Initially a simple eyespot with a handful of light-sensitive cells that provided information to the organism about an important source of the light, it developed into a recessed eyespot, where a small surface indentation filled with light-sensitive cells provided additional data on the direction of light; then into a deep recession eyespot, where additional cells at greater depth provide more accurate information about the environment; then into a pinhole camera eye that is able to focus an image on the back of a deeply recessed layer of light-sensitive cells; then into a pinhole lens eye that is able to focus the image; then into a complex eye found in such modern mammals as humans. All of these structures are expressed in modern eyes.

Further, *biological structures show signs of natural design.* The anatomy of the human eye, in fact, shows anything but "intelligence" in its design. It is built upside down and backwards, requiring photons of light to travel through the cornea, lens, aqueous fluid, blood vessels, ganglion cells, amacrine cells, horizontal cells, and bipolar cells before they reach the light-sensitive rods and cones that transduce the light signal into neural impulses—which are then sent to the visual cortex at the back of the brain for processing into meaningful patterns. For optimal vision, why would an intelligent designer have built an eye upside down and backwards? This "design" makes sense only if natural selection built eyes from available materials, and in the particular configuration of the ancestral organism's preexisting organic structures. The eye shows the pathways of evolutionary history, not of intelligent design.

Additionally, *vestigial structures stand as evidence of the mistakes, the misstarts, and, especially, the leftover traces of evolutionary history.* The cretaceous snake *Pachyrhachis problematicus,* for example, had small hind limbs used for locomotion that it inherited from its quadrupedal ancestors, gone in today's snakes. Modern whales retain a tiny pelvis for hind legs that existed in their land mammal ancestors but have disappeared today. Likewise, there are wings on flightless birds, and of course humans are replete with useless vestigial structures, a distinctive sign of our evolutionary ancestry. A short list of just ten vestigial structures in humans leaves one musing: Why would an Intelligent Designer have created these?

1. *Male nipples.* Men have nipples because females need them, and the overall architecture of the human body is more efficiently developed in the uterus from a single developmental structure.

2. *Male uterus.* Men have the remnant of an undeveloped female reproductive organ that hangs off the prostate gland for the same reason.

3. *Thirteenth rib.* Most modern humans have twelve sets of ribs, but 8 percent of us have a thirteenth set, just like chimpanzees and gorillas. This is a remnant of our primate ancestry: We share common ancestors with

chimps and gorillas, and the thirteenth set of ribs has been retained from when our lineage branched off six million years ago.

4. *Coccyx.* The human tailbone is all that remains from our common ancestors' tails, which were used for grasping branches and maintaining balance.

5. *Wisdom teeth.* Before stone tools, weapons, and fire, hominids were primarily vegetarians, and as such we chewed a lot of plants, requiring an extra set of grinding molars. Many people still have them, despite the smaller size of our modern jaws.

6. *Appendix.* This muscular tube connected to the large intestine was once used for digesting cellulose in our largely vegetarian diet before we became meat eaters.

7. *Body hair.* We are sometimes called "the naked ape"; however, most humans have a layer of fine body hair, again left over from our evolutionary ancestry from thick-haired apes and hominids.

8. *Goose bumps.* Our body hair ancestry can also be inferred from the fact that we retain the ability of our ancestors to puff up their fur for heat insulation, or as a threat gesture to potential predators. Erector pili— "goose bumps"—are a telltale sign of our evolutionary ancestry.

9. *Extrinsic ear muscles.* If you can wiggle your ears you can thank our primate ancestors, who evolved the ability to move their ears independently of their heads as a more efficient means of discriminating precise sound directionality and location.

10. *Third eyelid.* Many animals have a nictitating membrane that covers the eye for added protection; we retain this "third eyelid" in the corner of our eye as a tiny fold of flesh.

Evolutionary scientists can provide dozens more examples of vestigial structures—let alone examples of how we know evolution happened from all of these other various lines of historical evidence. Yet as a science, evolution depends primarily on the ability to test a hypothesis. How can we ever test an evolutionary hypothesis if we cannot go into a lab and create a new species naturally?

I once had the opportunity to help dig up a dinosaur with Jack Horner, the curator of paleontology at the Museum of the Rockies in Bozeman, Montana. As Horner explains in his book *Digging Dinosaurs,* "paleontology is not an experimental science; it's a historical science. This means that paleontologists are seldom able to test their hypotheses by laboratory experiments, but they can still test them." Horner discusses this process of historical science at the famous dig in which he exposed the first dinosaur eggs ever found in North America. The initial stage of the dig was "getting the fossils out of the ground." Unsheathing the bones from the overlying and surrounding stone is backbreaking work. As you move from jackhammers and pickaxes to dental tools and small brushes, historical interpretation accelerates as a function of the rate of bone unearthed. Then, in the second phase of a dig, he gets "to look at the fossils, study them, make hypotheses based on what we saw and try to prove or disprove them."

When I arrived at Horner's camp I expected to find the busy director of a fully sponsored dig barking out orders to his staff. I was surprised to come upon a patient historical scientist, sitting cross-legged before a cervical vertebra from a 140-million-year-old *Apatosaurus* (formerly known as *Brontosaurus*), wondering what to make of it. Soon a reporter from a local paper arrived inquiring of Horner what this discovery meant for the history of dinosaurs. Did it change any of his theories? Where was the head? Was there more than one body at this site? Horner's answers were those of a cautious scientist: "I don't know yet." "Beats me." "We need more evidence." "We'll have to wait and see." It was historical science at its best.

After two long days of exposing nothing but solid rock and my own ineptness at seeing bone within stone, one of the paleontologists pointed out that the rock I was about to toss away was a piece of bone that appeared to be part of a rib. If it was a rib, then the bone should retain its riblike shape as more of the overburden was chipped away. This it did for about a foot, until it suddenly flared to the right. Was it a rib, or something else? Horner moved in to check. "It could be part of the pelvis," he suggested. If it was part of the pelvis, then it should also flare out to the left when more was uncovered. Sure enough, Horner's prediction was verified by further digging.

In science, this process is called the *hypothetico-deductive method,* in which one forms a hypothesis based on existing data, deduces a prediction from the hypothesis, then tests the prediction against further data. For example, in 1981 Horner discovered a site in Montana that contained approximately thirty million fossil fragments of approximately ten thousand *Maiasaurs* in a bed measuring 1.25 miles by .25 miles. His hypothesizing began with a question: "What could such a deposit represent?" There was no evidence that predators had chewed the bones, yet many were broken in half lengthwise. Further, the bones were all arranged from east to west—the long dimension of the bone deposit. Small bones had been separated from bigger bones, and there were no bones of baby *Maiasaurs,* only those of individuals between nine and twenty-three feet long. What would cause the bones to splinter lengthwise? Why would the small bones be separated from the big bones? Was this one giant herd, all killed at the same time, or was it a dying ground over many years?

An early hypothesis—that a mud flow buried the herd alive—was rejected because "it didn't make sense that even the most powerful flow of mud could break bones lengthwise . . . nor did it make sense that a herd of living animals buried in mud would end up with all their skeletons disarticulated." Horner constructed another hypothesis. "It seemed that there had to be a twofold event," he reasoned, "the dinosaurs dying in one incident and the bones being swept away in another." Since there was a layer of volcanic ash 1.5 feet above the bone bed, volcanic activity was implicated in the death of the herd. Horner then deduced that only fossil bones would split lengthwise, and therefore the damage to the bones had occurred long after the dying event. His hypothesis and deduction led to his conclusion that the herd was "killed by the gases, smoke and ash of a volcanic eruption. And if a huge eruption killed them all at once, then it might have also killed everything else around." Then perhaps there was a flood, maybe from a breached lake, carrying the rotting bodies downstream, separating the big bones from the small, lighter bones, and giving the bones a uniform orientation.

A paleontological dig is a good example of how hypothetico-deductive reasoning and historical sciences can make predictions based on initial data that are then verified or rejected by later historical evidence. Evolutionary theory is rooted in a rich array of data from the past that, while nonreplicable in a laboratory, are nevertheless valid sources of information that can be used to piece together specific events and test general hypotheses. While the specifics of evolution—how quickly it happens, what triggers species change, at which level of the organism it occurs—are still being studied and unraveled, the general theory of evolution is the most tested in science over the past century and a half. Scientists agree: Evolution happened.

Critical Thinking

1. What is the point Shermer is trying to make in this article?
2. What was Darwin's contribution to our understanding of coral reefs?
3. Who was Darwin's "one long argument" with? What was his view? How was it different from the Darwinian one?

4. What did Ernst Mayr mean when he asserted that evolution has both "horizontal" and "vertical" dimensions?
5. What five tenets of evolution does Mayr outline? Describe each.
6. What, according to Shermer, is "one of the most important and difficult points to grasp about evolution?" Why do you think this is?
7. What are the random and non-random processes in evolution as identified by Richard Dawkins? What makes them random and non-random respectively?
8. What was wrong with Shermer's example of a "polar bear" as a transitional species when he was talking to his daughter?
9. Why are fossils so difficult to come by?
10. Why is it that genetic change can occur more quickly in small groups? Why is this important for the evolution of new species?
11. What does Shermer mean by the "convergence of evidence"?
12. How long ago did the domestic dog "evolve"? Why does Shermer use this as an example of the way science works?
13. What is the "comparative method"?
14. What other lines of evidence mentioned by Shermer support the evolution?
15. What human vestigial structures does he mention? What is the evolutionary reason for their existence? Discuss the likely original function of at least four of these supposedly meaningless features.

Internet References

American Anthropologist Association
   www.aaanet.org

Charles Darwin on Human Origins
   www.literature.org/Works/Charles-Darwin

Enter Evolution: Theory and History
   www.ucmp.berkeley.edu/history/evolution.html

Fossil Hominids FAQ
   www.talkorigins.org/faqs/homs

Harvard Dept. of MCB–Biology Links
   http://mcb.harvard.edu/BioLinks.html

Article

Prepared by: Elvio Angeloni

Evolution in Action

Finches, monkeyflowers, sockeye salmon, and bacteria are changing before our eyes.

JONATHAN WEINER

Learning Outcomes

After reading this article, you will be able to:

- Explain the ways in which human ecological pressure is bringing about "evolution in action" in wildlife.

- Discuss the various ways in which evolution is being observed and documented.

C harles Darwin's wife, Emma, was terrified that they would be separated for eternity, because she would go to heaven and he would not. Emma confessed her fears in a letter that Charles kept and treasured, with his reply to her scribbled in the margin: "When I am dead, know that many times, I have kissed and cryed over this."

Close as they were, the two could hardly bear to talk about Darwin's view of life. And today, those of us who live in the United States, by many measures the world's leading scientific nation, find ourselves in a house divided. Half of us accept Darwin's theory, half of us reject it, and many people are convinced that Darwin burns in hell. I find that old debate particularly strange, because I've spent some of the best years of my life as a science writer peering over the shoulders of biologists who actually watch Darwin's process in action. What they can see casts the whole debate in a new light—or it should.

Darwin himself never tried to watch evolution happen. "It may metaphorically be said," he wrote in the *Origin of Species,*

> that natural selection is daily and hourly scrutinizing, throughout the world, the slightest variations; rejecting those that are bad, preserving and adding up all that are good; silently and insensibly working, whenever and

wherever opportunity offers. . . . We see nothing of these slow changes in progress, until the hand of time has marked the lapse of ages.

Darwin was a modest man who thought of himself as a plodder (one of his favorite mottoes was, "It's dogged as does it"). He thought evolution plodded too. If so, it would be more boring to watch evolution than to watch drying paint. As a result, for several generations after Darwin's death, almost nobody tried. For most of the twentieth century the only well-known example of evolution in action was the case of peppered moths in industrial England. The moth had its picture in all the textbooks, as a kind of special case.

Then, in 1973, a married pair of evolutionary biologists, Peter and Rosemary Grant, now at Princeton University, began a study of Darwin's process in Darwin's islands, the Galápagos, watching Darwin's finches. At first, they assumed that they would have to infer the history of evolution in the islands from the distribution of the various finch species, varieties, and populations across the archipelago. That is pretty much what Darwin had done, in broad strokes, after the *Beagle*'s five-week survey of the islands in 1835. But the Grants soon discovered that at their main study site, a tiny desert island called Daphne Major, near the center of the archipelago, the finches were evolving rapidly. Conditions on the island swung wildly back and forth from wet years to dry years, and finches on Daphne adapted to each swing, from generation to generation. With the help of a series of graduate students, the Grants began to spend a good part of every year on Daphne, watching evolution in action as it shaped and reshaped the finches' beaks.

At the same time, a few biologists began making similar discoveries elsewhere in the world. One of them was John A. Endler, an evolutionary biologist at the University of California,

Santa Barbara, who studied Trinidadian guppies. In 1986 Endler published a little book called *Natural Selection in the Wild,* in which he collected and reviewed all of the studies of evolution in action that had been published to that date. Dozens of new field projects were in progress. Biologists finally began to realize that Darwin had been too modest. Evolution by natural selection can happen rapidly enough to watch.

Now the field is exploding. More than 250 people around the world are observing and documenting evolution, not only in finches and guppies, but also in aphids, flies, grayling, monkeyflowers, salmon, and sticklebacks. Some workers are even documenting pairs of species—symbiotic insects and plants—that have recently found each other, and observing the pairs as they drift off into their own world together like lovers in a novel by D.H. Lawrence.

The Grants' own study gets more sophisticated every year. A few years ago, a group of molecular biologists working with the Grants nailed down a gene that plays a key role in shaping the beaks of the finches. The gene codes for a signaling molecule called bone morphogenic protein 4 (BMP4). Finches with bigger beaks tend to have more BMP4, and finches with smaller beaks have less. In the laboratory, the biologists demonstrated that they could sculpt the beaks themselves by adding or subtracting BMP4. The same gene that shapes the beak of the finch in the egg also shapes the human face in the womb.

Some of the most dramatic stories of evolution in action result from the pressures that human beings are imposing on the planet. As Stephen Palumbi, an evolutionary biologist at Stanford University, points out, we are changing the course of evolution for virtually every living species everywhere, with consequences that are sometimes the opposite of what we might have predicted, or desired.

Take trophy hunting. Wild populations of bighorn mountain sheep are carefully managed in North America for hunters who want a chance to shoot a ram with a trophy set of horns. Hunting permits can cost well into the six figures. On Ram Mountain, in Alberta, Canada, hunters have shot the biggest of the bighorn rams for more than thirty years. And the result? Evolution has made the hunters' quarry scarce. The runts have had a better chance than the giants of passing on their genes. So on Ram Mountain the rams have gotten smaller, and their horns are proportionately smaller yet.

Or take fishing, which is economically much more consequential. The populations of Atlantic cod that swam for centuries off the coasts of Labrador and Newfoundland began a terrible crash in the late 1980s. In the years leading up to the crash, the cod had been evolving much like the sheep on Ram Mountain. Fish that matured relatively fast and reproduced relatively young had the better chance of passing on their genes; so did the fish that stayed small. So even before the population crashed, the average cod had been shrinking.

We often seem to lose out wherever we fight hardest to control nature. Antibiotics drive the evolution of drug-resistant bacteria at a frightening pace. Sulfonamides were introduced in the 1930s, and resistance to them was first observed a decade later. Penicillin was deployed in 1943, and the first penicillin resistance was observed in 1946. In the same way, pesticides and herbicides create resistant bugs and weeds.

Palumbi estimates that the annual bill for such unintended human-induced evolution runs to more than $100 billion in the U.S. alone. Worldwide, the pressure of global warming, fragmented habitats, heightened levels of carbon dioxide, acid rain, and the other myriad perturbations people impose on the chemistry and climate of the planet—all change the terms of the struggle for existence in the air, in the water, and on land. Biologists have begun to worry about those perturbations, but global change may be racing ahead of them.

To me, the most interesting news in the global evolution watch concerns what Darwin called "that mystery of mysteries, the origin of species."

The process whereby a population acquires small, inherited changes through natural selection is known as microevolution. Finches get bigger, fish gets smaller, but a finch is still a finch and a fish is still a fish. For people who reject Darwin's theory, that's the end of the story: no matter how many small, inherited changes accumulate, they believe, natural selection can never make a new kind of living thing. The kinds, the species, are eternal.

Darwin argued otherwise. He thought that many small changes could cause two lines of life to diverge. Whenever animals and plants find their way to a new home, for instance, they suffer, like emigres in new countries. Some individuals fail, others adapt and prosper. As the more successful individuals reproduce, Darwin maintained, the new population begins to differ from the ancestral one. If the two populations diverge widely enough, they become separate species. Change on that scale is known as macroevolution.

In *Origin,* Darwin estimated that a new species might take between ten thousand and fourteen thousand generations to arise. Until recently, most biologists assumed it would take at least that many, or maybe even millions of generations, before microevolutionary changes led to the origin of new species. So they assumed they could watch evolution by natural selection, but not the divergence of one species into separate, reproductively isolated species. Now that view is changing too.

Not long ago, a young evolution-watcher named Andrew Hendry, a biologist at McGill University in Montreal, reported the results of a striking study of sockeye salmon. Sockeye tend to reproduce either in streams or along lake beaches. When the glaciers of the last ice age melted and retreated, about ten thousand years ago, they left behind thousands of new lakes. Salmon from streams swam into the lakes and stayed. Today their descendants tend to breed among themselves rather than with sockeyes that live in the streams. The fish in the lakes and streams are reproductively isolated from each other. So how fast did that happen?

In the 1930s and 1940s, sockeye salmon were introduced into Lake Washington, in Washington State. Hundreds of thousands of their descendants now live and breed in Cedar River, which feeds the lake. By 1957 some of the introduced sockeye also colonized a beach along the lake called Pleasure Point, about four miles from the mouth of Cedar River.

Hendry could tell whether a full-grown, breeding salmon had been born in the river or at the beach by examining the rings on its otoliths, or ear stones. Otolith rings reflect variations in water temperature while a fish embryo is developing. Water temperatures at the beach are relatively constant compared with the river temperatures. Hendry and his colleagues checked the otoliths and collected DNA samples from the fish—and found that more than a third of the sockeye breeding at Pleasure Point had grown up in the river. They were immigrants.

With such a large number of immigrants, the two populations at Pleasure Point should have blended back together. But they hadn't. So at breeding time many of the river sockeye that swam over to the beach must have been relatively unsuccessful at passing on their genes.

Hendry could also tell the stream fish and the beach fish apart just by looking at them. Where the sockeye's breeding waters are swift-flowing, such as in Cedar River, the males tend to be slender. Their courtship ritual and competition with other males requires them to turn sideways in strong current—an awkward maneuver for a male with a deep, roundish body. So in strong current, slender males have the better chance of passing on their genes. But in still waters, males with the deepest bodies have the best chance of getting mates. So beach males tend to be rounder—their dimensions greater from the top of the back to the bottom of the belly—than river males.

What about females? In the river, where currents and floods are forever shifting and swirling the gravel, females have to dig deep nests for their eggs. So the females in the river tend to be bigger than their lake-dwelling counterparts, because bigger females can dig deeper nests. Where the water is calmer, the gravel stays put, and shallower nests will do.

So all of the beachgoers, male and female, have adapted to life at Pleasure Point. Their adaptations are strong enough that reproductive isolation has evolved. How long did the evolution take? Hendry began studying the salmon's reproductive isolation in 1992. At that time, the sockeyes in the stream and the ones at Pleasure Point had been breeding in their respective habitats for at most thirteen generations. That is so fast that, as Hendry and his colleagues point out, it may be possible someday soon to catch the next step, the origin of a new species.

And it's not just the sockeye salmon. Consider the three-spined stickleback. After the glaciers melted at the end of the last ice age, many sticklebacks swam out of the sea and into new glacial lakes—just as the salmon did. In the sea, sticklebacks wear heavy, bony body armor. In a lake they wear light armor. In a certain new pond in Bergen, Norway, during the past century, sticklebacks evolved toward the lighter armor in just thirty-one years. In Loberg Lake, Alaska, the same kind of change took only a dozen years. A generation for sticklebacks is two years. So that dramatic evolution took just six generations.

Dolph Schluter, a former finch-watcher from the Galápagos and currently a biologist at the University of British Columbia in Vancouver, has shown that, along with the evolution of new body types, sticklebacks also evolve a taste for mates with the new traits. In other words, the adaptive push of sexual selection is going hand-in-hand with natural selection. Schluter has built experimental ponds in Vancouver to observe the phenomenon under controlled conditions, and the same patterns he found in isolated lakes repeat themselves in his ponds. So adaptation can sometimes drive sexual selection and accelerate reproductive isolation.

There are other developments in the evolution watch, too, many to mention in this small space. Some of the fastest action is microscopic. Richard Lenski, a biologist at Michigan State University in East Lansing, watches the evolution of *Escherichia coli*. Because one generation takes only twenty minutes, and billions of *E. coli* can fit in a petri dish, the bacteria make ideal subjects for experimental evolution. Throw some *E. coli* into a new dish, for instance, with food they haven't encountered before, and they will evolve and adapt—quickly at first and then more slowly, as they refine their fit with their new environment.

And then there are the controversies. Science progresses and evolves by controversy, by internal debate and revision. In the United States these days one almost hates to mention that there are arguments among evolutionists. So often, they are taken out of context and hyperamplified to suggest that nothing about Darwinism is solid—that Darwin is dead. But research is messy because nature is messy, and fieldwork is some of the messiest research of all. It is precisely here at its jagged cutting edge that Darwinism is most vigorously alive.

Not long ago, one of the most famous icons of the evolution watch toppled over: the story of the peppered moths, familiar to anyone who remembers biology 101. About half a century ago, the British evolutionist Bernard Kettlewell noted that certain moths in the British Isles had evolved into darker forms when the trunks of trees darkened with industrial pollution. When the trees lightened again, after clean air acts were passed, the moths had evolved into light forms again. Kettlewell claimed that dark moths resting on dark tree trunks were harder for birds to see; in each decade, moths of the right color were safer.

But in the past few years, workers have shown that Kettlewell's explanation was too simplistic. For one thing, the moths don't normally rest on tree trunks. In forty years of observation, only twice have moths been seen resting there. Nobody knows where they do rest. The moths did evolve rapidly, but no one can be certain why.

To me what remains most interesting is the light that studies such as Hendry's, or the Grants', may throw on the origin of species. It's extraordinary that scientists are now examining the very beginnings of the process, at the level of beaks and fins, at the level of the genes. The explosion of evolution-watchers is a remarkable development in Darwin's science. Even as the popular debate about evolution in America is reaching its most heated moment since the trial of John Scopes, evolutionary biologists are pursuing one of the most significant and surprising voyages of discovery since the young Darwin sailed into the Galápagos Archipelago aboard Her Majesty's ship *Beagle*.

Not long ago I asked Hendry if his studies have changed the way he thinks about the origin of species. "Yes," he replied without hesitation, "I think it's occurring all over the place."

Critical Thinking

1. Did Darwin ever see evolution in action? Why or why not?

2. Who are Rosemary and Peter Grant? What did they study? Where? How did they show that natural selection occurs?

3. How many people around the world are documenting evolution now?

4. What recent advance has been found in the Grants' research?

5. How have trophy hunting and fishing impacted the evolution of species according to the research presented by Weiner?

6. When was penicillin first deployed? How soon did resistance show up?

7. What is "microevolution"?

8. How many generations did Darwin think it would take for a new species to arise? Did more recent scholars agree with this? Was Darwin right, too optimistic, or too pessimistic?

9. What happened with the sockeye salmon? What did they show about the number of generations these changes took?

10. What selection pressure drove differences in morphology (body shape and size) between males and females of the river and lake types?

11. How do the stickleback findings show that "adaptations sometimes drive sexual selection and accelerate reproductive isolation"?

12. Why does Weiner say "in the United States these days one almost hates to mention that there are arguments among evolutionists"?

13. What is the classic story about the peppered moths? Why has this icon been "toppled"?

Internet References

American Anthropologist Association
www.aaanet.org

Charles Darwin on Human Origins
www.literature.org/Works/Charles-Darwin

Enter Evolution: Theory and History
www.ucmp.berkeley.edu/history/evolution.html

Harvard Dept. of MCB–Biology Links
http://mcb.harvard.edu/BioLinks.html

JONATHAN WEINER began writing about evolution in 1990, when he met Peter and Rosemary Grant, who observe evolution firsthand in finch populations in the Galápagos. Weiner's book *The Beak of the Finch* (Alfred A. Knopf) won a Pulitzer Prize in 1994. He is a professor in the Graduate School of Journalism at Columbia University, in New York City. He is also working on a book about human longevity for Ecco Press.

Article   Prepared by: Elvio Angeloni

Beauty Happens

Darwin's theory that mate choice is explicitly aesthetic was a really dangerous idea.

RICHARD O. PRUM

Learning Outcomes

After reading this article, you will be able to:

- Discuss "sexual selection" in terms of the Charles Darwin viewed versus the way it is seen today by most evolutionary biologists.

- Discuss the "Smucker's principle" as an explanation mate choice.

In *On the Origin of Species*, Charles Darwin made two transcendent scientific discoveries: the mechanism of evolution by natural selection and the concept that all organisms are historically descended from a single common ancestor. But despite these successes, Darwin had three gnawing problems after publication of the *Origin*. The first was the absence of any working theory of genetics, which was fundamental to natural selection. The second was human evolution, which he left unaddressed in the *Origin*. And the third problem was the origin of impracticable beauty.

If natural selection was driven by the differential survival of heritable variations, what could explain the elaborate beauty of the peacock's tail? Obviously, the tail did not help the male peacock to survive; if anything, the huge tail would be a hindrance, slowing him down and making him much more vulnerable to predators.

Darwin was especially obsessed with the peacock's "eyespots." He had argued that the human eye could be explained as the result of many small, incremental, and functional advances over time. Each advance produced slight improvements in the ability of the eye to detect light, to distinguish shadows from light, to focus, to create images, to differentiate among colors, and so forth, all of which would have contributed to the animal's survival. But what purpose could the intermediate stages in the evolution of the eyespots have served? Indeed, what function do the eyespots on a peacock serve? In 1860, Darwin wrote to his American friend, Harvard botanist Asa Gray: "The sight of a feather in a peacock's tail, whenever I gaze at it, makes me sick!"

In *The Descent of Man, and Selection in Relation to Sex*, published in 1871, Darwin boldly addressed both the problem of human origins and the evolution of beauty. In *Descent*, Darwin proposed a second, distinct, and independent mechanism of evolution—sexual selection. If natural selection results from differential survival of heritable variations, then sexual selection is the result of their differential sexual success (i.e., the success of heritable variations that contribute to obtaining more mates and fertilizing more offspring).

Within sexual selection, Darwin envisioned two different evolutionary mechanisms at work. The first, which he called the "Law of Battle," was the struggle between individuals of one sex—often male—for sexual control over individuals of the other sex. This process would result in the evolution of large body size and weapons of aggression such as horns, antlers, and spurs. The second mechanism, which he called the "Taste for the Beautiful," concerned the process by which the members of one sex—often female—choose their mates based on their own innate preferences. Darwin hypothesized that mate choice had resulted in the evolution of the ornamental features of nature that are so beautiful and pleasing to the senses—from the songs, colorful plumages, and displays of birds to the brilliant blue face and hindquarters of the mandrill. The most distinct and revolutionary feature of Darwin's theory of mate choice was that it was explicitly aesthetic. Darwin described the evolutionary origin of beauty in nature as a consequence of the fact that animals had evolved to be beautiful to their own species. Darwin viewed organisms—especially females—as active agents in the evolution of their own species. Unlike natural selection, which emerges passively from external forces, such as geography, climate, predation, and competition acting on the organism, sexual selection is a self-directed process in which the desires of the organisms themselves (mostly female) were in charge. Darwin described females as having a "taste for the beautiful" and an "aesthetic faculty." He described males as trying to "charm" their mates. He wrote: If female birds had been incapable of appreciating the beautiful colors, the ornaments, and voices of their male partners, all the labor and anxiety by the latter in displaying their charms before the females would have been thrown away; and this is impossible to admit.

Darwin concluded, "On the whole, birds appear to be the most aesthetic of all animals, excepting of course man, and they have nearly the same taste for the beautiful as we have." Today, Darwin's choice of aesthetic language can seem quaint, anthropomorphic, and possibly even embarrassingly silly. Clearly, Darwin did not have our contemporary fear of anthropomorphism. Indeed, he was engaged in breaking down the previously unquestioned barrier between humans and other forms of life. Darwin's use of aesthetic language was not just a curious mannerism, or a quaint Victorian affectation, but an integral feature of his scientific argument about the nature of evolutionary process. Darwin used ordinary aesthetic language to make an extraordinary scientific claim: mate choices based on the subjective evaluations of animals drive the evolution of sexual ornaments in nature. By using the words beauty, taste, charm, appreciate, admire, and love, Darwin proposed that mating preferences evolved for displays that had no utilitarian value, other than the pleasure they evoked to the chooser. Darwin wrote:

The case of the male Argus Pheasant is eminently interesting, because it affords good evidence that the most refined beauty may serve as a sexual charm, and for no other purpose.

In this way, Darwin viewed sexual selection as a distinct evolutionary mechanism from natural selection with independent, potentially nonadaptive consequences. Darwin's theory of mate choice was also coevolutionary. Darwin hypothesized that specific display traits and the "standards of beauty" used to evaluate them evolved together, mutually influencing and reinforcing one another over time. Thus, he wrote:

. . . the male Argus Pheasant acquired his beauty gradually through the preference of the females during many generations for the more highly ornamented males; the aesthetic capacity of females advanced through exercise or habit just as our own taste is gradually improved.

To Darwin, behind every sexual ornament is an equally elaborate, coevolved sensory/cognitive preference that has driven, shaped, and been shaped by that ornamental trait.

Upon its publication, Darwin's theory of sexual selection was swiftly and brutally attacked. Or more precisely, part of it was. Darwin's concept of male–male competition—the Law of Battle—was immediately and almost universally accepted. Clearly, the notion of male–male competition for dominance over female sexuality was not a hard sell in the patriarchal Victorian culture of Darwin's time. But, immediately after its publication, the confirmed evolutionist St. George Mivart launched an all-out attack on Darwinian mate choice:

Even in Mr. Darwin's specially selected instances, there is not a tittle of evidence tending, however slightly, to show that any brute possesses the representative reflective faculties.

In discussing the role of the peahen in the evolution of the peacock's tail, Mivart wrote:

such is the instability of vicious feminine caprice, that no constancy of coloration could be produced by its selective actions.

To Mivart, female sexual whims were so malleable (i.e., fickle females preferring one thing one minute and another the next) that they could never lead to the evolution of something as marvelously complex as the peacock's tail.

Mivart's language also reveals the deep misogyny and moral judgment that Darwin's concept of mate choice evoked. At that time, the word "vicious" meant immoral, depraved, or wicked—literally, characterized by vice. Likewise, to Victorians, "caprice" was a "turn of mind made without apparent or adequate motive." Thus, to Darwin's critics, female mate choice had overtones not just of fickleness but of immorality and sin.

Mivart was also the first to portray Darwin as a traitor to his own great legacy—a traitor to true Darwinism:

The assignment of the law of "natural selection" to a subordinate position is virtually an abandonment of the Darwinian theory; for the one distinguishing feature of that theory was the all-sufficiency of "natural selection."

Mivart established an attack on Darwin's concept of aesthetic evolution that is still in use today—citing the *Origin* to argue against *Descent*.

The most consistent and effective critique of sexual selection came from Alfred Russel Wallace. Darwin and Wallace never agreed on sexual selection, but Wallace's critique was so successful that sexual selection was almost completely marginalized within evolutionary biology until the 1970s.

Wallace's view of sexual selection was motivated by his religious faith. Wallace believed that humans had been specially created by God and divinely endowed with cognitive capacities and free will that animals lacked. Animal choices were inconceivable to him. But Wallace was never able to reject evolution by mate choice entirely. When forced to admit the possibility, he insisted that sexual ornaments could only have evolved because they had an adaptive, utilitarian value. In Tropical Nature, and Other Essays, Wallace wrote:

> The only way in which we can account for the observed facts is by supposing that colour and ornament are strictly correlated with health, vigor, and general fitness to survive.

Here, Wallace was the first to articulate the idea that sexual displays constitute "honest" indicators of the objective quality and condition of mates—an entirely orthodox view in sexual selection today. But how can it be that Wallace, the man justly credited with having destroyed sexual selection theory for over a century, invented the viewpoint that would be entirely at home in any modern biology textbook? The answer is that contemporary mainstream views of mate choice are as stridently anti-Darwinian as Wallace's were.

Today, most evolutionary biologists would agree with Wallace that all sexual selection is simply a form of natural selection. But Wallace went further than they do, by rejecting the term sexual selection entirely. If adaptive natural selection is always driving the show, he reasoned, then the concept of sexual selection should be abandoned entirely.

Then, in the introduction to his 1886 book Darwinism, Wallace wrote:

> . . . [I]n rejecting that phase of sexual selection depending on female choice, I insist on the greater efficacy of natural selection. This is pre-eminently the Darwinian doctrine, and I therefore claim for my book the position of being the advocate of pure Darwinism. Here, Wallace claims to be more Darwinian than Darwin! Just a few years after Darwin's death, Wallace had begun to reshape Darwinism in his own image. In these passages, we witness the birth of "adaptationism"—the belief that adaptive natural selection is a universally strong force that will always be predominant in the evolutionary process. In this way, Wallace transformed Darwin's fertile, creative, and diverse intellectual legacy into the monolithic, narrow, and intellectually impoverished theory with which Darwin is almost universally associated today.

The Darwin we have all inherited has been laundered, retailored, and cleaned up for ideological purity. The true breadth and creativity of Darwin's ideas have been nearly written out of history. Alfred Russel Wallace may have lost the battle for credit over the discovery of natural selection, but he won the war over what evolutionary biology and Darwinism would become in the twentieth century.

During the century-long dark ages of evolution by mate choice, there was one fundamental contribution to the field. In a 1915 paper and a 1930 book, British biologist and statistician Ronald Aylmer Fisher proposed a genetic mechanism for the evolution of mate choice that built on and extended Darwin's aesthetic ideas. Fisher proposed a two-stage evolutionary model—one phase for the initial origin of mating preferences and a second phase for the coevolutionary elaboration of trait and preference. The first phase is solidly Wallacean and proposes that mating preferences initially evolve for traits that are honest indices of health, vigor, and survival ability (i.e., objectively better mates). Then, in the second phase, Fisher predicts that the action of mate choice will unhinge the display trait from its original honest, quality information by creating a new, unpredictable, aesthetically driven evolutionary force: sexual attraction to the ornamental trait itself.

According to Fisher, the force that drives the evolution of mating preference is mate choice itself. In an exact reversal of the Wallacean view of natural selection as "neutralizing" sexual selection, Fisher proposes that arbitrary aesthetic choices (per Darwin) will trump choices made for adaptive advantage (per Wallace). Once the trait is attractive, its attractiveness and popularity become ends in themselves. To Darwin and Fisher, ornamental traits are meaningless and arbitrary—merely beautiful and lacking adaptive utility. In nature, the desire for beauty will endure and undermine the desire for truth.

How can this work? Fisher hypothesized the evolution of a positive feedback loop between the ornament and the preference for it. Because females who prefer mates with longer or shorter tails will choose corresponding males, genetic variation for display traits and preferences will become correlated (i.e., genes for long tails will be found in individuals with genes for preferring long tails and vice versa). As a consequence, when females exercise their mate choices for particular display traits, they will also be selecting indirectly on genes for mating preference. The result is a positive feedback loop in which mate choice becomes the selective agent in the evolution of mate choice itself. Fisher called this self-reinforcing sexual selection mechanism a "runaway process."

Like Darwin's idea, Fisher's model is coevolutionary. The form of sexual beauty and the desire for it shape each other through a coevolutionary process. In this way, Fisher provided a mechanism of how the display trait and mating preference can "advance together," as Darwin envisioned.

Later, in the early 1980s, biologists Russell Lande at the University of Chicago and Mark Kirkpatrick at the University of Texas, Austin, developed explicit mathematical models of Fisher's long-ignored mechanism of trait and preference evolution. However, this renascent interest in Darwinian mate choice was soon overtaken by neo-Wallacean theories of adaptative mate choice. Of course, contemporary adaptive mate choice theories had to be reinvented from scratch because no one remembered Wallace's version of honest advertisement. But all these theories shared Wallace's original logic.

The chief proponent of adaptive mate choice in the 1970s and 1980s was Amotz Zahavi, a charismatic and energetic Israeli ornithologist with a fierce independent streak. In 1975, Zahavi published his "handicap principle," which was a huge stimulus to the adaptive mate choice paradigm. Echoing Wallace, Zahavi wrote that "sexual selection is effective because it improves the ability of the selecting sex to detect quality in the selected sex."

Zahavi then added his own distinctive twist to Wallacean logic. To Zahavi, the entire point of any sexual display is that it is a costly burden to the signaler—literally, a handicap. By its very existence, the ornamental handicap demonstrates the superior quality of the signaler because the signaler has been able to survive it. Zahavi wrote that "sexual selection is effective only by selecting for a character that lowers the survival of the organism. . . . It is possible to consider a handicap as a kind of test."

The more elaborate the trait, the greater the costs, the bigger the handicap, the more rigorous the test, and the better the mate. Accordingly, the individual who is attracted to a mate with such a costly trait is responding not to its beauty, which is incidental to its costs, but to what it tells her about that male's ability to rise above its cost.

In what way was the handicapped male better? To Zahavi, it was clear that he could be better in every imaginable way. However, those who followed Zahavi established that the adaptive benefits of mate choice could be either direct or indirect. The direct benefits of mate choice include any advantages to the health, survival, or fecundity of the choosers themselves, such as a mate with no sexually transmitted diseases, a greater capacity to invest in the feeding offspring, better protection from predators, or a better territory with more food or better nesting sites. Alternatively, the adaptive indirect benefits are in the form of good genes that are inherited by the chooser's male and female offspring and contribute to their survival and fecundity.

To understand the logic of Zahavi's handicap principle, let's consider a corollary to it that I call the "Smucker's

principle." Smucker's Jelly takes its name from its founder, Jerome Monroe Smucker, who opened a cider press in Orrville, OH, in 1897. Since the early 1950s, the company has used the catchy advertising slogan: "With a name like Smucker's, it has to be good!" The slogan claims that the Smucker's brand name is so unappealing, so off-putting, and so costly that the fact that the company has survived with this name proves that its jelly is of really superior quality. The Smucker's slogan embodies the handicap principle.

But what if Smucker's Jelly were suddenly in competition with another jelly with an even worse, costlier name? Wouldn't an even worse, more off-putting name indicate a jelly of even higher quality? What limits the possibility of ever worsening and costlier names indicative of ever higher-quality jellies? The "Smucker's principle" reveals the logical flaw of Zahavi's "handicap principle." If the sexual benefit of a signal is directly related to its costs, the signaler will never gain an advantage, unless a small increase in cost yields a large increase in sexual benefit. Rather, handicaps will fail under their own costly burden. The "Smucker's principle" also reveals that the handicap principle is fundamentally incompatible with the aesthetic nature of sexual display. Sexual displays evolve because they are aesthetically attractive.

The Darwin versus Wallace debate over mate choice remains vital to science today. Unfortunately, it is not a fair fight because the framework of modern evolutionary biology was designed to make neo-Wallacean logic inevitable. For example, let's examine the history of the word "fitness." To Darwin, fitness had the ordinary language meaning of physical fitness. Fitness meant fit to do a task. Darwinian fitness was the physical capacity to do the tasks necessary to ensure one's survival and capacity for reproduction. However, during the development of population genetics in the early twentieth century, fitness was redefined mathematically as the differential success of one's genes in subsequent generations. This broader and more general definition combined differential survival, fecundity, and mating/fertilization success into a single new variable, under the common umbrella of adaptive natural selection. Of course, the redefinition of fitness was accomplished in the early twentieth century when sexual selection by mate choice had been rejected as irrelevant to evolution.

The effect of redefining fitness was to flatten and eliminate the original, subtle, Darwinian distinction between natural selection on traits that ensured survival and fecundity and sexual selection on traits that resulted in differential mating and reproductive success. Ever since, this mathematically convenient but intellectually muddled new concept of fitness has shaped how people think evolution works and made it difficult to even articulate the possibility of a distinct, independent, non-adaptive mechanism of sexual selection.

To restore the promise of Darwin's insights to contemporary evolutionary biology, we need to recognize sexual selection as a distinct mechanism of evolution, alongside the classic mechanisms of mutation, recombination, drift, and natural selection. This conceptual change will require us to realize that mate choice is not always an adaptive process, and that adaptive mate choice—whenever it occurs—requires a specific and special interaction between sexual and natural selection.

Adaptation by natural selection is justly considered to be among the most successful and influential scientific ideas in history. Because of its profound impact on science and culture despite the persistent resistance to it, the philosopher Daniel Dennett referred to natural selection as *Darwin's Dangerous Idea*. However, Darwin's really dangerous idea is the concept of aesthetic evolution by mate choice. Why so dangerous? Because Darwinian mate choice establishes that there are limits to the power of natural selection as an evolutionary force and as a scientific explanation of the origin of diversity in the living world. Natural selection cannot be the only mechanism at work in evolution, Darwin reasoned, because it fails to fully account for the extraordinary diversity of sexual ornaments we see in the biological world. Darwin's really dangerous idea is his insight that natural selection is not the only source of design in nature. We are still awaiting the full impact of this revolutionary idea on science and human culture.

Critical Thinking

1. How did Darwin define sexual selection as distinct from natural selection?
2. How do evolutionary biologists explain sexual selection today?

Internet References

Beauty and the Beast: Mechanisms of Sexual Selection in Humans
  https://www.ehbonline.org/article/S1090-5138%2810%2900027-9/abstract

Charles Darwin on Human Origins
  www.literacture.org/Works/Charlesl-Darwin

Sexual Selection in Humans
  https://en.wikipedia.org/wiki/Sexual_selection_in_humans

RICHARD O. PRUM is a William Robertson Coe Professor of Ornithology at Yale University and a head curator of Vertebrate Zoology at the Yale Peabody Museum of Natural History.

Article Prepared by: Elvio Angeloni

The Age of Disbelief

Skepticism about science is on the rise, and polarization is the order of the day. What's causing reasonable people to doubt reason?

JOEL ACHENBACH

Learning Outcomes

After reading this article, you will be able to:

- Explain why there is so much public distrust of science today.
- Describe the scientific method.
- Explain why we cling to our intuitions even in the face of evidence for such ideas as a sun-centered solar system and organic evolution.
- Discuss "confirmation bias" and the scientific approach to overcome it.

There's a scene in Stanley Kubrick's comic masterpiece *Dr. Strangelove* in which Jack D. Ripper, an American general who's gone rogue and ordered a nuclear attack on the Soviet Union, unspools his paranoid worldview—and the explanation for why he drinks "only distilled water, or rainwater, and only pure grain alcohol" to Lionel Mandrake, a dizzy-with-anxiety group captain in the Royal Air Force.

RIPPER: Have you ever heard of a thing called fluoridation? Fluoridation of water?

MANDRAKE: Ah, yes, I have heard of that, Jack. Yes, yes.

RIPPER: Well, do you know what it is?

MANDRAKE: No. No, I don't know what it is. No.

RIPPER: Do you realize that fluoridation is the most monstrously conceived and dangerous communist plot we have ever had to face?

The movie came out in 1964, by which time the health benefits of fluoridation had been thoroughly established, and antifluoridation conspiracy theories could be the stuff of comedy. So you might be surprised to learn that, half a century later, fluoridation continues to incite fear and paranoia. In 2013 citizens in Portland, Oregon, one of only a few major American cities that don't fluoridate their water, blocked a plan by local officials to do so. Opponents didn't like the idea of the government adding "chemicals" to their water. They claimed that fluoride could be harmful to human health.

Actually fluoride is a natural mineral that, in the weak concentrations used in public drinking water systems, hardens tooth enamel and prevents tooth decay—a cheap and safe way to improve dental health for everyone, rich or poor, conscientious brusher or not. That's the scientific and medical consensus.

To which some people in Portland, echoing antifluoridation activists around the world, reply: We don't believe you.

We live in an age when all manner of scientific knowledge—from the safety of fluoride and vaccines to the reality of climate change—faces organized and often furious opposition. Empowered by their own sources of information and their own interpretations of research, doubters have declared war on the consensus of experts. There are so many of these controversies these days, you'd think a diabolical agency had put something in the water to make people argumentative. And there's so much talk about the trend these days—in books, articles, and academic conferences—that science doubt itself has become a pop-culture meme. In the recent movie *Interstellar,* set in a futuristic, downtrodden America where NASA has been forced into hiding, school textbooks say the Apollo moon landings were faked.

In a sense all this is not surprising. Our lives are permeated by science and technology as never before. For many of us this new world is wondrous, comfortable, and rich in rewards—but also more complicated and sometimes unnerving. We now face risks we can't easily analyze.

We're asked to accept, for example, that it's safe to eat food containing genetically modified organisms (GMOs) because, the experts point out, there's no evidence that it isn't and no reason to believe that altering genes precisely in a lab is more dangerous than altering them wholesale through traditional breeding. But to some people the very idea of transferring genes between species conjures up mad scientists running amok—and so, two centuries after Mary Shelley wrote Frankenstein, they talk about Frankenfood.

The world crackles with real and imaginary hazards, and distinguishing the former from the latter isn't easy. Should we be afraid that the Ebola virus, which is spread only by direct contact with bodily fluids, will mutate into an airborne superplague? The scientific consensus says that's extremely unlikely: No virus has ever been observed to completely change its mode of transmission in humans, and there's zero evidence that the latest strain of Ebola is any different. But type "airborne Ebola" into an Internet search engine, and you'll enter a dystopia where this virus has almost supernatural powers, including the power to kill us all.

In this bewildering world we have to decide what to believe and how to act on that. In principle that's what science is for. "Science is not a body of facts," says geophysicist Marcia McNutt, who once headed the U.S. Geological Survey and is now editor of *Science,* the prestigious journal. "Science is a method for deciding whether what we choose to believe has a basis in the laws of nature or not." But that method doesn't come naturally to most of us. And so we run into trouble, again and again.

The trouble goes way back, of course. The scientific method leads us to truths that are less than self-evident, often mind-blowing, and sometimes hard to swallow. In the early 17th century, when Galileo claimed that the Earth spins on its axis and orbits the sun, he wasn't just rejecting church doctrine. He was asking people to believe something that defied common sense—because it sure looks like the sun's going around the Earth, and you can't feel the Earth spinning. Galileo was put on trial and forced to recant. Two centuries later Charles Darwin escaped that fate. But his idea that all life on Earth evolved from a primordial ancestor and that we humans are distant cousins of apes, whales, and even deep-sea mollusks is still a big ask for a lot of people. So is another 19th-century notion: that carbon dioxide, an invisible gas that we all exhale all the time and that makes up less than a tenth of one percent of the atmosphere, could be affecting Earth's climate.

Even when we intellectually accept these precepts of science, we subconsciously cling to our intuitions—what researchers call our naive beliefs. A recent study by Andrew Shtulman of Occidental College showed that even students with an advanced science education had a hitch in their mental gait when asked to affirm or deny that humans are descended from sea animals or

that Earth goes around the sun. Both truths are counterintuitive. The students, even those who correctly marked "true," were slower to answer those questions than questions about whether humans are descended from tree-dwelling creatures (also true but easier to grasp) or whether the moon goes around the Earth (also true but intuitive). Shtulman's research indicates that as we become scientifically literate, we repress our naive beliefs but never eliminate them entirely. They lurk in our brains, chirping at us as we try to make sense of the world.

Most of us do that by relying on personal experience and anecdotes, on stories rather than statistics. We might get a prostate-specific antigen test, even though it's no longer generally recommended, because it caught a close friend's cancer—and we pay less attention to statistical evidence, painstakingly compiled through multiple studies, showing that the test rarely saves lives but triggers many unnecessary surgeries. Or we hear about a cluster of cancer cases in a town with a hazardous waste dump, and we assume pollution caused the cancers. Yet just because two things happened together doesn't mean one caused the other, and just because events are clustered doesn't mean they're not still random.

We have trouble digesting randomness; our brains crave pattern and meaning. Science warns us, however, that we can deceive ourselves. To be confident there's a causal connection between the dump and the cancers, you need statistical analysis showing that there are many more cancers than would be expected randomly, evidence that the victims were exposed to chemicals from the dump, and evidence that the chemicals really can cause cancer.

Even for scientists, the scientific method is a hard discipline. Like the rest of us, they're vulnerable to what they call confirmation bias—the tendency to look for and see only evidence that confirms what they already believe. But unlike the rest of us, they submit their ideas to formal peer review before publishing them. Once their results are published, if they're important enough, other scientists will try to reproduce them—and, being congenitally skeptical and competitive, will be very happy to announce that they don't hold up. Scientific results are always provisional, susceptible to being overturned by some future experiment or observation. Scientists rarely proclaim an absolute truth or absolute certainty. Uncertainty is inevitable at the frontiers of knowledge.

Sometimes scientists fall short of the ideals of the scientific method. Especially in biomedical research, there's a disturbing trend toward results that can't be reproduced outside the lab that found them, a trend that has prompted a push for greater transparency about how experiments are conducted. Francis Collins, the director of the National Institutes of Health, worries about the "secret sauce"—specialized procedures, customized software, quirky ingredients—that researchers don't share with their colleagues. But he still has faith in the larger enterprise.

"Science will find the truth," Collins says. "It may get it wrong the first time and maybe the second time, but ultimately it will find the truth." That provisional quality of science is another thing a lot of people have trouble with. To some climate change skeptics, for example, the fact that a few scientists in the 1970s were worried (quite reasonably, it seemed at the time) about the possibility of a coming ice age is enough to discredit the concern about global warming now.

Last fall the Intergovernmental Panel on Climate Change, which consists of hundreds of scientists operating under the auspices of the United Nations, released its fifth report in the past 25 years. This one repeated louder and clearer than ever the consensus of the world's scientists: The planet's surface temperature has risen by about 1.5 degrees Fahrenheit in the past 130 years, and human actions, including the burning of fossil fuels, are extremely likely to have been the dominant cause of the warming since the mid-20th century. Many people in the United States— a far greater percentage than in other countries—retain doubts about that consensus or believe that climate activists are using the threat of global warming to attack the free market and industrial society generally. Senator James Inhofe of Oklahoma, one of the most powerful Republican voices on environmental matters, has long declared global warming a hoax.

The idea that hundreds of scientists from all over the world would collaborate on such a vast hoax is laughable—scientists love to debunk one another. It's very clear, however, that organizations funded in part by the fossil fuel industry have deliberately tried to undermine the public's understanding of the scientific consensus by promoting a few skeptics.

The news media give abundant attention to such mavericks, naysayers, professional controversialists, and table thumpers. The media would also have you believe that science is full of shocking discoveries made by lone geniuses. Not so. The (boring) truth is that it usually advances incrementally, through the steady accretion of data and insights gathered by many people over many years. So it has been with the consensus on climate change. That's not about to go poof with the next thermometer reading.

But industry PR, however misleading, isn't enough to explain why only 40 percent of Americans, according to the most recent poll from the Pew Research Center, accept that human activity is the dominant cause of global warming.

The "science communication problem," as it's blandly called by the scientists who study it, has yielded abundant new research into how people decide what to believe—and why they so often don't accept the scientific consensus. It's not that they can't grasp it, according to Dan Kahan of Yale University. In one study he asked 1,540 Americans, a representative sample, to rate the threat of climate change on a scale of zero to ten. Then he correlated that with the subjects' science literacy. He found that higher literacy was associated with stronger views— at both ends of the spectrum. Science literacy promoted polarization on climate, not consensus. According to Kahan, that's because people tend to use scientific knowledge to reinforce beliefs that have already been shaped by their worldview.

Americans fall into two basic camps, Kahan says. Those with a more "egalitarian" and "communitarian" mind-set are generally suspicious of industry and apt to think it's up to something dangerous that calls for government regulation; they're likely to see the risks of climate change. In contrast, people with a "hierarchical" and "individualistic" mind-set respect leaders of industry and don't like government interfering in their affairs; they're apt to reject warnings about climate change, because they know what accepting them could lead to—some kind of tax or regulation to limit emissions.

In the U.S., climate change somehow has become a litmus test that identifies you as belonging to one or the other of these two antagonistic tribes. When we argue about it, Kahan says, we're actually arguing about who we are, what our crowd is. We're thinking, People like us believe this. People like that do not believe this. For a hierarchical individualist, Kahan says, it's not irrational to reject established climate science: Accepting it wouldn't change the world, but it might get him thrown out of his tribe.

"Take a barber in a rural town in South Carolina," Kahan has written. "Is it a good idea for him to implore his customers to sign a petition urging Congress to take action on climate change? No. If he does, he will find himself out of a job, just as his former congressman, Bob Inglis, did when he himself proposed such action."

Science appeals to our rational brain, but our beliefs are motivated largely by emotion, and the biggest motivation is remaining tight with our peers. "We're all in high school. We've never left high school," says Marcia McNutt. "People still have a need to fit in, and that need to fit in is so strong that local values and local opinions are always trumping science. And they will continue to trump science, especially when there is no clear downside to ignoring science."

Meanwhile the Internet makes it easier than ever for climate skeptics and doubters of all kinds to find their own information and experts. Gone are the days when a small number of powerful institutions—elite universities, encyclopedias, major news organizations, even *National Geographic*—served as gatekeepers of scientific information. The Internet has democratized information, which is a good thing. But along with cable TV, it has made it possible to live in a "filter bubble" that lets in only the information with which you already agree.

How to penetrate the bubble? How to convert climate skeptics? Throwing more facts at them doesn't help. Liz Neeley, who helps train scientists to be better communicators at an organization called Compass, says that people need to hear from believers they can trust, who share their fundamental values. She has personal experience with this. Her father is a climate change skeptic and gets most of his information on the issue from conservative media. In exasperation she finally confronted him: "Do you believe them or me?" She told him she believes the scientists who research climate change and knows many of them personally. "If you think I'm wrong," she said, "then you're telling me that you don't trust me." Her father's stance on the issue softened. But it wasn't the facts that did it.

If you're a rationalist, there's something a little dispiriting about all this. In Kahan's descriptions of how we decide what to believe, what we decide sometimes sounds almost incidental. Those of us in the science-communication business are as tribal as anyone else, he told me. We believe in scientific ideas not because we have truly evaluated all the evidence but because we feel an affinity for the scientific community. When I mentioned to Kahan that I fully accept evolution, he said, "Believing in evolution is just a description about you. It's not an account of how you reason."

Maybe—except that evolution actually happened. Biology is incomprehensible without it. There aren't really two sides to all these issues. Climate change is happening. Vaccines really do save lives. Being right does matter—and the science tribe has a long track record of getting things right in the end. Modern society is built on things it got right.

Doubting science also has consequences. The people who believe vaccines cause autism—often well educated and affluent, by the way—are undermining "herd immunity" to such diseases as whooping cough and measles. The anti-vaccine movement has been going strong since the prestigious British medical journal the *Lancet* published a study in 1998 linking a common vaccine to autism. The journal later retracted the study, which was thoroughly discredited. But the notion of a vaccine-autism connection has been endorsed by celebrities and reinforced through the usual Internet filters. (Anti-vaccine activist and actress Jenny McCarthy famously said on the Oprah Winfrey Show, "The University of Google is where I got my degree from.")

In the climate debate the consequences of doubt are likely global and enduring. In the U.S., climate change skeptics have achieved their fundamental goal of halting legislative action to combat global warming. They haven't had to win the debate on the merits; they've merely had to fog the room enough to keep laws governing greenhouse gas emissions from being enacted.

Some environmental activists want scientists to emerge from their ivory towers and get more involved in the policy battles. Any scientist going that route needs to do so carefully, says Liz Neeley. "That line between science communication and advocacy is very hard to step back from," she says. In the debate over climate change the central allegation of the skeptics is that the science saying it's real and a serious threat is politically tinged, driven by environmental activism and not hard data. That's not true, and it slanders honest scientists. But it becomes more likely to be seen as plausible if scientists go beyond their professional expertise and begin advocating specific policies.

It's their very detachment, what you might call the cold-bloodedness of science, that makes science the killer app. It's the way science tells us the truth rather than what we'd like the truth to be. Scientists can be as dogmatic as anyone else—but their dogma is always wilting in the hot glare of new research. In science it's not a sin to change your mind when the evidence demands it. For some people, the tribe is more important than the truth; for the best scientists, the truth is more important than the tribe.

Scientific thinking has to be taught, and sometimes it's not taught well, McNutt says. Students come away thinking of science as a collection of facts, not a method. Shtulman's research has shown that even many college students don't really understand what evidence is. The scientific method doesn't come naturally—but if you think about it, neither does democracy. For most of human history neither existed. We went around killing each other to get on a throne, praying to a rain god, and for better and much worse, doing things pretty much as our ancestors did.

Now we have incredibly rapid change, and it's scary sometimes. It's not all progress. Our science has made us the dominant organisms, with all due respect to ants and blue-green algae, and we're changing the whole planet. Of course we're right to ask questions about some of the things science and technology allow us to do. "Everybody should be questioning," says McNutt. That's a hallmark of a scientist. But then they should use the scientific method, or trust people using the scientific method, to decide which way they fall on those questions." We need to get a lot better at finding answers, because it's certain the questions won't be getting any simpler.

Critical Thinking

1. Why is there so much public distrust of science today?
2. What is the scientific method?
3. Why do we cling to our intuitions in spite of scientific evidence to the contrary?
4. What is meant by the "confirmation bias" and how should we use the scientific approach to overcome it?
5. Why is science literacy not always enough to overcome science denial?

Internet References

Faraday Institute for Science and Religion
   www.faraday-institute.org/
National Center for Science Education
   http://ncse.com/

Washington Post science writer **Joel Achenbach** has contributed to *National Geographic* since 1998.

Article   Prepared by: Elvio Angeloni

The Roots of Science Denial

It has nothing do with science itself.

KATHERINE HAYHOE AND JEN SCHWARTZ

Learning Outcomes

After reading this article, you will be able to:

- Describe and explain the anti-intellectualism that is rampant today in America.

- Describe the polarization implicit in today's "tribalism" and the author's suggestion as to how scientists should deal with it.

Although she's technically Canadian, atmospheric scientist Katharine Hayhoe might understand America's polarized attitudes toward science better than anyone. Her bona fides have serious range: she is codirector of the Climate Science Center and a political science professor at Texas Tech University, CEO of a climate-impact consulting group, creator of the myth-busting web series Global Weirding, and an electric-car-driving evangelical Christian. Self-described as "on the fringes of many tribes," Hayhoe is equally adept at presenting to church groups and speaking on panels alongside people like Barack Obama and Leonardo DiCaprio. As a result, she has become one of the most lauded and sought-after climate communicators in the country—and the recipient of much hate mail. Hayhoe spoke with *Scientific American* about the war on facts and the forces driving climate skepticism. Edited excerpts from that conversation follow.

Science denial is basically anti-intellectualism. It's a thread that has run though American society for decades, possibly even centuries. Back in 1980, Isaac Asimov said that it's "nurtured by the false notion that democracy means that 'my ignorance is just as good as your knowledge.'" Today we're dealing with its most recent manifestation, at its peak.

Climate change is a special case of science denial, which of course goes back to Galileo. The Catholic Church didn't push back on Galileo until he stuck his head out of the ivory tower and published in Italian rather than in Latin, so that he could tell the common people something that was in direct opposition to the church's official program. Same with Darwin. The church didn't have a problem with his theory of evolution until he published a popular book that everyone could read.

Similarly, we've known about the relationship between carbon dioxide and global warming since the 1890s. It's been about 50 years since scientists warned President Lyndon B. Johnson about the dangers of a changing climate. But scientists back then didn't get the deluge of hate mail that I get now. So what shifted? It started, possibly, with (Columbia University climate scientist) James Hansen's testimony before Congress in 1988. He announced that a resource we all rely on—and makes many of the world's biggest companies rich—is harming not just the environment but all of humanity. I think it's no accident that Hansen is the most vilified and attacked climate scientist in the United States because he was the first person to emerge from ivory tower and start talking about global warming in a sphere where its implications became apparent for policy and politics.

So you can see that the problem people have with science is never the actual science. People have a problem with the implications of science for their worldview and, even more important, for their ideology. When anti-intellectualism rises to the surface, it's because there are new, urgent results coming out of the scientific community that challenge the perspective and status quo of people with power. Renewable energy is now posing a very significant threat to them. The more viable the technologies, the greater the pushback. It's a last-ditch effort to resist change, which is why denial is at a fever pitch.

Today, although many of the objections to climate science are couched in science-y terms—it's just a natural cycle, scientists aren't sure, global cooling, could it be volcanoes—or even religious-y terms—God is in control—99 percent of the time, that language is just a smokescreen. If you refuse to engage these arguments and push through for even five minutes, the conversation will naturally lead to profound objections to climate change solutions.

What's Really at Play

The number-one question I get from people is, "Could you just talk to my father-in-law, my congressman, and my colleague? If you just explain the facts to them, I'm sure it will change their mind." This is a trap. It turns us into Don Quixote, willing to tilt with these people and say, "Here's how we know it's not a natural cycle!" It almost never works. The only way to have a constructive dialogue with a dismissive person is on the level at which he or she really has the issue.

How did the narrative of climate change become a polarized, faith-based system? If we look at the surveys, the level of political polarization in the United States now compared with 20 or 30 years ago is staggering. Polarization implies a rise in tribalism: an unthinking, unquestioning adherence to the tenets of my tribe. Unfortunately, because climate solutions appear to challenge the ideology of the right-hand side of the political spectrum, it's become one of the most polarized issues in the United States We've become so tribal that if you're on the left, it's like a statement of faith to say climate change is real. And if you're on the right, it's a tenet to say climate change isn't real. That's why this "belief" language has come in more naturally rather than artificially.

That said, climate change is deliberately framed as a false religion by those who want people of faith to reject it. You'll see some conservative politicians say, "I'm a true believer, I reject that God is not in charge." It's a very clever messaging technique because if I'm a Christian—and more than 70 percent of Americans are—I'm taught to beware of false prophets. Beware of people saying things that sound good but are actually leading you to worship the created instead of the creator, Earth instead of God.

After presentations to skeptical audiences, I've had people say to me, "You know, this makes sense, and I wish I could agree with you, but I just can't because that would mean I'm agreeing with Al Gore." Any perceived Earth worship immediately triggers an ingrained response to reject. One of the funny images I show in some of my talks is called the Church of Climatology, with Al Gore as the preacher and other politicians and celebrities as the choir. Once somebody photoshopped my head onto one of the choir members. And I thought it was absolutely hilarious because, yes, I get how people feel. We have to laugh together before we can move on to talk about beliefs versus evidence.

That's why Al Gore is one of the best and one of the worst messengers for climate change. The best because he's so passionate and informed and has such a great reach. At the same time—I know he recognizes this—in this politically polarized

society, he firmly belongs to only one tribe. So by definition, it means the other tribe must reject him—and everything he stands for.

Climate change, of course, is also a tragedy of the commons, and it requires communal action. Yet the United States is the number-one most individualistic country in the world, founded on a revolt against big government and taxes. For many Americans, we have to talk more about market-based and technological solutions that appeal to their values instead of trying to change their identity. Take (Australian cognitive scientist) John Cook who founded the blog Skeptical Science, which evaluates and pushes back on global warming denial. John couldn't even get his own father to accept climate change. But then his fiscally conservative dad used a rebate program to get solar panels on his house. He saved all kinds of money and started telling everyone how wonderful these panels are. And later, his dad says to John, "You know, this climate change thing, it's probably real, and I'm doing my part." He didn't need to be a wide-eyed tree hugger saving the whales; he could now align climate change with his own identity.

Even in the science community, there's so much confusion over how to communicate. The deficit model—just give them the facts!—does not work in public discourse unless everybody is politically neutral. That's why social science is increasingly important. It was the experimental method in a recent paper where a researcher asked me to speak at an evangelical Christian college. He asked the students about global warming before and after my talk and found statistically significant differences on their perspectives. Many people are now doing this kind of message testing. How humans interact with information is an emerging area of research that's desperately important.

Scientists also tend to understate the impact of climate change. We tend to, in the words of one researcher, "[err] on the side of least drama." We tracked 20 years' worth of studies and found that we systematically underestimate the rate and speed of change. Climate science is under such a microscope now that we like to be 99.9 percent sure of results before we say anything. But are we being too conservative? It's a challenge I confront every day.

The Work Ahead

LOOK, WE CAN'T FIX ALL these issues—cultural, political, and psychological—before we take necessary action on climate change. People say to me, "Well, if you could just get everyone onboard with the science. . . ." I'm like, good luck with that! How did that work out the past few centuries? This climate problem is urgent. The window is closing. We have to fix it with the flawed, imperfect society we have today.

We have to start by asking what people's values are, where they're coming from, what they love, what they fear, and what gets them up in the morning. I say, "We can agree to disagree, but don't you support solar energy bringing all these jobs to Texas? Did you know Fort Hood gets energy from solar because it's cheaper?" If someone thinks solar power protects us from immigrants or terrorists or the Antichrist, then great, fine. With some groups, I don't even use the words "climate" and "change" sequentially. With Christians, we talk about the Bible's message of stewardship. With libertarians, we talk about free-market strategies. With moms' groups, we talk about pollution affecting our kids' health. With farmers, I say, "Hey, you're the backbone of our food system, how have drought patterns changed?" I don't validate the concept that there is a left and right side to climate science. And neither should the media. We should focus instead on solutions and impacts.

My number-one piece of advice for people doing climate—or any science—outreach is, Don't focus on the dismissive people. They're really a very small part of the population, and they're primarily older white men. Granted, the majority of them seem to be clustered in Washington, DC, these days. Still, for people who react so emotionally, it's because they've staked their identity on that denial. It's as much a part of them as their kidneys or heart. When you're asking them to change their mind, you are literally seen as a threat. It's worth standing up to them in a public forum and saying, "You are lost. Here is the evidence." Not for the purpose of changing their mind but to show everybody else that we have answers.

Because here's the thing: if you look at Yale University's climate communication surveys, most Americans agree that climate change is real, that humans are causing it and that it's important to do something about it. But the number-one problem we're facing is that most Americans do not think climate change affects them personally. They think it's a problem for poor people in poor counties or for future generations. It's in our psychology to deny an overwhelming problem that isn't immediately bearing down on us. And until recently, we've been shielded by our infrastructure, our crop insurance, and home insurance programs. Of course, all of that is up against the wall now, and it's my job to connect those dots.

That's why we (the authors of the government's National Climate Assessment) decided to write a supplemental Climate Science Special Report this year. It's the first time we've done it, and it's the most comprehensive, definitive report on climate change that the government has ever published. It's going through federal clearance now, slated for release in November, so we'll see what happens. (Editors' note: A draft of the report was leaked to the press shortly after this interview was conducted.) We made a lot of effort to write in a language that people can understand, and I think it really shuts down the whole "blue versus red" debate. It brings the science down to the level of where we live. You can see how climate change is affecting our food, water, economy, agriculture, infrastructure, and security.

The goal of the report is to provide a scientific basis for anyone who wants to know both broadly and specifically why climate change matters to us, now. Many, many more people in this country are in the cautious, disengaged category, but they often seem very quiet. We have to filter out the noise from the dismissive people and talk with those who are lurking at the edges, listening, not sure what they think yet about what should be done but open to dialogue. So, forget this elaborate smoke screen. By falling for the illusion that climate deniers can be convinced with more facts, we are distracted from engaging with a much larger group of people who want to understand why and how we should move forward with solutions. And that's exactly what the deniers want.

Critical Thinking

1. How does the author describe and explain today's anti-intellectualism with regard to science?
2. How should scientists deal with science denial?

Internet References

Hartford Institute for Religion Research
Hirr.hartsem.edu/ency/Anthropology.htm
Harvard Department of Anthropology
https://anthropology.fas.harvard.edu/research/religion
Society for the Anthropology of Religion
Sar.americananthro.org/

KATHARINE HAYHOE is codirector of the Climate Science Center and political science professor at Texas Tech University.

JEN SCHWARTZ is a senior editor for technology and mind for *Scientific American*.

Article   Prepared by: Elvio Angeloni

Life Chances

Evolution is a tug of war between randomness and determinism. But which one wins, asks Bob Holmes.

BOB HOLMES

Learning Outcomes

After reading this article, you will be able to:

- Discuss the importance of random mutations versus the process of natural selection in evolution.

- Discuss the ways in which random events in general may limit the powers of natural selection.

- Discuss the importance of the "founder effect" in creating new species.

- Discuss the role of "genetic drift" in determining the make-up of our genomes.

- Discuss "convergent evolution" with respect to the predictability of evolution.

Take 100 newly formed planets of one Earth mass. Place each in the habitable zone of a G-type main sequence star. Set your timer for 4 billion years. What do you get? A hundred planets teeming with life forms quite similar to those on Earth, perhaps even dominated by naked apes? Or would evolution produce very different outcomes every time, if life even got started at all?

Some biologists argue that evolution is a deterministic process, that similar environments will tend to produce similar outcomes. Others, the most famous of whom was Stephen Jay Gould, think its course follows unpredictable twists and turns, and that the same starting point can lead to very different results.

The answer does matter. If the Gould camp is right, the study of evolution is like the study of history: something we can understand only in retrospect. If, however, the vagaries of chance play just a minor role, then biologists can predict the course of evolution to a large extent—and predicting evolution

is crucial to stopping tumours becoming drug-resistant, or bacteria shrugging off an antibiotic, or bedbugs becoming immune to pesticides, or viruses killing people who have been vaccinated against them and so on.

So which is it? We might not have 100 Earths and a time machine, but we can look at how evolution has turned out on, say, neighbouring islands, or even rerun it over and over in the lab. These kinds of studies are giving us a better idea of the role of chance.

First things first. Evolution does begin with chance events, in the form of mutations. But it is not a case of anything goes; far from it. Which mutations survive and spread depends on natural selection—the survival of the fittest. Put another way, chance is the creative partner that comes up with all the ideas—some brilliant, others hopeless—while natural selection is the ruthlessly practical one, picking what works.

Many biologists, most notably Richard Dawkins, therefore insist that although mutations may be random, evolution is not. This insistence might make sense when explaining evolution to people who have not grasped the basic concept. But there is an element of chance in evolution, even when natural selection is firmly in the driving seat.

Take the evolution of flu viruses. We can predict with confidence that, over the next few years, the structure of a viral surface protein called haemagglutinin will evolve so that the human immune system can no longer recognise and attack it. What's more, we can even be fairly sure that the mutations that allow new strains of flu to evade the immune system will happen at one of seven critical sites in the gene coding for haemagglutinin, says Trevor Bedford, an evolutionary biologist at Fred Hutchinson Cancer Research Center in Seattle. In this sense, the evolution of flu is non-random and predictable. But it's a matter of chance which of those seven sites mutate, and how. Predicting the course of flu's evolution is almost impossible more than a year or two in advance, says Bedford. This is why flu vaccine makers do not always get it right, and why this season's flu vaccine was largely ineffective.

What's more, as important as natural selection is, its powers are limited. The fittest do not always survive; instead, the course of evolution is often shaped by accidental events. If it hadn't been for an asteroid strike, for instance, we mammals might still be scurrying about in mortal fear of dinosaurs. And if a different bird had been blown to the far-off Galapagos Islands a few million years ago, we might talk about Darwin's crows instead of Darwin's finches.

We've long known about this "founder effect", but recent studies suggest it may be more important than thought. For example, a handful of little birds were the ancestors of several populations of Berthelot's pipit on the Selvagem and Madeira island chains, in the Atlantic. There are big variations among them in the shape and size of beaks, legs, and wings.

When Lewis Spurgin of the University of East Anglia in Norwich, UK, studied these populations, he expected to find environmental differences that explained this variation, but he did not. Instead, he concluded that the physical differences were not driven by natural selection but were just a result of the small number of founders: accidents of history, in other words (*Molecular Ecology*, vol 23, p 1028).

Accidental Process

The founder effect can even create new species without the need for natural selection. When Daniel Matute, now at the University of North Carolina in Chapel Hill, took a large population of fruit flies and created 1000 founder populations of a single male and female in identical vials in his lab, most populations simply went extinct because of inbreeding. But in three of the surviving populations, the founders produced offspring different enough that they were less able to interbreed with the larger parental population—the first step to the creation of a new species.

Effects like these might explain why the islands of Hawaii have such a rich diversity of fruit flies. In fact, a few biologists think speciation is almost always an accidental process, rather than one driven by natural selection (*New Scientist*, 13 March 2010, p 30).

Yet more evidence of the limits of natural selection comes from genomes, which are littered with the products of chance. Despite many claims to the contrary, most of the human genome is just junk, for instance. This junk has accumulated because natural selection has not been strong enough to remove it, says Michael Lynch, an evolutionary biologist at Indiana University in Bloomington. In small populations, even mutations that are slightly harmful can spread throughout the population simply by chance.

Does this kind of genetic drift really matter? At least sometimes, it does. Joe Thornton of the University of Chicago has

been turning back the clock and replaying evolution to see if it could have turned out differently. Think Jurassic Park, except rather than recreate extinct animals, Thornton has recreated ancient proteins. His team began with living vertebrates that each have their own version of the gene encoding the protein that detects the stress hormone cortisol. By comparing the versions, they could work out how it had evolved over hundreds of millions of years, from a protein that could detect another hormone.

Then Thornton's team went a lot further. They actually made some of these ancient proteins and tried them out to see what effect each mutation had. Switching to cortisol took five mutations: two to recognise cortisol and three to "forget" the previous hormone.

But when the team made only these five changes, they destabilised the protein and wrecked it. It turns out the transition to cortisol was possible only because two other mutations that stabilise the protein had occurred first. But these "permissive" mutations have no effect by themselves. They must have arisen by chance, not by natural selection (*Science*, vol 317, p 1544).

"We think of these permissive mutations as opening doors, so that evolution has the opportunity to follow pathways that were inaccessible without the permissive mutations," says Thornton. And there seems to be only one way the door to the cortisol-binding pathway could have opened. Thornton tested thousands of other mutations, but none did the trick. "There is nothing else in the neighbourhood around the ancestral protein that could have opened that door," he says.

In Thornton's view, the course of evolution often—although not always—hinges on such seemingly insignificant chance events. In this way, evolution is a lot like life, he notes: a seemingly inconsequential decision one night to go to one party rather than another might lead to meeting your future partner and thus change the course of your life.

Then again, who we hook up with seldom alters the course of history.

Although all these studies suggest that chance plays a bigger role in evolution than generally acknowledged, the big question is how much difference it makes in the long run. The detailed paths taken by evolving populations might depend largely on chance, yet still lead to similar outcomes. There are only so many ways of flying and swimming, for instance, which is why wings and fins have independently evolved on many occasions. If Thornton's protein hadn't evolved the ability to bind cortisol, perhaps another protein would have instead.

There are many examples of this kind of convergent evolution. Arctic and Antarctic fish have independently evolved antifreeze proteins that work in the same way, for example, while several snake lineages have separately come up with identical methods of coping with the poisons secreted by the newts they eat. In the Greater Antilles in the Caribbean, meanwhile, evolution has effectively been rerun on four islands—and turned out the same way. Each of the islands has long-legged Anolis lizards that run on the ground, short-legged ones that grasp twigs, and lizards with big toepads that stick to leaves. But each island's lizards seem to derive from a single founder population, meaning they independently evolved to fill the same niches. Does this mean Gould was wrong after all, that in the long run chance does not matter that much? Perhaps the closest we can get to an answer is the Long-Term Experimental Evolution Project, led by Richard Lenski of Michigan State University. On 24 February 1988, Lenski took samples of one kind of *E. coli* bacteria and used them to found 12 new populations. Every day since then—on weekends and holidays, despite blizzards and grant deadlines—someone has kept them growing by transferring samples to new nutrient medium.

Replaying Evolution

In the 27 years that have passed, Lenski's populations evolved for about 60,000 generations. For comparison, *Homo sapiens* has gone through perhaps 20,000 generations in its entire existence. All 12 populations have changed in similar ways, evolving larger cells and faster growth rates, showing that sometimes evolution really does unfold in predictable ways. But even without external events like asteroid strikes, its course was not always predictable. One population evolved into a mix of two lineages, each of which survive because they pursue slightly different strategies. Another suddenly developed, at about the 31,500th generation, the ability to feed on citrate, an additive to the culture medium that *E. coli* cannot normally use. "They started from the same place and were subjected to exactly the same conditions, and differences still pop up," says Zachary Blount, who works with Lenski on the project. "The differences arise purely out of the chance that is inherent in the evolutionary process."

Was the citrate-using mutation a lucky break, or could evolution find it again? Because Lenski's team freezes a sample of each culture every 500 generations, Blount was able to go back into the archives of this population and literally rerun evolution. When he did so, the only time citrate use evolved was when he began the replay with cells from the 20,000th generation or later.

Clearly, some mutation or mutations must have happened around the 20,000th generation that set the stage for citrate use to evolve much later, just as Thornton's hormone receptor required permissive mutations before it could switch to recognise a different target. "We still haven't figured out what that mutation was, which is really frustrating," says Blount. Until they can, the team will not know whether the permissive mutation offered some other advantage to the bacteria. Even if it did, however, it seems clear that its role in permitting citrate use must have been just a lucky by-product.

So what would we get if we could replay evolution over and over on a planetary scale? One possibility is an awful lot of slime. Nick Lane of University College London thinks that the emergence of complex cells depended on a highly unlikely merger of two kinds of simple cell (*New Scientist*, 23 June 2012, p 32). If he's right, bacteria-like life forms are common on other worlds but rarely give rise to more sophisticated organisms.

No Naked Apes

But assuming life did get past the slime stage on our worlds, what would it be like? "There is a fairly good chance that such replays would often yield worlds that look broadly like ours in terms of what niches are filled, and what sorts of major traits you see," says Blount. In other words, you'd still expect to see photosynthesisers and predators, and parasites and decomposers. But the details are likely to differ sharply from one replay to the next, he says. Even if we replayed evolution a hundred times, it's highly unlikely that we would end up again with a big-brained primate ruling the planet.

But would some other brainy, social animal take over the planet? Maybe. "There's clearly an adaptive zone in most habitats that involves intelligence," says David Jablonski, a palaeontologist at the University of Chicago. And it has become clear that many traits we once thought of as uniquely human, from language to tool-making, exist to some extent in many other animals. So although naked apes might not emerge on any of the 100 planets, other smart tool-users might. It is a question we might even be able to answer one day. Thousands of exoplanets have now been discovered and even though we've yet to find any just like ours, all the evidence suggests there are plenty of Earth-like planets close enough that we might not only determine whether they support life, but also learn a little about it. The answer may be in the stars.

Critical Thinking

1. How do the processes of random mutation and natural selection interact to bring about evolution?
2. What role does the "founder effect" have in creating new species?
3. How does "genetic drift" help to explain variations that were not selected for?
4. Discuss convergent evolution as a way of explaining similar characteristics evolving separately in different species.

Internet References

Understanding Evolution
http://evolution.berkeley.edu
Human Evolution
https://en.wikipedia.org/wiki/Human_evolution

BOB HOLMES is a correspondent for *New Scientist* based in Edmonton, Canada.

Article   Prepared by: Elvio Angeloni

The Good Dinosaur

JONATHAN B. LOSOS

Learning Outcomes

After reading this article, you will be able to:

- Explain *convergent evolution* and the evidence for it.

- Discuss Stephen Jay Gould's argument for *contingency* in evolution as a counterargument to the notion that a human-like creature would not have evolved if an asteroid had not destroyed the large reptiles.

- Explain the author's point of view regarding the debate about contingency versus determinism.

The trailer for the Pixar movie *The Good Dinosaur* begins with an asteroid belt packed full of oversized boulders. One asteroid shoots through the rock pile, slamming into another, which ricochets into a third, sending it zooming off into space, straight toward a distant object. As the object gets larger, its identity becomes obvious: a blue planet with patches of green and wisps of white. "Millions of years ago, an asteroid six miles wide destroyed every dinosaur on Earth," the narrator intones. We see the asteroid entering Earth's atmosphere, turning orange, sizzling.

You know what comes next: the impact in the Gulf of Mexico, earthquakes around the world, forests in the Northern Hemisphere spontaneously bursting into flames, the sky blackened for months by soot. The dinosaurs, and many other creatures, wiped out. A sad day, indeed. This Pixar offering, apparently, is darker than most of their movies, a tragedy, ending with the demise of the great reptiles. Or maybe it isn't.

"But what if," the trailer asks, and then shows the asteroid streaking through the Cretaceous sky. Grazing behemoths—sauropods, duck-billed dinosaurs—look up momentarily, then go back to filling their cavernous bellies with leafy food. The asteroid flies by, a near miss instead of a fatal impact. Life goes on. The dinosaurs' salad days continue.

I know the answer to the question "What if?" The dinosaurs were at the peak of their reign 66 million years ago. They had dominated the world for more than 100 million years. Sans asteroid, the dinos would have continued their global rule: *Tyrannosaurus rex*, *Triceratops*, *Velociraptor*, *Ankylosaurus*—they all would have survived. New dinosaurs would have evolved, replacing the old ones. The ever-changing dinosaurian parade would have marched on. In all likelihood, the dinosaurs would still be walking the Earth today.

And who wouldn't be here today? We wouldn't, that's who. Even though we mammals evolved about 225 million years ago, almost exactly at the same time as the dinosaurs, for the first 160 million years of our existence, we didn't amount to much. The dinosaurs saw to that. Our furry forebears were an insignificant afterthought in the global biosphere, generally much smaller than the smallest dinosaur, active at night to avoid their reptilian overlords, scurrying in the underbrush, eating whatever scraps they could find. If you think of an opossum, you have a good idea of the looks and lifestyle of our Cretaceous kin, though most were probably even smaller.

It wasn't until the asteroid wiped out the dinosaurs that Team Mammal got its evolutionary opportunity—and we certainly took advantage of it, quickly proliferating to fill the empty ecosphere, transforming the last 66 million years into the *Age of Mammals*. But we owe all of that to the asteroid.

We—scientists and laypersons alike—once thought that the rise of mammals was inevitable, that we mammals are inherently superior to those reptilian brutes, thanks to our big brains and our internal combustion engines generating body heat. It took some time, so the idea went, but we eventually supplanted the dinosaurs, perhaps by eating their eggs into extinction or otherwise showing them who's who.

We now know this is nonsense. Mammals had bit parts in the Mesozoic evolutionary play. The dinos were doing just fine on that lovely day in 66 million BC, their dominance in no manner challenged by the vermin underfoot. Without the asteroid, life would have continued on its merry way, with reptilian intrigue and machinations, new species evolving, others going extinct, as they had for millions of years. There's little reason to think that we mammals would have emerged from the shadows to become major players in the ecosystem. The dinosaurs were already there, filling the ecological niches, using the resources—it was only after they were gone that we had our evolutionary turn.

No asteroid, no mass extinction, no mammal evolutionary flowering, no you and me. So, these first few moments of the movie trailer had me excited. Pixar had made a movie all about dinosaurs and how the world would have turned out differently if the asteroid had sailed on by. Forty-five seconds into the preview, I knew the movie was going to be a winner.

The trailer continued with a *T. rex* chasing a herd of plant eaters, causing them to stampede, a pell-mell rush of enormous herbivores, long-necked brontosaurs, and three-horned *Triceratops*, a typical day in the Mesozoic. But then I did a double take—some of those beasts looked more like hairy, big-horned bison than ceratopsians. And the next scene shows a brontosaur bounding along with something on its head—a human child!

If the asteroid was a near miss, what are mammals doing there? This is a Pixar movie, after all, so one expects a few liberties to be taken (e.g., dinosaurs speaking English), but is there any scientific evidence supporting the juxtaposition of *Brontosaurus*, bison, and baby? If the dinosaurs hadn't been wiped out, might mammals have diversified anyway, producing bison and—more importantly—us? Dinosaurs had kept mammals in their place—that place being tiny and in the underbrush—for millions of years. Is it possible that somehow, after all that time, mammals could have cut loose evolutionarily and prospered, even while the rule of the big reptiles continued?

There is one possibility, at least according to British paleontologist Simon Conway Morris. Dinosaurs, being reptiles, liked it hot. Their low metabolic rates did not produce much internal heat. When it was warm outside, that wasn't a problem—they could get their heat from the ambient environment, supplementing it when necessary by sitting in the Sun. The dinosaur dynasty was enabled by a long stretch of global warming, a time when much of the world was tropical, a good time to be a reptile.

But Conway Morris points out that the climate finally began to change about 34 million years ago. The world got cooler. Eventually, the ice ages came, glaciers expanded, much of the world became chilly. There's a reason you don't find reptiles in the far north and south today—it's too cold for them. Conway Morris suggests that even with dinosaurs still extant, this global cooldown would have sprung the mammals, kick-starting their evolutionary radiation. Dinosaurs would have had to retreat to the tropical equator, leaving the higher and midlatitudes free, giving mammals their evolutionary chance at last.

Let's humor Conway Morris for the moment and assume his scenario is correct. Mammals start diversifying, occupying ecological niches long filled by dinosaurs, becoming bigger, more diverse. Maybe this Ice Age—enabled evolutionary diversification would have led to an Age of Mammals equally as magnificent and multifarious as the one the asteroid spawned.

But would it have been the same Age of Mammals? Would there be elephants and rhinos and tigers and aardvarks? Or would this alternative world have produced a very different ensemble of animals—species completely unrecognizable to us, dividing up the world's resources and filling its ecological niches, but in different ways than the creatures around us today? Or, to place the question closer to home, would we have evolved? Would there be humans to produce babies to sit atop Pixar's *Brontosaurus*?

Conway Morris responds with an emphatic "yes." To him and other scientists in his camp, evolution is deterministic, predictable, following the same course time after time. The reason, they argue, is that there are only so many ways to make a living in the world. To each problem posed by the environment, a single, optimal solution exists, leading natural selection to produce the same evolutionary outcomes over and over.

As evidence, they point to convergent evolution, the phenomenon that species independently evolve similar features. If there are limited ways to adapt to a given environmental circumstance, then we would expect species occupying similar environments to convergently evolve the same adaptations, and that's exactly what happens. There's a reason that dolphins and sharks look so much alike—they evolved the same body shape to move rapidly through the water in pursuit of prey. The eyes of octopuses and humans are nearly indistinguishable because the ancestors of both evolved very similar organs to detect and focus light. The list of evolutionary convergences goes on and on, as we shall soon see. Conway Morris and his colleagues see it as ubiquitous and inevitable, allowing us to predict how evolution would have unfolded, what a late-blooming mammal radiation might have looked like. Conway Morris concludes that "the rise of active, agile, and arboreal ape-like mammals, and ultimately a hominid-like form would have been postponed, not cancelled . . . without the end-Cretaceous asteroid impact . . . the appearance of the hominids would have been delayed by approximately 30 million years." Pixar, in other words, was on solid ground in commingling babies and brontos.

But let's take this argument one step further. Even if the mammals forever stayed in the shadows, could a species like us have evolved from some other ancestral lineage? If convergence is so ineluctable, the push to particular solutions so unrelenting, there's no reason to think the rise of mammals was a necessary prerequisite. A big-brained, bipedal, highly social species with forward-facing eyes and forelimbs capable of manipulating objects could have evolved from some other ancestor. But if not from mammals, then descended from what?

Answering that question requires no more than switching from *The Good Dinosaur* to the bad dinosaur. Specifically, to *Velociraptor*, the villain of *Jurassic Park* (and, in an unexpected case of redemption 20 years later, the hero of *Jurassic World*). Talk about smarts! These wily reptiles worked as a team, outwitted the hardened safari hunter, and even figured out how to open doors with their three-fingered hands. And they were visually oriented and bipedal. Beginning to sound familiar?

With a few exceptions, *Jurassic Park*'s portrayal of *Velociraptor* was reasonably accurate. Of course, we don't know how smart they were, but they did have large brains, and some paleontologists have speculated that they may have been social, living in groups, and coordinating their predatory attacks like lions or wolves. If you were looking for a jumping-off point for the evolution of a hominid-like animal, *Velociraptor* would seem like a good place to start.

And that's just where Canadian paleontologist Dale Russell began in the early 1980s. He studied a close relative of *Velociraptor*, another small theropod dinosaur named *Troodon* that also lived at the end of the Cretaceous period. *Troodon* had the largest brain relative to its body weight of any dinosaur, a brain comparable in size to that of an armadillo or a guinea fowl. In other words, these reptiles were no geniuses, but they weren't completely clueless, either. Russell noted that over the course of hundreds of millions of years, animals have steadily evolved bigger brains. The fact that the largest dinosaur brain occurred in a species that lived at the end of their tenure suggested that dinosaurs, too, were following this evolutionary trend of increasing brain size through time. What would have happened, Russell asked, if the asteroid hadn't wiped them out? How would *Troodon*'s descendants have evolved if natural selection pushed them toward ever larger brains?

Russell went through a chain of logic to speculate what a modern-day descendant of *Troodon* would have looked like: larger brains require larger braincases, bigger braincases usually are associated with a shortening of the facial region, heavier heads are more easily balanced by placement directly on top of the body, this in turn favors an upright posture, which means that a tail is no longer needed as a counterweight to the no longer forward-leaning front half of the body. A few more assumptions about the best leg and ankle structure for walking upright and, voilà, what was termed inelegantly the "dinosauroid," a green, scaly creature with an uncanny resemblance to a human, right down to the butt cheeks and fingernails.

Remember, Russell did not set out to ask how a dinosaur could evolve into a humanoid. Rather, his goal was to think about how selection for increased brain size would lead to other anatomical changes. The end result of this project led to envisioning a creature strikingly similar to us, a reptilian humanoid.

Russell's evolutionary projection, though conjured years in advance, is consistent with Conway Morris' ideas that the evolution of hominid-like life-forms is inevitable. So consistent, in fact, that Conway Morris even appeared in a BBC documentary, sipping coffee at a café next to a dinosauroid reading a newspaper.

So Pixar had a couple of plot options. If the Cretaceous asteroid had, indeed, missed Earth, then according to Conway Morris and others, humans or something like us would have evolved one way or another. The only question was whether they would have been hairy, the result of delayed mammalian evolutionary diversification, or scaly, an outcome of natural selection on increased dinosaur brain size.

. . .

It's fun to think counterfactually to wonder what might have transpired if history had unfolded differently. But questions about the inevitability of humanoid evolution transcend speculation about Earth's history.

We now know there are a lot of planets in the universe that potentially could harbor life as we know it. These "habitable exoplanets" are neither too hot nor too cold and have liquid water on the surface. A recent study indicated that billions of such planets may exist in the Milky Way galaxy alone. The nearest may be only four light-years away.

Suppose life has evolved on some of these planets. What would it look like? Would the life-forms resemble those here? And what about intelligent life-forms, as smart as us, or even much smarter? How much, if at all, would they be like humans?

Quite a lot, if we believe what we see in the movies, and some well-renowned scientists agree. "If we ever succeed in communicating with conceptualizing beings in outer space," wrote the late biologist Robert Bieri, "they won't be spheres, pyramids, cubes, or pancakes. In all probability, they will look an awful lot like us." David Grinspoon, doyen of the emerging interdisciplinary field of astrobiology, goes a step further: "when they [aliens] do finally land on the White House lawn, whatever walks or slithers down the gangplank may look strangely familiar." Not surprisingly, Conway Morris agrees, suggesting that "the constraints of evolution and the ubiquity of convergence make the emergence of something like ourselves a near-inevitability." But before exploring the scientific basis for these scientists' extraterrestrial predictions, let's return to Planet Earth.

. . .

More specifically, to southeast Africa. Darkness comes quickly in the Zambian woodlands. I'm a herpetologist—a lizard guy—so tracking nocturnal lions is not my day job, but I've come to Zambia for a little R & R prior to fieldwork in South Africa. Amazingly, lions can become accustomed to the presence of vehicles and will allow you to shadow them as they go on the prowl, and that's just what we're doing.

Off to the right, there's a movement, something not too large approaching, unaware that it's on a collision course with a pride of lions. As it shuffles closer, its identity becomes clear—a crested porcupine, the sixty-pound rodent covered head to tail with pointy spines, some a foot and a half long. Its spines, of course, are for defense, for situations just like this, but they're not always effective. Lions have a counterstrategy, slipping a paw underneath the porcupine's body to flip it over, exposing the vulnerable belly. You can imagine the rest.

There's a *Seinfeld* episode in which Jerry's watching a nature documentary on antelopes, and the lions attack, and Jerry's yelling, "Run, antelope, run! Use your speed. Get away!" And the next night, he's watching another nature flick, this time focused on lions, and they go for an antelope, and he's shouting, "Get the antelope; eat him; bite his head! Trap him; don't let him use his speed!" But even though tonight we've been following the lions, I'm rooting for the porcupine. Leave him alone and go after something your own size!

But, of course, they don't. One of the lionesses wanders over to the porcupine. He turns his backside to her, erects his spines, sort of like a cat arching its back and bristling its hair, and then he starts shaking the tail spines against each other, clackity-clack, clackity-clack.

And, amazingly, it works. After a moment, the lioness turns away and rejoins the pride, and the porcupine wanders off into the night.

At the end of the evening, I replayed the events in my head, mulling over my previous porcupine encounters. As well as Africa and Asia, porkies also occur throughout most of the New World. I've only seen the North American porcupine in the wild once, in a tree of all places—30 feet up as I glided by on a ski lift. In the rainforests of Costa Rica, however, I've seen prehensile-tailed porcupines a number of times, again mostly in trees. Two porcupines: the North American porcupine and the African crested porcupine.

Certainly, there are differences among these species. The most obvious is size: the crested porcupine is twice the weight of its North American counterpart and 30 times that of the diminutive Rothschild's porcupine from Panama. The quills correspondingly vary in length—14 inches in the crested, four inches in the North American, shorter yet in the Rothschild's. Some species have red noses, others brown; prehensile-tailed porcupines have no quills on their tails. Yet, the differences pale in comparison to the similarities: not only possession of quills but also a similar stocky body with short legs, small eyes, spiky hairdo. Given these similarities, I never questioned my assumption that porcupines were one happy evolutionary family, all descended from the same ancestral spiny ur-porcupine.

Imagine my surprise, then, when I learned that I had it all wrong. Despite their shared prickliness, New and Old World porcupines do not share a common evolutionary heritage. Rather than owing their pointy good looks to descent from a common, bristly ancestor, the two lineages have independently evolved their quills from different, unquilled rodent species. They are the result of convergent evolution.

. . .

I'm not the first person in the history to be fooled by convergence. In fact, I'm in pretty good company. Charles Darwin himself was bamboozled on his famous visit to the Galápagos Islands. There he discovered the small birds that now bear his name, the Darwin's finches. But Darwin did not realize that these bird species were all closely related to each other, descendants of a single ancestral finch that colonized the islands sometime in the past. Rather, he thought the species represented four groups with which he was familiar from home: true finches, grosbeaks, blackbirds, and wrens.

It was only when Darwin returned to London and turned his specimens over to the noted ornithologist John Gould that he learned his mistake. The species were not representatives of a diverse set of familiar types after all but instead members of a single group of birds unique to the Galápagos—Darwin had been hoodwinked by convergent evolution. This revelation fit in with other findings from Darwin's voyage, all pointing in one direction, toward the "transmutability" of species. By the time that he revised his best-selling *Voyage of the Beagle* in 1845, the finch story intimated what was to come a decade later: "Seeing this gradation and diversity of structure in one small, intimately related group of birds, one might really fancy that from an original paucity of birds in this archipelago, one species had been taken and modified for different ends."

The broader implication of the story—that the finches had diversified on the Galápagos to mirror species using a variety of habitats elsewhere—was also not lost on Darwin. Although he didn't allude to convergent evolution in the *Voyage*, he clearly articulated the idea 14 years later in the *Origin*: "in nearly the same way as two men have sometimes hit on the very same invention, so natural selection . . . has sometimes modified in very nearly the same manner two parts in two organic beings, which owe but little of their structure in common to inheritance from the same ancestor."

Darwin was not the only early naturalist so fooled by convergence. When Captain Cook landed in Botany Bay in 1770 on his first South Pacific voyage, the naturalist on the expedition, Joseph Banks, sent specimens and drawings of Australian birds back to England. This began a flood of material dispatched to the motherland by colonists and explorers over the next half century, revealing the existence of many new species.

The key figure in making sense of this profusion of new species was John Gould. At around the same time that he was consulting with Darwin on the finches, Gould decided to take up a comprehensive description of Australian birds. Quickly realizing that he needed to go to Australia to do the job right, he picked up and relocated Down Under, spending three years there and eventually producing a mammoth seven-volume series of paintings and descriptions.

But Gould, so right about Darwin's finches, turned out to be equally wrong about the evolutionary affinities of Australia's avifauna. Many Aussie birds are very similar in appearance and habit to species in Europe, such as wrens, warblers, babblers, flycatchers, robins, nuthatches, and others. As a result, Gould assigned the newly discovered Australian birds to the familiar Northern Hemisphere families.

Gould's error is understandable. Over the course of the next century and a half, many very knowledgeable ornithologists were equally deceived and treated these birds as colonial outposts, the result of a wave of invasions of Australia by many types of birds.

However, genetic studies starting in the 1980s showed that, in fact, most of the species are part of a large Australian bird radiation that evolved in situ. In other words, these Australian birds are closely related to each other; they are not members of many different Northern Hemisphere families but convergent with them.

The discovery of unexpected cases of convergent evolution continues to this day. Indeed, with the flood of genetic data now available for so many different species, our understanding of evolutionary relationships is advancing by leaps and bounds, producing a much firmer grasp on the evolutionary tree of life. One consequence is that we are increasingly finding new cases in which we had been misled by anatomical similarity, only now realizing that it results not from descent from a similar common ancestor but from independent derivation.

How can we explain this rampant convergent evolution? There's a commonsense explanation, the one Darwin proposed. If species live in similar environments and face similar challenges to their survival and reproduction, then natural selection will lead to the evolution of similar traits: the existence of large seeds is a resource for birds, requiring big beaks to crack them open, and so similar, big-beaked birds evolve in numerous seedy locations; threatened by big cats, oversized rodents repeatedly evolve a spiny defense, as effective against lions in Africa as it is against pumas in the Americas.

In the last two decades, some biologists have extended this view to the cosmos. Here on Earth, species face the same challenges around the world and through time, and they evolve the same solutions. These scientists argue that the same physical challenges that occur here will also be faced by life-forms on similar planets and will lead to the same biological solutions. George McGhee, a paleontologist from Rutgers University, argues that there's only one way to build a fast-swimming aquatic organism, and that's why dolphins, sharks, tunas, and ichthyosaurs (extinct marine reptiles from the Age of Dinosaurs) all look alike.

Taking this a step further, he argues that "if any large, fast-swimming organisms exist in the oceans of Jupiter's moon Europa, swimming under the perpetual ice that covers their world, I predict with confidence that they will have streamlined, fusiform bodies . . . very similar to a porpoise, an ichthyosaur, a swordfish, or a shark." Conway Morris agrees, saying, "Certainly it's not the case that every Earth-like planet will have life let alone humanoids. But if you want a sophisticated plant it will look awfully like a flower. If you want a fly, there's only a few ways you can do that. If you want to swim, like a shark, there's only a few ways you can do that. If you want to invent warm-bloodedness, like birds and mammals, there's only a few ways to do that."

. . .

Not everyone agrees with this viewpoint. Let's go back to the movies to see why.

In the climactic scene of the classic 1946 film *It's a Wonderful Life*, George Bailey (played by Jimmy Stewart) despairs that his life has been a failure and wishes that he'd never been born. Clarence Odbody, George's guardian angel, then shows him how life in Bedford Falls would have been radically different—and much for the worse—if George had never existed: his brother dead; his friends and family unhappy, homeless, and institutionalized; a boat full of soldiers sunk; the town a den of iniquity. George realizes that his life has been worthwhile and abandons his suicidal plans, then subsequently is redeemed when the townspeople come to his rescue in appreciation of all his good deeds.

The American Film Institute in 2006 named *It's a Wonderful Life* the most inspirational movie of all time. Stephen Jay Gould, the famed paleontologist and evolutionary biologist, was among those inspired by it but in a way different than most. To him, the movie was a parable for the evolutionary history of life, so much so that the title of his 1989 book, *Wonderful Life*, paid homage to the movie. In the book,

Gould argued for the dominating importance of historical contingency in evolution. By contingency, he meant that the particular sequence of events critically determines the course of history: A leads to B, B to C, C to D, and so on. In a historically contingent world, if you alter A, you don't get D. If George Bailey is never born, events in New Bedford unfold differently. Gould argued that life is full of George Bailey events—some major, most minor—but any of which could send life in a different direction. Lightning strikes, falling trees, asteroid impacts, even the flip-of-a-coin determination of which genetic variant a mother passes on to her daughter—any of these could make a difference that would ramify through the eons. Like New Bedford without George Bailey, Gould wrote, "any replay [of the history of life] altered by an apparently insignificant jot or tittle at the outset, would have yielded an . . . outcome of entirely different form."

This view has important implications for understanding the diversity of life we see around us. If evolution is dominated by contingency, then there can be no predictability, no Conway Morrisian determinism. The end result is so influenced by contingencies that there is no way one could predict at the beginning what would happen at the end. Start over again, and a completely different result might unfold. Hitting home where it matters the most, Gould concluded, "Replay the tape [of life] a million times . . . and I doubt that anything like *Homo sapiens* would ever evolve again."

. . .

Gould's argument, elegantly and persuasively made, resonates with us all. Who hasn't rued that "if I hadn't done X, then Y wouldn't have happened," where X could be anything minor (mispronouncing a name) or major (having a drink too many) and Y is something you wish hadn't taken place?

Still, sensible as the argument may be, what is the evidence? There's only one history of life. How can we test the repeatability of evolution? Gould proposed a thought experiment to address such questions. Replay the tape of life, he suggested, go back to the same starting conditions and see if the same result ensues. Such "gedankenexperiments," as the Germans call them, have a long pedigree in science and philosophy, and this one has been taken up by many and proven particularly fruitful.

Conway Morris and colleagues, of course, disagree with Gould's basic premise—changing an earlier event need not substantially alter the downstream outcome. They argue that the ubiquity of convergent evolution demonstrates the impotence of contingency, that in many cases more or less the same outcome would ensue regardless of the specific historical sequence of events.

The issue of convergence and evolutionary determinism had not yet been raised when Gould wrote *Wonderful Life*. However, in an exchange with Conway Morris published nine years later, Gould's response was simple: the importance of convergence is "overestimated," he said, and pointed to Australia as state's evidence number one.

Let's again consider Captain Cook's expedition to the Antipodes. Among the first animals, they encountered was a kangaroo. Kangaroos are the major native plant eaters in Australia today. Functionally, they fill the same role as deer, bison, and myriad other herbivores in the rest of the world. And yet, as Gould (Stephen Jay, not John) noted, kangaroos haven't converged upon these other types of herbivores—even a toddler can tell that a kangaroo and a deer are different sorts of animals.

And then there's the koala, that lovable, bearish tree hugger that lives life in the slow lane, sleeping 20 hours a day as it detoxifies the eucalyptus leaves that comprise its diet (and that make its fur reek of menthol). Nothing like it exists anywhere else in the world, now or, according to the fossil record, ever.

But when we're talking evolutionary one-offs, there's only one king. Venomous ankle spurs, luxurious pelt, the ability to detect the electrical discharges of their prey's muscles with electroreceptors on their snout. Powerful flat tail, webbed feet, lays eggs. Bill like a duck. The world's greatest animal, the duck-billed platypus, a mishmash of parts borrowed from throughout the animal kingdom. An animal so confused that when the first specimens arrived in England at the end of the eighteenth century, shipped from Sydney across the Indian Ocean, scientists searched for hours in vain to locate the stitches by which crafty Chinese merchants must have assembled their hoax.

These examples have come from Down Under, but evolutionary one-offs occur everywhere. Giraffes, elephants, penguins, and chameleons—these are all species exquisitely adapted to their specific ecological niches, with no evolutionary facsimile now or in the past (note that an "evolutionary one-off" is not necessarily a single species. For example, there are three living species of elephant, and many more that occurred in the past, like mastodons and mammoths. However, all elephant species are descended from a single ancestral elephant. That is why elephants can be considered evolutionarily unique—the proboscidean way of life only evolved a single time).

. . .

Convergent evolution is a scientific phenomenon, and you'd think that science should have been able to settle the question of its ubiquity by now. But the problem is that figuring out what happened in the past is not easy. We are taught in grade school about the scientific method, how observations lead to the formulation of a hypothesis that is then tested with a decisive experiment in the laboratory. That formulation in a very simplistic way captures the operation of mechanistically oriented sciences—that is, the sciences involved in understanding how something like a cell or an atom works. Think that a particular gene is important in producing a particular trait? Use molecular biology wizardry to disable the gene and see if the trait still develops.

But evolutionary biology is a historical science. Like astronomers and geologists, we evolutionary biologists try to figure out what happened in the past. And like historians, we are bedeviled by the asymmetry of time's arrow—we can't go back in time to see what happened. Moreover, evolution occurs notoriously slowly, seemingly making it impossible to watch it as it occurs.

Stephen Jay Gould laid out the experiment we'd like to do: replay evolution time and time again, and see how sensitive the outcome is to various experimental perturbations. But we call such ideas thought experiments for a reason—in the real world, they can't be conducted. Or so we used to think.

It turns out that Darwin and a century of biologists following him were wrong in one key respect: evolution does not always plod along at a snail's pace. When natural selection is strong—as occurs when conditions change—evolution can rip along at light speed.

The reality of rapid evolution allows us to go beyond simply observing whether and how species respond. In a development that would have astonished Darwin, researchers are creating their own evolution experiments, altering conditions in a controlled and statistically designed way. Just like lab biologists, we can test evolutionary mechanisms, but out in nature, in real populations. Researchers are placing light- and dark-colored mice in half-acre-sized cages in the Nebraska sand dunes, moving guppies in Trinidad from stream pools with predators to those without, and switching walking stick insects from one habitat to another.

I've conducted some of these experiments myself, testing hypotheses about why small lizards in the Bahamas evolve longer or shorter legs. I know what you're thinking, but my colleagues and I are willing to sacrifice for science. It's a dirty job, hanging out on beautiful, windswept islands surrounded by ocean, but someone's got to do it, and we're the ones. I'll go into much greater detail but for now suffice to say that if you go back to the Bahamas year after year and measure the legs of thousands of lizards with a portable X-ray machine, you'll see that lizard populations can evolve rapidly. Moreover, if you experimentally alter the conditions the lizards experience, causing them to change their habitat use, populations on those islands will evolve quickly and in predictable directions.

Although evolution experiments in nature are still in their infancy, laboratory scientists have been conducting such work for decades. These studies trade the realism of nature for the hyper-precision of the lab, providing exquisite control over conditions experienced by the evolving populations. Moreover, the shorter life span of lab organisms, particularly microbes, means that these studies can be longer term, encompassing more generations and creating more opportunity for evolution to occur. One laboratory experiment has been following microbial evolution for more than a quarter century, studying the extent to which 12 populations evolve in the same way.

. . .

I often compare evolutionary biology to a detective story, a whodunit. A crime has been committed—or in this case, something has evolved—and we want to know what happened. If we had a time machine, we could go back and watch for ourselves. If we could replay the tape, we'd just set things up like they were back then and start it again.

But neither of these is possible. Instead, we're left with a bunch of clues, and, like Sherlock Holmes, we have to figure it out as best we can. We can see the patterns of evolutionary history, the species that occur today and the fossils of what existed in the past, allowing us to assess the extent to which evolution has repeatedly produced the same outcome. And we can study the evolutionary process as it operates today. By conducting experiments, we can see how repeatable and predictable evolution is: if you start at the same point, will you always end up with the same outcome? And if you start at different points, but select in the same way, will you converge on the same result? So even though we can't replay the tape, we can study evolutionary pattern and process. By putting the two together, scientists are now well on the way to understanding evolutionary repeatability.

. . .

Seven billion and counting, sometimes we are the resource being exploited. Malaria, HIV, hantavirus, influenza—to microorganisms, our bodies are like any other crop and they are evolving to take advantage of us. We, in turn, combat them as we do crop pests, with chemicals, and they rapidly evolve resistance.

This is where the debate between contingency and determinism becomes personal. If we can predict not only when rapid evolution will occur but what form it will take, we will be able to derive general principles and thus be better positioned to respond effectively. But if each case of rapid evolution is contingent on the specific circumstances, then we'll have to start from scratch each time we face a new weed, pest, or disease, figuring out how our evolutionary foe is adapting and what we can do about it.

. . .

Debate about contingency versus determinism affects us in another, more ethereal way. Humans are no less subject to convergent evolution than other species. Our ability to drink milk as adults, for example, is unique among animals; it was, of course, irrelevant until we domesticated livestock in the last few 1,000 years, and since then has evolved convergently in several pastoral societies around the world. Skin color, so important in the course of human history, is also the result of convergent evolution, as is the ability to survive at high elevations, and many other traits.

The human species itself, of course, is not convergent. We are one of the singletons, lacking an evolutionary duplicate. Does our understanding of evolutionary determinism have anything to say about how we evolved, or why? If we hadn't come along, would some other lineage have taken our place, and would that species have ended up much like us, perhaps so much so that someone—something—else would have been writing this very book, albeit with scaly, three-fingered hands? And if not here, perhaps on the moons of Jupiter or xh3-9?

Critical Thinking

1. What is *convergent evolution?*
2. What is *contingency in evolution?*

3. How is it that the author can claim that "scientists are now well on the way to understanding evolutionary repeatability?

Internet References

Biology Dictionary
    https://biologydictionary.net/convergent-evolution/

Convergent Evolution
    https://en.wikipedia.org/wiki/Convergent_evolution

Travels in the Great Tree of Life
    http://peabody.yale.edu/exhibits/tree-of-life/convergent-evolution-recurrence-form

Article Prepared by: Elvio Angeloni

Evolution Evolves

KEVIN LALAND

Learning Outcomes

After reading this article, you will be able to:

- Discuss the "modern synthesis" regarding how evolution works and how the discovery of "epigenetic changes" and "developmental plasticity" necessitate an "extended evolutionary synthesis."

- Discuss the role of "developmental bias" as a limiting factor regarding on the evolutionary developments.

WHY is life so diverse? And why are living things so exquisitely suited to their environments? To understand these two striking features of the natural world, you need look no further than evolution. Darwin's beautiful idea explains why there are hundreds of thousands of species of beetles and flowering plants, why birds' feathers are ideal for flight and insulation, and why a desert plant possesses hairy leaves to reduce water loss. The Origin of Species was published in 1859, and time has not eroded Darwin's insights.

Yet all scientific theories must incorporate new ideas and findings, and evolution is no exception. In recent years, our understanding of biology has taken huge strides. Advances in genetics, epigenetics, and developmental biology challenge us to think anew about the relationship between genes, organisms, and the environment, with implications for the origins of diversity and the direction and speed of evolution. In particular, new findings undermine the idea, encapsulated by the "selfish gene" metaphor, that genes are in the driving seat. Instead, they suggest that organisms play active, constructive roles in their own development and that of their descendants, so that they impose direction on evolution.

Some biologists are trying to shoehorn the new knowledge into traditional evolutionary thinking. Others, myself included, believe a more radical approach may be required. We don't deny the roles of genetic inheritance and natural selection, but think we should look at evolution in a markedly different way. It is time for the theory of evolution to evolve.

Our current framework for thinking about evolution emerged only in the 1940s, with the integration of new knowledge about evolutionary processes and biological inheritance. This so-called modern synthesis is at the heart of how most people understand evolution. According to this view, the evolution of the features of an organism—collectively known as its phenotype—comes down to random genetic mutation, genetic inheritance, and selection of those gene variants that bestow traits best adapted to the environment.

The modern synthesis has served us well: evolutionary biology is developing and thriving. But discoveries made over the past two decades are starting to reveal cracks in some of its central ideas.

Not by Genes Alone

Take the notion that heredity happens via genes alone. In a classic 19th-century experiment, German biologist August Weismann cut off the tails of generations of mice, bred from the amputees, and found no reduction in tail length. This led to the view that genetic mutations in the germ line (eggs and sperm) are the only changes passed on to the next generation. But recent experiments suggest a more complex picture.

We now know that things other than genes are transmitted from parents to offspring. These include components of the egg, hormones, symbionts (microorganisms that live inside bodies), epigenetic marks (compounds that bind to DNA and turn genes on and off), antibodies, ecological resources, and learned knowledge. At least some of these can lead to stable inheritance of phenotypes. For example, the transmission of epigenetic marks across generations is extremely widespread and, in plants, it can account for differences in fruit size, flowering time, and many other traits. Epigenetic changes are often induced by changes in conditions within cells or the external environment, such as temperature, stress or diet, and unlike random mutations are often adaptive. Likewise, many animals inherit knowledge from their parents. Cultural inheritance occurs in hundreds of species, not just humans or vertebrates, but invertebrates such as bees and crickets too, creating similarities between even unrelated individuals.

These and many other findings suggest that the current focus on genetic mutations only captures part of the story of adaptive evolution—the slowly changing part. The broader view shows there are other ways to generate heritable variety. It also undermines the clean separation of development and heredity that Weismann's theory promoted. It is time to let go of the idea that the genes we inherit are a blueprint to build our bodies. Genetic information is only one factor influencing how an individual turns out.

And that's not all. We now also know that a given set of genes has the potential to produce a variety of phenotypes, depending on the environment in which the organism develops. This ability, called developmental plasticity, used to be dismissed as "noise" or mere "fine-tuning," but recent research suggests it may play a far more active role in the evolutionary process. As well as being able to respond in specific ways to particular conditions, organisms seem to have evolved the ability to respond flexibly to whatever conditions they experience. This adaptability results from a sort of Darwinian evolution occurring within organisms. It's as if each organism evolves as it develops, by generating new variation and selecting what works. This allows systems such as the immune system, nervous system, and behavioural systems (through learning) to adjust to meet whatever environment the individual faces.

A flexible phenotype allows organisms to survive in the short term, and may then initiate evolutionary episodes—with genetic change following later. Consistent with this idea, several experiments reveal that organisms exposed to new environments develop characteristics that resemble those of closely related species adapted to these same environments.

For instance, marine sticklebacks reared on diets that are either benthic (bottom-feeding) or limnetic (mid-water) grow to resemble populations adapted to life in the corresponding environment. This suggests that adaptations may commonly arise through immediate responses to the environment, with natural selection favouring such individuals and subsequently cementing the useful features through genetic evolution.

There is also experimental evidence in insects, fish, and amphibians that environmentally induced forms can evolve reproductive isolation, meaning that after a while they can no longer interbreed with other members of their species—a key step toward speciation. So developmental plasticity may play a critical role in both adaptation and speciation.

Features of development also undermine orthodox ideas about what factors influence the direction of evolution. The modern synthesis places natural selection in control, regarding it as the sole explanation for adaptation. Evolutionary biologists have tended to think that evolution is not biased in any particular direction, since genetic mutation is assumed to occur at random. However, this idea is challenged by "developmental bias"—the fact that certain characteristics can develop more easily than others. This raises the intriguing possibility that the diversity of life may not only reflect the survival of the fittest but also the arrival of the frequentest.

Developmental bias could help explain some fascinating quirks of evolution. Consider parallel radiation, in which a species in one location diversifies into several distinct forms and, independently, the same diversification occurs in a different location. A famous example is cichlid fishes living in Lakes Malawi and Tanganyika in Africa. Here many species exhibit striking similarities in body shape with different species from the other lake, despite being more closely related to species from their own lake. These body shapes are adaptive, so natural selection has certainly been at play. But the forms we see are not necessarily the only possible adaptive solutions. This suggests there are features of cichlid development that make certain forms particularly likely to arise. Developmental bias could also help explain why cichlids—and some other groups of organisms—are so diverse. It is perhaps because they are particularly good at producing novel variants that can exploit ecological opportunities.

This creative role for development contrasts with its traditional role of imposing Constraints explain the absence of evolution or adaptation, so have been of limited interest. Many evolutionary biologists are now questioning whether this is the best way to think. Perhaps, rather than merely setting limits on what forms are available for selection, developmental bias directs evolution by generating the tramlines along which the engine of selection can proceed.

Not Passive Observers

There is a further way in which organisms might direct their own evolution. Selection is portrayed as a process in which external agents, such as environmental conditions, sort between alternative variants according to their suitability. This is too passive. Organisms are not merely buffeted around by the forces of nature; through their habitat choices and the way they modify their environment, they play active roles in determining which of their characteristics are useful. So they create some of the conditions of their existence, and this influences their evolution.

By building a nest, which reduces temperature fluctuations, for example, a bird weakens selection on the need for physiological regulation of egg temperature, but creates selection for refinements in nest design. Likewise, selection shapes a mammal that digs a burrow less for ways to counter predation, and more for resistance to fungal diseases. Such niche construction is not random, but systematic and directional. The animal manipulates the environment in a consistent, reliable way, to suit itself. In doing so, it biases the action of natural selection, imposing a direction on its own evolution, in much the same way that an animal breeder selects for particular traits in livestock.

Taken together, these discoveries challenge some of the fundamental assumptions of the modern synthesis (see "Modern vs. postmodern," page 41). This new approach gives organisms a central role in their own evolution, and suggests that novel variation frequently begins not with mutation, but with changes in phenotypes. It indicates that the direction of evolution does not depend on selection alone.

There are two ways to view these new findings: we can try to incorporate them into the old framework, or we can extend the framework. Most evolutionary biologists take the first course, viewing plasticity and niche construction as being under genetic control, and seeing non-genetic inheritance as rare, unstable or functionally equivalent to genes. This view allows genes and selection to retain their explanatory prominence, at the price of downplaying new evidence. The alternative approach is to accept that the modern synthesis struggles to account for the new findings and to propose a broader alternative—an extended evolutionary synthesis (EES). The two types of explanation can then be compared for their predictive power and ability to explain evidence, as well as their productivity in spawning new research questions and methods.

Evolutionary biologists who embrace this second approach are now acting on it. Earlier this year, an international consortium of 50 biologists and philosophers from eight universities announced a new research programme to investigate the evolutionary consequences of nongenetic inheritance, developmental plasticity and bias, and niche construction (see "Time for change?," right). These are exciting times for evolutionary biology, as the full ramifications of these ideas are explored rigorously for the first time. It remains to be seen whether our efforts will change the orthodox view. What is certain is that over the coming years, these advances will increasingly become the focus for evolutionary biologists.

My own view is that a new conceptualisation of evolution is emerging. The selfish gene has proved to be a powerful and instructive metaphor, but the evidence now suggests it is misleading. Far from being master molecules, genes turn out to be just one of many channels through which cells respond to environmental inputs, and just one of several sources of heredity. Organisms are not the "throwaway survival machines" envisaged by Richard Dawkins and others, but instead often take the lead in their own evolution, dragging genetic change along in their wake. Move over selfish gene, and make way for the orchestrating organism.

Modern versus Postmodern

Orthodox ideas about how evolution works are being challenged by new discoveries in genetics, epigenetics, and developmental biology. This has led some researchers to propose that the current framework, known as the modern synthesis, be broadened into an EES. The fundamentals remain the same, but they rest on quite different assumptions:

Modern Synthesis

The major directing influence in evolution is natural selection. It alone explains why the properties of organisms are adapted to match those of their environments.

Genes are the only widespread system of inheritance. Acquired characters—nongenetic traits that develop during an organism's lifetime—are not inherited and play no role in evolution.

Genetic variation is random. Mutations that occur are not necessarily fitness-enhancing. It is mere chance if mutations give rise to features that improve the ability of organisms to survive and thrive.

Evolution typically occurs through multiple small steps, leading to gradual change. That's because it rests on incremental changes brought about by random mutations.

The perspective is gene-centred: evolution requires changes in gene frequencies through natural selection, mutation, migration, and random losses of gene variants.

Microevolutionary processes explain macroevolutionary patterns. The forces that shape individuals and populations also explain major evolutionary changes at the species level and above.

EES

Natural selection is not solely in charge. The way that an organism develops can influence the direction and rate of its own evolution and its fit to its environment.

Inheritance extends beyond genes to include epigenetic, ecological, behavioural, and cultural inheritance. Acquired characters can be passed to offspring and play diverse roles in evolution.

Phenotypic variation is nonrandom. Individuals develop in response to local conditions, so any novel features they possess are often well suited to their environment.

Evolution can be rapid. Developmental processes allow individuals to respond to environmental challenges, or to mutations, with coordinated changes in suites of traits.

The view is organism-centred, with broader conceptions of evolutionary processes. Individuals adjust to their environment as they develop, and modify selection pressures.

Additional phenomena explain macroevolutionary changes by increasing e volvability—the ability to generate adaptive diversity. They include developmental plasticity and niche construction.

Time for Change?

A growing number of biologists believe we need to extend our ideas of how evolution works. This conviction rests on accumulating evidence that genes do not have sole control over development and heredity, and that organisms play active roles in their own fate and that of their descendants. We have launched a wide-ranging research programme to make the case for the so-called EES. One aim is to identify conceptual differences between the EES and orthodox thinking and to test the distinctive predictions they make.

For instance, the traditional perspective sees biological novelty arising as a result of random genetic mutation, so it predicts that new forms are rarely advantageous. By contrast, the EES predicts that new forms are often adaptive because novelty commonly originates as a result of individuals adjusting to their environment as they develop. We will explore the extent to which this occurs, using a statistical analysis of published results describing how organisms respond to variation in environmental conditions.

Another group will focus on coral reefs to investigate the causes of biodiversity. Traditional thinking says that natural selection gives rise to organisms suited to diverse ecological conditions: the more different kinds of environments there are, the more species are expected to have evolved. The EES suggests that diversity also depends on properties of organisms— their evolvability. Organisms create their own habitats through niche construction, and they can also adjust to new conditions through developmental plasticity. Researchers will quantify how much of the diversity of coral reef fauna can be explained by the evolvability of corals, and how much by factors corals do not control.

We will also explore how well the EES can explain long-term evolutionary trends. These include parallel evolution, in which geographically separated groups display similar trajectories of change; and convergence, where unrelated organisms evolve similar traits.

We aim to develop new ways to model the processes underpinning evolution. Among other things, this will help us understand how the genes an organism inherits relate to the features it displays—that is, how genotype maps to phenotype. At the same time, philosophers and biologists will work together to update definitions of evolution, heredity and fitness. Our aim is to help develop a theory of evolution fit for the 21st century.

The form a stickleback takes is a response to its environment.

Why are some groups of organisms so much more diverse than others?

By building a nest, a bird changes the selection pressures it faces.

Critical Thinking

1. What new findings have undermined the "selfish gene" idea?

2. What is the "modern synthesis?"

3. How have the findings of epigenetic changes and developmental plasticity resulted the need for an extended evolutionary synthesis?

Internet References

Epigenetics and Developmental Biology
   http://www.port.ac.uk/school-of-biological-sciences/research/epigenetics-and-developmental-biology/
MIT Department of Biology
   https://biology.mit.edu/research/stemcell_epigenetics
Riken Center for Developmental Biology
   http://www.cdb.riken.jp/en/research/laboratory/hiratani.html

---

KEVIN LALAND is a professor of behavioral and evolutionary biology at the University of St Andrews, UK, and leads the project to test the extended evolutionary synthesis (synergy.st-andrews.ac.uk/ees/the-project/).

Unit 2

UNIT

Prepared by: Elvio Angeloni

Primates

Primates are fun. They are active, intelligent, colorful, emotionally expressive, and unpredictable. Because, in some ways, they are very much like us, observing them is like holding up an opaque mirror to ourselves. The image may not be crystal-clear or, indeed, what some would consider flattering, but it is certainly familiar enough to be illuminating.

Primates are, of course, one of the many orders of mammals that adaptively radiated into the variety of ecological niches, which were vacated at the end of the Age of Reptiles about 65 million years ago. Whereas some mammals took to the sea (cetaceans), and some took to the air (chiroptera, or bats), primates took to the trees and are characterized by an arboreal or forested adaptation. While some mammals can be identified by their food-getting habits, such as the meat-eating carnivores, primates have a penchant for eating almost anything and are best described as omnivorous. After ascending into the trees, primates did not simply develop a full-blown set of distinguishing characteristics that set them off easily from other orders of mammals, the way the rodent order can be readily identified by its gnawing set of front teeth. Rather, each primate seems to represent degrees of anatomical, biological, and behavioral characteristics on a continuum of change, in the direction of the particular traits in which we humans happen to be interested.

None of this is meant to imply, of course, that the living primates are our ancestors. Because the prosimians, monkeys, and apes are contemporaries, they are no more our ancestors than we are theirs, and, as living end-products of evolution, we have all descended from a common stock in the distant past. So, if we are interested primarily in our own evolutionary past, why study primates at all? Because, by the criteria we have set up as significant milestones in the evolution of humanity, an inherent reflection of our own bias, primates have not evolved as far as we have. They and their environments, therefore, may provide a glimmer of the evolutionary stages and ecological circumstances through which our own ancestors may have gone. What we stand to gain, for instance, is an educated guess as to how our own ancestors might have appeared and behaved as semi-erect creatures before becoming bipedal. Aside from being

a pleasure to observe, then, living primates can teach us something about our past.

The kind of answers obtained in doing research on primates depend upon the kind of questions asked, and so we have to be very careful in making inferences about the motivations of any given species of primate, including humans, based on limited study. This goes for theory as well. Ever since Darwin published *On the Origin of Species* in 1859, for instance, some prominent economists have embraced it as supportive of laissez-faire capitalism. This interpretation, however, says more about the theorists and their socioeconomic agenda than it does about the actual facts of human nature or even the social context in which human beings evolved.

Still another benefit of primate field research is that it provides us with perspectives that the bones and stones of the fossil hunters will never reveal: a sense of the richness and variety of social patterns that must have existed in the primate order for many tens of millions of years.

Even if we had the physical remains of the earliest hominids in front of us, which we do not, there is no way such evidence could thoroughly answer the questions that physical anthropologists care most deeply about: How did these creatures move about and get their food? Did they cooperate and share? At what levels did they think and communicate? Did they have a sense of family, let alone a sense of self? But what sets off the study of our closest relatives from other aspects of anthropology is how primatologists attempt to deal with these matters head-on, even in the absence of direct fossil evidence. Thus, the finding that chimpanzees cooperatively hunt for meat and share food indicates that at least some aspects of "hominization" (the acquisition of humanlike qualities) may have actually begun while our own ancestors were still in the African rain forest rather than in the dry savanna, as has been proposed usually.

Although extrapolating from primate behavior to that of humans may seem like a reach may generate irreconcilable differences among theorists, a readiness to entertain new ideas should be welcomed for what it is—a stimulus for more intensive and meticulous research.

Article   Prepared by: Elvio Angeloni

No Alpha Males Allowed

STEVE KEMPER

Learning Outcomes

After reading this article, you will be able to:

- Discuss Karen Strier's findings in her study of the Muriqui monkeys and how it contrasts with primatology's traditional emphasis upon aggression.

- Contrast the muriqui "alternative life style" with other primate societies.

It's 9 o'clock on a June morning in a muggy tropical forest not far from Brazil's Atlantic coast and brown howler monkeys have been roaring for an hour. But the muriquis—the largest primates in the Americas after human beings, and the animals that the anthropologist Karen Strier and I have huffed uphill to see—are still curled high in the crooks of trees, waiting for the morning sun to warm them.

As they begin to stir, the adults scratch, stretch, and watch the suddenly frisky youngsters without moving much themselves. A few languidly grab leaves for breakfast. They are striking figures, with fur that varies between gray, light brown, and russet. Their black faces inspired the Brazilian nickname "charcoal monkey," after the sooty features of charcoal makers.

Strier knows these faces well. At age 54, the University of Wisconsin-Madison professor has been observing muriquis here for three decades. One of the longest-running studies of its kind, it has upended conventional wisdom about primates and may have a surprising thing or two to say about human nature.

"Louise!" Strier says, spotting one of her old familiars. Louise belongs to Strier's original study group of 23—clássicos, Strier's Brazilian students call them. "She's the only female who's never had a baby," says Strier. "Her friends are some of the old girls."

Above us, two youngsters frolic near their mother. "That's Barbara," says Strier, "and her three-year-old twins Bamba and Beleco." Female muriquis typically emigrate out of their natal group at about age 6, but Barbara has never left hers, the Matão study group, named after a valley that bisects this part of the forest. Even today, more than two years after I visited Brazil, Barbara remains in the group.

Strier first came to this federally protected reserve in 1982, at the invitation of Russell Mittermeier, now president of Conservation International and chairman of the primate specialist group of the International Union for Conservation of Nature's Species Survival Commission, who had been conducting a survey of primates in eastern Brazil. The reserve at the time held only about 50 muriquis, and Strier, a Harvard graduate student, was smitten with the lanky creatures cavorting in the canopy.

"As soon as I saw the muriquis," says Strier, "I said, 'This is it.'" She stayed for two months and then returned for 14 more.

In those days, to reach this patch of forest, she rode a bus almost 40 miles from the nearest town and walked the last mile to a simple house without electricity. Often alone, she rose before dawn to look for the monkeys and didn't leave the forest until they had settled down at dusk. She cut her own network of footpaths, collecting data on births, relationships, diets, dispositions, daily locations, and emigrations. At night, she sorted the data by the light of gas lanterns.

"As my contact with the animals increased, they introduced me to new species of food that they ate, and allowed me to witness new behaviors," Strier wrote in her 1992 book *Faces in the Forest*, now a classic of primatology. As a personal account of a field biologist's extraordinary, often lonely efforts to become acquainted with a wild primate, Strier's work has been compared to Jane Goodall's *In the Shadow of Man* and Dian Fossey's *Gorillas in the Mist*.

When Strier was first getting to know the muriquis, primatology was still largely focused on just a handful of species that had adapted to life on the ground, including baboons, or that had close evolutionary relationships with humans, such as apes. This emphasis came to shape public perception of primates as essentially aggressive. We picture chest-beating, teeth-flashing dominant male gorillas competing to mate with any female they choose. We picture, as Goodall had witnessed beginning in 1974, chimpanzees invading other territories, biting and beating other chimps to death. Primates, including possibly the most violent one of all—us—seemed to be born ruffians.

In reality, as Strier's work would underscore, the primates are a varied group, with diverse social structures and far more complex behavior. Descended from a tree-dwelling ancestor living some 55 million years ago in Africa or Asia, the group includes tarsiers, lemurs, lorises, monkeys, apes (such as gorillas, chimps, bonobos, and gibbons), and hominids. Monkeys, characterized by long tails and flat, hairless faces, are generally divided into two types: Old World monkeys, such as baboons and macaques, live in Asia and Africa. New World monkeys, including muriquis, are descended from ancestors that found their way from Africa to South America perhaps 35 million years ago.

For a long time, New World monkeys were the second-class citizens of primatology. "New World primates were considered not so smart, not so interesting, and not so relevant to human evolution," says Frans de Waal, director of the Living Links Center at Emory University's Yerkes National Primate Research Center. "They were sidelined—totally inappropriately, as Karen has demonstrated."

Strier's research introduced the world to an alternative primate lifestyle. Female muriquis mate with a lot of males and males don't often fight. Though bonobos, known for their casual sex, are often called the "hippie" primates, the muriquis in Strier's study site are equally deserving of that reputation. They are peace-loving and tolerant. Strier also showed that the muriquis turn out to be incredibly cooperative, a characteristic that may be just as important in primate societies as vicious rivalry.

Strier's ideas shook up primatology, making her an influential figure in the field. Her widely used textbook, *Primate Behavioral Ecology*, is in its fourth edition and "has no peers," according to the American Society of Primatologists. In 2005, at age 45, Strier was elected to the National Academy of Sciences, a rare honor. The University of Wisconsin recently recognized her with an endowed professorship. The money is being used to support her research in Brazil, where the muriquis she knows so well continue to surprise her.

Lately, they've been doing something arboreal primates aren't supposed to do. In an unusual behavioral twist, they're coming down out of the trees.

Muriquis are acrobats, spending much of the day swinging through the treetops in search of food. They ride branches down and scurry across vines like tightrope walkers. Hanging fully extended, muriquis appear 5 feet tall but weigh only 20 pounds, an elongated physique allowing for quick and astonishingly nimble movement.

As Strier and I walk through the forest, the muriquis sound like a herd of horses flying overhead. They neigh to maintain long-distance contact. A staccato hnk hnk hnk keeps them out of one another's way, and an excited chirp summons the others when a monkey has found a fruiting tree.

Muriquis' cooperative behaviors are often on display when they're eating. A few days into my visit, Strier and I watch nine males demonstrate their manners as they eat pods in a legume tree. When one monkey scoots past another on a branch, it pauses to hug its neighbor, as if to say, "Pardon, so sorry."

Muriquis almost never fight over food with members of their own group. They will chase howler monkeys or capuchins out of fruiting trees, and they loudly protest incursions by muriquis from other parts of the forest. But males and females, young and old, behave toward members of their own group in ways that can fairly be described as considerate.

Some of the muriquis in the legume tree exchange little pats as they brush by each other. Two of them, on a short break from eating, sit haunch to haunch, one resting his hand on top of the other's head. Before they resume picking pods, they hug.

Affectionate gestures, including full-body face-to-face embraces, are common. It's not unusual to see five or more muriquis in a tangled furry cuddle. Strier says that some males become more popular as they age, and younger males seek the company of the elders and solicit hugs during times of tension. Squabbles are rare. "Maybe their drive for social cohesion and conformity is much stronger than their aggression," says Strier.

They also tend to be easygoing about the other big activity that agitates almost all other primates: sex. Unlike chimpanzees and baboons, male muriquis don't attack rivals to keep them from females, Strier says. There are no alphas in these societies, so muriqui twosomes don't have to sneak off to evade punishment by jealous suitors. What's more, female muriquis don't need to form coalitions to protect infants from murderous males. Strier has called muriqui mating a "passive affair." Males don't chase down females or bully them into sexual submission. Instead, a male waits for an invitation from a female, who selects her partners and copulates openly. Instead of battling each other for access to females, males bond into extensive brotherhoods, and Strier suspects they have replaced fighting with "sperm competition." In proportion to their slight frames, muriquis have oversized testicles. It may be that the male producing the most sperm has the most tickets in the reproductive raffle.

When Strier first observed these behaviors, she thought muriquis were anomalies in the primate world. But as research documented the behaviors of a broader range of primates, Strier realized that there was actually a lot of variation—more than was generally acknowledged. In 1994, she wrote a paper titled "Myth of the Typical Primate" that urged her colleagues to reconsider the emphasis on aggression as a mediator of primate relationships, which "prevailed despite repeated efforts to demonstrate the limitations of such arguments." She contended that the roots of primate social behavior, including that of people, might be more accurately reflected in the flexibility, tolerance, cooperation, and affection that predominate among most primates and that these qualities are at least as recognizably human as aggressiveness, competition, and selfishness. Strier's paper was pivotal in initiating a new way of thinking about primate behavior.

"We have this idea that competition is good," says Robert Sussman, professor of anthropology at Washington University in St. Louis and co-author of *Man the Hunted: Primates, Predators, and Human Evolution*, "that everybody is out for themselves and that the people at the top are by nature superior. But there's now lots of evidence that competition among primates only occurs when the environment changes because of outside influence. The ultimate goal of evolution is to reach an ecological equilibrium and avoid competition and aggression, a very different point of view. Karen Strier has become one of the leaders in this alternative paradigm about the evolution of cooperation."

So as not to influence the behavior of the muriquis themselves, Strier decided at the start only to observe them and not interact with them. She has never trapped or tranquilized a monkey to take a blood sample or to affix a radio collar, and she won't use feeding stations to lure them to convenient spots for observations, as some researchers studying chimps in the wild have been known to do. For years she has collected hormone data on individual females by positioning herself to catch falling feces. She says they smell like cinnamon.

Though Strier maintains a kind of clinical detachment from the muriquis in the field that doesn't mean she's uninvolved. She has in fact become their impassioned advocate. No matter how cooperative they are, they can't by themselves overcome the forces at work to destroy them.

Once called woolly spider monkeys, muriquis occur in two closely related species that scientists didn't officially split until 2000: northern (Brachyteles hypoxanthus) and southern (Brachyteles arachnoides). Both species live only in Brazil, in scattered remnants of the once-vast Atlantic coastal forest, now greatly reduced by clearing for pasture and agricultural land. Because of extensive habitat fragmentation, both muriqui species are classified as endangered, the northern one critically: Only 1,000 of them survive, spread across about a dozen patches of forest, one of which is Strier's study site. Early in Strier's career, colleagues asked her why she wanted to study monkey behavior in such an altered habitat. But Strier didn't see the environment as an obstacle; she wanted to know how the monkeys adapt.

Born in New Jersey, Strier grew up in southern California, western New York, and then Maryland. She enjoyed the outdoors, hiking, and backpacking with friends, but she doesn't trace her deep fascination with primates to any childhood "aha" moment, unlike Jane Goodall, who recalls receiving a toy chimpanzee as a youngster. As an undergraduate studying biology and anthropology at Swarthmore College, Strier actually thought she might go on to conduct research on bears in the United States. But during her junior year she was offered the opportunity to work on the Amboseli Baboon Project in Kenya. She had never taken a course in primatology.

"It was a catharsis," she says. "Everything about who I was and what I liked came together—the outdoors, the animals, science." It was in graduate school that her adviser connected her with Mittermeier, who connected her with the muriquis. "She's one of the great leaders in primatology today," says Mittermeier. "She's had a huge influence in Brazil. She has trained some of the key people there, the richest country on earth for primates."

Her research is situated in the 2,365-acre federally protected Reserva Particular do Patrimônio Natural Feliciano Miguel Abdala, named after the coffee farmer who owned the land. After Abdala's death in 2000, his heirs followed his wishes and put the forest into permanent trust as a reserve. More than four dozen Brazilian students have conducted research there under Strier, with pairs and trios rotating in and out every 14 months. Strier typically spends about a month each year at the reserve, conversing with the students and making quips in Portuguese, which she studied for one semester but largely picked up during her fieldwork. She spends the rest of her time in Madison, where she lives with her husband and their cats. She prefers dogs, but her travel schedule makes caring for them difficult.

Acting on her profound concern for the muriquis' future, she has discussed in public lectures and scientific papers the need for national and international investment in wildlife preservation and for educational programs and employment opportunities that get the local community involved. She is a key member of the committee that advises the Brazilian government on its plans for muriqui conservation. Largely thanks to her efforts, the muriquis have become something of a cause célèbre of conservation in Brazil, featured on T-shirts and postage stamps. In June, the city of Caratinga, Brazil, not far from the reserve, made Strier an honorary citizen, and used her project's thirtieth anniversary to announce a new long-term sustainability program.

Though northern muriquis are critically endangered, the population in Strier's study site, which is protected from further deforestation and hunting, has increased. There are now 335 individuals in four groups, a sixfold increase since Strier started her study.

That's a development worth celebrating, but it's not without consequences. The monkeys appear to be outgrowing the reserve and, in response to this population pressure, altering millennia of arboreal behavior. These tree-dwellers, these born aerialists, are spending more and more time on the ground. At first, the behavior was surprising. Over time, though, Strier made some sense of it. "They're on an island, with no place to go but up or down. When humans didn't have enough food, they invented intensive agriculture. Monkeys come to the ground. It makes me think of how hominids had to eke out an existence in a hostile environment. Our ancestors would have brought to that challenge the plasticity we're seeing here."

Initially the muriquis descended only briefly and only for necessities, Strier says. Now they're staying down for up to four hours—playing, resting, and even mating. One of Strier's students shot a video of a big group of monkeys lounging on the ground, leaning against each other, and casually hugging, as if they're at a picnic. "Next they'll lose their tails," jokes Carla Possamai, a Brazilian postdoctoral researcher who's been working with Strier at the reserve for a decade.

One day we watch muriquis eat white berries on low bushes. At first the monkeys hang from their tails above the bushes, but soon they drop to the ground and stand there like customers at a pick-your-own patch. Upright but awkward, they are out of their element. "You're watching an animal whose body is adapted for something else, using it in new ways," says Strier.

In another unexpected break with predictable behavior, five female muriquis emigrated to another forest on the far side of 200 yards of bare pasture. Two of these adventurers made the dangerous trip back into the reserve, where it's suspected that one of them mated before again crossing the open ground to the new forest.

Eking out a living on the ground might sound like a radical departure with no real consequences, but it makes the muriquis more vulnerable to predators. Camera traps have captured images of ocelots and a family of cougars in the reserve, and feral dogs and other carnivores are known to roam the pastures.

"Basically they're telling us they need more space," Strier says. To give it to them, Preserve Muriqui, the Abdala family foundation that runs the reserve, is working with local ranchers and landowners to connect the forest to the archipelago of small forest fragments on the reserve's periphery.

Strier wonders about the potential for other changes. What will peaceful, egalitarian primates do if crowding becomes more severe and resources run short? "I predict a cascade of effects and demographic changes," she says. Will the monkeys become more aggressive and start to compete for food and other essentials the way chimps and baboons do? Will the clubby camaraderie between males fall apart? Will the social fabric tear or will the muriquis find new ways to preserve it? Strier has learned that there is no fixed behavior; instead, it's driven by circumstances and environmental conditions. Context matters.

"Nature is designing my experiment: the effects of population growth on wild primates," she says. Among the many unknowns there's one certainty: The muriquis will try to adapt. "It's not surprising that long-lived, intelligent, socially complex primates are capable of great behavioral plasticity," says Strier. "It gives me hope. After watching this group for 30 years," she adds, "I think anything is possible."

Critical Thinking

1. Explain primatology's emphasis on aggression before Karen Strier published her work.
2. Explain why New World monkeys were considered second-class citizens of primatology.
3. Describe the muriquis "alternative lifestyle."
4. Be familiar with muriqui social life and behavior, especially in contrast to other primates.
5. Discuss "sperm competition."
6. Why does Strier believe that muriqui behavior is not an anomaly among primates?
7. How has Strier been able to avoid influencing the behavior of the muriquis?
8. Why are the muriquis spending more time on the ground? What further changes might this involve, according to Strier?

Internet References

Electronic Zoo/NetVet-Primate Page
    http://netvet.wustl.edu/primates.htm
National Primate Research Center
    http://pin.primate.wisc.edu/factsheets

Article   Prepared by: Elvio Angeloni

Love in the Time of Monkeys

EDUARDO FERNANDEZ-DUQUE AND BENJAMIN FINKEL

Learning Outcomes

After reading this article, you will be able to:

- Discuss the rarity of monogamy among mammals.
- Discuss the relationship between monogamy, territoriality, and the distribution of food resources among owl monkeys.

Even though there is great diversity in the organization of human societies, we all fall in love. Many of us maintain long relationships with the person we love romantically—or, as biologists state it, establish pair bonds—and together we form families and raise children, albeit with different levels of paternal involvement. Although we cannot pinpoint when a predisposition for pair bonding and monogamy evolved, it was surely long ago, well before we organized ourselves with religion, law, government, and complex technology. Most likely love and pair bonding evolved due to the influence of a specific set of ecological and biological factors. We know this because we see it in other primates, nonhuman primates that allow us to examine the biological basis of monogamy without the influences of language, religion, and technology.

Monogamy comes in different shapes and sizes. Researchers have described it in taxa as diverse as amphibians, birds, shrimp, and termites, but monogamy is relatively rare in mammals—only about 10 percent of mammalian species and 25 percent of primates organize around a breeding adult pair. Why is monogamy so uncommon among mammals? First, because mammalian fertilization is internal, a "father" may risk investing time, energy, and resources in a baby that he cannot be sure he has sired. Even more important, a female mammal is reproductively limited by pregnancy and lactation, whereas a male is unfettered by these time and energy constraints. To illustrate the point, one can contrast the most reproductively prolific woman, Valentina Vassilyeva of eighteenth-century Russia, credited with the birth of 69 children (including many twins, triplets,

and even quadruplets), with the most reproductively prolific man, the Emperor of Morocco, Moulay Ismael (1672–1727), who allegedly had 888 children. Given that male and female mammals have such different reproductive potentials, how then did a mating strategy evolve that, without the guarantee of paternity, limits the male to breed with a single female?

Nearly two decades ago, I set off for Argentina in the hope of answering that question. I had just finished my doctoral dissertation investigating monogamy in titi monkeys (*Callicebus cupreus*) at the University of California, Davis, and was eager to study monogamous monkeys in the wild. My wife and I, along with our two young sons, moved to the rainforests of northeastern Argentina with a small grant from the Leakey Foundation and lots of dreams. To establish a field site and balance research with family life was a labor of love: my wife, Claudia Valeggia, a biological anthropologist as well, was beginning her field research on the reproductive ecology of the Toba-Qom indigenous communities of northern Argentina. We had to juggle our incipient projects with two kids attending school, along with a large number of volunteers and assistants in need of logistical (and emotional) support in the field. Some days, I would start at four or five o'clock in the morning, racing between home and the rainforest. Other times, it was more efficient to stay in the forest for several days at once. And so I started to study Azara's owl monkeys (*Aotus azarae*), known to locals as mirikiná, a species believed to find a partner, establish a monogamous pair bond, and share parental duties quite evenly.

In Argentina, owl monkeys live only in the eastern portion of the Formosa and Chaco provinces in the northern tip of the country. Both provinces are part of the South American Gran Chaco, a vast expanse of flat land that includes forests growing along rivers (gallery forests), savannas, and patches of forest immersed in those savannas. Most of the region is privately owned, and the main activity is raising cattle that graze on the open savannas. It was with the help of gauchos (Argentine cowboys) at Estancia Guaycolec, a 62,000-acre cattle ranch, that I was able to establish a research camp, carving out nearly ten miles of trails through 170 acres of forest. The owl monkey's habitat—a hot, dense and often mosquito-swarmed atmosphere—has earned the name el Infierno Verde, the Green Hell. Yet the Chaco's outstanding biodiversity is worth the effort, with more armadillo species than any other place in the world; a host of large mammals, including capybara, tapir, and puma; and two species of monkeys, the black and gold howler monkey (*Alouatta caraya*) and the owl monkey.

Owl monkeys are arboreal and relatively small primates, weighing roughly three pounds, which poses some challenges for detailed observation of their distant, scurrying bodies. To our eyes they are sexually mono-morphic: body size and coloring are identical between males and females. A lack of obvious differences between the sexes tends to be associated with pair-living species, as in the case of gibbons in southeast Asia, titi monkeys in the Amazon, and a number of lemurs in Madagascar. Fortunately, though, while the other 11 owl monkey species in Central and South America are nocturnal, the Azara's owl monkeys of the Chaco are cathemeral, with a mix of diurnal and nocturnal activity that allowed us to observe them in the daylight.

Early in my research, we made little progress in understanding the social behavior of owl monkeys, because this required the identification of individuals, their age, and their sex. Four years into the project, a description of a group would still frequently read, "3 adult-size individuals, 2 smaller, 1 dependent infant." Even so, we had begun to fill in our image of owl monkey life. We learned that their social lives centered on tightly affiliated and territorial units that consisted of two reproducing adults and one to three nonreproducing individuals. We suspected that these could be a pair of breeding adults and their offspring, but could not precisely define the relatedness between group members. Occasionally, a few animals looked distinctive to us. In 1998, we spotted an individual with a ten-inch tail, rather than the typical fifteen inches, and Cola Corta ("short tail" in Spanish) became easy to identify; he lived at least 14 years and sired five infants. Sometimes we classified individuals as female if we saw them nursing. Nonetheless, it became clear that we had to capture and mark the animals, examine their genitalia, measure them, and obtain genetic samples if we were going to have a groundbreaking project on primate monogamy. The project needed new tools.

A breakthrough came in 1999, once we were able to use radio collars and telemetry receivers to track individuals. The efficiency and reliability of locating the monkeys via telemetry was what finally let us address the questions about monogamy that had taken me to Argentina in the first place. As of today, we have tagged 166 individuals. My colleagues and I have found a surprising amount of biparental care. Mom is always around, but her main interaction with the infant is limited to nursing.

Males often play with and carry the infants, with equal or perhaps greater doggedness than the mother. When owl monkey males (presumed fathers) skitter through the trees, their young typically go along for the ride.

We also gathered valuable information on the relationships between pair bonding, monogamy, paternal care, and life-history traits. Owl monkeys have a remarkably slow life history for being so small: infants are wholly dependent until six months of age, and following weaning, both males and females continue to grow until four years of age, at which time they tend to disperse from their natal groups. Reproducing for the first time when they are at least six years old, individuals may produce in a lifetime four to six offspring, one at a time. Although our study has not lasted long enough to establish their lifespan conclusively, we estimate that some individuals have lived as long as 15 years.

So why are the mirikiná socially monogamous? We believe that the answer lies partly in how food is distributed in the forest. Their habitat is a subtropical forest where seasonal variation in both temperature and rainfall creates periods of food abundance and scarcity. There are sharp peaks in the abundance of preferred food items for owl monkeys and, conversely, lulls, which may constitute critical periods when the monkeys struggle to meet nutritional demands. We collaborated with botanists to examine the owl monkeys' feeding ecology: we created large plots within the forest to survey the production of leaves, flowers, and fruits, and we assembled a database detailing the forest structure, including the distribution and size of tree species. Since 2003, we have collected monthly data on food availability from 425 trees in those plots. We learned that owl monkey foods are not laid out in continuous buffets, but are distributed in smaller plates throughout the forest. While there are many dishes, they are separated, and each "plate" can only sustain a single female. Therefore, the distribution of food separates females who disperse into their individual plates, or territories. What are males to do given this spacious distribution of females? If a male wants to be close to one female, he will necessarily be far away from any other. In other words, the distribution of females may make it impossible for the male to control more than one of them.

Yet, this would only explain why there is social monogamy, not why the males are committed to the care of infants they may or may not have fathered. Just because a male stays with a female doesn't mean he will help with parenting. So why are male owl monkeys exceptionally good fathers? Genetic monogamy is a reasonable explanation. Social monogamy refers to the structure of groups, groups that only include one adult male and one adult female. Genetic, or reproductive, monogamy is about fidelity; it is about who has offspring with whom. This is a crucial distinction when attempting to understand the evolution of paternal care and monogamy, because what counts in evolution is the offspring produced.

Are male owl monkeys guaranteed of their parentage? For an answer, we examined jealousy and mate guarding in male and female owl monkeys. Absolute control of a mate's reproduction can be a behavioral mechanism to ensure fidelity. If one partner constantly watches out for and fends off competition, there won't be an opportunity for the other to mate outside of the pair; there won't be "extra-pair copulation." We have learned that owl monkeys are territorial, each group not only occupying a well-defined space within the forest, but actively defending a portion of it as well. Both adults take part in protecting the group from intruders who attempt to supplant one of them. Their young too will rally against the intruder, with serious consequences. When an intruder approaches the group and a fight ensues, sometimes one of the individuals may die in the aggressive encounter. Furthermore, when we examined demographic records from eighteen groups over 10 years, we discovered that owl monkeys that succeed in preserving their monogamous relationship produce 25 percent more offspring than those who are forced to take on a new partner. In other words, there are significant costs and benefits of this extreme mate guarding, and both sexes appear to be preserving their bond with equal stake. Such behavioral and demographic data supported the critical importance of monogamy to the mirikinás, but genetic data was still the Holy Grail to definitively confirm whether owl monkeys are reproductively monogamous and faithful in practice, not just in appearance.

Modern technology provided us much-needed answers. These days, a droplet of blood, a single baby hair, or a little saliva from a pacifier are enough to run a paternity test. The biological samples we had collected from 166 individuals during ten years allowed us to examine paternity relationships in owl monkeys. One of our first and most significant findings using genetic data was to confirm that the socially monogamous groups of owl monkeys are not always "families" of biological parents and offspring. We suspected this from the demographic data showing changes in the adult composition of these groups—many intruders were indeed successful. But the genetic data provided conclusive proof that intruders sometimes supplanted biological parents as stepparents, and the intense territoriality we observed was justified by legitimate threats. Still, the question remained: did a pair bond guarantee the father paternity of the offspring in his group?

To answer that question we examined the genetic relationships between 35 infants and 35 male and female pairs. In 100 percent of cases, the male in the group was the biological father of the infant. Combined with the absence of any observations of extra-pair copulation in 17 years, these findings strongly indicate that owl monkey mates are always faithful, making them socially and genetically monogamous. They are socially monogamous because of ecological issues that limit their chances of having multiple partners, and intolerance toward competitors protects the couple and keeps them genetically monogamous. Owl monkeys are the first primate species, and only the fifth mammal, for which there is substantial evidence of genetic monogamy. Our analyses show that, once social monogamy has evolved, paternal care, and potentially close bonds as well, may facilitate the evolution of genetic monogamy. This helps to explain why males play an unusually dominant role in parenting. With biparental care, the female can recover more easily from pregnancy; having two attentive parents increases an infant's chances of survival; and the male gets a better guarantee of replicating his own genes.

The study of monogamy, pair bonding, and alloparental care is of special interest to anthropologists and evolutionary biologists because pair bonding was likely a fundamental adaptation of our early ancestors. In human societies everywhere, couples develop relationships that are qualitatively different from the relationships they have with other adults. Psychologists, anthropologists, behavioral ecologists, economists, historians, and poets have all testified to this ubiquitous phenomenon: a pair bond, attachment, or love that develops between a couple with a commitment to share space, time, resources, offspring, and labor. As the research continues, under the auspices of the Owl Monkey Project of Argentina, we will continue to take advantage of one of the few primate models in which we can explore the interactions between behavior, ecology, demography, and genetics, in shaping primate behavior and life history.

Critical Thinking

1. Why is monogamy rare among mammals?
2. Why are owl monkeys monogamous?

Internet References

African Primates at Home
www.indiana.edu/~primate/primates.html
Living Links
www.emory.edu/LIVING_LINKS/dewaal.html
National Primate Research Center
http://pin.primate.wisc.edu/factsheets
Primate Society of Great Britain
http://www.psgb.org/

Article Prepared by: Elvio Angeloni

Becoming Jane

TONY GERBER

Learning Outcomes

After reading this article, you will be able to:

- Describe Jane Goodall's difficulties with a "primarily male science establishment."

- Discuss the many difficulties Jane had in doing her first film on chimpanzees with the National Geographic Society.

- Describe the polarization implicit in today's "tribalism" and the author's suggestion as to how scientists should deal with it.

"You may have heard my story before."
Jane Goodall told her audience at a 2015 lecture: "But it's like a campfire tale—it gets better with each telling." Her story is instantly recognizable from the many times it's been written, broadcast, or otherwise sent into the world: a young Englishwoman conducts chimpanzee research in Africa and winds up revolutionizing primate science. But how did it happen? How did a woman with a passion for animals but no formal background in research navigate the male-dominated worlds of science and media to make enormous discoveries in her field and become a world famous face of the conservation movement? This is that story.

Jane became widely known because of a film, *Miss Goodall and the Wild Chimpanzees*, which came out in 1965 and was produced by National Geographic. She hasn't seen it in years. But now I'm playing it for her on a laptop at the West London home of a friend. The primatologist, 83 this year, studies her 28-year-old self.

"Think how fun it would be to be that age again," Jane says with a smile. The young Jane on the screen is hiking through the forest of Gombe, Stream Game Reserve in what is now Tanzania. She's wearing high-top canvas sneakers and khaki shorts, and her blond hair is in the ponytail that became her signature. She appears to be doing field research—but in reality, Jane says,

she was reenacting events from her first six months at Gombe, so that photographer Hugo van Lawick could film them. Those months had been a remarkable period of solitude and discovery, a time before cameras were present. They've been present in her life ever since. National Geographic executives had specifically told Hugo which shots to get, Jane remembers: "They gave us a list: Jane in the boat, Jane with binoculars, Jane looking at a map." When *Miss Goodall and the Wild Chimpanzees* was broadcast on CBS on December 22, 1965, an estimated 25 million North American viewers tuned in—a huge audience, then and now.

The exposure brought Jane international acclaim and ignited what became a legendary career in primatology. In Jane, National Geographic found a telegenic researcher and storyteller with a film-ready setup: an attractive white woman doing scientific work in the African bush. It was especially poignant at a time when women typically were discouraged from pursuing careers in science.

Since then, Jane has completed a PhD at Cambridge University, authored dozens of books, mentored new generations of scientists, promoted conservation in the developing world, and established several sanctuaries for chimps. Today, the Jane Goodall Institute's Roots and Shoots program is in nearly a hundred countries, training young people to be conservation leaders. And Jane still travels about 300 days a year to lobby governments, visits schools, and gives speeches.

Jane has been the subject of more than 40 films and has made countless appearances on television. Now she is the subject of a new National Geographic Documentary Films release about her life and work. The two-hour feature, JANE, draws from never before seen footage to offer a revealing portrait of the woman whose devotion to chimpanzees made her famous.

When Hugo first went to Gombe in 1962 to document Jane's discoveries, he shot thousands of still images and more than 65 hours of 16-mm film footage. A fraction of the work made its way into the 1965 television special and *National Geographic* magazine. What the editors didn't use, the outtakes, went into film cans and boxes for storage and over time were forgotten. In 2015, they were found in an underground storage facility in rural Pennsylvania. These precious rolls of film held the promise of something rare: a new perspective on Jane.

. . .

Taken together, this trove of material provides an intimate view of Jane at a pivotal time: when a young woman who had known Africa only from *Tarzan* and *Dr. Dolittle* books was dropped into her fantasy and when a novice scientist's discoveries debunked long-held beliefs about humans' closest living relatives.

At Gombe, Jane withstood all manner of natural threats: malaria, parasites, snakes, storms. But in her dealings with the wider world, the challenges often required shrewd strategy and delicate diplomacy. Early in her career, Jane had to contend with a primarily male science establishment that didn't take her seriously, with media executives whose support hinged on her willingness to be scripted and glamorized and with men who said they'd be her partner or patron but also sought control, concessions, or relationships that she did not want.

Through it all, Jane's philosophy seemed the same: she would endure slights, accommodate demands, tolerate fools, and make sacrifices—if it served to sustain her work.

From her childhood in England, Valerie Jane Morris-Goodall professed a deep love of animals and a desire to work with them in Africa. Her family lacked the means to send her to college, so Jane went to secretarial school. She worked at Oxford and then for a documentary film company in London. In the summer of 1956, she returned home, where she waited tables to save for an ocean passage to Kenya.

In Nairobi, she boldly asked for an appointment with paleoanthropologist Louis S. B. Leakey whose interest in great apes grew from his pioneering research into human origins. Leakey hired Jane on the spot to do secretarial work and saw in her the makings of a scientist. He arranged for her to study primates while he raised funds, so she could conduct chimpanzee field research in Tanzania.

And within months of their first meeting, he told Jane he was in love with her.

Jane wrote to others that she was "horrified" by the overture from Leakey who was 30 years her senior and married. For months after Jane told him firmly that she'd never return his feelings, Leakey still sent her love letters.

In an interview years later with Virginia Morell, author of a book on the *Leakey family*, Jane said that "what I was most afraid of was what my rejection of him might mean for my study of the chimpanzees." But Leakey never withdrew his support—and by the summer of 1960 Jane was setting up camp in the Gombe Stream Reserve near the shores of Lake Tanganyika, with enough funding for six months of fieldwork.

Because government officials wouldn't allow a lone female to live in the reserve, Vanne Morris-Goodall came along as her daughter's chaperone.

From the start Jane followed her instincts for conducting research. Not knowing that the established scientific practice was to use numbers to identify animals under study, she recorded observations of the chimps by names she concocted: Fifi, Flo, Mr. McGregor, and David Greybeard. She wrote about the chimps as individuals with distinct traits and personalities— for example, when a female she called Mrs. Maggs was preparing a treetop nest for the night, Jane wrote that the chimp had "tested the branches exactly the way a person tests the springs of a hotel bed."

She spent most waking hours locating the animals through her binoculars, then trying to draw gradually closer, so they'd get used to her presence as she sat jotting notes. But with one month left in the study grant, she hadn't made the kind of significant discovery she felt would justify Leakey's faith in her.

As her study was approaching its end, Jane made three discoveries that would not only make Leakey proud but would also turn established science on its head.

In her first discovery, she observed a chimp gnawing on the carcass of a small animal, which belied the prevailing belief that apes don't eat meat. The chimp was memorable for his prominent gray goatee, and she would name him David Greybeard. He in turn would open the door for her to the hidden world of Gombe's chimpanzees. Within two weeks, Jane observed David Greybeard again, but this time what she witnessed was truly game-changing. Squatting by a termite mound, he picked a blade of grass and poked it into a tunnel. When he pulled it out, it was covered with termites, which he slurped down. In another instance, Jane saw him pick a twig and strip it of leaves before using it to fish for termites. David Greybeard had exhibited tool use and toolmaking—two things that previously only humans were believed capable of.

When Jane cabled the news to Louis Leakey, he sent this response:

NOW WE MUST REDEFINE TOOL STOP REDEFINE MAN STOP OR ACCEPT CHIMPANZEES AS HUMAN

In the wake of these discoveries, National Geographic gave Jane a grant to continue her work at Gombe.

As Jane began to write up and publish her field research, she met with skepticism from the scientific community. After all, she had no science training—no degree other than a secretarial certificate affirming that she could touch-type.

In the spring of 1962, Jane gave a presentation at the Zoological Society of London's primate symposium and impressed many in attendance, including zoologist and author

Desmond Morris. But she also faced derision. A society officer delivered a thinly veiled critique of her work as "anecdote and . . . speculation" that made no "real contribution to science." An Associated Press report began with this: "A willowy blonde with more time for monkeys than men told today how she spent 15 months in the jungle to study the habits of the apes."

A photographic record of Jane's discoveries would put them beyond dispute. But Jane rebuffed National Geographic's request to send a photographer, saying a stranger might disrupt the relationship she was building with the chimps. After spending months getting close enough to even be in camera range, "I want to do my own photos—or have a jolly good try," she wrote in a letter home.

National Geographic shipped a camera and several rolls of film to Africa with detailed instructions on how to use them. Jane made a valiant effort. But her dark-furred subjects tended to hide in the shadows, and the photos she submitted weren't up to the magazine editors' standards. Again, editors pressed to send a Geographic photographer, and again Jane held them off: her younger sister, Judy, had photography experience, and the two looked and sounded enough alike that the chimps might not be upset by the sister's presence.

Louis Leakey underwrote Judy's trip to Gombe, covering the expense by selling rights to print the first pictures to a British weekly. Ultimately the Geographic's editors found her photos unsatisfactory too.

National Geographic magazine wanted Jane to write an article about her work—but it couldn't go forward without "good pictures of the animals," an editor warned. Jane understood that if she couldn't get her work covered in the magazine, her funding from the National Geographic Society could be in jeopardy.

Leakey had helped Jane get into a PhD program at Cambridge University—she was one of the few individuals without an undergraduate degree to ever be admitted—and he asked National Geographic to support Jane as she wrote up her Gombe research and worked on her dissertation.

When the Geographic turned down the request, saying, "this lady . . . is unqualified in the sense that she holds no degree of any university," an outraged Leakey fired off a memo listing her accomplishments. National Geographic officials gave Jane the requested grant, but as part of the deal, she agreed to welcome a professional photographer to Gombe. On Leakey's recommendation, National Geographic hired Hugo van Lawick for the job.

The opportunity to work at Gombe with Jane would be a huge break for the 25-year-old Dutchman who had some experience in natural history filmmaking. Jane wrote to a friend that she actually looked forward to his arrival because she'd been told that Hugo was "a first-class photographer, wonderful with animals—well, it's just too good to be true."

When I interviewed Jane in 2015, she insisted that "Louis was definitely matchmaking when he sent Hugo. There's no question, and he admitted it." Jane believes that Leakey's enduring love for her was selfless in the end.

Hugo reached Gombe in August 1962. He smoked heavily; Jane detested the habit. Otherwise they were well matched, both ardent observers of wildlife and devoted to their work. In a letter to a friend, Jane wrote, "We are a very happy family. Hugo is charming and we get on very well."

As Jane and Hugo documented the chimps' behavior, neither felt it worthwhile to focus on Jane as well. But National Geographic executives were increasingly eager to turn the camera on her.

"I know you won't forget to get some pictures of straight camp life—cooking, the writing of reports into the night by lamp light, bathing, hair washing and the like," assistant illustrations editor Robert Gilka wrote in a letter to Hugo in the fall of 1962. "I bring up the hair washing bit because there came out of Jane's last trip to the chimp reserve just such a picture, but it was . . . so underexposed that it would not reproduce." Good shots of Jane washing her hair in a stream, Gilka stressed, "would be a big help."

In the london home, where *Miss Goodall and the Wild Chimpanzees* is still playing on the laptop, we've come to the hair-washing scene. Even today, it doesn't sit well with Jane.

"I was angry they filmed this," she says. Why? I ask. "I don't see why people should see me washing my hair. I couldn't see why it was interesting." Hugo's work pleased National Geographic's editors. He was checking off the boxes: capturing photographic proof of the chimps' toolmaking and use, nest building, and social hierarchies—and dutifully taking the human interest shots of Jane that Gilka had requested.

His photographs appeared with Jane's words in *National Geographic* magazine's August 1963 cover story, "My Life Among Wild Chimpanzees: A courageous young British scientist lives among these great apes in Tanganyika and learns hitherto unknown details of their behavior."

The issue was a resounding success. National Geographic Society President Melville Grosvenor paid Jane and Hugo bonuses and called the article "magnificent." On its first page, a short text introducing Jane captured the duality of the public image being crafted for her. In one paragraph, she was called "a modern scientific zoologist"—and in the next, "a charming young Englishwoman."

As Jane and Hugo expanded the research station at Gombe, they also developed ideas for new films, but National Geographic wanted to keep the spotlight on Jane in films being made for television and the lecture circuit. The requests were increasingly specific, as in this letter to Hugo from Joanne Hess of the National Geographic Society's lecture branch:

"It will be most important and helpful to have several shots of Jane, which you will have to pose, showing her looking through binoculars, laughing at chimps, staring up at chimps in trees, staring into distance at chimps, and writing notes in her book, etc.," Hess wrote. "I mean you should take about 200 feet of close-ups of Jane 'pretending' to do these things, so that we can cut pictures of her into the film."

The pressures to pose rankled Jane but she handled it diplomatically. In a letter to Melvin Payne, whose National Geographic committee oversaw her funding, Jane wrote, "Certainly I understand that it is necessary to build up a story around 'Jane Goodall' and we have cooperated with Joanne as much as we possibly could."

But when Hess came to Gombe to oversee some filming, Jane allowed herself a private act of rebellion. "We are already collecting large numbers of evil-looking spiders and centipedes to lay around casually in her tent, in an endeavor to shorten her visit," Jane wrote to her mother.

When I interviewed Jane years later, during a 2015 visit to Gombe, she could look back on the celebrity treatment more philosophically:

GOODALL: There's this glamorous young girl out in the jungle with potentially dangerous animals. People like romanticizing, and people were looking at me as though I was that myth that they had created in their mind. And the Geographic helped create it too.

GERBER: A lot of people would resist that and fight back and say, That's not me.

GOODALL: There was nothing I could do about it because as far as they knew, it was me. And there was no way I could be portrayed differently. It wasn't inaccurate. It's just that people take the facts and weave stories around them.

GERBER: But at some point you embraced it? You embellished it? You made it better?

GOODALL: Well, at some point I realized that if people were going to think this way, then they would listen to me, which is true. And this would help to conserve chimps and do all the other things I need to do.

As 1963 ended, Jane confided to friends that she and Hugo were "very much in love." During Christmas holidays at her family home in Bournemouth, on England's southern coast, she received a telegram: "WILL YOU MARRY ME STOP HUGO." She replied yes. They set March 28 as the wedding date, one month after what would be another red-letter day for Jane: her first major public lecture in the United States.

Jane was a little nervous about being on stage at the 3,700-seat DAR Constitution Hall in Washington, but the members of National Geographic's lecture committee seemed more nervous. She was to give her remarks against the backdrop of a film made from Hugo's Gombe footage. As the February 28 event neared, the committee asked for a draft of her speech. Jane hadn't written one.

Seeking assurance that the lecture would go well, Joanne Hess and her team asked Jane to join them in the editing room, to practice her remarks as the film played. When I interviewed her at Gombe in 2015, she recalled the scene:

"The Geographic naturally wanted to hear what it would be like," she recalled. "Well, it's very hard for me to practice something ahead; it comes out to the audience. I didn't know that then. I just knew that with three people listening to me in that cutting room, this isn't a lecture! Apparently they were all whispering to each other, "Shall we cancel it? It's going to be a disaster! Can we really have the Geographic associated with this young gal? She doesn't seem to know what she's going to say." I had every idea what I was going to say, but I wasn't going to give a whole speech to three people in a cutting room."

In her speech and film presentation at Constitution Hall, Jane reported on her scientific discoveries, which she called "results beyond my wildest dreams." She evoked scenes of Gombe's beauty and tranquility. And as she would throughout her career, she described chimps by their personalities and the names she'd given them. She called Fifi "agile and acrobatic" and described Fifi's older brother Figan as an adolescent who "feels he's a little bit superior." To a baby who was "just beginning to find her feet," Jane had impishly given the name Gilka, after the National Geographic editor.

And in describing the need to protect the chimps and prevent them from being shot or sold to circuses, Jane referred to David Greybeard, the trusting chimp who had opened the door to some of her most important discoveries.

"David Greybeard . . . has put his complete trust in man," she told the audience. "Shall we fail him? Surely it's up to us to do something to ensure that at least some of these fantastic, almost human creatures continue to live undisturbed in their natural habitat."

Her presentation was a triumph, and a milestone in her emergence as a public figure—a status she didn't start out seeking but was learning to manage to her advantage. It caught the attention of a National Geographic executive who was launching a television specials division. A good deal of the Gombe footage ended up in one of the division's first prime-time broadcasts: Miss Goodall and the Wild Chimpanzees, with narration by Hollywood luminary Orson Welles.

When Hugo and Jane first screened the finished film, they complained of its many inaccuracies. They found the Welles narration patently unscientific—and at Jane's insistence, the script was partially rewritten.

To this day, as she watches the film on the laptop, Jane points out flaws. That leopard wasn't photographed by Hugo, it was stock footage. That scene isn't in Gombe, it's somewhere in the Serengeti. And when Welles begins a sentence with "After two months' search in vain," Jane cuts him off: "It wasn't true that I didn't see any chimps for two months. That's an absolute lie."

The flaws seemed to matter only to Jane and Hugo; the film was a commercial success. The two hoped they might do another film project and have more creative control, but Geographic officials had other ideas. They wanted to do more with Jane and Gombe but not necessarily with Hugo. Jane was their star; Hugo, an accessory.

In the years after the filming at Gombe, Jane and Hugo took different paths. In 1967, Hugo and Jane welcomed a son, Hugo Eric Louis van Lawick, known by his nickname, Grub.

With Jane's work anchored in Gombe and Hugo's film-making passion in the Serengeti, nearly 400 miles away, the two grew apart. In 1974, Jane and Hugo divorced. In 1975, she married Derek Bryceson, a Tanzanian government official.

By the time Grub was eight, he was living with his grandmother and attending school in Bournemouth. Derek and Jane had been married for only five years when he died of cancer in 1980. After a career spanning four decades, Hugo died of emphysema in 2002.

When i interviewed Jane in Gombe, it had been 55 years since she'd climbed out of a skiff and onto a pebble beach there for the first time. In her mind's eye, she can see things as they were then, from that beach up to the high ridge known as the peak: "It's like another life, so long ago."

She can even watch herself pretending and today recount it with a smile.

In the film footage, Jane sees her 28-year-old self seated on the peak. It's magic hour, nightfall. Hugo's exposure is perfect. On screen, Jane pulls a blanket around her shoulders. She raises a tin cup to her mouth and sips.

Now it's Jane who's the narrator.

"That cup is empty, I swear," she says. "There's nothing inside it."

Critical Thinking

1. How did Jane cope with the "male science establishment?
2. In what ways did Jane follow her instincts for conducting research?
3. How did Jane manage to gain credibility with the scientific establishment as well as the public?

Internet References

African Primates at Home
www.indiana.edu/~primate/primates.html

Great Ape survival Project: United Nations
www.unep.org/grasp/ABOUT_/GRASO.ubdex.aso

Jane Goodall Institute for Wildlife Research, Education and Conservation
www.janegoodall.org

Article

Prepared by: Elvio Angeloni

The Gorillas Dian Fossey Saved

To some in Rwanda she was a menacing intruder, but her work kept mountain gorillas from being wiped out. Today the great apes face new challenges.

ELIZABETH ROYTE

Learning Outcomes

After reading this article, you will be able to:

- Discuss the difficulties in saving the mountain gorillas.

- Discuss Dian Fossey's struggles and why she was seen as a menacing intruder by some and was barely tolerated by others.

Shortly after dawn, two mountain gorillas swing gracefully over the shoulder-high stone wall that borders Volcanoes National Park in northwestern Rwanda. Landing lightly on cropped grass, the silverbacks stroll downhill through cultivated fields—knuckle-walking at first, then upright on two legs. The adult males belly up to eucalyptus trees and score the bark with their incisors. Then, joined by females and juveniles from their group, which researchers call Titus, they advance on a spindly stand of bamboo.

Later that morning, Veronica Vecellio, the gorilla program manager for the Dian Fossey Gorilla Fund International, settles onto a log inside the park, high on a thickly forested, mist-shrouded slope of the Virunga Mountains, and turns her attention to a silverback known as Urwibutso. A frequent wall hopper, Urwibutso is carefully folding thistle leaves before placing them in his mouth. When he turns toward Vecellio, an ebullient woman who studies gorilla group dynamics, she snaps a picture, then zooms in on a wound on his nose.

"He fought with another silverback from Titus this morning," she whispers intently. (Silverbacks get their name from the white hairs that blanket males, saddlelike, when they reach maturity.)

The Titus group has been sneaking over the park wall for 10 years, Vecellio says, and each year, it ventures farther. The situation isn't ideal. Gorillas don't eat the potatoes or beans that villagers plant—not yet. But they do kill trees, a valuable resource, and come into close contact with human and livestock waste, which is loaded with pathogens. The potential for disease spillover between species is high, and the chance gorillas could survive a virulent outbreak is low. So when the Titus group gets within a stone's throw of the mud-and-stick homes of Bisate, a village of about 10,000 people, park guards waving bamboo poles slowly shoo them back uphill. Vecellio sighs. "This is the price we're paying for success."

Dian Fossey, an american with no experience researching wild animals, arrived in Africa to study mountain gorillas in the late 1960s at the urging of anthropologist Louis Leakey and with financing from the *National Geographic* Society. By 1973, the population of these great apes in the Virunga Mountains had fallen below 275, but today, thanks to extreme conservation measures—constant monitoring, intensive anti-poaching efforts, and emergency veterinary interventions—there are now about 480.

More gorillas have been a boon for genetic diversity: for years, researchers have documented evidence of inbreeding, such as cleft palates and webbed fingers and toes. But the population uptick has a downside. "Group sizes are larger," Vecellio says. The Pablo group hit 65 members in 2006; it's now down to about 25—still almost three times as large as average gorilla groups in the Virunga Mountains in Uganda and the Democratic Republic of the Congo. "The density of groups in certain areas is also up," Vecellio adds.

Clashes between groups, which raise the odds gorillas will suffer injuries or commit infanticide to wipe out a competing male's genes, are six times as frequent now as 10 years ago. "We're seeing an increase in the level of stress too," Vecellio says, and possibly increased exposure to stress-related diseases.

These problems would not be so acute if the mountain gorillas had unlimited room to roam. But Volcanoes National Park is just 62 square miles, and a rising sea of humanity, hungry for more farm and grazing land, laps at its boundary. Villagers routinely flout park rules and clamber over the stone wall to cut firewood, hunt meat, gather honey, and in the dry season, collect water.

From the morning's eucalyptus and bamboo raid, it's obvious the Titus group is comfortable outside the forest. But the gorillas have little immunity to human diseases, and their blasé attitude toward people leaves them vulnerable.

Such dynamics are largely hidden to the park's visitors. Researchers who study Rwanda's mountain gorillas, however, understand that they're documenting a unique moment—not only the increase in population of a critically endangered species but also the possible revision of the rules assumed to govern its social behavior.

On an overcast morning, with temperatures in the mid-50s, it takes me nearly two hours to hike from the outskirts of Bisate through calf-deep mud and shoulder-high nettles to the research site established in 1967 by Fossey in the high-elevation saddle between Mounts Karisimbi and Visoke. The camp, which Fossey named Karisoke, began with two tents and grew to include more than a dozen cabins and outbuildings in a grove of moss-shrouded Hagenia trees, 80 feet tall. Today, as in Fossey's day, a profusion of ferns, vines, and grasses seems to tint the humid air green, and a stream flows past the clearing. When the corpse of an infant gorilla disappeared, Fossey spent countless hours hunched on this stream bank examining adult dung for irrefutable evidence of cannibalism, but she never found it.

After an intruder murdered Fossey in her bed in 1985—a crime that remains a mystery—researchers continued to work at Karisoke. The camp shut down in 1994 during the Rwandan genocide, and rebels traversing the forest ransacked it. Today the much expanded Karisoke Research Center operates out of a modern office building in nearby Musanze, and the only man-made traces of Fossey's site are foundation stones and the occasional stovepipe.

Despite the climb, drenching rains, and temperatures that can drop into the 30s, some 500 pilgrims a year trek to Karisoke to pay tribute to Fossey. Many know her from her book Gorillas in the Mist, which inspired the 1988 movie. On my visit, though, I have the place mostly to myself. As I explore the grounds, trying to imagine Fossey's life here, porters quietly scrape lichen from the wooden signs that mark the graves of 25 gorillas. Just outside this rustic cemetery, a bronze plaque rises over Fossey herself.

The tall, outspoken Fossey was not universally beloved. Many locals considered her an interloper or a witch who not only confounded cultural norms but also presented an existential threat to those who depended on the forest for sustenance. From the start, Fossey made clear her priorities. She chased herders and their cattle out of the park: the animals trampled the plants that gorillas favored and forced them upslope to temperatures they couldn't withstand. Every year she destroyed thousands of traps and snares intended to catch antelope and buffalo. The snares didn't kill gorillas outright but often pinched off limbs that became gangrenous or fatally infected. Fossey captured and beat poachers with stinging nettles, burned down their huts, confiscated their weapons, and once even took a poacher's child hostage. But her most effective tactic—and an enduring part of her legacy—was paying locals to patrol the park and insisting that Rwandan authorities enforce anti-poaching laws. Fossey was a polarizing figure, but as Jane Goodall, the chimpanzee expert, once said, "If Dian had not been there, probably there might have been no mountain gorillas in Rwanda today."

Contemplating the simple plaque on Fossey's headstone, I'm struck by all that was extraordinary about this pioneer: her 18 years in the forest, her epic battles for funding, and her struggles for academic legitimacy, physical health, and emotional connection. It's beyond irony that Fossey showed the world a largely peaceable realm of affectionate gorilla families, while her own life was characterized by bitterness and mistrust. "She was alone and hated by many," says Vecellio who describes herself as a lifelong Fossey "superfan."

Fossey's grave lies just a few steps from that of Digit, the silverback whom she reluctantly turned into a fund-raising bonanza—by creating the Digit Fund—after he was stabbed and decapitated by poachers. Fossey was desperate for money to pay her trackers and anti-poaching teams. But she hated the idea of generating revenue from ecotourism, and she considered gorilla tourists—who began arriving at Karisoke, against her wishes, in 1979—a driver of gorilla extinction. And yet it was Fossey's knack for publicizing her studies through lectures and articles that turned the gorillas into causes célèbres. It was also Fossey who figured out how to habituate gorillas to humans, without which the tourist trade wouldn't exist.

Rwanda barely tolerated Fossey when she was alive—authorities repeatedly denied her visa applications and stymied her efforts to halt poaching. But the country was quick to realize that her death and burial within a national park, Vecellio says, "had enormous symbolic value. It created a sense of urgency and brought international support for gorilla conservation." Last year more than 30,000 people hiked into the park, each paying the Rwanda Development Board, which oversees the nation's tourism, $750 for a gorilla-group encounter limited to one hour. The fees, which recently jumped to $1,500, pay for security and monitoring, and they ensure the government's commitment to protecting the species.

For the safety of animals and humans, the development board allows only eight people in each trekking group. But with more groups of gorillas, more visitors than ever can have their primal moment. Higher visitation means more money is funneled, through a revenue-sharing plan, into local communities, and it creates ripple opportunities for businesses. During the high season, tourists fill more than 20 hotels and guesthouses in and around Musanze—the town had just one when Fossey arrived—generating income for drivers, housekeepers, waiters, chefs, bartenders, guards, farmers, park guides, porters, and trackers.

Tourism opportunities may expand even more. The Rwandan government, in collaboration with the Massachusetts Institute of Technology, is considering the construction of a climate research station on the summit of Mount Karisimbi, at 14,787 feet. A cable car would whisk scientists to their instruments and tourists to crater-top zip lines. Worried that the project could destroy gorilla habitat, conservation groups are calling for a comprehensive study of its environmental impacts.

It's late morning before my guide locates the Sabyinyo group, a short hike from the park boundary, through a dim bamboo forest. As the rain that has been pelting lets up, we hear the animals—stripping and munching the scenery—well before we spot them. A mountain of muscle, the silverback Gihishamwotsi sits in a clearing of crushed ferns and giant lobelias, calmly overseeing a harem of females and their babies. Now and then he grunts, eliciting guttural responses from gorillas just out of sight. When he rises suddenly to beat his chest, he gets more of a reaction—alarm—from me than from anyone else.

I'd suspected that a lifetime of watching nature documentaries and knowing that gorillas and humans share 98 percent of their DNA would diminish the thrill of seeing these animals in the flesh. But from six feet away, I'm dumbstruck by that flesh: the babies' feet, as smooth and meaty as yams, the mothers' kielbasa-size fingers, the silverback's forearms, which resemble muffs fit for giants. I'm entranced too by the familiarity of their gestures: like us, they scratch! They play with their toes! They hug their babies to their faces! On the heels of this epiphany, however, comes guilt—for intruding upon their privacy.

When my hour is up, I dash down the mountain to meet Winnie Eckardt in a small room in the Karisoke Research Center. Leaning against a freezer, the research manager gestures to the trove of frozen samples at her back. "Welcome to the poop lab," she says with a grin. Eckardt, who jumps at any chance to summit the nearby volcanoes, has been studying mountain gorillas since 2004 and now supervises the monthly collection and processing of fecal samples—which contain hormones, enzymes, and DNA, in addition to viruses and parasites—from 130 animals. (Disposable bags are a key component of ranger gear.)

"Wildlife endocrinology is an increasingly significant field," Eckardt says, "and it's a very powerful tool." Karisoke researchers are extracting from gorilla feces the stress hormone cortisol and correlating it with observed interactions. "Now we can say this or that type of interaction is causing stress," she says.

In 2014, researchers compared observations on demographics and behavior in gorilla groups with genetic analyses of DNA extracted from fecal samples. Their results shed light on key differences between how far males and females disperse from their natal group—one of the main factors that determine a population's genetic structure.

DNA sequencing is also telling researchers about gorilla paternity. "From these studies, we've learned that the dominant silverback is the father of most babies in a group but not all," Eckardt says. The number two and three silverbacks are also passing on their genes. This raises more interesting questions: how do nondominant silverbacks decide whether to stay in a group or to try to seduce females into establishing a new group? What factors are linked with reproductive success? How do you stay number one? "There is a lot of competition out there," Eckardt notes.

By revealing evidence of inbreeding and the success of various family lineages, DNA analysis also informs conservation decisions. "If managers can save only a few groups of gorillas," Eckardt says, "you want to choose groups that are distantly related. If they're inbred, they won't behave normally or may have health complications, which you may need to monitor differently." Less genetic diversity also means gorillas are more vulnerable to disease and to climate-change disruptions.

RESEARCHERS HAVE PUBLISHED nearly 300 papers based on data collected at Karisoke, but there's still much to learn. "If you'd done a study from 1997 till 2007, which is a long study," says Tara Stoinski, president and chief scientific officer of the Fossey Fund, "you'd think there was no infanticide here. But we know, from before and after that period, that it's not an uncommon behavior."

Through the 1970s gorillas lived at low densities with a lot of human disturbance—like poaching and cattle herding—which shattered groups and drove lone males to lure females from their groups, then kill their babies to trigger estrus. As poaching declined, so did infanticide. "Now we have a high density of groups and low human disturbance," Stoinski says, "and infanticide is up because of increased intergroup interactions. It's fascinating to see how the gorillas react."

Perhaps one of the biggest surprises to park officials and Stoinski, who has published nearly a hundred papers on primate behavior and conservation, was the reappearance in January of a silverback presumed dead. Cantsbee, one of the last two gorillas named by Fossey, was the longest lived male recorded by researchers. He reigned over Pablo, Karisoke's largest group, and according to an analysis that ended in 2013, fathered at least 28 babies—a record among studied gorillas. After the rufous-browed legend disappeared last October, at the age of 37, scores of trackers spent a fruitless month scouring the forest for his body. Finally, the Fossey Fund published an obituary, noting that he was born during a time of intense poaching but lived to a ripe age thanks to conservation measures.

Cantsbee's return upended many assumptions about dominant male behavior. "For a leader of his age and status to go and then come back—that's never been seen," Stoinski says, with a note of wonder. "Plus, he looked great—superfit."

In Cantsbee's absence, his son Gicurasi had become Pablo's leader; upon his return, Cantsbee sometimes led the group but by no means dominated. Then, in February, looking weak, he slipped away for the last time. His body was found in May.

To Karisoke researchers, everything happening in the park today demonstrates how flexible mountain gorillas, like most big-brained primates, can be. In Fossey's time, groups under observation contained just two or three males. In the 1990s and early 2000s when human interference declined, groups grew considerably in size and had as many as eight silverbacks. More recently, researchers have observed many group splits, often after the death of a dominant male, resulting again in groups that look more like those of Fossey's time. "This shows us that behavior doesn't exist in a vacuum. It depends on a larger context," Stoinski says. "As their environment and circumstances change, so do things like gorilla social organization." And because gorillas take a long time to mature, it takes long-term studies to even hint at what "normal" means.

WHILE HUMAN ACTIVITIES are propelling about 60 percent of wild primate species toward extinction, one great ape population is rising. Even so, the mountain gorillas of the Virungas are still vulnerable. "The population is incredibly small and fragile," Stoinski warns.

And so the Fossey Fund continues to monitor animals and help remove snares, even as it invests in social programs. The organization created a school library and computer center in Bisate, where it also built a maternity ward; it runs conservation education programs that reach about 13,000 Rwandans a year; and it plans to help villagers find ways to make a living that don't include scrambling over the park's stone wall.

Gorillas are already shifting into areas of the park with fewer groups. But humans may need to cede land to gorillas too. The government has proposed a buffer zone that would force people, their livestock, and their farm plots farther downhill. That would be enormously controversial, since 1,813 people per square mile call Musanze District home. "We need to make sure that the communities understand the value of the park," Stoinski says. After all, gorilla trekking is the mainstay of the nation's tourism industry, which brought in $367 million in 2015, and the park shares 10 percent of its revenue with local communities.

Watching a mother gorilla dandle a tiny puff of an infant while a pair of adolescents wrestle on a mattress of vines, it's easy to forget the human gymnastics that make such a delightful tableau possible. Critics ask whether these extreme conservation efforts consume money that might better be spent on other species, and some have suggested they may even disrupt natural selection by helping less fit individuals survive.

But Vecellio steadfastly defends the work. "We are keeping these gorillas alive, reversing the human impacts," she says, "because it's humans who have made them endangered." ®© Elizabeth Royte, a regular contributor, last visited Africa to write about the decline of vultures in the January 2016 issue. Ronan Donovan, who trained as a wildlife biologist, discovered a talent and passion for photography while researching chimpanzees in Uganda.

FIVE DECADES OF GROWTH

Here are the trajectories of the primary groups and some key gorillas that Fossey studied. Groups typically split after the deaths of alpha males or disputes over dominance, with a new male luring away females to start another group.

DIGIT| Fossey's favorite
Digit was killed by poachers in 1977 while defending Group Four. The death of the famed gorilla was announced on CBS News.

CANTSBEE| Longestreigning With 28 offspring, he's the most reproductively successful male gorilla ever tracked. Cantsbee led the Pablo group for a record 21 years.

GASORE| Survivedinfancy Gasore is one of Maggie's three babies that survived their early years; 25 percent of mountain gorillas die before age three, often from trauma.

On the night of December 26, 1985, Fossey—threatened for her anti-poaching work—is murdered in her cabin at Karisoke.

MAGGIE| Prolificmother Maggie had 10 offspring and spent decades in the Pablo group. Later solitary, she was 35 when her trail was lost in 2015.

GUFASHA| Lost female

Like many females, Gufasha left her birth group when she reached sexual maturity—in 2005, at age seven. She hasn't been seen since.

INSHUTI| Solitary male

Born into Group Five, Inshuti has lived mostly on his own, with short stays within groups, as is typical of many males. He was last sighted in May 2017.

POPPY| Returned home

At 41, Poppy is the oldest gorilla tracked by the Fossey Fund. Born under Fossey's watch, she left the Karisoke population in 1984 but rejoined it 30 years later.

Critical Thinking

1. Why is it so difficult to maintain mountain gorillas on a suitable amount of land?
2. In what ways was Dian Foseey effective in saving the mountain gorillas?
3. Why is DNA sequencing important for preserving the mountain gorillas?

Internet References

African Primates at Home
www.indiana.edu/~primate/primates.html

Great Ape survival Project: United Nations
www.unep.org/grasp/ABOUT_/GRASO.ubdex,aso

The Dian Fossey Gorilla Fund International
www.gorillafund.org

Article   Prepared by: Elvio Angeloni

The 2% Difference

Now that scientists have decoded the chimpanzee genome, we know that 98 percent of our DNA is the same. So how can we be so different?

ROBERT SAPOLSKY

Learning Outcomes

After reading this article, you will be able to:

- Discuss the similarities and differences between chimps and humans.

- Explain why we humans are so different from chimpanzees even though we share 98% of our DNA with them.

I f you find yourself sitting close to a chimpanzee, staring face to face and making sustained eye contact, something interesting happens, something that is alternately moving, bewildering, and kind of creepy. When you gaze at this beast, you suddenly realize that the face gazing back is that of a sentient individual, who is recognizably kin. You can't help but wonder, What's the matter with those intelligent design people?

Chimpanzees are close relatives to humans, but they're not identical to us. We are not chimps. Chimps excel at climbing trees, but we beat them hands down at balance-beam routines; they are covered in hair, while we have only the occasional guy with really hairy shoulders. The core differences, however, arise from how we use our brains. Chimps have complex social lives, play power politics, betray and murder each other, make tools, and teach tool use across generations in a way that qualifies as culture. They can even learn to do logic operations with symbols, and they have a relative sense of numbers. Yet those behaviors don't remotely approach the complexity and nuance of human behaviors, and in my opinion there's not the tiniest bit of scientific evidence that chimps have aesthetics, spirituality, or a capacity for irony or poignancy.

What makes the human species brainy are huge numbers of standard-issue neurons.

What accounts for those differences? A few years ago, the most ambitious project in the history of biology was carried out: the sequencing of the human genome. Then just four months ago, a team of researchers reported that they had likewise sequenced the complete chimpanzee genome. Scientists have long known that chimps and humans share about 98 percent of their DNA. At last, however, one can sit down with two scrolls of computer printout, march through the two genomes, and see exactly where our 2 percent difference lies.

Given the outward differences, it seems reasonable to expect to find fundamental differences in the portions of the genome that determine chimp and human brains—reasonable, at least, to a brainocentric neurobiologist like me. But as it turns out, the chimp brain and the human brain differ hardly at all in their genetic underpinnings. Indeed, a close look at the chimp genome reveals an important lesson in how genes and evolution work, and it suggests that chimps and humans are a lot more similar than even a neurobiologist might think.

DNA, or deoxyribonucleic acid, is made up of just four molecules, called nucleotides: adenine (A), cytosine (C), guanine (G), and thymine (T). The DNA codebook for every species consists of billions of these letters in a precise order. If, when DNA is being copied in a sperm or an egg, a nucleotide is mistakenly copied wrong, the result is a mutation. If the mutation persists from generation to generation, it becomes a DNA difference—one of the many genetic distinctions that separate one species (chimpanzees) from another (humans). In genomes involving billions of nucleotides, a tiny 2 percent difference translates into tens of millions of ACGT differences. And that 2 percent difference can be very broadly distributed. Humans and chimps each have somewhere between 20,000 and 30,000 genes, so there are likely to be nucleotide differences in every single gene.

To understand what distinguishes the DNA of chimps and humans, one must first ask: What is a gene? A gene is a string of nucleotides that specify how a single distinctive protein should be made. Even if the same gene in chimps and humans differs by an A here and a T there, the result may be of no consequence. Many nucleotide differences are neutral—both the mutation and the normal gene cause the same protein to be made. However, given the right nucleotide difference between the same gene in the two species, the resulting proteins may differ slightly in construction and function.

One might assume that the differences between chimp and human genes boil down to those sorts of typographical errors: one nucleotide being swapped for a different one and altering the gene it sits in. But a close look at the two codebooks reveals very few such instances. And the typos that do occasionally occur follow a compelling pattern. It's important to note that genes don't act alone. Yes, each gene regulates the construction of a specific protein. But what tells that gene *when* and *where* to build that protein? Regulation is everything: It's important not to start up genes related to puberty during, say, infancy, or to activate genes that are related to eye color in the bladder.

In the DNA code list, that critical information is contained in a short stretch of As and Cs and Gs and Ts that lie just before each gene and act as a switch that turns the gene on or off. The switch, in turn, is flicked on by proteins called transcription factors, which activate certain genes in response to certain stimuli. Naturally, every gene is not regulated by its own distinct transcription factor; otherwise, a codebook of as many as 30,000 genes would require 30,000 transcription factors—and 30,000 more genes to code for them. Instead, one transcription factor can flick on an array of functionally related genes. For example, a certain type of injury can activate one transcription factor that turns on a bunch of genes in your white blood cells, triggering inflammation.

Accurate switch flickers are essential. Imagine the consequences if some of those piddly nucleotide changes arose in a protein that happened to be a transcription factor: Suddenly, instead of activating 23 different genes, the protein might charge up 21 or 25 of them—or it might turn on the usual 23 but in different ratios than normal. Suddenly, one minor nucleotide difference would be amplified across a network of gene differences. (And imagine the ramifications if the altered proteins are transcription factors that activate the genes coding for still other transcription factors!) When the chimp and human genomes are compared, some of the clearest cases of nucleotide differences are found in genes coding for transcription factors. Those cases are few, but they have far-ranging implications.

The genomes of chimps and humans reveal a history of other kinds of differences as well. Instead of a simple mutation, in which a single nucleotide is copied incorrectly, consider an insertion mutation, where an extra A, C, G, or T is dropped in, or a deletion mutation, whereby a nucleotide drops out. Insertion or deletion mutations can have major consequences: Imagine the deletion mutation that turns the sentence "I'll have the mousse for dessert" into "I'll have the mouse for dessert," or the insertion mutation implicit in "She turned me down for a date after I asked her to go bowling with me." Sometimes, more than a single nucleotide is involved; whole stretches of a gene may be dropped or added. In extreme cases, entire genes may be deleted or added.

More important than how the genetic changes arise—by insertion, deletion, or straight mutation—is where in the genome they occur. Keep in mind that, for these genetic changes to persist from generation to generation, they must convey some evolutionary advantage. When one examines the 2 percent difference between humans and chimps, the genes in question turn out to be evolutionarily important, if banal. For example, chimps have a great many more genes related to olfaction than we do; they've got a better sense of smell because we've lost many of those genes. The 2 percent distinction also involves an unusually large fraction of genes related to the immune system, parasite vulnerability, and infectious diseases: Chimps are resistant to malaria, and we aren't; we handle tuberculosis better than they do. Another important fraction of that 2 percent involves genes related to reproduction—the sorts of anatomical differences that split a species in two and keep them from interbreeding.

That all makes sense. Still, chimps and humans have very different brains. So which are the brain-specific genes that have evolved in very different directions in the two species? It turns out that there are hardly any that fit that bill. This, too, makes a great deal of sense. Examine a neuron from a human brain under a microscope, then do the same with a neuron from the brain of a chimp, a rat, a frog, or a sea slug. The neurons all look the same: fibrous dendrites at one end, an axonal cable at the other. They all run on the same basic mechanism: channels and pumps that move sodium, potassium, and calcium around, triggering a wave of excitation called an action potential. They all have a similar complement of neurotransmitters: serotonin, dopamine, glutamate, and so on. They're all the same basic building blocks.

The main difference is in the sheer number of neurons. The human brain has 100 million times the number of neurons a sea slug's brain has. Where do those differences in quantity come from? At some point in their development, all embryos—whether human, chimp, rat, frog, or slug—must have a single first cell committed toward generating neurons. That cell divides and gives rise to 2 cells; those divide into 4, then 8, then 16. After a dozen rounds of cell division, you've got roughly enough neurons to run a slug. Go another 25 rounds or so and you've got a human brain. Stop a couple of rounds short of that and, at about one-third the size of a human brain, you've got one for a chimp. Vastly different outcomes, but relatively few genes regulate the number of rounds of cell division in the nervous system before calling a halt. And it's precisely some of those genes, the ones involved in neural development, that appear on the list of differences between the chimp and human genomes.

That's it; that's the 2 percent solution. What's shocking is the simplicity of it. Humans, to be human, don't need to have evolved unique genes that code for entirely novel types of neurons or neurotransmitters, or a more complex hippocampus (with resulting improvements in memory), or a more complex frontal cortex (from which we gain the ability to postpone gratification). Instead, our braininess as a species arises from having humongous numbers of just a few types of off-the-rack neurons and from the exponentially greater number of interactions between them. The difference is sheer quantity: Qualitative distinctions emerge from large numbers. Genes may have something to do with that quantity, and thus with the complexity of the quality that emerges. Yet no gene or genome can ever tell us what sorts of qualities those will be. Remember that when you and the chimp are eyeball to eyeball, trying to make sense of why the other seems vaguely familiar.

Critical Thinking

1. What are the similarities and differences between chimps and humans?

2. How much of our DNA differs from chimps? How do these differences come about?

3. What is the structure of DNA? How much of this material is different between chimps and humans, given the 2% overall difference between us?

4. What does Sapolsky mean when he says "genes don't act alone"?

5. What is a transcription factor? Is every gene regulated by its own transcription factor?

6. Where are "some of the clearest cases of nucleotide differences" between chimps and humans found?

7. What is the difference between a "simple mutation," an "insertion mutation," and a "deletion mutation"?

8. What type of genes do chimps have more of than we do? What other types of genes are disproportionately impacted by the 2% difference? What are four areas of difference?

9. How are chimp brains and human brains similar and how are they different?

10. What is shocking about the "2% solution"?

Internet References

Electronic Zoo/NetVet-Primate Page
http://netvet.wustl.edu/primates.htm

Laboratory Primate Newsletter
www.brown.edu/Research/Primate/other.html

Wellcome Trust Sanger Institute
www.sanger.ac.uk/research/projects/humanevolution

Max Planck Institute for Evolutionary Biology
wwwstaff.eva.mpg.de/~paabo

Article

Prepared by: Elvio Angeloni

Dim Forest, Bright Chimps

In the rain forest of Ivory Coast, chimpanzees meet the challenge of life by hunting cooperatively and using crude tools.

CHRISTOPHE BOESCH AND HEDWIGE BOESCH-ACHERMANN

Learning Outcomes

After reading this article, you will be able to:

- Discuss the implications of tool use, social hunting, and food sharing by the Ivory Coast chimpanzees for human evolution.

- Discuss the environmental circumstances that may have caused the common ancestor of apes and humans to divergence into two separate evolutionary paths.

Taï National Park, Ivory Coast, December 3, 1985. Drumming, barking, and screaming, chimps rush through the undergrowth, little more than black shadows. Their goal is to join a group of other chimps noisily clustering around Brutus, the dominant male of this seventy-member chimpanzee community. For a few moments, Brutus, proud and self-confident, stands fairly still, holding a shocked, barely moving red colobus monkey in his hand. Then he begins to move through the group, followed closely by his favorite females and most of the adult males. He seems to savor this moment of uncontested superiority, the culmination of a hunt high up in the canopy. But the victory is not his alone. Cooperation is essential to capturing one of these monkeys, and Brutus will break apart and share this highly prized delicacy with most of the main participants of the hunt and with the females. Recipients of large portions will, in turn, share more or less generously with their offspring, relatives, and friends.

In 1979, we began a long-term study of the previously unknown chimpanzees of Taï National Park, 1,600 square miles of tropical rain forest in the Republic of the Ivory Coast (Côte d'Ivoire). Early on, we were most interested in the chimps' use of natural hammers—branches and stones—to crack open the five species of hard-shelled nuts that are abundant here. A sea

otter lying on its back, cracking an abalone shell with a rock, is a familiar picture, but no primate had ever before been observed in the wild using stones as hammers. East Africa's savanna chimps, studied for decades by Jane Goodall in Gombe, Tanzania, use twigs to extract ants and termites from their nests or honey from a bees' nest, but they have never been seen using hammerstones.

As our work progressed, we were surprised by the many ways in which the life of the Taï forest chimpanzees differs from that of their savanna counterparts, and as evidence accumulated, differences in how the two populations hunt proved the most intriguing. Jane Goodall had found that chimpanzees hunt monkeys, antelope, and wild pigs, findings confirmed by Japanese biologist Toshida Nishida, who conducted a long-term study 120 miles south of Gombe, in the Mahale Mountains. So we were not surprised to discover that the Taï chimps eat meat. What intrigued us was the degree to which they hunt cooperatively. In 1953 Raymond Dart proposed that group hunting and cooperation were key ingredients in the evolution of *Homo sapiens*. The argument has been modified considerably since Dart first put it forward, and group hunting has also been observed in some social carnivores (lions and African wild dogs, for instance), and even some birds of prey. Nevertheless, many anthropologists still hold that hunting cooperatively and sharing food played a central role in the drama that enabled early hominids, some 1.8 million years ago, to develop the social systems that are so typically human.

We hoped that what we learned about the behavior of forest chimpanzees would shed new light on prevailing theories of human evolution. Before we could even begin, however, we had to habituate a community of chimps to our presence. Five long years passed before we were able to move with them on their daily trips through the forest, of which "our" group appeared to claim some twelve square miles. Chimpanzees are alert and shy animals, and the limited field of view in the rain forest—about sixty-five feet at best—made finding them more difficult. We had to rely on sound, mostly their vocalizations and drumming on trees. Males often drum regularly while moving through the forest: pant-hooting, they draw near a big buttress tree; then, at full speed they fly over the buttress, hitting it repeatedly with their hands and feet. Such drumming may resound more than half a mile in the forest. In the beginning, our ignorance about how they moved and who was drumming led to failure more often than not, but eventually we learned that the dominant males drummed during the day to let other group members know the direction of travel. On some days, however, intermittent drumming about dawn was the only signal for the whole day. If we were out of earshot at the time, we were often reduced to guessing.

During these difficult early days, one feature of the chimps' routine proved to be our salvation: nut cracking is a noisy business. So noisy, in fact, that in the early days of French colonial rule, one officer apparently even proposed the theory that some unknown tribe was forging iron in the impenetrable and dangerous jungle.

Guided by the sounds made by the chimps as they cracked open nuts, which they often did for hours at a time, we were gradually able to get within sixty feet of the animals. We still seldom saw the chimps themselves (they fled if we came too close), but even so, the evidence left after a session of nut cracking taught us a great deal about what types of nuts they were eating, what sorts of hammer and anvil tools they were using, and—thanks to the very distinctive noise a nut makes when it finally splits open—how many hits were needed to crack a nut and how many nuts could be opened per minute.

After some months, we began catching glimpses of the chimpanzees before they fled, and after a little more time, we were able to draw close enough to watch them at work. The chimps gather nuts from the ground. Some nuts are tougher to crack than others. Nuts of the *Panda oleosa* tree are the most demanding, harder than any of the foods processed by present-day hunter-gatherers and breaking open only when a force of 3,500 pounds is applied. The stone hammers used by the Taï chimps range from stones of ten ounces to granite blocks of four to forty-five pounds. Stones of any size, however, are a rarity in the forest and are seldom conveniently placed near a nut-bearing tree. By observing closely, and in some cases imitating the way the chimps handle hammerstones, we learned that they have an impressive ability to find just the right tool for the job at hand. Taï chimps could remember the positions of many of the stones scattered, often out of sight, around a panda tree. Without having to run around rechecking the stones, they would select one of appropriate size that was closest to the tree. These mental abilities in spatial representation compare with some of those of nine-year-old humans.

To extract the four kernels from inside a panda nut, a chimp must use a hammer with extreme precision. Time and time again, we have been impressed to see a chimpanzee raise a twenty-pound stone above its head, strike a nut with ten or more powerful blows, and then, using the same hammer, switch to delicate little taps from a height of only four inches. To finish the job, the chimps often break off a small piece of twig and use it to extract the last tiny fragments of kernel from the shell. Intriguingly, females crack panda nuts more often than males, a gender difference in tool use that seems to be more pronounced in the forest chimps than in their savanna counterparts.

After five years of fieldwork, we were finally able to follow the chimpanzees at close range, and gradually, we gained insights into their way of hunting. One morning, for example, we followed a group of six male chimps on a three-hour patrol that had taken them into foreign territory to the north. (Our study group is one of five chimpanzee groups more or less evenly distributed in the Taï forest.) As always during these approximately monthly incursions, which seem to be for the purpose of territorial defense, the chimps were totally silent, clearly on edge and on the lookout for trouble. Once the patrol was over, however, and they were back within their own borders, the chimps shifted their attention to hunting. They were after monkeys, the most abundant mammals in the forest. Traveling in large, multi-species groups, some of the forest's ten species of monkeys are more apt than others to wind up as a meal for the chimps. The relatively sluggish and large (almost thirty pounds) red colobus monkeys are the chimps' usual fare. (Antelope also live in the forest, but in our ten years at Taï, we have never seen a chimp catch, or even pursue, one. In contrast, Gombe chimps at times do come across fawns, and when they do, they seize the opportunity—and the fawn.)

The six males moved on silently, peering up into the vegetation and stopping from time to time to listen for the sound of monkeys. None fed or groomed; all focused on the hunt. We followed one old male, Falstaff, closely, for he tolerates us completely and is one of the keenest and most experienced hunters. Even from the rear, Falstaff set the pace; whenever he stopped, the others paused to wait for him. After thirty minutes, we heard the unmistakable noises of monkeys jumping from branch to branch. Silently, the chimps turned in the direction of the sounds, scanning the canopy. Just then, a diana monkey spotted them and gave an alarm call. Dianas are very alert and fast; they are also about half the weight of colobus monkeys. The chimps quickly gave up and continued their search for easier, meatier prey.

Shortly after, we heard the characteristic cough of a red colobus monkey. Suddenly Rousseau and Macho, two twenty-year-olds, burst into action, running toward the cough. Falstaff seemed surprised by their precipitousness, but after a moment's hesitation, he also ran. Now the hunting barks of the chimps mixed with the sharp alarm calls of the monkeys. Hurrying behind Falstaff, we saw him climb up a conveniently situated tree. His position, combined with those of Schubert and Ulysse, two mature chimps in their prime, effectively blocked off three of the monkeys' possible escape routes. But in another tree, nowhere near any escape route and thus useless, waited the last of the hunters, Kendo, eighteen years old and the least experienced of the group. The monkeys, taking advantage of Falstaff's delay and Kendo's error, escaped.

The six males moved on and within five minutes picked up the sounds of another group of red colobus. This time, the chimps approached cautiously, nobody hurrying. They screened the canopy intently to locate the monkeys, which were still unaware of the approaching danger. Macho and Schubert chose two adjacent trees, both full of monkeys, and started climbing very quietly, taking care not to move any branches. Meanwhile, the other four chimps blocked off anticipated escape routes. When Schubert was halfway up, the monkeys finally detected the two chimps. As we watched the colobus monkeys take off in literal panic, the appropriateness of the chimpanzees' scientific name—*Pan* came to mind: with a certain stretch of the imagination, the fleeing monkeys could be shepherds and shepherdesses frightened at the sudden appearance of Pan, the wild Greek god of the woods, shepherds, and their flocks.

Taking off in the expected direction, the monkeys were trailed by Macho and Schubert. The chimps let go with loud hunting barks. Trying to escape, two colobus monkeys jumped into smaller trees lower in the canopy. With this, Rousseau and Kendo, who had been watching from the ground, sped up into the trees and tried to grab them. Only a third of the weight of the chimps, however, the monkeys managed to make it to the next tree along branches too small for their pursuers. But Falstaff had anticipated this move and was waiting for them. In the following confusion, Falstaff seized a juvenile and killed it with a bite to the neck. As the chimps met in a rush on the ground, Falstaff began to eat, sharing with Schubert and Rousseau. A juvenile colobus does not provide much meat, however, and this time, not all the chimps got a share. Frustrated individuals soon started off on another hunt, and relative calm returned fairly quickly: this sort of hunt, by a small band of chimps acting on their own at the edge of their territory, does not generate the kind of high excitement that prevails when more members of the community are involved.

So far we have observed some 200 monkey hunts and have concluded that success requires a minimum of three motivated hunters acting cooperatively. Alone or in pairs, chimps succeed less than 15 percent of the time, but when three or four act as a group, more than half the hunts result in a kill. The chimps seem well aware of the odds; 92 percent of all the hunts we observed were group affairs.

Gombe chimps also hunt red colobus monkeys, but the percentage of group hunts is much lower: only 36 percent. In addition, we learned from Jane Goodall that even when Gombe chimps do hunt in groups, their strategies are different. When Taï chimps arrive under a group of monkeys, the hunters scatter, often silently, usually out of sight of one another but each aware of the others' positions. As the hunt progresses, they gradually close in, encircling the quarry. Such movements require that each chimp coordinate his movements with those of the other hunters, as well as with those of the prey, at all times.

Coordinated hunts account for 63 percent of all those observed at Taï but only 7 percent of those at Gombe. Jane Goodall says that in a Gombe group hunt, the chimpanzees typically travel together until they arrive at a tree with monkeys. Then, as the chimps begin climbing nearby trees, they scatter as each pursues a different target. Goodall gained the impression that Gombe chimps boost their success by hunting independently but simultaneously, thereby disorganizing their prey; our impression is that the Taï chimps owe their success to being organized themselves.

Just why the Gombe and Taï chimps have developed such different hunting strategies is difficult to explain, and we plan to spend some time at Gombe in the hope of finding out. In the meantime, the mere existence of differences is interesting enough and may perhaps force changes in our understanding of human evolution. Most currently accepted theories propose that some three million years ago, a dramatic climate change in Africa east of the Rift Valley turned dense forest into open, drier habitat. Adapting to the difficulties of life under these new conditions, our ancestors supposedly evolved into cooperative hunters and began sharing food they caught. Supporters of this idea point out that plant and animal remains indicative of dry, open environments have been found at all early hominid excavation sites in Tanzania, Kenya, South Africa, and Ethiopia. That the large majority of apes in Africa today live west of the Rift Valley appears to many anthropologists to lend further support to the idea that a change in environment caused the common ancestor of apes and humans to evolve along a different line from those remaining in the forest.

Our observations, however, suggest quite another line of thought. Life in dense, dim forest may require more sophisticated behavior than is commonly assumed: compared with their savanna relatives, Taï chimps show greater complexity in both hunting and tool use. Taï chimps use tools in nineteen different ways and have six different ways of making them, compared with sixteen uses and three methods of manufacture at Gombe.

Anthropologist colleagues of mine have told me that the discovery that some chimpanzees are accomplished users of hammerstones forces them to look with a fresh eye at stone tools turned up at excavation sites. The important role played by female Taï chimps in tool use also raises the possibility that in the course of human evolution, women may have been decisive in the development of many of the sophisticated manipulative skills characteristic of our species. Taï mothers also appear to pass on their skills by actively teaching their offspring. We have observed mothers providing their young with hammers and then stepping in to help when the inexperienced youngsters encounter difficulty. This help may include carefully showing how to position the nut or hold the hammer properly. Such behavior has never been observed at Gombe.

Similarly, food sharing, for a long time said to be unique to humans, seems more general in forest than in savanna chimpanzees. Taï chimp mothers share with their young up to 60 percent of the nuts they open, at least until the latter become sufficiently adept, generally at about six years old. They also share other foods acquired with tools, including honey, ants, and bone marrow. Gombe mothers share such foods much less often, even with their infants. Taï chimps also share meat more frequently than do their Gombe relatives, sometimes dividing a chunk up and giving portions away, sometimes simply allowing beggars to grab pieces.

Any comparison between chimpanzees and our hominid ancestors can only be suggestive, not definitive. But our studies lead us to believe that the process of hominization may have begun independently of the drying of the environment. Savanna life could even have delayed the process; many anthropologists have been struck by how slowly hominid-associated remains, such as the hand ax, changed after their first appearance in the Olduvai age.

Will we have the time to discover more about the hunting strategies or other, perhaps as yet undiscovered abilities of these forest chimpanzees? Africa's tropical rain forests, and their inhabitants, are threatened with extinction by extensive logging, largely to provide the Western world with tropical timber and such products as coffee, cocoa, and rubber. Ivory Coast has lost 90 percent of its original forest, and less than 5 percent of the remainder can be considered pristine. The climate has changed dramatically. The harmattan, a cold, dry wind from the Sahara previously unknown in the forest, has now swept through the Taï forest every year since 1986. Rainfall has diminished; all the rivulets in our study region are now dry for several months of the year.

In addition, the chimpanzee, biologically very close to humans, is in demand for research on AIDS and hepatitis vaccines. Captive-bred chimps are available, but they cost about twenty times more than wild-caught animals. Chimps taken from the wild for these purposes are generally young, their

mothers having been shot during capture. For every chimp arriving at its sad destination, nine others may well have died in the forest or on the way. Such priorities—cheap coffee and cocoa and chimpanzees—do not do the economies of Third World countries any good in the long run, and they bring suffering and death to innocent victims in the forest. Our hope is that Brutus, Falstaff, and their families will survive, and that we and others will have the opportunity to learn about them well into the future. But there is no denying that modern times work against them and us.

Critical Thinking

1. To what extent does cooperation and sharing of food exist among the Ivory Coast chimpanzees?

2. What were the researchers interested in at first? What was unique about it? What did they find that was not surprising? What was surprising?

3. What is the purpose of drumming?

4. How do the authors describe the chimps' mental abilities with regard to hammerstones? What manual skills are required? In what respect is there a gender difference in tool use?

5. What is the purpose of the "patrol" into foreign territories?

6. What is their favorite hunting target and why?

7. Describe the hunting strategies. What is the minimum number for success? In what ways do these chimps contrast with the Gombe chimps and what is the partial explanation given?

8. How did chimps and humans diverge, according to most currently accepted theories?

9. How do comparisons between forest-dwelling chimps and the savanna-dwelling Gombe chimps lead the authors to different conclusions from the above? (Include in this the important role of females in tool use and food sharing.)

10. In what ways are chimpanzee populations threatened?

Internet References

Great Ape Survival Project: United Nations
www.unep.org/grasp/ABOUT_GRASP/index.asp
Jane Goodall Institute for Wildlife Research, Education, and Conservation
www.janegoodall.org

Boesch, Christophe; Boesch-Achermann, Hedwige. "Dim Forest, Bright Chimps," *Natural History*, September 1991, pp. 50, 52–56. Reprinted by permission of Natural History Magazine.

Article   Prepared by: Elvio Angeloni

One for All

Our ability to cooperate in large societies has deep evolutionary roots in the animal kingdom.

FRANS DE WAAL

Learning Outcomes

After reading this article, you will be able to:

- Discuss the traditional scenario as to how humanity became the dominant form of life and why it is unlikely.
- Discuss the findings of recent studies of primate cooperation.

Traditional discussions of how humanity became the dominant form of life, with a population of more than seven billion and counting, have focused on competition. Our ancestors seized land, so the story goes, wiped out other species—including our brethren the Neandertals—and hunted big predators to extinction. We conquered nature, red in tooth and claw.

Overall, however, this is an unlikely scenario. Our forebears were too small and vulnerable to rule the savanna. They must have lived in constant fear of pack-hunting hyenas, 10 different kinds of big cats and other dangerous animals. We probably owe our success as a species more to our cooperativeness than our capacity for violence.

Our propensity to cooperate has old evolutionary roots. Yet only humans organize into groups capable of achieving colossal feats. Only humans have a complex morality that emphasizes responsibilities to others and is enforced through reputation and punishment. And sometimes we do incredible things that put a lie to the idea of humans as purely self-interested actors.

Consider this scene that unfolded last year in a Metrorail station in Washington, D.C. A passenger's motorized wheelchair malfunctioned, and the man ended up sprawled on the tracks. Within seconds, multiple bystanders jumped down to bring him back up before the next train. An even more dramatic rescue occurred in 2007 in the New York City subway, when Wesley Autrey, a 50-year-old construction worker, saved a man who

had fallen in front of an approaching train. Too late to pull him up, Autrey jumped between the tracks and lay on top of the other man while five cars rolled overhead. Afterward, he downplayed his heroism: "I don't feel like I did something spectacular."

What he did was spectacular, of course. But what propelled him to put his own life in jeopardy to help a fellow stranger in the subway? For answers to this question and to how we came to cooperate in other ways, we must first look at similar behavior in our evolutionary cousins, particularly our closest living relatives: chimpanzees and bonobos.

Primate Cooperation

I regularly watch less dramatic cases of selfless cooperation in these animals at the Yerkes National Primate Research Center at Emory University. My office overlooks a large, grassy enclosure, in which an aging female, Peony, spends her days in the sun with other chimpanzees. Whenever her arthritis flares up, she has trouble walking and climbing. But while Peony is huffing and puffing to get up into the climbing frame, an unrelated younger female may move behind her, place both hands on her ample behind and push her up. We have also seen others bring water to Peony, for whom the walk to the spigot is strenuous. When she starts out in that direction, others run ahead to pick up a mouthful of water, then stand in front of the old lady, who opens her mouth to let them spit a jet of water into it.

A host of recent studies have carefully documented primate cooperation, reaching three main conclusions. First, cooperation does not require family ties. Even though these animals favor kin, they do not limit their cooperation to family. DNA extracted from chimpanzee feces collected in the African forest has allowed field-workers to examine which animals hunt and travel together. Most close partnerships in the forest involve unrelated individuals. Friends mutually groom one another, warn each other of predators and share food. We know the same is true for bonobos.

Second, cooperation is often based on reciprocity. Experiments indicate that chimpanzees remember received favors. One study measured grooming in a captive colony in the morning before feeding time. On introduction of sharable food, such as watermelons, the few lucky possessors would be surrounded by beggars holding out a hand, whimpering and whining. Researchers found that an individual that earlier in the day had groomed another was more likely to obtain a share from this partner later on.

Third, cooperation may be motivated by empathy, a characteristic of all mammals, from rodents to primates. We identify with others in need, pain or distress. This identification arouses emotions that tend to prompt helping action. Scientists now believe that primates, in particular, go further and care about the well-being of others. In a typical experiment, two monkeys are placed side by side, while one of them selects a token based on color. One color rewards only the monkey itself but the other rewards both of them. After a few rounds, the choosing monkey opts most often for the "prosocial" token. This preference is not based on fear of the other monkey, because dominant monkeys (which have the least to fear) are the most generous.

Sometimes caring about others costs primates nothing, such as in the above test, but they also help one another at a substantial cost, such as when they lose half their food in the process. In nature, chimpanzees are known to adopt orphans or defend others against leopards—both extremely costly forms of altruism.

Deeper Roots of Helping

These caring tendencies in primates probably evolved from the obligatory maternal care demanded of all mammals. Whether a mouse or an elephant, mothers need to respond to their young's signals of hunger, pain or fear—otherwise the infants might perish. This sensitivity (and the neural and hormonal processes that support it) was then co-opted for other relationships, helping to enhance emotional bonding, empathy and cooperation within the larger society.

Cooperation affords substantial benefits, so it is not surprising that it was co-opted in these ways. The most ubiquitous form in the animal kingdom is known as mutualistic cooperation and is presumably so widespread because it produces immediate payoffs, such as providing food or defending against predators. It is marked by working together toward an obvious goal that is advantageous to all—say when hyenas bring down a wildebeest together or when a dozen pelicans in a semicircle drive fish together with their feet in a shallow lake, which allows them to simultaneously scoop up mouthfuls of prey. Such cooperation rests on well-coordinated action and shared payoffs.

This kind of cooperation can spawn more subtle cooperative behaviors such as sharing. If one hyena or one pelican were to monopolize all rewards, the system would collapse. Survival depends on sharing, which explains why both humans and animals are exquisitely sensitive to fair divisions. Experiments show that monkeys, dogs and some social birds reject rewards inferior to those of a companion performing the same task; chimpanzees and humans go even further by moderating their share of joint rewards to prevent frustration in others. We owe our sense of fairness to a long history of mutualistic cooperation.

The Human Difference

Humans provide sharp examples of how sharing is linked with survival. Lamaleran whale hunters in Indonesia roam the open ocean in large canoes, from which a dozen men capture whales almost bare-handed. The hunters row toward the whale, the harpoonist jumps onto its back to thrust his weapon into it, and then the men stay nearby until the leviathan dies of blood loss. With entire families tied together around a life-threatening activity, their men being literally in the same boat, distribution of the food bonanza is very much on their mind. Not surprisingly, the Lamalera people are the champions of fairness, as measured by anthropologists using a tool called the Ultimatum Game, which measures preferences for equitable offers. In societies with greater self-sufficiency, such as those in which every family tends its own plot of land, equity is less important.

One oft-mentioned difference between humans and other primates is that we are the only species to cooperate with outsiders and strangers. Although our willingness to cooperate depends on the circumstances (after all, we may also kill those who do not belong to our group), primates in nature are mostly competitive between groups. The way human communities allow outsiders to travel through their territories, share meals with them, exchange goods and gifts, or band together against common enemies is not a typical primate pattern.

Yet this openness does not need a special evolutionary explanation, as some have argued. Most likely, cooperation among strangers is an extension of tendencies that arose for in-group use. In nature, it is not unusual for existing capacities to be applied outside their original context, a bit the way primates use hands (which evolved for tree climbing) to cling to their mothers. Experiments in which capuchin monkeys and bonobos interact with unfamiliar outsiders have shown them capable of exchanging favors and sharing food. In other words, the potential for cooperating with outsiders is present in other species even if they rarely encounter situations in nature that prompt them to do so.

One way we may be truly unique, though, is in the highly organized nature of our cooperativeness. We have the capacity to create hierarchical collaborations that can execute large-scale projects of a complexity and magnitude not found elsewhere in nature. Consider the terraced rice paddies of the Mekong Delta—or the technology that went into CERN's Large Hadron Collider.

Most animal cooperation is self-organized in that individuals fulfill roles according to their capacities and the "slots" open to them. Sometimes animals divide roles and closely coordinate, such as when synchronized killer whales make a wave that washes a seal off an ice floe or when several chimpanzee males organize as drivers and blockers to chase a group of monkeys through the canopy, as if they agreed on their roles beforehand. We do not know how the shared intentions and goals of this kind of cooperation are established and communicated, but they do not seem to be orchestrated from above by leaders, as is typical of humans.

Humans also have ways of enforcing cooperation that thus far have not been documented in other animals. Through repeated interactions, we build reputations as reliable friends, or poor ones, and may get punished if our efforts fall short. The potential for punishment also discourages individuals from cheating the system. In the laboratory, humans punish freeloaders, even at a cost to themselves, a practice that, in the long run, would tend to promote cooperation in a population. There is much debate about how typical such punishment is in real life, outside the lab, but we do know that our moral systems include expectations about cooperation and that we are hypersensitive to public opinion. In one experiment, people donated more money to a good cause if a picture of two eyes were mounted on the wall to watch them. Feeling observed, we worry about our reputation.

These concerns over reputation could have been the primordial glue that enabled early *Homo sapiens* to stick together in ever larger societies. During much of human prehistory, our ancestors lived nomadic lives much like current hunter-gatherers. These modern peoples demonstrate a robust potential for peace and trade between communities, which suggests that early *H. sapiens* had these traits, too.

Without denying our violent potential, I am convinced that it is these cooperative tendencies that have brought us as far as we have come. Building on tendencies that evolved in nonhuman primates, we have been able to shape our societies into complex networks of individuals who cooperate with one another in all kinds of ways.

Critical Thinking

1. Why are caring tendencies rooted in primate maternal care and what are the substantial benefits afforded by cooperation?

2. In comparison to other primates, how are humans unique with respect to cooperation?

More to Explore

The Human Potential for Peace. Douglas P. Fry. Oxford University Press, 2005.

The Age of Empathy. Frans de Waal. Harmony Books, 2009.

Prosocial Primates: Selfish and Unselfish Motivations. Frans B. M. de Waal and Malini Suchak in Philosophical Transactions of the Royal Society B, Vol. 365, No. 1553, pages 2711–2722; September 12, 2010.

From our Archives

Why We Help. Martin A. Nowak; July 2012. scientificamerican.com/magazine/sa

In Brief

Human beings have a unique ability to cooperate in large, well-organized groups and employ a complex morality that relies on reputation and punishment.

But much of the foundation for this cooperation—including empathy and altruism—can also be observed in our primate cousins.

Homo sapiens' unique cooperative abilities are what have allowed the species to become the dominant one on the earth.

Internet References

Electronic Zoo/NetVet-Primate Page
  http://netvet.wustl.edu/primates.htm
Living Links
  www.emory.edu/LIVING_LINKS/dewaal.html
National Primate Research Center
  http://pin.primate.wisc.edu/factsheets

FRANS DE WAAL is **C. H. CANDLER** Professor of Primate Behavior at Emoiy University and director of the Living Links Center at the Yerkes National Primate Research Center. His books include Our Inner Ape (Riverhead, 2005) and The Bonobo and the Atheist (W. W. Norton, 2013).

Unit 3

UNIT

Prepared by: Elvio Angeloni

Sex and Gender

Any account of hominid evolution would be remiss if it did not attempt to explain that which is the most mystifying of all human experiences—our sexuality. No other aspect of humanity—whether it be upright posture, tool-making ability, or intelligence in general—seems to elude our intellectual grasp at least as much as it dominates our subjective consciousness. While we are a long way from reaching a consensus as to why it arose and what it is all about, there is widespread agreement that our very preoccupation with sex is, in itself, one of the hallmarks of being human. Even as we experience it and analyze it, we exalt it and condemn it. Beyond seemingly irrational fixations, however, there is the further tendency to project our own values onto the observations we make and the data we collect.

There are many who argue quite reasonably that the anthropological bias has been too male-oriented and that the recent "feminization" of the field has resulted in new kinds of research and refreshingly new theoretical perspectives. Not only should we consider the source when evaluating the old theories, but we should also welcome the source when considering the new.

One reason for studying the sexual and social lives of primates is that they allow us to test certain notions too often taken for granted. For instance, are primate males always dominant over females? Is it always the adolescent females that leave the group in which they were born? Does sexual exclusivity always result from pair-bonding between males and females? Are males always larger than females within a species? Primate research has shown that the answers to these questions are not as simple and straightforward as some have thought—that primates vary in their behavior just as humans do, depending upon the particular circumstances of their lives.

Finally, it should be noted that the study of primate social and sexual lives enables us to better comprehend our own. The more we know about why they do as they do in the context of their particular adaptations, the more insight we gain as why we may be similar to them, often because we are trying to solve similar problems, or differ from them, because our circumstances are not the same as theirs. It is these kinds of comparisons and contrasts, in other words, that help us to understand who we are.

Article   Prepared by: Elvio Angeloni

Powers of Two

Coupling up might have been the best move our ancestors ever made.

BLAKE EDGAR

Learning Outcomes

After reading this article, you will be able to:

- Discuss the benefits of monogamy for humans.
- Discuss the various theories that have been proposed for the rise of monogamy in human evolution.

In Brief

Even in societies where polygamy is permitted, monogamy is by far the most common human mating arrangement. In this regard, we are unusual animals: fewer than 10 percent of mammals form exclusive sexual relationships.

How humans got this way has been the subject of scientific debate for decades, and it is still an open question. But new research is clarifying matters.

We now know that the first hominins, which emerged more than seven million years ago, might have been monogamous. Humans stayed (mostly) monogamous for good reason: it helped them evolve into the big-brained world conquerors they are today.

Mammals are not big on monogamy. In fewer than 10 percent of species is it common for two individuals to mate exclusively. The primate wing of the group is only slightly more prone to pairing off. Although 15 to 29 percent of primate species favor living together as couples, far fewer commit to monogamy as humans know it—an exclusive sexual partnership between two individuals.

Humans obviously have an imperfect track record. People have affairs, get divorced and, in some cultures, marry multiple mates. In fact, polygamy appears in most of the world's societies. Yet even where polygamy is permitted, it is the minority arrangement. Most human societies are organized around the assumption that a large fraction of the population will pair off into enduring, sexually exclusive couples. And monogamy

seems to have done our species good. "Pair bonds," as scientists call monogamous relationships, were a crucial adaptation that arose in an archaic forebear that became central to human social systems and our evolutionary success. "We have a very big advantage over many other species by having pair bonds," says University of Montreal anthropologist Bernard Chapais.

The monogamous couple also forms the basis for something uniquely human—the vast, complex social networks in which we live. Other primate young establish kinship links only through their mother; humans trace kinship from both parents, broadening each generation's family ties. Among humans, social networks extend to include other families and even unrelated groups in widening ripples of relationships. In Chapais's view, such group ties, along with monogamy, constitute "two of the most consequential features of human society."

Scientists have struggled for decades to understand the origins and implications of human monogamy. Basic questions such as when we started to pair up for life, why it was advantageous and how coupling might have spurred our success as a species remain unresolved and contentious, but new research has brought us closer to solving the mystery.

The Origins of Coupling

It is entirely possible that our most distant ancestors were monogamous. Fossil evidence, says anthropologist C. Owen Lovejoy of Kent State University, suggests that monogamy predates even *Ardipithecus ramidus,* the species best known from a 4.4-million-year-old partial female skeleton, nicknamed "Ardi," discovered in the Middle Awash region of Ethiopia. In Lovejoy's hypothesis, soon after the split from the last common ancestor between the great ape and human evolutionary branches more than seven million years ago, our predecessors adopted a transformative trio of behaviors: carrying food in arms freed by bipedal posture, forming pair bonds and concealing external signals of female ovulation. Evolving together, these innovations gave hominins, the tribe that emerged when early humans diverged from chimpanzees, a reproductive edge over apes.

According to this hypothesis, an ancestral polygamous mating system was replaced by pair bonding when lower-ranked hominin males diverted energy from fighting one another toward finding food to bring females as an incentive to mate. Females preferred reliable providers to aggressive competitors and bonded with the better foragers. Eventually females lost the skin swelling or other signs of sexual receptivity that would have attracted different males while their partners were off gathering food.

For evidence, Lovejoy points to *Ar. ramidus's* teeth. Compared with living and fossil apes, *Ar. ramidus* shows a stark reduction in the differences between male and female canine-tooth size. Evolution has honed the dagger-like canines of many male primates into formidable weapons used to fight for access to mates. Not so for early hominins. Picture the canines in a male gorilla's gaping jaws; now peer inside your own mouth. Humans of both sexes have small, stubby canines—an unthreatening trait unique to hominins, including the earliest *Ardipithecus* specimens.

A rough correlation also exists between mating behavior in primates and sexual dimorphism—that is, differences in body mass and size between males and females of the same species. The more dimorphic a primate species is, the more likely it is that males fight over females. At one extreme, polygamous gorilla males grow to be more than twice as massive as females. At the opposite extreme, both male and female gibbons, which are mainly monogamous, are nearly equal in mass. Humans lie closer to gibbons on the dimorphism spectrum: human males can be up to 20 percent more massive than females.

There is only so much we can make of the fossil record, though. Paleoanthropologist J. Michael Plavcan of the University of Arkansas urges caution in making the leap from fossilized bones to social behavior in hominins. Consider *Australopithecus afarensis,* the species to which "Lucy" belonged, which lived between 3.9 million and 3 million years ago. Like *Ardipithecus, A. afarensis* had small canines, but its skeleton displays a level of dimorphism between that of modern chimpanzees and gorillas. "You have [a level of] body-size dimorphism suggesting that [*A. afarensis*] males were competing for females and [a] loss of canine dimorphism that suggests they weren't," Plavcan says. "It's a puzzle."

Many anthropologists also dispute Lovejoy's conclusion that monogamy nurtured by males providing food for their mates and offspring has been a hominin strategy for millions of years. Last year in the journal *Evolutionary Anthropology,* Chapais argued that the unique features of human family and social structure (monogamy, kinship ties through both parents and expanding social circles) emerged in a stepwise sequence.

Before the first step, Chapais said, both male and female hominins were, like chimpanzees, promiscuous with partners. Then came a transition to polygamy, which is found in gorillas. But keeping many mates is hard work. It involves a lot of fighting other males and guarding females. Monogamy might have emerged as the best way to reduce the effort of polygamy.

Chapais declines to speculate about when this shift happened and what species were involved. But other researchers are homing in on the period between 2 million and 1.5 million years ago, after the origin of our genus *Homo* and coincident with physical changes that show up in *Homo erectus,* most likely the first hominin species to successfully migrate beyond Africa. *H. erectus* possessed a much larger body, proportioned more like that of a modern human, than its predecessors. Roughly twice the size of Lucy's species, *H. erectus* also seems to be less sexually dimorphic than australopithecines and the earliest members of *Homo.* Limited fossil evidence suggests that *H. erectus* females started to approach the physical stature of males and to have a similar degree of dimorphism as in modern humans, which together could suggest that *H. erectus* had a less competitive way of life than its ancestors. Because primates with similar body sizes tend to be monogamous, this change could signal a shift toward more exclusive mating behavior.

A Strategic Partnership

If scientists cannot agree on when humans became monogamous, we can hardly expect them to agree on why it happened. In 2013, two independent research teams published separate statistical studies of existing literature to determine which behaviors could have been drivers of monogamy. Both studies aimed to determine the best explanation for monogamy from three persistent hypotheses, generally known as female spacing, infanticide avoidance and male parental care.

The female-spacing hypothesis posits that monogamy arises after females begin to establish larger territories to gain more access to limited food resources and, in the process, put more distance between one another. With females farther apart, males have a harder time finding and keeping multiple mates. Settling down with a single partner makes life easier, reducing a male's risk of being injured while patrolling his territory and enabling him to ensure that his mate's offspring are his own.

Zoologists Dieter Lukas and Tim Clutton-Brock, both at the University of Cambridge, found evidence for this idea in a statistical analysis of 2,545 species of mammals. They described their findings in a paper published in *Science.* The data indicated to them that mammals started out solitary, but then one species or another switched to monogamy 61 different times during their evolutionary history. Monogamy most frequently emerged in carnivores and primates, suggesting that species will tend toward mating in pairs when its females require a rich but rare diet (such as protein-rich carcasses or ripe fruits) that can usually be obtained only by searching a large area. Their findings provided the strongest statistical support for the conclusion that increasingly scattered, solitary females drove males to solicit single partners.

Lukas acknowledges that although the hypothesis may work for nonhumans, it might not be so apt for humans: it is difficult to reconcile the inherent sociality of humans with a hypothesis that depends on a low density of available females. It may be that our ancestors were too social for females to have been scattered across the savanna like other mammals. But the theory could potentially hold for humans if monogamy arose in hominins before our tendency to dwell in groups did.

The second leading hypothesis holds that monogamy originated from the threat of lethal violence toward offspring. If a rival male challenged or supplanted a dominant male in a community, the usurper could kill infants that he had not sired. Mothers would stop lactating and start ovulating again, giving the marauding male a chance to spread his genes. To prevent infanticide, a female would select a male ally who could defend her and her baby.

Anthropologist Kit Opie of University College London cites evidence for the infanticide-avoidance hypothesis in a study published in the *Proceedings of the National Academy of Sciences USA*. Opie and his colleagues ran computer simulations of primate evolutionary history for 230 primate species; they then applied what is called a Bayesian statistical analysis to determine which of the three prominent hypotheses for the origin of monogamy had the highest probability of being correct. They identified a significant correlation between monogamy in primates and each of the three hypothetical triggers, but only an increase in the threat of infanticide consistently preceded the appearance of monogamy in multiple primate lineages.

The biology and behavior of modern primates add some plausibility to the conclusion that infanticide is a spur to monogamy. Primates are uniquely at risk for infanticide: they have big brains that need time to develop, which leaves babies dependent and vulnerable for long periods after birth. And the killing of babies has been observed in more than 50 primate species; it typically involves a male from outside a group attacking an unweaned infant in a bid for dominance or access to females. But there are limits to the evidence: nearly all these species have either promiscuous or polygamous mating systems, so the distribution of infanticide in living primates does not fit the prediction that monogamy should evolve when infanticide is a big threat.

The third hypothesis for why monogamy evolved highlights a male pulling his weight with parental duties. When a baby becomes too costly in terms of calories and energy for a mother to raise on her own, the father who stays with the family and provides food or other forms of care increases his offspring's chances of survival and encourages closer ties with the mother A related idea, proposed by anthropologist Lee Gettler of the University of Notre Dame, holds that the mere carrying of offspring by fathers fosters monogamy. Mothers have to meet the considerable nutritional demands of nursing infants. Yet for primates and human hunter-gatherers, hauling an infant, especially without the benefit of a sling or other restraint, required an expense of energy comparable to breast-feeding. Carrying by males could have freed females to fulfill their own energetic needs by foraging.

South America's Azara's owl monkey may offer some insight into how paternal care would reinforce monogamy. These monkeys live in small family groups, with an adult male-and-female pair and an infant, plus a juvenile or two. A mother monkey carries a newborn on her thigh just after birth. But the baby's father assumes most of the carrying and caretaking—grooming, playing and feeding—from the time the baby is two weeks old. The adult partners literally stay in touch with frequent tail contact, and the male's mere proximity to both the female and his young may promote deeper emotional ties.

Indeed, a study published in March in the *Proceedings of the Royal Society B* presented genetic evidence that Azara's owl monkey pairs remain monogamous—the first genetic confirmation for any nonhuman primate. DNA collected from several study groups revealed that all the females and all but one of the males in 17 pairs were the most likely parents of 35 offspring. "They go all the way and commit to a monogamous relationship in genetic terms," says anthropologist Eduardo Fernandez-Duque, now at Yale University and a co-author of the study. Mating bonds between Azara's owl monkeys last an average of nine years, and monkeys that stay with the same partner achieve greater reproductive success—the end game of evolution under any mating system.

What do the two recent statistical studies have to say about the paternal care hypothesis? Both concluded that paternal care seemed the least likely among the competing hypotheses to trigger monogamous mating—but, Lukas says, "paternal care may still explain why a species stays monogamous."

It Takes a Village

A Monogamous set of parents is not enough to raise an ape as smart and social as a human, says anthropologist Sarah Hrdy of the University of California, Davis. A human baby consumes some 13 million calories on its long journey from birth to maturity, a heavy burden for a mother to bear even with a mate helping. This demand might explain why in many societies, human mothers rely on "alloparents" (such as the kin of either parent or other group members) to help provide food and child care. "Human mothers are willing to let others hold their babies right from birth," Hrdy notes. "That's amazing, and it's remarkably unapelike." No ape engages in anything like alloparenting.

Hrdy maintains that cooperative breeding, a social system in which alloparents help care for young, evolved among our ancient ancestors starting with *H. erectus* nearly two million years ago. This species had a much larger body and brain than its ancestors; by one estimate, it took 40 percent more metabolic energy to run an *H. erectus* body relative to previous hominins. If *H. erectus* started down a humanlike path of delayed development and prolonged dependency, cooperative alloparents might have been required to support the energetic demands of raising bigger-brained babies.

Without cooperative breeding, conclude Karin Isler and Carel van Schaik, both at the University of Zurich, early *Homo* would not have broken through the hypothetical "gray ceiling" that constrains an ape's brain to a maximum volume of about 700 cm^3. To pay the energetic cost of having an enlarged brain, an animal must reduce its rate of birth or its rate of growth, or both. But humans have achieved shorter weaning periods and greater reproductive success than a creature with a brain volume ranging from 1,100 to 1,700 cm^3 should have been able to. Isler and van Schaik attribute this success to alloparenting, which enabled *H. erectus* to have offspring more frequently while providing those offspring enough energy to grow a large brain.

It was cooperation, then, whether in the form of monogamous pairs, nuclear families or tribes, that enabled humans to succeed when all our fossil ancestors and cousins went extinct. In fact, cooperation may be the greatest skill we have acquired during the past two million years—one that enabled our young genus to survive through periods of environmental change and stress and one that may well determine our geologically young species' future.

Critical Thinking

1. Discuss the relationship between mating behavior and sexual dimorphism in primate species.

2. What have been the various theories proposed for the rise of monogamy among humans and what has been the evidence for them?

3. What is "cooperative breeding" and why does it seem to have been important in human evolution?

More to Explore

Reexamining Human Origins in Light of Ardipithecus ramidus. C. Owen Lovejoy in Science, Vol. 326, pages 74,74e1–74e8; October 2, 2009.

Monogamy, Strongly Bonded Groups, and the Evolution of Human Social Structure. Bernard Chapais in Evolutionary Anthropology, Vol. 22, No. 2, pages 52–65; March/April 2013.

The Evolution of Social Monogamy in Mammals. D. Lukas and T. H. Clutton-Brock in Science, Vol. 341, pages 526–530; August 2, 2013.

Male Infanticide Leads to Social Monogamy in Primates. Christopher Opie et al. in Proceedings of the National Academy of Sciences USA, Vol. 110, No. 33, pages 13,328–13, 332; August 13, 2013.

From our Archives

Evolution of Human Walking. C. Owen Lovejoy; November 1988.
scientificamerican.com/magazine/sa

Internet References

Electronic Zoo/NetVet-Primate Page
http://netvet.wustl.edu/primates.htm

Journal of Mammology
http://www.bioone.org/doi/abs/10.1644/06-MAMM-A-417.1Evolutionary Demography Group

National Primate Research Center
http://pin.primate.wisc.edu/factsheets

BLAKE EDGAR is co-author of From Lucy to Language and other books and a contributing editor at Archaeology Magazine. He is a senior acquisitions editor at the University of California Press.

Article   Prepared by: Elvio Angeloni

When Do Girls Rule the Womb?

JENNIFER ABBASI

Learning Outcomes

After reading this article, you will be able to:

- Discuss the ways in which a sex ratio imbalance within populations might lead to reproductive success.

- Describe "integrated evolutionary social demography."

As a demographer, Shige Song was trained to focus on the social forces that change the proportion of males and females in a population. His studies of sex ratio in China, India, and South Korea, where the birth of boys has significantly outpaced girls over the past few decades, had focused exclusively on the effect of cultural preferences for sons. Demographic studies since the 1980s have suggested son preference and sex-selective abortions of girls were the main causes of the skewed sex ratio in these countries.

What demographers have not been able to explain is why trends in sex ratio at birth also exist in societies that don't value sons more than daughters. In the second half of the 1900s, more girls were born than usual in North America and most of Europe, while boy births significantly outpaced girls in Ireland, France, Italy, and Spain. "It became clear to me that the standard social science model may not be adequate to explain sex ratio," Song says. His controversial new theory has less to do with social forces among people, and more to do with simple biology.

Enter Adaptations

While demographers were struggling to understand sex ratio anomalies in the context of culture, evolutionary biologists had largely embraced an idea put forth in 1973 by biologist Robert Trivers and mathematician Dan Willard. The Harvard-based pair theorized that as the physical condition of a female declines—if she's nutritionally deprived, for example—she'll tend to produce a lower ratio of male to female offspring. Evidence of the theory came from red deer and humans; in both species, adverse conditions in the mother's environment during pregnancy are correlated with a shift toward female births.

Although natural selection ideally favors a 50/50, or .500, sex ratio in a population, mammals typically produce slightly more males than females. Because sex ratio is biased toward males, the figure is expressed by dividing male births by total births. It's estimated that women give birth to 3 percent more boys, for a standard .515 sex ratio (with 48.5 percent female births). When fewer boys and more girls are born than that, it's described as a sex ratio decline.

Evolutionary biologists say male mortality, which is overall higher than that of females, explains the male bias in sex ratio: A slightly skewed sex ratio at birth that favors males ensures that there are roughly an equal number of males and females of reproductive age. (Theoretically, a .500 sex ratio at birth may be possible if the gender difference in mortality is eliminated.)

But under certain conditions, biologists say, an imbalance favoring female births can improve the reproductive success of an individual organism. Trivers and Willard argued that the strongest and most dominant males of a species were far more likely to leave offspring than weaker males, while virtually all females would reproduce. According to this so-called adaptive sex ratio adjustment hypothesis, healthy mothers were better off producing sons, who would likely be fit and go on to reproduce, whereas mothers in less prime condition would benefit more from daughters, who would reproduce regardless of their low health status. The strategy allowed a mother to "maximize her eventual reproductive success," the two wrote in their seminal paper.

Just how adaptive sex selection may occur is unknown, but there's evidence that poor maternal nutrition disproportionately affects male offspring. Plentiful food sources are consistently linked with a male-biased sex ratio in nonhuman mammals, and a 2008 study found that British women with the best nutrition during conception were significantly more likely to give birth to boys than women with the poorest diet. (The researchers found no socioeconomic link to fetal gender.)

Glucose levels, which may drop in women who don't get enough to eat, could have something to do with it, says Elissa Cameron, an evolutionary biologist at the University of Tasmania. In 2008 she showed that in the pre-embryonic stage of development, males have lower survival rates than females when glucose levels are low, causing more females to be born. Trivers believes sex selection may happen even earlier, at the time of conception.

Famine as Experiment

While working as a social demographer at the Chinese Academy of Social Sciences in 2008, Song became interested in the sex ratio decline that came out of the devastating Great Chinese Famine in the mid-twentieth century. Scholars had noticed a drop in male births during the 1960s, but they attributed it to data error "because they focused exclusively on the search for social explanations, and there were none," says Song, like a cultural son preference. He saw the famine as a natural experiment for the adaptive sex ratio adjustment hypothesis.

In a paper published recently in the journal *Proceedings of the Royal Society B* (Biological Sciences) that looked at demographic data from more than 310,000 Chinese women, Song demonstrated a dramatic sex ratio decrease more than a year after the two-year famine began and lasting about two years after it ended, followed by an equally significant bounce back to pre-famine proportions.

Trivers says the findings are consistent with previous studies of post-communist Poland and historical Portugal in which poor economic conditions, and in turn poor nutrition, predicted the birth of more girls. "Evolutionary theories provide a simple and elegant framework to explain and even predict such changes," says Song, who is now a sociologist at Queens College of the City University of New York.

To that end, Song wants to reexamine sex ratio phenomena through a new framework he calls "integrated evolutionary social demography." This type of cross-disciplinary model might help explain, for example, why the sex ratio returned to normal levels around 2007 in South Korea, despite enduring cultural son preference there. And the sex ratio decline in the West, where the proportion of boys and girls moves closer to 1-to-1, might be explained by improved life expectancies reducing the gender difference in mortality in some regions, Song says.

But there's still a long way to go before demographers embrace evolutionary theory. A panel of sociologists at the National Science Foundation recently turned down three of Song's funding proposals; one reviewer even used the term "grade school reasoning" to describe the logic behind the adaptive sex ratio hypothesis. "The only way to make this change happen is to bring more funding, federal and private, into the field," Song says—a grim solution in today's economic climate. "As an individual researcher, the only thing I can do is to try to publish."

Critical Thinking

1. Explain why the standard social science model is not adequate for understanding sex ratios in some societies.

2. What sex ratio does natural selection seem to favor and what constitutes a "decline"? How do evolutionary biologists explain the favored ratio?

3. Discuss the "sex ratio adjustment hypothesis" and how and why it might work. What do glucose levels have to do with it?

4. How did the Great Chinese Famine and the decline of economic conditions in post-communist Poland and historical Portugal seem to support the sex ratio adjustment hypothesis?

5. Describe "integrated evolutionary social demography."

Internet References

Evolutionary Demography Group
    http://blogs.lshtm.ac.uk/evolutionarydemography/
Evolutionary Demography Society
    http://www.sdu.dk/en/om_sdu/institutter_centre/maxo/evodemos

---

JENNIFER ABBASI is a Portland-based science writer and a frequent contributor to *Discover*.

Jennifer Abassi. "When Do Girls Rule the Womb?" *Discover*, November 2013. Reprinted by permission of PARS International.

Article   Prepared by: Elvio Angeloni

Brains Are Not Male or Female

JESSICA HAMZELOU

Learning Outcomes

After reading this article, you will be able to:

- Discuss the issue as to whether or not gender is binary with respect to human brains.

- Discuss whether differences in skills between males and females have to do with biology or culture.

- Discuss gender stereotypes with respect to the actual evidence.

You may have read that having a male brain will earn you more money. Or maybe that female brains are better at multitasking. But there is no such thing as a female or male brain, according to the first search for sex differences across the entire human brain. Scans of 1400 brains reveal most have a mix of male and female features. The work also supports the idea that gender is not binary and that gender classifications in many situations are meaningless.

"This evidence that human brains cannot be categorised into two distinct classes is new, convincing, and somehow radical," says Anelis Kaiser at the University of Bern, Switzerland.

The idea that people have either a "female" or "male" brain is an old one, says Daphna Joel at Tel Aviv University in Israel. "The theory goes that once a fetus develops testicles, they secrete testosterone which masculinises the brain," she says. "If that were true, there would be two types of brain."

To test this, Joel and her colleagues looked for differences in brain scans taken from 1400 people aged between 13 and 85. The team looked for variations in the size of brain regions as well as the connections between them. Overall, they identified 29 brain regions that generally seem to be different sizes in people who self-identify as male or female. These include the hippocampus, which is involved in memory, and the inferior frontal gyrus, thought to play a role in risk aversion.

When the group looked at each individual brain scan, however, they found that very few people had all of the brain features they might be expected to have, based on their sex. Across the sample, between 0 and 8 percent of people had "all-male" or "all-female" brains, depending on the definition used (PNAS, doi.0rg/gk4). "Most people are in the middle," says Joel.

This means that, averaged across many people, sex differences in brain structure do exist, but an individual brain is likely to be just that: individual, with a mix of features. "There are not two types of brain," says Joel.

Although the team only looked at brain structure, and not function, their findings suggest that we all lie along a continuum of what are traditionally viewed as male and female characteristics.

"The study is very helpful in providing biological support for something that we've known for some time—that gender isn't binary," says Meg John Barker, a psychologist at the Open University in Milton Keynes, UK.

The findings will still come as a surprise to many, including scientists, says Bruce McEwen at the Rockefeller University in New York. "We are beginning to realise the complexity of what we have traditionally understood to be 'male' and 'female', and this study is the first step in that direction," he says. "I think it will change people's minds."

Cultural Expectations

Markus Hausmann at Durham University, UK, isn't surprised by the findings, however. He has been studying sex differences in cognition, such as whether men, as commonly believed, really do have better spatial awareness.

"Across all kinds of spatial skills, we find very, very few that are sensitive to sex," says Hausmann. "We have also identified spatial problems where women outperform men; the black-and-white idea of a male or female brain is clearly too simple."

Despite persisting stereotypes, girls are no worse than boys at science and maths subjects, either (see "Gender Myths").

"People get wedded to the idea that being male or female is highly predictive of having different aptitudes or career choices," says Margaret McCarthy at the University of Maryland in Baltimore. "This study fights against the idea that these outcomes are based on biological differences, as opposed to cultural expectations."

Some other parts of the body, such as the immune system, are also often wrongly considered to be either male or female, says Joel.

Alexandra Kautzky-Wilier, head of the Gender Medicine Unit at the Medical University of Vienna in Austria, agrees that things aren't so simple. "There are differences between men and women when you look in large groups, and these are important for diagnosis and treatment," she says. "But there are always more differences within genders. We always need to look at culture, environment, education and a person's role in society," she says.

Genderless Future

If a neuroscientist was given someone's brain without their body or any information, they would still probably be able to guess if it had belonged to a man or a woman. Men's brains are larger, for example, and are likely to have a larger number of "male" features overall. But the new findings suggest that it is impossible to predict what mix of brain features a person is likely to have based on their sex alone.

Joel envisions a future in which individuals are not so routinely classified based on gender alone. "We separate girls and boys, men and women all the time," she says. "It's wrong, not just politically, but scientifically—everyone is different."

But other scientists contacted by *New Scientist* don't think that will ever be possible—as a sexually reproductive species, identifying a person's biological sex will always be of paramount importance to us, they say.

Even so, Joel's findings can be used to help people understand the non-binary nature of gender, says Barker. After all, some people don't identify as either male or female, and others feel their gender identity shift over time. "It's a shame that people's experience alone isn't enough for us to recognise as a society that non-binary gender is legitimate."

"We need to start thinking a lot more carefully about how much weight we give to gender as a defining feature of human beings, and stop asking for it in situations where it simply isn't relevant," says Barker.

Gender Myths

Plenty of gender stereotypes have little evidence.

Men Are Obsessed with Sex

Many studies have found that men report having more casual sex than women. But female sexual appetites may be underestimated because women are more likely to downplay use of pornography or masturbation, while men tend to exaggerate theirs.

Women Are Bigger Gossips

We've all heard that women are better communicators. In reality, the gender differences in verbal abilities are small, and for some specific skills, men outperform women. Some studies find that girls are better at reading, but it might only seem that way because boys are more likely to have learning difficulties.

Boys Are Better at Maths

A large meta-analysis of 242 studies found that girls and boys are equally competent when it comes to maths. Tellingly, girls tend to perform as well as boys in countries with more gender equality. Not so different.

"The study gives biological support to something we've known for some time—gender isn't binary."

Critical Thinking

1. Are human brains binary? Explain.
2. Are differences in gender behavior determined biologically or culturally?
3. What does the evidence show with respect to commonly-held gender stereotypes?

Internet References

The Clayman Institute for Gender Research
   http://gender.stanford.edu/
Sexuality Studies—San Francisco State University
   https://sxs.sfsu.edu/Elvio Angeloni

Article   Prepared by: Elvio Angeloni

Promiscuous Men, Chaste Women, and Other Gender Myths

The Notion that Behavioral Differences Between the Sexes Are Innate and Immutable does not Hold Up Under Scrutiny.

CORDELIA FINE AND ELGAR MARKA

Learning Outcomes

After reading this article, you will be able to:

- Discuss the reasons why the supposed behavioral differences between the sexes are not so innate and immutable as once thought.

- Discuss the importance of gender equity in erasing the differences between women and men with regard to behavior and values.

One of australia's more provocative art museums, the Museum of Old and New Art in Hobart, Tasmania, recently hosted an exhibition on the evolution of art. Three evolutionary scientists who guest-curated the show offered their perspectives on how evolution explains not only just the characteristics of amoebas, ants, and antelopes but also the uniquely human endeavor of art. One of these explanations sees art as an evolved trait akin to the peacock's effervescently colored tail, which increases its bearer's reproductive success by signaling superiority as a mate.

Hands up if this scenario conjures in your mind, the image of a much feted female artist, famous for fearlessly pushing the boundaries of artistic convention, pleasurably making her way through a series of handsome young male muses? We didn't think so.

The stereotype of the daring, promiscuous male—and his counterpart, the cautious, chaste female—is deeply entrenched. Received wisdom holds that behavioral differences between men and women are hardwired, honed by natural selection over

millennia to maximize their differing reproductive potentials. In this view, men, by virtue of their innate tendencies toward risk-taking and competitiveness, are destined to dominate at the highest level of every realm of human endeavor, whether it is art, politics, or science.

But a closer look at the biology and behavior of humans and other creatures shows that many of the starting assumptions that have gone into this account of sex differences are wrong. For example, in many species, females benefit from being competitive or playing the field. And women and men often have similar preferences where their sex lives are concerned. It is also becoming increasingly clear that inherited environmental factors play a role in the development of adaptive behaviors; in humans, these factors include our gendered culture. All of which means that equality between the sexes might be more attainable than previously supposed.

Fast Males, Finicky Females

The origin of the evolutionary explanation of past and present gender inequality is Charles Darwin's theory of sexual selection. His observations as a naturalist led him to conclude that, with some exceptions, in the arena of courtship and mating, the challenge to be chosen usually falls most strongly on males. Hence, males, rather than females, have evolved characteristics such as a large size or big antlers to help beat off the competition for territory, social status, and mates. Likewise, it is usually the male of the species that has evolved purely aesthetic traits that appeal to females, such as stunning plumage, an elaborate courtship song, or an exquisite odor.

It was, however, British biologist Angus Bateman who, in the middle of the 20th century, developed a compelling explanation of why being male tends to lead to sexual competition. The goal of Bateman's research was to test an important assumption from Darwin's theory. Like natural selection, sexual selection results in some individuals being more successful than others. Therefore, if sexual selection acts more strongly on males than females, then males should have a greater range of reproductive success, from dismal failures to big winners. Females, in contrast, should be much more similar in their reproductive success. This is why being the animal equivalent of a brilliant artist, as opposed to a mediocre one, is far more beneficial for males than for females.

Bateman used fruit flies to test this idea. Although the technology for paternity testing did not exist at the time, he inferred parentage and the number of different mates of males and females as best he could. He did this rather ingeniously, by using fruit flies with different genetic mutations, including one that makes the bristles on the wings extra long, another that makes the wings curl upward, and yet another that renders the eyes very small or absent. These mutations are sometimes evident in offspring, so Bateman could estimate how many offspring each adult produced by counting the number of different mutants among the surviving offspring. From his data, he concluded that males were indeed more variable than females in their reproductive success (measured as offspring). Bateman also reported that only male reproductive success increased with the number of mates. This result, he argued, is why males compete and females choose: a male's reproductive success is largely limited by the number of females he can inseminate, whereas a female reaches her plateau with a single mate that provides her with all the sperm she needs.

Scholars mostly ignored Bateman's study at first. But some two decades later evolutionary biologist Robert Trivers, now at Rutgers University, catapulted it into scientific fame. He expressed Bateman's idea in terms of greater female investment in reproduction—the big, fat egg versus the small, skinny sperm—and pointed out that this initial asymmetry can go well beyond the gametes to encompass gestation, feeding (including via lactation, in the case of mammals), and protecting. Thus, just as a consumer takes far more care in the selection of a car than of a disposable, cheap trinket, Trivers suggests that the higher investing sex—usually the female—will hold out for the best possible partner with whom to mate. And here is the kicker: the lower investing sex—typically the male—will behave in ways that, ideally, distribute cheap, abundant seed as widely as possible.

The logic is so elegant and compelling it is hardly surprising that contemporary research has identified many species to which the so-called Bateman-Trivers principles seem to apply, including species in which, unusually, it is males that are the higher investing sex. For example, in some species of katydids, also known as bush crickets, the male's investment in reproduction is greater than the female's, thanks to a nutrient-rich package he provides, along with sperm, during copulation. Females thus fight one another for access to males.

The Bateman-Trivers principles also seem to provide a plausible explanation of the gender dynamics of human societies. Women are commonly understood to have less interest in casual sex with multiple partners, for instance, and to be more caring and less competitive and risk-taking. Applying the Bateman-Trivers logic, these behaviors serve to protect their investment. Contemporary advice from Facebook's chief operating officer Sheryl Sandberg to women to "lean in" at work to rise to the top thus appears to be undercut by arguments that predispositions to take risks and compete have evolved more strongly in males than in females because of greater reproductive return.

Breaking The Rules

But it turns out that nature is not nearly so simple and neat as this line of reasoning would suggest, even for nonhuman animals. In the decades since the Bateman-Trivers principles were forged, many of their foundational assumptions have been overturned. One such change in thinking concerns the supposed cheapness of reproduction for males. Sperm is not always cheap nor is it always abundant: for instance, male stick insects can take several weeks to recover their libido after a lengthy copulation. And more recent scrutiny of the fruit fly's reproductive habits found that males do not always take up mating opportunities. Male selectivity has consequences for females of many insects, because if they mate with a male that has copulated extensively, they risk acquiring insufficient sperm. Scarce or limited sperm is not an uncommon challenge for females, which may mate repeatedly with different males precisely to acquire enough sperm.

In fact, a reexamination of Bateman's data from the lab of Patricia Gowaty of the University of California, Los Angeles, revealed, crucially, that a female fruit fly's reproductive success also increased with her mating frequency, a pattern that has emerged for a great many other species of animals. Furthermore, field studies show that mating for females is not the given scientists once assumed it to be. In a surprisingly large number of species, a significant proportion of females do not encounter a male and are thus unable to reproduce. Nor is promiscuous mating standard practice for males. Monogyny, in which males mate only once, is not uncommon and can be an effective means of maximizing reproductive success.

Insects are not the only creatures that challenge the Bateman-Trivers principles. Even in mammals, for which investment in reproduction is particularly skewed because of the costs of gestation and lactation for females, competition is important not only just for male reproductive success but also for female reproductive success. For example, the infants of higher ranking female chimpanzees have higher rates of both arrival and survival than those of lower ranking females.

In our own species, the traditional story is additionally complicated by the inefficiency of human sexual activity. Unlike many other species, in which coitus is hormonally coordinated to a greater or lesser degree to ensure that sex results in conception, humans engage in a vast amount of nonreproductive sex. This pattern has important implications. First, it means that any one act of coitus has a low probability of giving rise to a baby, a fact that should temper overoptimistic assumptions about the likely reproductive return on seed spreading. Second, it suggests that sex serves purposes beyond reproduction—strengthening relationships, for example.

Cultural and societal changes further necessitate rethinking the application of Bateman-Trivers principles to humans. The dichotomous view of the sexes that held sway in the last century has given way to one that sees differences mainly in degree rather than kind. Increased female sexual autonomy wrought by the birth-control pill and the sexual revolution has led to marked increases in premarital sex and numbers of sexual partners in women especially. And women and men report largely similar preferences for their sex lives. For example, the second British National Survey of Sexual Attitudes and Lifestyles, based on a random sample of more than 12,000 people between the ages of 16 and 44 surveyed around the turn of this century, found that 80 percent of men and 89 percent of women preferred monogamy.

Meanwhile, the feminist movement increased women's opportunities to enter, and excel in, traditionally masculine domains. In 1920, there were just 84 women studying at the top 12 law schools that admitted women, and those female lawyers found it nearly impossible to find employment. In the 21st century, women and men are graduating from law school in roughly equal numbers, and women made up about 18 percent of equity partners in 2015.

Risks and Benefits

As we zoom in from this broad-brush perspective on gender patterns to a fine-grained examination of sex differences in behavior, the familiar evolutionary story becomes even muddier. Consider risk-taking, once assumed to be a masculine personality trait, thanks to its role in enhancing male reproductive success. It turns out that people are quite idiosyncratic in the kinds of risks they are willing to take. The skydiver is no more likely to gamble money than the person who prefers to exercise in the safety of the gym. It is people's perception of the potential costs and benefits of a particular risky action, not their attitude toward risk per se, that explains their willingness

to take risks. These perceived costs and benefits can include not only material losses and gains but also less tangible impacts on reputation or self-concept.

This nuance is important because sometimes the balance of risks and benefits is not the same for men and women because of physical differences between the sexes or gendered norms, or both. Consider, for example, the risk of a casual sexual encounter. For a man, the gains include the near certainty of an orgasm and perhaps a burnishing of his reputation as a "stud." For a woman, sexual pleasure is far less likely from casual sex, according to a large-scale study of North American students published in 2012 by Elizabeth Armstrong of the University of Michigan and her colleagues. And thanks to the sexual double standard, her reputation is more likely to be damaged by the episode. Among young Australians, for example, sociologist Michael Flood, now at the Queensland University of Technology, found that the label "slut" retains a stronger "moral and disciplinary weight . . . when applied to women." Moreover, a woman bears greater physical risks, including pregnancy, sexually transmitted disease, and even sexual assault.

The lens of different risks and benefits can also clarify the sexes' different propensity to assert themselves at work, as Sandberg has advised women to do. It is hard to see how a young female lawyer, looking first at the many young women at her level and then at the very few female partners and judges, can be as optimistic about the likely payoff of leaning in and making sacrifices for her career as a young male lawyer. And this is before one considers the big-picture evidence of sexism, sexual harassment and sex discrimination in traditionally masculine professions such as law and medicine.

Still, the idea that a nonsexist society could erase the psychological effects of timeless, enduring sex differences in reproductive investment seems implausible to many. A recent article in *The Economist*, for example, equated the marketing-inspired tradition of the diamond engagement ring with the strutting peacock's extravagant tail, an evolved courtship ritual that signals a man's resources and commitment. The journalist wrote that "greater equality for women might seem to render male-courtship displays redundant. But mating preferences evolved over millennia and will not change quickly."

Environmental Influence

Although sex certainly influences the brain, this argument overlooks the growing recognition in evolutionary biology that offspring do not just inherit genes. They also inherit a particular social and ecological environment that can play a critical role in the expression of adaptive traits. For example, adult male moths that hailed, as larvae, from a dense population develop particularly large testes. These enhanced organs stand the moths in good stead for engaging in intense copulatory competition against the many other males in the population. One would be forgiven for assuming that these generously sized gonads are a genetically determined adaptive trait. Yet adult male moths of the same species raised as larvae in a lower-density population instead develop larger wings and antennae, which are ideal for searching for widely dispersed females.

If the development of sex-linked physical characteristics can be influenced by the social environment, it stands to reason that sex-linked behavior can be, too. One striking example comes from the previously mentioned female katydids, which compete for the males that bring them both sperm and food, in line with the Bateman–Trivers principles. Remarkably, when their environment becomes rich with nutritious pollen, their competitive "nature" wanes.

The environment is similarly important for adaptive behavior in mammals. Research published starting in the late 1970s found that rat mothers care for male and female pups differently. The males get licked more than the females in the anogenital region because the mothers are attracted to the higher level of testosterone in male pups' urine. Intriguingly, the greater stimulation from this higher-intensity licking plays a part in the development of sex differences in parts of the brain involved in basic masculine mating behavior.

As University of Sydney philosopher of science Paul Griffiths has observed, we should not be surprised that environmental factors or experiences that reliably recur every generation should be incorporated as inputs into the developmental processes that bring about evolved traits.

In our own species, these developmental inputs include the rich cultural inheritance bestowed on every human newborn. And although social constructions of gender vary across time and place, all societies weight biological sex with heavy cultural meaning. Gender socialization starts at birth, and it would only make sense if the ruthless process of natural selection were to exploit it. It may well have been adaptive in our evolutionary past for males to take these and those risks or for females to avoid them. But when culture changes—creating a very different pattern of rewards, punishments, norms, and consequences, compared with those in the past—so, too, will patterns of sex differences in behavior.

Thus, *The Economist* writer was not quite right in stating that human "mating preferences evolved over millennia and will not change quickly." True, they are unlikely to change as quickly as those of katydids, with a sprinkling of pollen (although we suspect that is not what was meant). There is usually nothing simple and quick about creating cultural shifts. But change certainly can, and certainly has, taken place over timescales shorter than millennia.

Take, for example, gender gaps in the importance men and women place on a partner's financial resources, attractiveness, and chastity. The very quaintness of the term "chastity" to Western ears today compared with several decades ago speaks to rapid changes in cultural gender expectations. Cross-culturally, women and men from countries with greater gender equity are more similar in all these dimensions of partner preferences than those from countries with lower equity between the sexes, according to a 2012 study by Marcel Zentner and Klaudia Mitura, both then at the University of York in England. Research has also shown that in the United States, men now place more importance on a female partner's financial prospects, education, and intelligence—and care less about her culinary and housekeeping skills—than they did several decades ago. Meanwhile, the cliché of the pitiable bluestocking spinster is a historical relic: although wealthier and better-educated women were once less likely to marry, now they are more likely to do so.

Could we, then, see the day when the world's finest art galleries display as much art by women as by men? We certainly shouldn't let Bateman's fruit flies tell us no.

Critical Thinking

1. Are males inherently more risk-taking than females? Explain.
2. How have cultural and societal changes necessitated a rethinking of the application of the Bateman Trivers principles to humans?

Internet References

Hartford Institute for Religion Research
Hirr.hartsem.edu/ency/Anthropology.htm
Harvard Department of Anthropology
https://anthropology.fas.harvard.edu/research/religion
Society for the Anthropology of Religion
Sar.americananthro.org/

Article   Prepared by: Elvio Angeloni

Evolution, Sex, and Language

DEBORAH CAMERON

Learning Outcomes

After reading this article, you will be able to:

- Discuss the notion that human language developed in a way that women would be more socially skilled with it than men.

- Discuss Robin Dunbar's theory that the primary purpose for language had to do with gossip.

- Describe the belief that language could be a product of sexual selection.

It is a basic assumption of evolutionary theory that there is no "intelligent designer" directing the progress of organisms toward some predetermined goal. Evolution happens because in any population, there will be genetic variations: over time, some of these will spread at the expense of others because they prove to be advantageous for survival.

"Survival" in modern evolutionary theory means ensuring the survival of your genes by passing them on to offspring. To say that a gene is advantageous for survival is to say that individuals who possess it are more successful at reproducing themselves than those who do not. The drive to maximize reproductive success—pass your genes on to as many offspring as possible—is fundamental for both sexes. Evolutionary scientists argue, however, that the biological facts of sexual reproduction give it different implications for males and females.

In theory, there is virtually no limit to the number of offspring a human male can father. Females, on the other hand, can only conceive a certain number of times, and for them, conception is only the beginning of a much longer process involving gestation, giving birth, and caring for a dependent infant. This restricts female sexual availability, making women a scarce resource which men must compete for. It also gives women a reason to be picky about who they mate with: for them, every sexual encounter represents what could be a huge investment of time and energy. The result is that males do the courting, and females do the choosing.

Theorists reason that among our prehistoric ancestors, reproductive success demanded not only differences in the anatomy and physiology of the two sexes, but differences in their ways of thinking, feeling, and behaving. The most successful males were those who maximized their opportunities to mate—who were aggressive in competition with other males and who possessed qualities (such as hunting skills) which females considered desirable. The most successful females, by contrast, were those who chose their mates wisely and nurtured their children well.

It is not hard to see how language might be incorporated into this picture. Socially skilled, nurturant women would also have been more fluent, articulate, and "caring" communicators; men would have placed more emphasis on nonverbal abilities like those required to hunt, and their talk—when they did talk—would have reflected their generally competitive mentality. All of which is, of course, exactly what the myth of Mars and Venus says about male and female language-use today.

Many evolutionary scientists embrace the myth wholeheartedly. But they have different ways of weaving it into the larger story of the descent of Man and Woman. These differences are bound up with the answers they give to another big question about human evolution: how and why language itself evolved.

It might seem self-evident that the ability to speak would be an advantage in the struggle to survive and reproduce, but the advantages of any characteristic have to be set against the costs. In the case of language, the cost is heavy: to accommodate it, humans need very large brains. Large brains demand a lot of energy; they also take time to develop. Because their brains at birth are immature, human infants remain helpless and dependent for several years. What advantage could language have conferred on our species that outweighed these significant disadvantages?

Gathering, Mothering, and Gossiping

In the past, it was often suggested that the big advantage conferred by language was that it enabled hunters to coordinate their activities more efficiently. Since hunters were assumed to be male, it followed that men were the driving force in the evolution of language. But the general assumptions of evolutionary psychology fit better with stories in which women were the driving force; today there are several competing stories of this kind.

One of these stories suggests that the main advantage language offered had to do with the management of social relationships in prehistoric human groups. Humans are social animals who survive by cooperating as well as competing. To succeed as a social animal, it is necessary both to maintain social relationships and to keep track of them—you need to be aware of who is doing what with whom and where they are in the pecking order.

Our closest nonhuman relatives, apes, negotiate their relationships through grooming each other. But when a group gets beyond a certain size, one-to-one physical contact becomes a time-consuming and inefficient way of keeping up your social networks. According to the evolutionary scientist Robin Dunbar, this may have been a decisive factor in the evolution of language. Dunbar believes that in the course of human evolution, environmental conditions made it advantageous for the size of the average human group to increase. As groups grew too large for grooming to be manageable, language provided a more efficient substitute. The ability to speak enabled people to maintain social relationships and exchange social information many-to-many as well as one-to-one. It also meant they could do it without having to put aside every other task (since unlike grooming, talking leaves your hands free).

In Dunbar's story, the primary purpose for which language was selected was to enable humans to gossip—that is, to engage in the kind of talk that conveys information about, and passes judgment on, the activities and relationships of group members. He also argues that women rather than men were the driving force behind this development. Females are at the center of most stable primate social networks, whereas males tend to be more peripheral. If that was also true of early human groups, the women would have been better placed to act as conduits for gossip.

Some stories which also accord women a primary role in language evolution give more weight to two other aspects of their roles in prehistoric society. Women were mothers and would presumably have vocalized to the children they cared for. They were also gatherers rather than hunters. As one writer, Rhawn Joseph, summarizes:

Over the course of human evolution . . . female mothers and female gatherers were able to freely chatter with their babies or amongst themselves. . . . Unlike the men who must remain quiet for long time periods in order to not scare off game, the women are free to chatter and talk to their hearts' delight.

Whereas gathering and childcare responsibilities allowed women to develop verbal skill, hunting inhibited this development in men because it required them to spend long periods without talking. What men needed to hunt successfully was not verbal skill but spatial skill—the ability to plan routes, judge distances, and calculate angles. This fits perfectly with what is claimed on the cover of *Why Men Don't Iron*—that among modern humans, "boys excel in tasks that require three-dimensional thought processing, girls in verbal skills." The Stone Age story explains both how that difference came into existence, and also why it became a hard-wired characteristic of the human species.

On closer inspection, though, there are reasons to doubt that this story explains much at all. To begin with, there is a logical problem: the so-called explanation presupposes what it is meant to be explaining. Modern women's superior verbal skills and modern men's superior spatial skills are explained by saying that prehistoric conditions favored the development of just those skills in our ancestors: we modern humans have simply inherited them. But there is no independent evidence that early human females had superior verbal skills. The only evidence for the prehistoric sex-difference is the modern sex-difference which it is supposed to explain.

What about the argument that hunters (male) had to be silent, whereas gatherers (female) were free to talk? Isn't that a point in favor of the theory? Maybe: but a lot of what is said about early humans is based on anthropological studies of groups who have maintained the hunter-gatherer way of life into modern times. And for these groups, "men hunt, women gather" is now considered to be an oversimplification. In general, it is gathering which provides the bulk of what modern hunter-gatherers subsist on. Gathering is a regular activity and is often engaged in by both sexes, whereas hunting tends to be more sporadic. While it is typical for the hunting of large animals to be a male preserve, women do hunt smaller game.

In addition, hunting is something men generally do in groups. It needs planning and coordination and often involves lengthy periods spent travelling to where the animals are. Some hunters have been observed to perform rituals at the site of a kill and to spend time butchering and partially consuming the meat before beginning the journey back. If we assume (as evolutionary psychologists usually do) that early human practices were similar to those of hunter-gatherer peoples today, it does not seem plausible to claim that their role as hunters deprived prehistoric men of opportunities to talk. It seems more likely that hunting expeditions were not an everyday occurrence, and that when they did take place, they were occasions for male bonding, in which verbal interaction played a part.

Lekking and Listening

Some evolutionary scientists tell a different story about how and why language evolved: they suggest that it was a product of "sexual selection." Sexual selection is the concept which explains why some characteristics get selected despite the fact that they do not have any obvious survival value. They may even appear to be counterproductive—the peacock's large and gaudy tail, for instance, makes it more conspicuous to predators. The theory of sexual selection proposes that these characteristics do have a value: they make their possessors more attractive to the opposite sex and thus enable them to mate more often. It is not a coincidence that many of them are specifically male characteristics (like bright plumage or large horns). This is linked to the principle that males court and females choose. The lavishly ornamented peacock's tail says to peahens: "choose me!"

It would be hard to argue that language was purely ornamental, but some theorists do argue that if utility had been the only consideration, we could have got by with something much less elaborate. Human verbal abilities go far beyond what is needed for efficient communication, and in that sense do not justify their high cost. Their selection might be explicable, however, if the capacity for language also made individuals more attractive to potential mates—if it gave human males a new and powerful tool for advertising themselves to human females.

Robin Dunbar (who believes that this self-advertising function was a by-product of the evolution of language rather than the main purpose for which it evolved) cites an interesting finding as evidence for this theory. His research on present-day humans found that although both sexes spent much the same amount of time exchanging social information, men spent more time than women talking about themselves, as opposed to about other people. Dunbar explains this as a form of what is called "lekking" in peacocks and certain other species. The lek is a kind of courtship ritual in which males display themselves and females select the best ones to mate with.

This account seems to overlook the fact that modern advice on human courtship consistently recommends showing an interest in the other person as a more effective strategy than talking endlessly about yourself. Leaving that detail aside, however, what is most puzzling about the self-advertisement theory is its apparent incompatibility with the idea that women are more verbally skilled than men. If language enabled prehistoric men to show off to their womenfolk, shouldn't verbal skill be a guy thing?

This contradiction is inventively addressed by Geoffrey Miller, a scholar who believes that language, art, and culture evolved mainly as tools for courtship (for him the principle that males court and females choose explains why most of the world's art and public culture has been produced by men). He gets over the objection that in that case, men should be the more verbal sex by suggesting that the main area in which women's linguistic abilities outstrip men's is not talking but listening. Women evolved into the proverbial "good listeners" because they spent millennia judging the quality of men's verbal displays in order to choose the best mates to father their children.

This claim underscores a problem with evolutionary psychology which I have already drawn attention to—the inherently speculative nature of its arguments. These are often ingenious, but in the absence of direct evidence about prehistoric language-use, impossible to verify or falsify. There are too many different and incompatible stories that can be made to fit the supposed facts—especially if, like many of the writers I have mentioned, you approach the (modern) evidence like a peahen at a lek, fastening enthusiastically on the splashiest generalizations while disregarding the more serviceable but drabber specimens.

Factual Selection?

The argument that a sex-difference is "in the genes" will always be stronger if the difference in question appears consistently across a wide range of cultures and in different historical eras. If it is variable in time and space, that suggests that it is more likely to reflect social and cultural factors. The way evolutionary psychologists talk about sex differences in language implies that they think the Mars and Venus generalizations they use to back up their story—for instance, that women like to talk more than men, have better verbal skills than men, are less competitive and less direct in their speech than men, and so on—apply, if not universally, then very widely across cultures. But if that is what they think, they are overlooking a fair amount of evidence to the contrary.

In Chapter 2, we visited the people of Gapun, in Papua New Guinea, and the Malagasy people of the island of Madagascar—two of many nonwestern societies in which the stereotypical Mars and Venus patterns are absent or reversed. Women are more assertive and more direct in their speech than men; men are believed by both sexes to be more verbally skilled than women, largely because of their greater facility with the highly elaborate language used on ritual occasions.

For evolutionary psychologists trying to argue that certain patterns of linguistic behavior reflect innate characteristics, the existence of such striking cross-cultural variation is a problem in itself. But the form that variation takes is arguably an even bigger problem. Evolutionary psychologists usually reason that the less a society has been affected by very recent cultural and technological developments, the more it should be able to tell us about the lives and behavior of ancestral humans. On that reasoning, the pattern of sex differences found in more traditional societies should be a better model for reconstructing prehistory than patterns which—like modern industrial society itself—may only go back a couple of centuries. (As well as having evidence of cross-cultural variation in patterns of gender difference, we have evidence that those patterns have varied historically: some male–female differences which are reported consistently in modern western speech communities apparently did not exist in the same communities in earlier periods.)

Their failure to deal with the cross-cultural and historical evidence is not the only respect in which evolutionary psychologists are selective in their use of research. Most versions of the Stone Age narrative assume that females have superior verbal skills and that their story needs to explain that. But the research evidence suggests that they are overexplaining it: sex differences in verbal ability are really not very large. In Chapter 3, I quoted one linguist's estimate that the overlap between men and women is about 99.75 percent.

Another generalization which is often used to support the thesis that "men's brains are built for action and women's for talking" is that women talk more than men. According to Rhawn Joseph, they inherit their loquacity from prehistoric women who were "free to chatter and talk to their heart's delight." But the idea of the "chattering" woman is a stereotype which research has repeatedly contradicted.

In Chapter 1, I discussed the claim that the average woman utters 20,000 words in a day to the average man's 7,000. As we saw, these figures were based on no reliable evidence, and in any case, there is too much variation among individuals to make an average male or female daily word-count meaningful. If we are going to try to generalize about which sex talks more, a more reliable way to do it is to observe both sexes in a single interaction, and measure their respective contributions. This cuts out extraneous variables that are likely to affect the amount of talk (like whether someone is spending their day at a Buddhist retreat or a high school reunion) and allows for a comparison of male and female behavior under the same contextual conditions.

Numerous studies have been done using this approach, and while as always, the results have been mixed, by far the commonest finding is that men talk more than women. One review of 56 research studies categorizes their findings as shown in Table 2.

The reviewers are inclined to believe that this is a case of the "missing link" phenomenon I explained in Chapter 3. Gender and amount of talk are linked indirectly rather than directly: the more direct link is with status, in combination with the

Table 2

Pattern of Difference Found	Number of Studies
Men talk more than women	34 (60.8%)
Women talk more than men	2 (3.6%)
Men and women talk the same amount	16 (28.6%)
No clear pattern	4 (7.0%)

Source: Based on Deborah James and Janice Drakich, 'Understanding Gender Differences in Amount of Talk' in Deborah Tannend (ed.), *Gender and Conversational Interaction,* New York: Oxford University Press, 1991, 281–312.

formality of the setting (status tends to be more relevant in formal situations). The basic trend, especially in formal and public contexts, is for higher-status speakers to talk more than lower-status ones. The gender pattern is explained by the observation that in most contexts where status is relevant, men are more likely than women to occupy high-status positions; if all other things are equal, gender itself is a hierarchical system in which men are regarded as having higher status.

Regarded' is an important word here because conversational dominance is not just about the way dominant speakers behave; it is also about the willingness of others to defer to them. Some experimental studies have found that you can reverse the "men talk more" pattern, or at least reduce the gap, by instructing subjects to discuss a topic which both sexes consider a distinctively female area of expertise. In a discussion of fashion, or pregnancy, men will more readily cede the floor to women. Status, then, is not a completely fixed attribute but can vary relative to the setting, subject, and purpose of conversation.

That may be why some studies find that women talk more in domestic interactions with partners and family members: in the domestic sphere, women are often seen as being in charge. In other spheres, however, the default assumption is that men outrank women, and men are usually found to talk more. In informal contexts where status is not an issue, the commonest finding is not that women talk more than men, it is that the two sexes contribute about equally.

If it does not reflect reality, why is the folk-belief that women talk more than men so persistent? The feminist Dale Spender once suggested an explanation: she said that people overestimate how much women talk because they think that ideally, women would not talk at all. While that may be rather sweeping, it is true that belief in female loquacity is generally combined with disapproval of it. The statement "women talk more than men" tends to imply the judgment "women talk too much." (As one old proverb charmingly puts it: "Many women, many words; many geese, many turds.")

The folk-belief that women talk more than men persists because it provides a justification for an ingrained social prejudice. Evolutionary psychology is open to a similar criticism: that it takes today's social prejudices and projects them back into prehistory, thus elevating them to the status of timeless truths about the human condition.

Champions of the evolutionary approach often say it is their opponents whose arguments are based on prejudice rather than facts or logic. They complain that feminists and other "PC" types are unwilling even to consider the idea that sex differences might have biological rather than social causes. Instead of judging the arguments on their merits, these politically motivated critics just denounce them, and those who advance them, as reactionary and bigoted. . . .

Critical Thinking

1. Why did language develop in the human species and not among apes?
2. Is there an innate difference between men and women with respect to language?

Internet References

Hartford Institute for Religion Research
Hirr.hartsem.edu/ency/Anthropology.htm
Harvard Department of Anthropology
https://anthropology.fas.harvard.edu/research/religion
Society for the Anthropology of Religion
Sar.americananthro.org/

Unit 4

UNIT

Prepared by: Elvio Angeloni

The Fossil Evidence

A primary focal point of this book, as well as of the whole of physical anthropology, is the search for, and the interpretation of, fossil evidence for hominid (meaning human or humanlike) evolution. Paleoanthropologists carry out this task by conducting painstaking excavations and detailed analyses that serve as a basis for understanding our past. Every fragment found is cherished like a ray of light that may help to illuminate the path taken by our ancestors in the process of becoming "us." At least, that is what we would like to believe. In reality, each discovery leads to further mystery, and for every fossil-hunting paleoanthropologist who thinks his or her find supports a particular theory, there are many others anxious to express their disagreement. How wonderful it would be, we sometimes think, in moments of frustration over inconclusive data, if the fossils would just speak for themselves, and every primordial piece of humanity were to carry with it a self-evident explanation for its place in the evolutionary story. Paleoanthropology would then be more of a quantitative, mechanical problem of amassing enough material to reconstruct our ancestral development than a qualitative problem of interpreting what it all means. It would certainly be a simpler process, but would it be as interesting?

Most scientists tolerate, welcome, or even (dare it be said?) thrive on controversy, recognizing that diversity of opinion refreshes the mind, rouses students, and captures the imagination of the general public. After all, where would paleoanthropology be without the gadflies, the near-mythic heroes, and, lest we forget, the research funds they generate? Consider, for example, the issue of the differing roles played by males and females in the transition to humanity and all that it implies with regard to bipedalism, tool-making, and the origin of the family. Did bipedalism

evolve in the grasslands or in the forests of equaltorial Africa? Did bipedalism develop as a means of gathering fruits and vegetables or pursuing prey? Should the primary theme of human evolution be summed up as "man the hunter" and "woman the gatherer"? Indeed, for early hominid evolution, how about "man the hunted"?

Not all the research and theoretical speculations taking place in the field of paleoanthropology are controversial. Most students of human evolution, in fact, go about their work quietly and methodically, each year finding more hominid fossil sites and increasing our understanding of the general environmental circumstances in which our human predecessors lived. The hypotheses formed from this systematic and thought-provoking work have had the cumulative effect of enriching our understanding of the details of human evolution.

As we mull over the controversies, we should not take them as reflecting an inherent weakness of the field of paleoanthropology, but rather as reflective of its strength: the ability and willingness to scrutinize, question, and reflect (endlessly) on every bit of evidence.

Contrary to the way that the proponents of creationism or "intelligent design theory" would have it, an admission of doubt is not an expression of ignorance but simply a frank recognition of the imperfect state of our knowledge. If we are to increase our understanding of ourselves, we must maintain an atmosphere of free inquiry without preconceived notions and unquestioning commitment to a particular point of view.

To paraphrase anthropologist Ashley Montagu, "while creationism embraces certainty without proof, science embraces proof without certainty."

Article   Prepared by: Elvio Angeloni

Mystery Man

A trove of fossils found deep in a South African cave adds a baffling new branch to the human family tree.

JAMIE SHREEVE

Learning Outcomes

After reading this article, you will be able to:

- Discuss the astonishingly unique combination of characteristics exhibited by *H. naledi*.

- Discuss the various possibilities as to how the remains of *H. naledi* got into the Rising Star cave and what possibilities seem to be ruled out.

- Discuss the implications of the mixture and advanced characteristics of *H. naledi*.

- Understand the implications of the age of *H. naledi*— whether it is quite "old" or quite "young."

O n September 13, 2013, two recreational cavers named Steven Tucker and Rick Hunter entered a dolomite cave system called Rising Star, some 30 miles northwest of Johannesburg. Rising Star has been a popular draw for cavers since the 1960s, and its filigree of channels and caverns is well mapped. Tucker and Hunter were hoping to find some less trodden passage.

In the back of their minds was another mission. In the first half of the 20th century, this region produced so many fossils of our early ancestors that it later became known as the Cradle of Humankind. Though the heyday of fossil hunting there was long past, the cavers knew that a scientist at the University of the Witwatersrand in Johannesburg was looking for bones. The odds of happening upon something were remote. But you never know.

Deep in the cave, Tucker and Hunter worked their way through a constriction called Superman's Crawl—because most people can fit through only by holding one arm tightly against the body

and extending the other above the head, like the Man of Steel in flight. Crossing a large chamber, they climbed a jagged wall of rock called the Dragon's Back. At the top they found themselves in a pretty little cavity decorated with stalactites. Hunter got out his video camera, and to remove himself from the frame, Tucker eased himself into a fissure in the cave floor. His foot found a finger of rock, then another below it, then—empty space.

Dropping down, he found himself in a narrow, vertical chute, in some places less than eight inches wide. He called to Hunter to follow him. Both men have hyper-slender frames, all bone and wiry muscle. Had their torsos been just a little bigger, they would not have fit in the chute, and what is arguably the most astonishing human fossil discovery in half a century—and undoubtedly the most perplexing—would not have occurred.

Lee Berger, the paleoanthropologist who had asked cavers to keep an eye out for fossils, is a big-boned American with a high forehead, a flushed face, and cheeks that flare out broadly when he smiles, which is a lot of the time. His unquenchable optimism has proved essential to his professional life. By the early 1990s, when Berger got a job at the University of the Witwatersrand ("Wits") and had begun to hunt for fossils, the spotlight in human evolution had long since shifted to the Great Rift Valley of East Africa.

Most researchers regarded South Africa as an interesting sidebar to the story of human evolution but not the main plot. Berger was determined to prove them wrong. But for almost 20 years, the relatively insignificant finds he made seemed only to underscore how little South Africa had left to offer.

What he most wanted to find were fossils that could shed light on the primary outstanding mystery in human evolution: the origin of our genus, *Homo*, between 2 million and 3 million years ago. On the far side of that divide are the ape-like *australopithecines*, epitomized by *Australopithecus afarensis* and its most famous representative, Lucy, a skeleton discovered in Ethiopia in 1974. On the near side is *Homo erectus*, a tool-wielding, fire-making, globe-trotting species with a big brain and body proportions much like ours. Within that murky million-year gap, a bipedal animal was transformed into a nascent human being, a creature not just adapted to its environment but able to apply its mind to master it. How did that revolution happen?

The fossil record is frustratingly ambiguous. Slightly older than *H. erectus* is a species called *Homo habilis*, or "handy man"—so named by Louis Leakey and his colleagues in 1964 because they believed it responsible for the stone tools they were finding at Olduvai Gorge in Tanzania. In the 1970s teams led by Louis's son Richard found more *H. habilis* specimens in Kenya, and ever since, the species has provided a shaky base for the human family tree, keeping it rooted in East Africa. Before *H. habilis* the human story goes dark, with just a few fossil fragments of *Homo* too sketchy to warrant a species name. As one scientist put it, they would easily fit in a shoe box, and you'd still have room for the shoes.

Berger has long argued that *H. habilis* was too primitive to deserve its privileged position at the root of our genus. Some other scientists agree that it really should be called *Australopithecus*. But Berger has been nearly alone in arguing that South Africa was the place to look for the true earliest *Homo*. And for years the unchecked exuberance with which he promoted his relatively minor finds tended only to alienate some of his professional colleagues. Berger had the ambition and personality to become a famous player in his field, like Richard Leakey or Donald Johanson, who found the Lucy skeleton. Berger is a tireless fund-raiser and a master at enthralling a public audience. But he didn't have the bones.

Then, in 2008, he made a truly important discovery. While searching in a place later called Malapa, some ten miles from Rising Star, he and his 14-year-old son, Matthew, found some hominin fossils poking out of hunks of dolomite.

Over the next year Berger's team painstakingly chipped two nearly complete skeletons out of the rock. Dated to about 2 million years ago, they were the first major finds from South Africa published in decades. (An even more complete skeleton found earlier has yet to be described.) In most respects they were very primitive, but there were some oddly modern traits too.

Berger decided the skeletons were a new species of australopithecine, which he named *Australopithecus sediba*. But he also claimed they were "the Rosetta stone" to the origins of *Homo*. Though the doyens of paleoanthropology credited him with a "jaw-dropping" find, most dismissed his interpretation of it. *A. sediba* was too young, too weird, and not in the right place to be ancestral to *Homo*: It wasn't one of us. In another sense, neither was Berger. Since then, prominent researchers

have published papers on early *Homo* that didn't even mention him or his find.

Berger shook off the rejection and got back to work—there were additional skeletons from Malapa to occupy him, still encased in limestone blocks in his lab. Then one night, Pedro Boshoff, a caver and geologist Berger had hired to look for fossils, knocked on his door. With him was Steven Tucker. Berger took one look at the pictures they showed him from Rising Star and realized that Malapa was going to have to take a backseat.

After contorting themselves 40 feet down the narrow chute in the Rising Star cave, Tucker and Rick Hunter had dropped into another pretty chamber, with a cascade of white flowstones in one corner. A passageway led into a larger cavity, about 30 feet long and only a few feet wide, its walls and ceiling a bewilderment of calcite gnarls and jutting flowstone fingers. But it was what was on the floor that drew the two men's attention. There were bones everywhere. The cavers first thought they must be modern. They weren't stone heavy, like most fossils, nor were they encased in stone—they were just lying about on the surface, as if someone had tossed them in. They noticed a piece of a lower jaw, with teeth intact; it looked human.

Berger could see from the photos that the bones did not belong to a modern human being. Certain features, especially those of the jawbone and teeth, were far too primitive. The photos showed more bones waiting to be found; Berger could make out the outline of a partly buried cranium. It seemed likely that the remains represented much of a complete skeleton. He was dumbfounded. In the early hominin fossil record, the number of mostly complete skeletons, including his two from Malapa, could be counted on one hand. And now this. But what was this? How old was it? And how did it get into that cave?

Most pressing of all: how to get it out again, and quickly, before some other amateurs found their way into that chamber. (It was clear from the arrangement of the bones that someone had already been there, perhaps decades before.) Tucker and Hunter lacked the skills needed to excavate the fossils, and no scientist Berger knew—certainly not himself—had the physique to squeeze through that chute. So Berger put the word out on Facebook: Skinny individuals wanted, with scientific credentials and caving experience; must be "willing to work in cramped quarters." Within a week and a half he'd heard from nearly 60 applicants. He chose the six most qualified; all were young women. Berger called them his "underground astronauts."

With funding from *National Geographic* (Berger is also a *National Geographic* explorer-in-residence), he gathered some 60 scientists and set up an aboveground command center, a science tent, and a small village of sleeping and support tents. Local cavers helped thread two miles of communication and power cables down into the fossil chamber. Whatever was happening there could now be viewed with cameras by Berger and his team in the command center. Marina Elliott, then a graduate student at Simon Fraser University in British Columbia, was the first scientist down the chute.

"Looking down into it, I wasn't sure I'd be OK," Elliott recalled. "It was like looking into a shark's mouth. There were fingers and tongues and teeth of rock."

Elliott and two colleagues, Becca Peixotto and Hannah Morris, inched their way to the "landing zone" at the bottom, then crouched into the fossil chamber. Working in two-hour shifts with another three-woman crew, they plotted and bagged more than 400 fossils on the surface, then started carefully removing soil around the half-buried skull. There were other bones beneath and around it, densely packed. Over the next several days, while the women probed a square-yard patch around the skull, the other scientists huddled around the video feed in the command center above in a state of near-constant excitement. Berger, dressed in field khakis and a Rising Star Expedition cap, would occasionally repair to the science tent to puzzle over the accumulating bones—until a collective howl of astonishment from the command center brought him rushing back to witness another discovery. It was a glorious time.

The bones were superbly preserved, and from the duplication of body parts, it soon became clear that there was not one skeleton in the cave, but two, then three, then five . . . then so many it was hard to keep a clear count. Berger had allotted three weeks for the excavation. By the end of that time, the excavators had removed some 1,200 bones, more than from any other human ancestor site in Africa—and they still hadn't exhausted the material in just the one square yard around the skull. It took another several days digging in March 2014 before its sediments ran dry, about six inches down.

There were some 1,550 specimens in all, representing at least 15 individuals. Skulls. Jaws. Ribs. Dozens of teeth. A nearly complete foot. A hand, virtually every bone intact, arranged as in life. Minuscule bones of the inner ear. Elderly adults. Juveniles. Infants, identified by their thimble-size vertebrae. Parts of the skeletons looked astonishingly modern. But others were just as astonishingly primitive—in some cases, even more ape-like than the *australopithecines*.

"We've found a most remarkable creature," Berger said. His grin went nearly to his ears.

In paleoanthropology, newly discovered specimens are traditionally held close to the vest until they can be carefully analyzed and the results published, with full access to them granted only to the discoverer's closest collaborators. By this protocol, answering the central mystery of the Rising Star find—What is it?—could take years, even decades. Berger wanted the work done and published by the end of the year. In his view everyone

in the field should have access to important new information as quickly as possible. And maybe he liked the idea of announcing his find, which might be a new candidate for earliest *Homo*, in 2014—exactly 50 years after Louis Leakey published his discovery of the reigning first member of our genus, *Homo habilis*.

In any case there was only one way to get the analysis done quickly: Put a lot of eyes on the bones. Along with the 20-odd senior scientists who had helped him evaluate the Malapa skeletons, Berger invited more than 30 young scientists, some with the ink still wet on their PhDs, to Johannesburg from some 15 countries, for a blitzkrieg fossil fest lasting six weeks. To some older scientists who weren't involved, putting young people on the front line just to rush the papers into print seemed rash. But for the young people in question, it was "a paleofantasy come true," said Lucas Delezene, a newly appointed professor at the University of Arkansas. "In grad school you dream of a pile of fossils no one has seen before, and you get to figure it out."

The workshop took place in a newly constructed vault at Wits, a windowless room lined with glass-paneled shelves bearing fossils and casts. The analytical teams were divided by body part. The cranial specialists huddled in one corner around a large square table that was covered with skull and jaw fragments and the casts of other well-known fossil skulls. Smaller tables were devoted to hands, feet, long bones, and so on. The air was cool, the atmosphere hushed. Young scientists fiddled with bones and calipers. Berger and his close advisers circulated among them, conferring in low voices.

Delezene's own fossil pile contained 190 teeth—a critical part of any analysis, since teeth alone are often enough to identify a species. But these teeth weren't like anything the scientists in the "tooth booth" had ever seen. Some features were astonishingly human-like—the molar crowns were small, for instance, with five cusps like ours. But the premolar roots were weirdly primitive. "We're not sure what to make of these," Delezene said. "It's crazy."

The same schizoid pattern was popping up at the other tables. A fully modern hand sported wackily curved fingers, fit for a creature climbing trees. The shoulders were apish too, and the widely flaring blades of the pelvis were as primitive as Lucy's—but the bottom of the same pelvis looked like a modern human's. The leg bones started out shaped like an *australopithecine's* but gathered modernity as they descended toward the ground. The feet were virtually indistinguishable from our own.

"You could almost draw a line through the hips—primitive above, modern below," said Steve Churchill, a paleontologist from Duke University. "If you'd found the foot by itself, you'd think some Bushman had died."

But then there was the head. Four partial skulls had been found—two were likely male, two female. In their general morphology they clearly looked advanced enough to be called *Homo*. But the braincases were tiny—a mere 560 cubic centimeters for the males and 465 for the females, far less than *H. erectus*'s average of 900 cubic centimeters, and well under half the size of our own. A large brain is the sine qua non of humanness, the hallmark of a species that has evolved to live by its wits. These were not human beings. These were pinheads, with some human-like body parts.

"Weird as hell," paleoanthropologist Fred Grine of the State University of New York at Stony Brook later said. "Tiny little brains stuck on these bodies that weren't tiny." The adult males were around five feet tall and a hundred pounds, the females a little shorter and lighter.

"The message we're getting is of an animal right on the cusp of the transition from *Australopithecus* to *Homo*," Berger said as the workshop began to wind down in early June. "Everything that is touching the world in a critical way is like us. The other parts retain bits of their primitive past."

In some ways the new hominin from Rising Star was even closer to modern humans than *Homo erectus* is. To Berger and his team, it clearly belonged in the *Homo* genus, but it was unlike any other member. They had no choice but to name a new species. They called it *Homo naledi*, tipping a hat to the cave where the bones had been found: In the local Sotho language, naledi means "star."

Back in November, as Marina Elliott and her mates were uncovering that startling trove of bones, they were almost as surprised by what they weren't finding. "It was day three or four, and we still hadn't found any fauna," Elliott said. On the first day a few little bird bones had been found on the surface, but otherwise there was nothing but hominin bones.

That made for a mystery as perplexing as that of *H. naledi*'s identity: How did the remains get into such an absurdly remote chamber? Clearly the individuals weren't living in the cave; there were no stone tools or remains of meals to suggest such occupation. Conceivably a group of *H. naledi* could have wandered into the cave one time and somehow got trapped—but the distribution of the bones seemed to indicate that they had been deposited over a long time, perhaps centuries. If carnivores had dragged hominin prey into the cave, they would have left tooth marks on the bones, and there weren't any. And finally, if the bones had been washed into the cave by flowing water, it would have carried stones and other rubble there too. But there is no rubble—only fine sediment that had weathered off the walls of the cave or sifted through tiny cracks.

"When you have eliminated the impossible," Sherlock Holmes once reminded his friend Watson, "whatever remains, however improbable, must be the truth."

Having exhausted all other explanations, Berger and his team were stuck with the improbable conclusion that bodies of *H. naledi* were deliberately put there, by other *H. naledi*. Until now only *Homo sapiens*, and possibly some archaic humans such as the *Neanderthals*, are known to have treated their dead in such a ritualized manner. The researchers don't argue that these much more primitive hominins navigated Superman's Crawl and the harrowing shark-mouth chute while dragging corpses behind them—that would go beyond improbable to incredible. Maybe back then Superman's Crawl was wide enough to be walkable, and maybe the hominins simply dropped their burden into the chute without climbing down themselves. Over time the growing pile of bones might have slowly tumbled into the neighboring chamber.

Deliberate disposal of bodies would still have required the hominins to find their way to the top of the chute through pitch-black darkness and back again, which almost surely would have required light—torches, or fires lit at intervals. The notion of such a small-brained creature exhibiting such complex behavior seems so unlikely that many other researchers have simply refused to credit it. At some earlier time, they argue, there must have been an entrance to the cave that afforded more direct access to the fossil chamber—one that probably allowed the bones to wash in. "There has to be another entrance," Richard Leakey said after he'd paid a visit to Johannesburg to see the fossils. "Lee just hasn't found it yet."

But water would inevitably have washed rubble, plant material, and other debris into the fossil chamber along with the bones, and they simply aren't there. "There isn't a lot of subjectivity here," said Eric Roberts, a geologist from James Cook University in Australia, svelte enough to have examined the chamber himself. "The sediments don't lie."

Disposal of the dead brings closure for the living, confers respect on the departed, or abets their transition to the next life. Such sentiments are a hallmark of humanity. But *H. naledi*, Berger emphatically stresses, was not human—which makes the behavior all the more intriguing.

"It's an animal that appears to have had the cognitive ability to recognize its separation from nature," he said.

The mysteries of what *H. naledi* is, and how its bones got into the cave, are inextricably knotted with the question of how old those bones are—and for the moment no one knows. In East Africa, fossils can be accurately dated when they are found above or below layers of volcanic ash, whose age can be measured from the clocklike decay of radioactive elements in the ash. At Malapa, Berger had gotten lucky: The *A. sediba* bones lay between two flowstones—thin layers of calcite deposited by running water—that could also be dated radiometrically. But the bones in the Rising Star chamber were just lying on the cave floor or buried in shallow, mixed sediments. When they got into the cave is an even more intractable problem to solve than how.

Most of the workshop scientists fretted over how their analysis would be received without a date attached. (As it turned out, the lack of a date would prove to be one impediment to a quick publication of the scientific papers describing the finds.) But Berger wasn't bothered one bit. If *H. naledi* eventually proved to be as old as its morphology suggested, then he had quite possibly found the root of the *Homo* family tree. But if the new species turned out to be much younger, the repercussions could be equally profound. It could mean that while our own species was evolving, a separate, small-brained, more primitive-looking *Homo* was loose on the landscape, as recently as anyone dared to contemplate. A hundred thousand years ago? Fifty thousand? Ten thousand? As the exhilarating workshop came to an end with that fundamental question still unresolved, Berger was sanguine as always. "No matter what the age, it will have tremendous impact," he said, shrugging.

A few weeks later, in August of last year, he traveled to East Africa. To mark the occasion of the 50th anniversary of Louis Leakey's description of *H. habilis*, Richard Leakey had summoned the leading thinkers on early human evolution to a symposium at the Turkana Basin Institute, the research center he (along with the State University of New York at Stony Brook) had established near the western shore of Lake Turkana in Kenya.

The purpose of the meeting was to try to come to some consensus over the confounding record of early *Homo*, without grandstanding or rancor—two vices endemic to paleoanthropology. Some of Lee Berger's harshest critics would be there, including some who'd written scathing reviews of his interpretation of the *A. sediba* fossils. To them, he was an outsider at best, a hype artist at worst. Some threatened not to attend if he were there. But given the Rising Star discovery, Leakey could hardly not invite him.

"There's no one on Earth finding fossils like Lee is now," Leakey said.

For four days the scientists huddled together in a spacious lab room, its casement windows open to the breezes, casts of all the important evidence for early *Homo* spread out on tables. One morning Meave Leakey (who's also a *National Geographic* explorer-in-residence) opened a vault to reveal brand-new specimens found on the east side of the lake, including a nearly complete foot. When it was his turn to speak, Bill Kimbel of the Institute of Human Origins described a new *Homo* jaw from Ethiopia dated to 2.8 million years ago—the oldest member of our genus yet. Archaeologist Sonia Harmand of Stony Brook University dropped an even bigger bombshell—the discovery of dozens of crude stone tools near Lake Turkana dating to 3.3 million years ago. If stone tools originated half a million years before the first appearance of our genus, it would

be hard to argue anymore that the defining characteristic of *Homo* was its technological ingenuity.

Berger meanwhile was uncommonly subdued, adding little to the discussion, until the topic turned to a comparison of *A. sediba* and *H. habilis*. It was time.

"More of interest perhaps to this debate is Rising Star," he offered. For the next 20 minutes he laid out all that had happened—the serendipitous discovery of the cave, the crash analysis in June, and the gist of its findings. While he talked, a couple of casts of Rising Star skulls were passed hand to hand.

Then came the questions. Have you done a cranio-dental analysis? Yes. The *H. naledi* skull and teeth place it in a group with *Homo erectus*, *Neanderthals*, and modern humans. Closer to *H. erectus* than *H. habilis* is? Yes. Are there any tooth marks on the bones from carnivores? No, these are the healthiest dead individuals you'll ever see. Have you made progress on the dating? Not yet. We'll get a date sometime. Don't worry.

Then, when the questions were over, the gathered doyens did something no one expected, least of all Berger. They applauded.

When a major new find is made in human evolution—or even a minor new find—it's common to claim it overturns all previous notions of our ancestry. Perhaps having learned from past mistakes, Berger doesn't make such assertions for *Homo naledi*—at least not yet, with its place in time uncertain. He doesn't claim he has found the earliest *Homo*, or that his fossils return the title of "Cradle of Humankind" from East to South Africa. The fossils do suggest, however, that both regions, and everywhere in between, may harbor clues to a story that is more complicated than the metaphor "human family tree" would suggest.

"What naledi says to me is that you may think the record is complete enough to make up stories, and it's not," said Stony Brook's Fred Grine. Maybe early species of *Homo* emerged in South Africa and then moved up to East Africa. "Or maybe it's the other way around."

Berger himself thinks the right metaphor for human evolution, instead of a tree branching from a single root, is a braided stream: a river that divides into channels, only to merge again downstream. Similarly, the various hominin types that inhabited the landscapes of Africa must at some point have diverged from a common ancestor. But then farther down the river of time they may have coalesced again, so that we, at the river's mouth, carry in us today a bit of East Africa, a bit of South Africa, and a whole lot of history we have no notion of whatsoever. Because one thing is for sure: If we learned about a completely new form of hominin only because a couple of cavers were skinny enough to fit through a crack in a well-explored South African cave, we really don't have a clue what else might be out there.

Critical Thinking

1. What are the kinds of behavior implied by the mixture of physical characteristics of *H. naledi*?
2. What are the likely as well as the unlikely ways in which the bones of *H. naledi* came to be deposited in the Rising Star Cave?
3. What would be the implications of where *H. naledi* stands in relation to *Homo sapiens* depending upon its age?

Internet References

Evolutionary Demography Group
http://blogs.lshtm.ac.uk/evolutionarydemography/

Evolutionary Demography Society
http://www.evodemos.org/

Fossil Hominids FAQ
www.talkorigins.org/faqs/homs

Institute of Human Origins
http://iho.asu.edu/node/27

Article   Prepared by: Elvio Angeloni

Who Apes Whom?

FRANS DE WAAL

Learning Outcomes

After reading this article, you will be able to:

- Discuss the "teleological view" fostered by *Homo naledi* and why we should not necessarily put it on an evolutionary branch that led to us.

- Discuss the notion that there is no single point at which our ancestors became human.

The fabulous find, named *Homo naledi,* has rightly been celebrated for both the number of fossils and their completeness. It has *australopithecine*-like hips and an ape-size brain, yet its feet and teeth are typical of the genus *Homo.*

The mixed features of these prehistoric remains upset the received human origin story, according to which bipedalism ushered in technology, dietary change and high intelligence. Part of the new species' physique lags behind this scenario, while another part is ahead. It is aptly called a mosaic species.

We like the new better than the old, though, and treat every fossil as if it must fit somewhere on a timeline leading to the crown of creation. Chris Stringer, a prominent British paleoanthropologist who was not involved in the study, told BBC News: "What we are seeing is more and more species of creatures that suggests that nature was experimenting with how to evolve humans, thus giving rise to several different types of human-like creatures originating in parallel in different parts of Africa."

This represents a shockingly teleological view, as if natural selection is seeking certain outcomes, which it is not. It doesn't do so any more than a river seeks to reach the ocean.

News reports spoke of a "new ancestor," even a "new human species," assuming a ladder heading our way, whereas what we are actually facing when we investigate our ancestry is a tangle of branches. There is no good reason to put *Homo naledi* on the branch that produced us. Nor does this make the discovery any less interesting.

Every species in our lineage tells us something about ourselves, because the hominoids (humans, apes and everything in between) are genetically extremely tight. We have had far less time to diverge than the members of many other animal families, like the equids (horses, zebras, donkeys) or canids (wolves, dogs, jackals). If it hadn't been for the human ego, taxonomists would long ago have squeezed all hominoids into a single genus.

The standard story is that our ancestors first left the apes behind to become *australopithecines*, which grew more sophisticated and brainier to become us. But what if these stages were genetically mixed up? Some scientists have claimed early hybridization between human and ape DNA. Did our ancestors, after having split off, keep returning to the apes in the same way that today's grizzlies and polar bears still interbreed occasionally?

Instead of looking forward to a glorious future, our lineage may have remained addicted to the hairy embrace of its progenitors. Other scientists, however, keep sex out of it and speak of incomplete lineage separation. Either way, our heritages are closely intertwined.

The problem is that we keep assuming that there is a point at which we became human. This is about as unlikely as there being a precise wavelength at which the color spectrum turns from orange into red. The typical proposition of how this happened is that of a mental breakthrough—a miraculous spark—that made us radically different. But if we have learned anything from more than 50 years of research on chimpanzees and other intelligent animals, it is that the wall between human and animal cognition is like a Swiss cheese.

We know, for example, that apes plan ahead. They carry tools over long distances to places where they use them, sometimes up to five different sticks and twigs to raid a bee nest or probe for underground ants. In the lab, they fabricate tools in anticipation of future use. Animals think without words, as do we most of the time.

Undeterred by *Homo naledi*'s relatively small brain, however, the research team sought to stress its humanity by pointing at the bodies in the cave. But if taking this tack implies that only humans mourn their dead, the distinction with apes is being drawn far too sharply.

Apes appear to be deeply affected by the loss of others to the point of going totally silent, seeking comfort from bystanders and going into a funk during which they don't eat for days. They may not inter their dead, but they do seem to understand death's irreversibility. After having stared for a long time at a lifeless companion—sometimes grooming or trying to revive him or her—apes move on.

Since they never stay in one place for long, they have no reason to cover or bury a corpse. Were they to live in a cave or settlement, however, they might notice that carrion attracts scavengers, some of which are formidable predators, like hyenas. It would absolutely not exceed the ape's mental capacity to solve this problem by either covering odorous corpses or moving them out of the way.

The suggestion by some scholars that this requires belief in an afterlife is pure speculation. We simply don't know if *Homo naledi* buried corpses with care and concern or unceremoniously dumped them into a faraway cave to get rid of them.

It is an odd coincidence that "naledi" is an anagram of "denial." We are trying way too hard to deny that we are modified apes. The discovery of these fossils is a major paleontological breakthrough. Why not seize this moment to overcome our anthropocentrism and recognize the fuzziness of the distinctions within our extended family? We are one rich collection of mosaics, not only genetically and anatomically, but also mentally.

Critical Thinking

1. Using *Homo naledi* as an example, discuss the teleological view of human evolution as a ladder leading to us versus the notion that our human-like ancestors represent a tangle of branches.
2. How do studies of contemporary apes show that there was no particular point at which our ancestors became human?

Internet References

Animal Intelligence
http://www.animalintelligence.org/

Fossil Hominids FAQ
www.talkorigins.org/faqs/homs

Institute of Human Origins
https://iho.asu.edu/

FRANS DE WAAL, a primatologist and professor of psychology at Emory University, is the author of the forthcoming book *Are We Smart Enough to Know How Smart Animals Are?*

Article
Prepared by: Elvio Angeloni

Four Legs Good, Two Legs Fortuitous:
Brains, Brawn, and the Evolution of Human Bipedalism

DANIEL E. LIEBERMAN

Learning Outcomes

After reading this article, you will be able to:

- Discuss the concept of "contingency in evolution" in the context of hour our ancestors became bipedal.

- Understand the shifting environment circumstances in which our ancestors became bipedal.

- Discuss "persistence hunting" as a key adaptation in the evolution of modern humanity.

O n The Origin of Species, the greatest achievement in the history of biological thought is remarkably silent on the evolution of one important species: Homo sapiens. Darwin was understandably reticent to speculate in The Origin on the role of natural selection in human evolution. One reason was tactical. To many of his readers, it was difficult enough to accept the idea that an agentless process, rather than divine creation, was responsible for the diversity of various plants and nonhuman animals. Going the next step to suggest that humans arose in a similar manner, rather than at the hand of the Divine Creator (and in His image), would have been far too radical. Another reason for Darwin's silence on human evolution was ignorance. Although Darwin had amassed much information on variation and evolutionary change in all sorts of living things, he had very few facts at his disposal about what happened during the evolution of the human species. In 1859, it was clearly premature to address the topic directly. By 1871, Darwin had changed his mind. His next book, *The Descent of Man and Selection in Relation to Sex*, grapples directly with many aspects of human evolution, notably evidence that humans are related to other mammals,

the nature of human variation, and the evolution of intelligence and morality. The book is largely an effort to demonstrate that humans evolved through the same mechanisms as other animals, and little of The Descent addresses what events actually occurred in human evolution—and for good reason. By 1871, a few fossil Neanderthals had been discovered, as had stone tools associated with extinct mammals, but Darwin and his contemporaries knew almost nothing about the intermediate evolutionary stages between humans and nonhuman primates. In spite of this ignorance, Darwin made a number of prescient speculations. For one, following T. H. Huxley and others, he reasoned that humans evolved in Africa and were most closely related to the African great apes. In addition, Darwin also inferred that the origin of bipedal locomotion was a key initial event that set humans on a separate evolutionary trajectory from our ape cousins. In his words (Darwin, 1871:140–142):

Man alone has become a biped; and we can, I think, partly see how he has come to assume his erect attitude, which forms one of his most conspicuous characters. Man could not have attained his present dominant position in the world without the use of his hands, which are so admirably adapted to act in obedience to his will . . . . But the hands and arms could hardly have become perfect enough to have manufactured weapons, or to have hurled stones and spears with a true aim, as long as they were habitually used for locomotion and for supporting the whole weight of the body, or, as before remarked, so long as they were especially fitted for climbing trees . . . . If it be an advantage to man to stand firmly on his feet and to have his hands and arms free, of which, from his pre-eminent success in the battle of life, there can be no doubt, then I can see no reason why it should not have been advantageous to the progenitors of man to have become more and more erect or bipedal. They would thus have been better able to defend themselves with stones or clubs, to attack their prey, or otherwise to obtain food. The best built individuals would in the long run have succeeded best and have survived in larger numbers.

In other words, contrary to what the animals in George Orwell's Animal Farm initially proclaim, "Four legs good, two legs bad," Darwin reasoned that, under the right circumstances, bipedalism could be a powerful force for evolutionary change by freeing up the hands, thus permitting natural selection to promote tool use and other special human characteristics. Put differently, "Four legs good, two legs fortuitous." Darwin was a famously cautious scientist, loathe to speculate without cause. When he did make unsubstantiated guesses, he was always careful to admit so openly and to provide some justification. So why did Darwin feel comfortable enough to guess, without much evidence, that bipedalism was a key initial driving force in human evolution? There are several answers to this question, but I think the chief one is that any satisfying theory of human evolution must address not only what happened to make humans the way they are but also why humans are so special. It is one thing to speculate on the evolution of the giraffe's long neck or the varied beaks of Galápagos finches, but it is a far taller order to speculate on the origin of human peculiarities. Every species is unique, but we humans tend to be keenly attuned to how our species is astonishingly different from other animals, and we want to understand why. Why, of all the earth's species, do we have such big brains, complex language and culture, the ability to make and use sophisticated tools, to grow food, to build cities, and to exercise dominion over all other creatures? To provide a compelling alternative to creationist myths, Darwin, in 1871, just like his successors today, needed to address how and why natural selection made humans so special. But explaining the evolutionary origin of human uniqueness poses a conundrum for evolutionary biologists. The essence of Darwin's theory is that natural selection is an agentless process by which random, heritable mutations change their frequency from one generation to the next, depending on whether they increase or decrease an organism's odds of reproducing successfully in particular circumstances. How and why did such chance events make humans so special? Darwin's hypothesis that bipedalism was an initial driving force in human evolution is a superb example of the critical role of contingency in evolution. One of Darwin's key insights is that natural selection is a highly contingent process in which evolutionary changes are constrained and/or influenced by prior events. Species evolve differently not only because of their unique environmental circumstances but also because of their particular history. For example, fins evolved in fish to help them swim, but, by chance, they acted occasionally as weight-bearing appendages in certain fish, permitting natural selection to favor one lineage of fish with more limblike fins. Without fins, limbs might never have evolved. And so it

was, thought Darwin, with bipedalism. At some point, natural selection favored an ape that stood upright, thus emancipating its hands to carry objects and to make tools. These capabilities, in turn, favored early humans that had larger brains, hence more advanced linguistic and cognitive abilities. In short, Darwin's speculation was that, without bipedalism, humans might never have evolved.

When Did Hominins and Bipedalism First Arise?

It has taken more than 100 years to amass sufficient evidence to test Darwin's hypothesis, and, until the last few years, most of the strongest clues about human origins have been genetic and comparative rather than fossil. Since Darwin's day, anatomical studies have indicated that humans are most closely related to the African great apes (chimpanzees, bonobos, and gorillas). Given the many similarities between chimpanzees, bonobos, and gorillas, it was reasonable to infer that the great apes were more closely related to each other than to humans. However, an avalanche of genetic evidence from the last 20 years has proven this tree to be wrong, with important consequences for thinking about human origins. We now know that humans, chimpanzees, and bonobos are more closely related to each other than any of those three species are to gorillas. Further, by calibrating the lengths of the tree's branches against known fossil dates, we can estimate that the chimp and human lineages diverged sometime between 5 and 10 million years ago, and that gorillas diverged from the human–chimp lineage several million years before that. Our closer relationship to the chimpanzees is profoundly important because it means that the last common ancestor (LCA) of humans and chimpanzees must have resembled the African great apes in many ways. The basis for this inference is that gorillas and chimpanzees are remarkably similar: they share a unique, distinctive mode of terrestrial locomotion (knuckle-walking), and they are very similar to each other both behaviorally and anatomically, with most of their differences deriving from the effects of size. If one enlarges a chimpanzee skeleton, preserving the scaling relationships between size and shape, then one gets something that looks very much like a gorilla. Given that the many similarities shared by chimpanzees and gorillas are unlikely to have evolved independently, we can reliably infer that the LCA of these two species must have resembled in terms of anatomy a chimpanzee or a gorilla (which amounts to much the same thing), and that the LCA of chimpanzees and humans must have been more or less the same. In other words, it is a good bet that the first hominins (defined as a species more closely related to humans than to chimpanzees) evolved from a knuckle-walking LCA that bore some morphological resemblance to a chimpanzee. That said, it is unlikely the LCA was exactly like a chimpanzee. Knowing something about the LCA permits us to ask how different the first hominins were from the LCA of humans and chimpanzees. Were these hominins bipedal or were they different in other ways? Efforts to answer this question have been controversial, in large part because of differences of opinion on how to interpret the fossil record of early hominins, particularly the australopiths. The first known species of Australopithecus, A. africanus, was discovered in 1924 in South Africa by Raymond Dart. At the time, few scientists believed that A. africanus was a hominin because its small brain did not accord with the Piltdown forgery. This infamous forgery (a partial orangutan jaw whose teeth were filed down, mixed with fragments of a human cranial vault that had been stained and broken to make them appear to be ancient) supplied Edwardian "experts" with just what they were looking for: evidence that big brains had evolved early in human evolution, and that humans had originated in England. However, Dart's initial discovery was soon followed by many other fossil finds in Southern and Eastern Africa. By the 1970s we knew of at least four early hominin species, some more gracile, others more robust. The oldest and most primitive of these australopiths, A. afarensis (made famous by the partial skeleton known as Lucy), dates back to between three and four million years ago. Importantly, the australopiths were chimpanzee-like in many ways (they had big incisors, a long snout, and a small brain), but they also provided unambiguous evidence for habitual bipedalism. Key evidence for bipedalism (shown in Figure 3) included a lumbar curve that positions the upper body above, rather than in front of, the hips; femurs that angle inward so that the knees are more centrally positioned than the hips; hips that curve to the side, permitting the muscles along the side of the pelvis to stabilize the body's center of gravity when one foot is on the ground; and humanlike feet with robust heels, a large big toe partly in line with the other toes, and a partial arch. Even more definitive evidence that australopiths were habitually bipedal came from the spectacular 3.6 million-year-old trackway of footprints that Mary Leakey discovered at Laetoli, Tanzania. The chimpanzee-like nature of the australopiths, combined with evidence that they were bipedal, supported Darwin's hypothesis that bipedalism came first in human evolution. There were two big problems, however, with this inference. First, the oldest australopiths known prior to the 1990s were all less than 4 million years old. If chimpanzees and hominins diverged between 5 and 10 million years ago, then approximately 2 million to 6 million years of evolution were still unaccounted for by the fossil record. In addition, reappraisal of australopith fossils suggested that, although these hominins were bipeds, they were bipedal in ways substantially different from modern humans, because they retained many primitive features that would have

improved their ability to climb trees, some of which might have compromised their ability to walk efficiently. Among the many arboreal adaptations evident in such australopiths as Lucy were long, curved toes in both the hands and the feet; relatively short legs, combined with relatively long arms; somewhat more mobile ankles; and feet that had only a partial arch. To this day, a vigorous debate continues over whether australopiths walked with a slightly bent-hip and bent-knee gait, or more like you and me, with a long, striding gait. Regardless of how, exactly, the australopiths walked and climbed, several exciting new discoveries from the last decade have pushed the hominin fossil record back much closer to the time of the LCA. Darwin, no doubt, would have been delighted by these finds, which include remains of four new species (currently assigned to three different genera): Ardipithecus ramidus, Ardipithecus kadabba, Orrorin tugenensis, and Sahelanthropus tchadensis. Of these, Sahelanthropus tchadensis is especially exciting. Discovered in Chad in 2001 by an intrepid team led by Michel Brunet, this species includes a nearly complete cranium (nicknamed Toumaï) along with some teeth and jaw fragments, dated to between 6 and 7.2 million years ago. Sahelanthropus thus falls within the predicted time range of the chimpanzee–human divergence. Not surprisingly, Toumaï's cranium is ape-like in many ways, but it differs unmistakably from chimpanzee and gorilla crania in several features shared with other, later hominins: it has smaller canines; larger, thicker cheek teeth; and a somewhat forward-positioned foramen magnum oriented downward rather than backward. When Toumaï (which was a likely male) was looking forward—as animals typically do—his neck would have been vertical like a biped's (see Figure 4). Not enough has yet been published about Orrorin (which dates from 6 million years ago in Kenya), but recently we have learned much more about Ardipithecus ramidus, a younger species dated to about 4.4 million years ago in Ethiopia. Ardipithecus ramidus has a cranium very much like Sahelanthropus with a downwardly pointing foramen magnum suggestive of bipedalism, along with slightly smaller canines and somewhat bigger, thicker cheek teeth than chimpanzees. The rest of the skeleton of Ardipithecus, however, is very primitive, including an ape-like foot with long curved toes and a highly divergent big toe. Just what kind of biped it was remains to be seen.

Why Be Bipedal?

As far as we can tell, the earliest known hominins resembled chimpanzees in many respects, and they differed in just a few ways, such as smaller canines; bigger, flatter, and thicker cheek teeth; and, crucially, being bipedal. These differences raise many questions, including why early hominins were bipedal and what the evolutionary consequences of becoming bipedal might have been. Again, contingency plays a central role in the answer to both questions because bipedalism appears to be a special solution to some particular problems posed by being a knuckle-walker. Knuckle-walking, the manner in which chimpanzees and gorillas walk on the middle digits of their hands, is a classic example of the kinds of compromise solutions that evolution can favor, given the right conditions. Like their cousins, orangutans and gibbons, chimpanzees and gorillas evolved from frugivorous apes that were well adapted to hanging below the branches of trees—thanks to several specialized features, such as highly mobile shoulders, elongated arms, flexible wrists, and long, curved fingers. At some point, chimps and gorillas apparently re-evolved a unique form of quadrupedalism, knuckle-walking, which is really a way of walking on all four limbs while retaining features in their shoulders, forelimbs, and hands that are useful for climbing and hanging. Knuckle-walking enables chimps to be spectacular arboreal athletes while also permitting them to trek across the forest in search of areas with more plentiful food. But knuckle-walking has an energetic cost. Experiments that measure the cost of transport (the amount of oxygen consumed per unit of body mass to move a given distance) find that knuckle-walking by chimpanzees is about 75 percent more expensive than either normal quadrupedalism or bipedalism. This cost is not very significant to chimpanzees, who typically trek only 2 to 3 km per day, but it would have been very costly to apes that needed to travel longer distances. Under such circumstances, there probably would have been strong selection against knuckle-walking. Which brings us back to bipedalism and the earliest hominins. We will never know precisely why the earliest bipeds stood up—perhaps they did so to feed on fruits on branches and in bushes—but we can guess that, at some point, a group of early hominins found themselves in a habitat that required them to travel longer distances but also to remain adept at climbing trees. Under these conditions, hominins with such features as lumbar spines that were more curved, hips that faced more laterally, and extended hips and knees that were better suited to a bipedal gait, would have had a selective advantage over hominins trying to trek long distances with a more ape-like anatomy. This scenario is difficult, perhaps impossible, to test definitively, but is supported by the few lines of evidence so far available. First, all of the earliest hominins (Sahelanthropus, Ardipithecus, and Orrorin) appear to have lived in woodland habitats that were apparently more open than the forests typically inhabited by chimpanzees and gorillas. In addition, selection for bipedal locomotion to forage efficiently for more widely dispersed foods accords with the derived dental characteristics of the first hominins. As noted above, early hominins also differ from chimps in having bigger, thicker cheek teeth as well as smaller canines. Studies of dental functional morphology show that bigger, thicker molars

and premolars are useful for chewing harder, tougher foods that require more forceful grinding. Chimps have thinner, smaller molar teeth because they feed primarily on a diet of high-quality fruit. Chimps also have large canines, which are useful for fighting, but such canines restrict how much they can move their jaws from side to side when grinding food with their back teeth. Viewed together, all of the derived features evident in the earliest hominins point to a suite of adaptations for an ape-like animal that occasionally had to range more widely to find and to chew tougher, harder food than chimps typically eat.

Early Homo, and the Downside to Standing Upright

Darwin was characteristically prescient when he speculated that upright locomotion evolved early in human evolution—but what of the rest of his theory, that emancipating the arms and hands from terrestrial locomotion set the stage for future developments? Darwin was well aware of the pitfalls of viewing evolution as a teleological process in which past events inevitably lead to present conditions. Bipedalism may have been a critical precursor to the evolution of big brains, toolmaking, and other hallmark features of humankind, but these developments cannot have been inexorable consequences of an upright posture. Indeed, what little we know suggests that the early hominin way of life, once evolved, persisted with only minor variations for at least 4 million years. After Sahelanthropus and Ardipithecus, more than a half dozen species of different australopiths evolved, but the differences between them are not very extensive, and mostly reflect anatomical features involved in mastication. For the most part, the australopiths lived in woodland habitats and frequently ate fruits, but they probably also ventured out into more open habitats, either to travel long distances between patches of woods, or perhaps to dig up tubers and other foods unavailable in forest and woodland habitats. Unfortunately, the hominin fossil record is very poor between 3 million and 2 million years ago, but we do know that the genus Homo evolved sometime during this period. Many details remain obscure, but we can characterize the major features of this transformation by comparing H. erectus, which followed the transition, with earlier australopith species. Australopiths vary to some extent, but they were generally the size of chimpanzees (25–50 kg in weight and 100–150 cm tall), with relatively long arms, short legs, and, as noted above, retaining many adaptations for climbing trees. Australopiths also had small brains, ranging from 400 to 550 cm3, and they had big, thick, cheek teeth that were set in large, muscular faces well adapted for chewing hard, tough foods. H. erectus remains, which first appear 1.9 million years ago, vary considerably, but they generally have larger brains, ranging from 600 cm^3 to 900 cm^3, along with bigger bodies, with body masses ranging from 45 kg to 70 kg and heights ranging from 150 cm to 185 cm. In addition, H. erectus had smaller, thinner cheek teeth set in a vertical, less snoutlike face and a much more modern body with long legs and short arms poorly suited for climbing, but better suited for long-distance trekking and running. H. erectus was a long-enduring and widespread species that dispersed out of Africa and into Eurasia by 1.8 million years ago, and it persisted in Asia until quite recently, maybe less than 50,000 years ago. It is important to recognize, however, that the derived features evident in H. erectus did not evolve all at once, and the transformation from Australopithecus to Homo was complex in nature. Early individuals of H. erectus were highly variable, and along with their likely ancestor, H. habilis, displayed a mixture of primitive australopith features, especially in its postcranium, as well as more derived cranial and dental features. The first appearance of the genus Homo corresponds very approximately to the first appearance of stone tools, around 2.6 million years ago. No doubt many factors selected for the transition from Australopithecus to Homo, but changing environments probably played a major role. Gradual cooling over the last 5 million years was responsible for a general trend in Africa of shrinking forests and expanding savannas, but there is evidence that the pace of these changes increased after 3 million years ago. As more open habitats became more prevalent, the genus Homo apparently evolved a new way of life that was more energy intensive. Key evidence for this shift comes from the unusual combination of bigger bodies and bigger brains along with smaller teeth. As a rule, metabolic costs scale to body mass to the power of 0.75, which means that larger-bodied H. erectus individuals would have needed absolutely more calories per day than australopiths, although they would have needed relatively fewer calories per unit body mass. Bigger brains were also a major added cost because brain is one of the most expensive tissues in the body, consuming 20 kcal/kg/h, about 20 times the energy cost of muscle tissue. In practical terms, this means that the human brain consumes approximately 20–25 percent of an adult's metabolism and as much as 50 percent of an infant's. Increased energetic demands in H. erectus were especially onerous for reproducing females, who not only had to supply their own energetic needs but also the energetic needs of their infants. Daily energy requirements for gestating and lactating mothers increase by 25 percent and 50 percent, respectively. According to estimates by Aiello and Key (2002), a nursing H. erectus mother would have needed to eat about 2,500 kcal per day, about 800 kcal more than a nursing australopith. How did H. erectus mothers obtain this extra energy? Most animals cope with increasing energetic demands by taking advantage of scaling laws. Because basal metabolic rates scale to body mass to the power of 0.75, bigger animals

have relatively slower rates of metabolism and can lengthen the time it takes for food to pass through their guts, thereby making use of fermentation processes in the gut to digest foods of lower quality and with a higher content of fiber. These principles account for why gorillas can eat a more fibrous and less fruit-rich diet than smaller-bodied chimpanzees. H. erectus, however, did not employ this strategy, as we can tell from its relatively smaller chewing muscles and the smaller, thinner teeth compared with Australopithecus. Instead of getting more energy by eating foods of lower quality, H. erectus appears to have been more reliant on foods of higher quality that required less energy to chew. Since fruits are not abundant in the savanna, and cooking was probably not invented until fire was first controlled by hominins less than 750,000 years ago, the major source of high-quality food was animal tissue: meat, marrow, and brains. The archaeological record provides corroborating evidence that Homo species became carnivores of sorts. By 2.6 million years ago, hominins were making simple stone tools, getting access to animal carcasses (perhaps initially by scavenging), and then extracting marrow and cutting meat off bones. By 1.8 million years ago, H. erectus was able to hunt big animals, such as wildebeest and kudu.

Brains, Brawn, and Endurance Running

The problem of how early Homo species become hunters brings us back to the topic of bipedal locomotion. In particular, it is useful to consider some of the constraints and opportunities of being a carnivorous, bipedal primate. Most carnivores hunt using a mixture of stealth and power, ultimately relying on speed, agility, and force to overcome their prey. In this respect, having only two legs would have posed a problem for an unprepossessing early hominin hunter. Bipedal walking and running may be less costly than knuckle-walking, but bipeds cannot gallop and thus can run only comparatively slowly. Today, the world's fastest humans can sprint approximately 10 meters per second for only about 20 to 30 seconds, not nearly fast enough or long enough to keep up with most quadrupeds, most of whom can easily run faster than 15 meters per second for several minutes. In addition, bipeds are much less stable and less maneuverable than quadrupeds (as anyone who has tried to chase a dog well knows). Because of these constraints, most paleoanthropologists have assumed that bipedal hominin hunters were able to compensate for these deficiencies by using tools and having the ability to throw. Until recently, human hunters relied on such technologies as the bow and arrow, nets, and the spear thrower. And, as Darwin (1871) argued in The Descent of Man and Selection in Relation to Sex, such adaptations were probably contingent upon bipedalism, which freed up the hands and arms from a role in locomotion, permitting natural selection to modify them for other uses. But there is one problem with this deeply entrenched idea: it turns out that effective projectile weapons were invented only fairly recently. The bow and arrow and the spear thrower first appear less than 100,000 years ago, and the first stone spearheads were invented between 200,000 and 300,000 years ago. According to the archaeological record, the most lethal technology available to a H. erectus hunter 2 million years ago was a club or a sharpened wooden stick. To those of us who forage in supermarkets (hunting at most for bargains), this fact may seem unremarkable, but untipped spears pose several challenges that make them unsuitable weapons for even the most foolhardy and desperate of hunters. Untipped wooden spears have a limited ability to penetrate an animal's hide when thrown, and, even if they do penetrate the hide, they seldom cause death because, unlike spearheads, untipped spears rarely cause lacerations and internal bleeding. Thus, early hominin hunters who wished to kill large animals with untipped spears probably would have had to get up very close to the animals and risk being gored or kicked by their prey. No experienced modern hunter is so foolhardy, and one can easily imagine that such risky behaviors would dramatically lower any early Homo hunter's fitness, quickly selecting against them. So to answer the question, "How did early hominins hunt?," we need to return to the issue of contingency and the power of natural selection to favor novel solutions using whatever variations are at its disposal. As noted above, once hominins became bipedal, they gave up speed in order to be more economical. Indeed, the obvious fact that humans lack speed and power when compared with most animals is deeply rooted in our psyche. Many creation myths tell stories about how we humans have triumphed over nature, red in tooth and claw, by using our superior wits. Darwin (1871, p. 157) also believed in this idea: "The slight corporeal strength of man, his little speed, his want of natural weapons, etc., are more than counterbalanced, firstly by his intellectual powers, through which he has, whilst remaining in a barbarous state, formed for himself weapons and tools, etc., and secondly by his social qualities which lead him to give aid to his fellow-men and to receive it in return." Put simply, by becoming bipedal, hominins were set on a trajectory that favored brains over brawn. I am loathe to disagree with Darwin, but I think the notion that humans became hunters through the triumph of brains over brawn is partly wrong for several reasons. The first is that large brains and sophisticated weapons did not evolve until later in human evolution. Brain size in early Homo species is a little bigger than in Australopithecus species, but so is body size, keeping the ratio of brain to body size about the same in early H. erectus and Australopithecus. In addition, although

humans are slow and lack power compared with most mammals, humans are actually remarkable endurance athletes, particularly when running long distances in high heat. Such endurance athleticism is actually quite rare in the animal world. Most mammals, even dogs and horses, can trot for long distances, but they cannot gallop for long because quadrupeds cannot pant while galloping. Unless it is very cold, galloping quadrupeds overheat rapidly. In contrast, humans are able to run under aerobic capacity in the heat for hours on end at speeds up to 6 m/s, well above the trot-to-gallop transition speed of most mammals, even large quadrupeds weighing as much as 500 kg. Humans can actually outrun horses over long distances, such as the marathon (42 km), especially in hot weather. The superb endurance running capabilities of humans are hardly a fluke, but, instead, derive from a suite of novel features. Many of these features are such musculoskeletal adaptations as long legs, a large gluteus maximus muscle, and long tendons in our legs that help us to run with a bounding, springy gait that is the biomechanical basis for energy exchange during running. (When running, we use our legs as springs, first storing and then releasing elastic energy in the tendons and muscles of our legs.) As my colleague Dennis Bramble and I have argued, many of these features first appear in Homo erectus and play no role in walking, which uses a different, pendular form of mechanics. In addition, humans are unique among mammals in being able to thermoregulate effectively by sweating. We are the champion sweaters of the animal world, thanks to our absence of fur and a many-fold increase in the number of eccrine glands (2 to 5 million) that we have all over our bodies. We do not yet know when sweating and furlessness evolved, but my prediction is that it occurred at least 2 million years ago. The evolution of running capabilities in humans in combination with the origins of meat eating raises the hypothesis that H. erectus evolved endurance capabilities—brawn of a special sort—in order to compete with other carnivores and, thus, to pay for bigger bodies and bigger brains. The hypothesis is that, long before the invention of the bow and arrow, H. erectus became the first diurnal, endurance-running carnivore by practicing a special form of predation called persistence hunting. During persistence hunts, hunters chase an animal above its trot-to-gallop transition speed during the middle of the day when it is hot. Because the prey cannot pant while galloping, it quickly overheats as it runs from the hunter. Like the tortoise chasing the hare, the hunter keeps coming, tracking the animal whenever it hides. And the faster the hunter can track his prey, the less time the animal has in which to cool itself down between bouts of galloping. Eventually, usually in 10 to 15 km, the exhausted prey collapses from hyperthermia and the hunter can kill it safely with nothing more than a simple spear or a club. All a H. erectus hunter would have needed was a good drink of water before (and after) he started running, and a hot, open habitat in which to chase his prey. Further, persistence hunting is not very costly when compared with its potential returns. The cost of transport (kcal/kg/km) for running at endurance speeds is only about 30–40 percent higher than walking, so chasing an animal for 15 km costs a hunter only about 1,100 kcal, about 300 more kcal than walking the same distance. According to ethnographic accounts by Louis Liebenberg, persistence hunting is remarkably effective (50 percent of persistence hunts by Bushmen in the Kalahari desert are successful) and was practiced until recently by hunter-gatherers in many hot, arid parts of the world, such as Africa, America, and Australia. Persistence hunting is rare today not because it is ineffective but because it has been rendered unnecessary by such recently invented technologies as the bow and arrow, nets, hunting dogs, and guns. Why run 10–15 km to kill an animal when you can shoot it or buy it shrink-wrapped at the butcher's shop? In short, walking was initially very important in human evolution, but, at some point, running also became important by enabling hominins to become carnivores. Although traces of our history as walkers and runners are abundant in our physiology and anatomy, many aspects of the endurance-running hypothesis are difficult to test. Although a number of musculoskeletal features that would have enabled hominins to run long distances were first evident in fossil remains attributed to Homo erectus, many key adaptations, such as greater tendon length or the elaboration of sweat glands, are hard to assess from fossil evidence. Therefore, we do not know if H. erectus was as good at endurance running, hence persistence hunting, as modern humans. In addition, although archaeological traces suggest that H. erectus hunters were able to kill medium- to large-sized animals, we don't actually know how those animals were hunted. That said, the endurance-running hypothesis not only explains how early hominins could have hunted such big animals as wildebeest armed with nothing more lethal than a sharpened wooden stick or a club, but it also accounts for why humans apparently evolved the ability to run long distances in the midday sun. In addition, the hypothesis also explains another important fact—namely, that the increase in brain size in human evolution occurred well after hominids became proficient hunters. The first individuals of H. erectus had brains between 600 cm^3 and 900 cm^3, but, by a million years ago, H. erectus brains were larger than 1000 cm^3. It is reasonable to speculate that the evolution of endurance-running capabilities, which permitted persistence hunting, released a constraint on the size of the brain, a costly organ to grow and to maintain. In turn, bigger brains set the stage for the evolution of our own species, H. sapiens, in Africa sometime in the last 300,000 years. But that's another story.

Final Thoughts and Future Directions

To some, the idea of evolution is most threatening because it leads one to realize that the world around us is really the result of innumerable chance events, many of them contingent upon previous chance events. It follows that, although we humans are indeed a special species with dozens of unusual features and traits that make us unique in myriad ways, those qualities evolved for no particular reason, other than through the cold calculus of natural selection. Further, the characteristics that make us human and have given us some measure of dominion over the other animals and plants of the Earth derive from a long chain of fortuitous occurrences, each of which set up conditions that made subsequent changes either possible or impossible. After 150 years of concerted research, we know far more than Darwin did about how, when, and why humans evolved, but much of our species' evolutionary history remains unknown or in dispute. The hypothesis recounted above just scratches the surface of what we know and need to explain about human evolution. I have not touched upon the evolution of language, aggression, moral sense, concealed ovulation, and other important aspects of human biology and behavior that make us special. That said, Darwin made some pretty good guesses in The Descent of Man, including the hypothesis that becoming bipedal was one of the first major shifts that helped set our first hominin ancestors off an a new path from the apes. Being bipedal had some advantages over knuckle-walking, reducing costs, and freeing up the hands, but upright locomotion also constrained our ancestors to be slow and awkward creatures. Hence, selection for walking in the earliest hominins appears to have set the stage for final selection for endurance running, which helped species of the genus Homo to become carnivores of sorts, gaining access to high-quality food as the savannas expanded sometime about 2.5 million years ago. Thus, as Darwin speculated, becoming bipedal was one of those chance events that made possible a suite of later shifts, including toolmaking, hunting, bigger brains, language, and the ability to run a marathon. Paradoxically, humans have become essentially sedentary today, in part because the evolution of walking and running helped us to evolve large, complex brains that freed us from the need to walk or run much anymore. Today, many humans walk very little, and few people run except to keep fit. Should civilization collapse tomorrow, few of us would know how to hunt or gather. If and when this collapse occurs, and if our species does not go extinct, then perhaps natural selection will go to work again, this time constrained by a new set of contingencies, many of which will trace back to some knuckle-walking apes about 6 million years ago that could walk better than their cousins.

Suggested Readings

Aiello, L. C., and C. Key. 2002. The energetic consequences of being a Homo erectus female. *Am. J. Hum. Biol.* 14:551–565.

Bramble, D. M., and D. E. Lieberman. 2004. Endurance running and the evolution of Homo. *Nature* 432:345–352.

Darwin, C. 1871. *The Descent of Man, and Selection in Relation to Sex.* John Murray: London.

Liebenberg, L. 2006. Persistence hunting by modern hunter-gatherers. *Curr. Anthropol.* 47:1017–1026.

Lieberman, D. E., D. M. Bramble, D. A. Raichlen, and J. J. Shea. 2007. Endurance running and the tyranny of ethnography. *J. Hum. Evol.* 53:439–444.

Wrangham, R., J. H. Jones, G. Laden, D. Pilbeam, and N. L. Conklin-Brittain. 1999. The raw and the stolen: Cooking and the ecology of human origins. *Curr. Anthropol.* 40:583–584.

Zollikofer, C. P., M. S. Ponce de Leon, D. E. Lieberman, F. Guy, D. Pilbeam, A. Likius, H. T. Mackaye, P. Vignaud, and M. Brunet. 2005. Virtual cranial reconstruction of Sahelanthropus tchadensis. *Nature* 434:755–759.

Critical Thinking

1. What is meant by "contingency in evolution" and how does it apply to the understanding of how humans evolved?

2. What were the most important stages in the development of our species from our primate ancestors and how are these stages documented in the fossil evidence?

3. What is "persistence hunting" and how is it crucial to the understanding of human evolution?

Internet References

Bradshaw Foundation
http://www.bradshawfoundation.com/origins/

Daniel E. Lieberman
https://scholar.harvard.edu/dlieberman/research

Lieberman, Daniel E. "Four Legs Good, Two Legs Fortuitous: Brains, Brawn, and the Evolution of Human Bipedalism," *In the Light of Evolution: Essays from the Laboratory and Field,* January 2011. Copyright ©2011 by Palgrave Macmillan. Used with permission.

Article   Prepared by: Elvio Angeloni

Stone Cold Science

Researchers Develop New Ways to Discover How Our Oldest Tech—and Our Brains—Evolved.

BRIDGET ALEX

Learning Outcomes

After reading this article, you will be able to:

- Discuss the importance of stone tools for the survival of the human lineage.

- Discuss the methods used by archaeologists to determine how stone tools were made and how they were used.

- Discuss the ways in which we differ from other primates and when our unique human traits emerged.

In the Kent State University laboratory for experimental archaeology, the Spot Hogg Hooter Shooter, an automatic bow launcher, fires arrows filmed by high-speed cameras. The arrows are tipped with stone points, which are replicas of ancient artifacts.

The replicas are "worthless . . . so we can break them and use them in ways that we can't with the real artifacts that are priceless," explains archaeologist Metin I. Eren who leads the lab. To better understand ancient stone tools, his team creates facsimiles and tests their mechanical properties.

It's just one of the cutting-edge ways archaeologists study humanity's oldest—and arguably most pivotal—technology. Without stone tools, says Eren, "we wouldn't be the species we are today."

As early as 3.3 million years ago, human ancestors began bashing rocks into tools—a move that set our lineage on a distinct evolutionary path. For the next 99 percent of our time on this planet, our ancestors depended on stones to survive: for hunting, food preparation, constructing clothes, and shelter. While artifacts made of wood and other perishable materials degraded, those made from rock endured. Thus, stone tools provide the richest record of human behavior across time and space. Archaeologists have dug up billions of them.

Every one of those artifacts "has a story. It has a history of the people that made it and used it," says Christian Tryon, an archaeologist at Harvard University. It's just a matter of learning to read the stones.

Make or Break

"Here's the problem: stone tools are the least-familiar things we excavate," says archaeologist John Shea of Stony Brook University. "When you find a pot, you can say it looks like a pot. Or you find a temple. It looks like a temple."

Because stone tools are a forgotten technology, the purpose behind different styles is not self-evident. Scholars in the 19th century devised names, like scraper, point, and burin, based on shape and assumed function. But they had no evidence that scrapers scraped or points impaled.

Unsure how stone tools were used, archaeologists fared better at determining how they were made. Typically, a rock (the hammerstone) was used to strike another rock (the core) to remove a slender piece (the flake) that was further sculpted into the desired form, such as an arrowhead or knife. To ensure the flake fractured with the right proportions, toolmakers often first shaped the core by knocking off scrap pieces in a systematic way.

Researchers deduced these steps through feats of reverse engineering. In the 1894 book *Man, the Primeval Savage*, Worthington G. Smith reported his efforts to reassemble flakes and scraps into their original cores, like 3-D jigsaw puzzles. For three years, he studied 2,259 pieces recovered from a site in England, managing to rejoin more than 500 of them (and concluding that shellac dissolved in spirit was the best adhesive for the job).

Though tedious, this methodology of refitting has proven essential for understanding stone tool production. Some reassembled cores have dozens of pieces, each a step in a complicated sequence of premeditated maneuvers.

"Making a stone tool is not a random procedure," says Tryon.

It's not easy, either. Every year Tryon teaches archaeology undergrads basic toolmaking; the students struggle to produce forms perfected long ago by human ancestors.

"Most people think you need to beat the hell out of these things," says Tryon. "That it requires brute strength. It does not. It's more finesse . . . It's rhythm. It's gesture."

The Point of It All

Eren started making stone tools in college classes, but to become an expert, he trained at the University of Exeter under Bruce Bradley, as well as with Jacques Pelegrin and Robert J. Patten, all renowned for their toolmaking skills. "It was like a true apprenticeship," Eren recalls.

For two years, Eren practiced the craft about eight hours a day—save one day per week, when he restocked his rock supply by hiking the beaches of South England, loading a backpack with 150 pounds of flint.

Now he can create any tool type by hand from the 6,000 pounds of rocks his lab houses, shipped from around the world. When identical copies of tools are required, his team uses lapidary equipment, or rock-cutters, to mass-produce them. This unlimited supply of replicas—"as many as we need for statistical validity," Eren says—enables them to conduct destructive experiments, like firing from the Spot Hogg Hooter Shooter. The goal is to test why tools had certain properties: Was a form preferred because it was aerodynamic, durable, or just in fashion?

Eren recently investigated tools made by early Americans some 13,000 years ago called Clovis points, which have distinctive channel-like divots known as flutes. Based on debris found at archaeological sites, Clovis people broke about 15–20 percent of their points while trying to flute them. The risky habit has perplexed scholars, with some speculating that it was an artistic flourish, a way for toolmakers to show off. But in a study this year in the *Journal of Archaeological Science*, Eren and coauthors found that fluting was practical. Through computer simulations and experiments that included mechanically crushing replicas with controlled force, they showed that flutes provided shock absorption, preventing points from breaking upon impact.

Know Your Gunk

Replication experiments demonstrate what different types of stone tools could have done, but they do not reveal what any particular artifact did. About a decade ago that question drove Gilliane Monnier, an archaeologist at the University of Minnesota, to put an artifact under an electron beam.

"It was clear there was stuff on that tool. I didn't know what kind of stuff, but there was stuff," recalls Monnier. She became intrigued by the possibility that artifacts might preserve particles from softer materials they once contacted, such as animal hides and wood.

Residue analysis got started in the 1970s, but materials were often identified by their visual appearance under a microscope—a highly subjective method. Other approaches, which measured elemental or molecular composition, were considered reliable but destroyed the residues.

Monnier wanted to find an accurate but nondestructive approach. So she began gunking up tools with known substances, the same way our ancestors might have done: whittling wood, slicing roots and grasses, even processing animal parts.

"Getting blood wasn't too difficult in Minnesota," she adds. "I was able to call my butcher, who knows me pretty well now."

Monnier had colleagues perform traditional residue analysis on the objects and found that most residues cannot be visually distinguished with confidence under a normal microscope: in one study, trained researchers misidentified Monnier's modern specimens nearly one in four times.

Since then, Monnier and colleagues have experimented using infrared and other forms of radiation to measure residue composition. Results on modern materials as well as artifacts with known residues have been promising.

In a 2013 study, for example, researchers removed bits of residue from stone points up to 130,000 years old and used a destructive technique to identify the substance as bitumen. This natural tar likely adhered the points to wooden spears that had long since decomposed. That same year, Monnier analyzed some remaining gunk on the same tools with X-ray and infrared beams and also identified bitumen, proving it was possible to do nondestructively.

Having verified her methods, Monnier is eager to analyze unstudied artifacts "and probably get some surprises."

Tooling Around the Brain

Some researchers think stone tools can answer the big questions in human evolution: how do we differ from other primates and when did our unique human traits emerge?

Chimpanzees and some monkeys use tools to a limited extent; they crack open hard-shelled foods with stones as natural hammers and anvils. Prehuman ancestors began breaking rocks to get sharp edges as early as 3.3 million years ago. By 2.6 million years ago, they did so in a standard way, producing what archaeologists call Oldowan tools. But a major innovation transpired around 1.8 million years ago: *Homo erectus* began sculpting rocks into intentional forms, making teardrop-shaped tools known as Acheulean hand axes.

According to Shea, these hand axes were "shaped to be carried efficiently. The average length and width are identical to a Samsung Galaxy 7."

Researchers hypothesize that the technological leap was driven by a cognitive leap, an evolution in brain wiring.

To test this, Shelby Putt, an anthropologist at the Stone Age Institute and Indiana University, compared the brains of modern people making Oldowan and Acheulean tools in a study published earlier this year in *Nature Human Behavior*. As trained volunteers worked stones, they wore caps sprouting wires connected to functional near-infrared spectroscopy. This neuroimaging technique is like MRI but allows subjects to move freely.

When participants made Oldowan tools, brain areas lit up related to vision and movement. Chimps smashing nuts probably engage this level of cognition. Acheulean toolmaking, however, required integration of higher-order regions that are responsible for sensory and motor control, memory, and planning. In fact, it was a brain network nearly identical to what's activated when people play the piano.

"We don't see any chimps playing the piano," says Putt. She believes that Acheulean tools mark a turning point in our evolution from ape-like to human-like brains.

The species that made that turn went extinct long ago, but the stone tools that bore witness to it survive—"the common heritage of all humanity," says Shea.

Bridget Alex is an anthropologist at Harvard University and a frequent contributor to *Discover*.

Critical Thinking

1. How did stone tools contribute to the survival of the human lineage?
2. How do archaeologists determine how ancient stone tools were made and used?
3. What separates humans from other primates in terms of technology and cognition?

Internet References

Fossil Hominids FAQ
www.talkorigins.org/faqs/homs
Institute of Human Origins
http://iho.asu.edu/node/27
Smithsonian National Museum of Natural History
http://humanorigins.si.edu

Article   Prepared by: Elvio Angeloni

The New Origins of Technology

Ancient Stone Tools from Kenya Shatter the Classic Story of When and How Humans Became Innovators.

KATE WONG

Learning Outcomes

After reading this article, you will be able to:

- Discuss the conventional wisdom as to how and under what circumstances our techno dependence began and the evidence that has overturned such a view.

- Explain the greater sophistication as revealed in the Acheulian technology compared to that of the Oldowan.

The desert badlands on the northwestern shores of Kenya's Lake Turkana offer little to the people who live there. Drinking water is elusive, and most of the wild animals have declined to near oblivion. The Turkana scrape by as pastoralists, herding goats, sheep, cattle, donkeys, and the occasional camel in the hot, arid countryside. It is a hard life. But millions of years ago, the area brimmed with freshwater, plants, and animals. It must have been paradise for the human ancestors who settled here.

Sonia Harmand has come to this region to study the legacy these ancestors left in stone. Harmand is an archaeologist at Stony Brook University. She has an intense gaze and a commanding presence. On a hazy July morning, Harmand sits at a small, wood folding table, scrutinizing a piece of rock. It is brownish-gray, about the size of her pinkie fingernail, and utterly unremarkable to the untrained eye. But it is exactly what she has been looking for.

Nearby 15 workers from Kenya, France, the United States, and England are digging their way into the side of a low hill. They tap hammers against chisels to chip away at the buff-colored sediments, searching for any bits of rock that could signal ancient human activity. At the top of the hill, the workers' water bottles hang like Christmas ornaments on the thorny branches of an acacia tree; the early breeze will keep their contents cool a little longer before the heat of the day sets in. By afternoon, the air temperature will top 100°F, and the excavation floor, windless and sun-cooked, will live up to its nickname: the Oven.

In 2015, Harmand and her husband, Jason Lewis, a paleo-anthropologist at Stony Brook, announced that their team had discovered 3.3-million-year-old stone tools at this site, which is called Lomekwi 3. They were the oldest stone tools ever found by far—so old that they challenged a cherished theory of human evolution. The scientists want to learn who made the tools and why. But they also have a more immediate task: unearthing more evidence that the tools are, in fact, as old as they appear.

The fragment in Harmand's hand is the first evidence of ancient stone-tool production the researchers have recovered since they got here. It is a piece of debris produced by knapping—the act of striking one rock against another to produce a sharp-edged flake. Small and light, the fragment implies that the site has not been disturbed by flowing water in the millions of years since. That fact, in turn, supports the argument that the Lomekwi 3 tools come from this ancient sedimentary layer and not a younger one. Now that the excavators have hit the artifact-bearing level of the site, they must proceed with care pole," Harmand instructs them in Swahili. Slowly, slowly.

Paleoanthropologists have long viewed stone-tool production as one of the defining characteristics of the *Homo* genus and the key to our evolutionary success. Other creatures use tools, but only humans shape hard materials such as rock to suit their purposes. Moreover, humans alone build on prior innovations, ratcheting up their utility—and complexity—over time. "We seem to be the only lineage that has gone fully technological," says Michael Haslam of the University of Oxford. "It isn't even a crutch. It's like an addition to our bodies."

The conventional wisdom holds that our techno dependence began to form during a period of global climate change between 3 million and 2 million years ago, when Africa's woodlands transformed into savanna grasslands. Hominins, members of the human family, found themselves at a crossroads. Their old food sources were vanishing. They had to adapt or face extinction. One lineage, that of the so-called robust australopithecines, coped by evolving huge molars and powerful jaws to process the tougher plant foods available in grassland environments. Another—the larger-brained Homo—invented stone.

. . .

Workers dig into the side of a hill at Lomekwi 3 in July 2016, looking for artifacts (1). They sift each bucket of sediment they remove, hoping to recover even the smallest fragments of interest (2). Every pebble is studied for signs of human modification, tools that gave it access to a wide variety of food sources, including the animals that grazed on these new plants. With the rich stores of calories from meat, *Homo* could afford to fuel an even bigger brain, which could then invent new and better tools for getting still more calories. In short order, a feedback loop formed, one that propelled our brain size and powers of innovation to ever greater heights. By 1 million years ago, the robust australopithecines disappeared, and *Homo* was well on its way to conquering the planet.

The Lomekwi tools have smashed that scenario to pieces. Not only are they too old to belong to *Homo*, but they also predate the climate shift that supposedly kindled our ancestors' drive to create. And without any cut-marked bones or other signs of butchery at the site, it is not at all certain that the tools were used to process animal foods. What is more, such a vast expanse of time separates the Lomekwi tools from the next oldest implements on record that it is impossible to connect them to the rest of humanity's technological endeavoring, suggesting that the advent of stone tools was not necessarily the watershed moment that experts have always envisioned it to be.

These new discoveries have scientists scrambling to figure out when and how our predecessors acquired the cognitive and physical traits needed to conceptualize and fashion stone tools and to pass their craft to the next generation. If multiple lineages made tools from rock, researchers will need to rethink much of what they thought they knew about the origins of technology and how it shaped our branch of the family tree.

Dawn breaks gently in the bush—a slow brightening of sky, a creeping swell of birdsong—and the team's campsite, on the bank of a dry riverbed about a mile from Lomekwi 3, comes to life. By 6:30 AM, the workers emerge from their tents and head to the makeshift dining table for breakfast, walking along a gravel path lined with stones to deter the snakes and scorpions. Within the hour, they pile into Land Cruisers and set off on a bone rattling ride to the excavation. The team is down one vehicle and short on seats in the remaining two, so archaeologist Hélène Roche has decided to stay at camp. Roche is an emeritus director of research at the French National Center for Scientific Research and an expert in early stone-tool technologies. She has short, sand-colored hair, and she dresses in desert hues. Her voice is low and crisp. Roche led the archaeological research in western Turkana for 17 years before handing the reins to Harmand and Lewis in 2011. She has returned for the second half of this expedition to see how they are faring. I remain at camp for the day to ask her about the history of work in this region.

"When I started in archaeology, we were just getting used to having stone tools at 1.8 [million years ago] at Olduvai," Roche recalls. In 1964, Kenyan paleoanthropologist Louis Leakey announced that he had found *Homo*-like fossils in association with what were then the oldest known artifacts in the world, stone tools from Tanzania's Olduvai Gorge (referred to as Oldowan tools). He assigned the fossils to a new species, *Homo habilis*, the "handy man," cementing the idea that stone toolmaking was linked to the emergence of *Homo*.

Hints that stone tools might have originated before Homo soon arrived, however. In the 1970s, Roche, then a graduate student, discovered older Oldowan stone tools at a site in Ethiopia called Gona. When archaeologist Sileshi Semaw, now at the National Center for Research on Human Evolution in Burgos, Spain, and his colleagues eventually analyzed the tools, they reported them to be 2.6 million years old. Because no hominin remains turned up with the tools, researchers could not be sure which species made them. Semaw and his team proposed that a small-brained australopithecine species found at a different site nearby—*Australopithecus garhi*—was the toolmaker. Few were swayed by that argument, however. Homo was still the favorite candidate, even though, at the time, the oldest known *Homo fossil* was only 2.4 million years old. (A recent find has extended the fossil record of Homo back to 2.8 million years ago.)

Yet as old as they were, the Gona artifacts looked too skillfully wrought to represent humanity's first foray into stone-tool manufacturing. So did other ancient tools that began to emerge, including some from western Turkana. In the 1990s, Roche found 2.3-million-year-old Oldowan stone tools at a site five miles from here known as Lokalalei 2c. She realized that in many instances, the site preserved entire knapping sequences that she could piece together like a 3-D puzzle. By refitting the Lokalalei flakes to the cores from which they were detached, Roche and her colleagues could show that toolmakers struck as many as 70 flakes from a single core. This impressive feat required an understanding of the rock shape best suited to flaking (flat on one side and convex on the other) and careful planning to maintain that shape while knapping. "You cannot imagine what it is like to hold the pieces together and reconstruct what [the toolmaker] has done and how he has done it, to go inside the prehistoric mind," she says.

It was becoming clear that the sophistication evident in the tools from Gona, Lokalalei, and elsewhere could not have sprung fully formed from the minds of these knappers. Some kind of technological tradition must have preceded the Oldowan.

In 2010, far older signs of stone-tool technology came to light. Zeresenay Alemseged, now at the University of Chicago, and his colleagues reported that they had found two animal bones bearing what appeared to be cut marks from stone tools at the site of Dikika in Ethiopia. The bones dated to 3.4 million years ago, hundreds of thousands of years before the earliest known traces of *Homo*. The researchers credited the marks to *Australopithecus afarensis*, a species that was still apelike in many respects, with about as much gray matter as a chimpanzee has and a body that retained some adaptations to life in the trees—hardly the brainy, fully terrestrial hominin that researchers had traditionally expected the first butcher to be. The claims did not go unchallenged, however. Some experts countered that animals could have trampled the bones. Without the stone tools themselves, the critics argued, the Dikika scars could not qualify as tool-inflicted marks—and the question of just how far back in time technology originated remained unresolved. Around the time, the battle over the Dikika bones erupted, Harmand and Lewis began to hatch a plan to look for the older stone tools that the Dikika marks, along with the too-good-to-be-first tools from Gona and Lokalalei, implied should exist. In the summer of 2011, they set out in search of new archaeological sites on the western side of Lake Turkana.

The Turkana basin, as well as much of the Great Rift Valley in which it sits, is a paleoanthropologist's dream. Not only does it harbor an abundance of fossils and artifacts, but it preserves them in rocks that, with some sleuthing, can be dated with a relatively high degree of certainty. The region's history of volcanic eruptions and fluctuating water levels is recorded in the layers of sediment that have accumulated over eons to form a sort of layer cake. Water and wind erosion have exposed cross sections of the cake in locations throughout the basin. Tectonic activity has pushed some sections higher and other sections lower than they once were, but as long as any given exposure preserves at least a few layers of the cake, researchers can figure out where in the geologic sequence it comes from and thus how old it is.

To navigate the rough, roadless landscape, the team drives in the dry riverbeds, called lagas that snake through the region, running from the lake to points west. On July 9 of that year, the researchers were headed to a site where, 12 years earlier, a different team had found a 3.5-million-year-old skull of another hominin species, *Kenyanthropus platyops*, when they took the wrong branch of the Lomekwi laga and got lost. Climbing a nearby hillside to get a better view of the terrain, they realized that they had ended up in just the kind of place that is promising for finding ancient remains. Outcrops of soft lake sediments, which tend to preserve fossils and artifacts well, surrounded them. And the researchers knew from previous geologic mapping of the region that all the sediments along this laga were more than 2.7 million years old. They decided to look around.

Within a couple of hours, Sammy Lokorodi, one of the Turkana members of the team, found several rocks bearing hallmarks of knapping—adjacent, scoop-shaped scars where sharp flakes had been chipped off. Could these be the older, more primitive tools that the team was looking for? Maybe. But the tools were found on the surface. A modern-day human—perhaps a passing Turkana nomad—could have made them and left them there. The researchers knew that to make a convincing case that the tools were ancient, they would have to find more of them, sealed in sediments that had lain undisturbed since their deposition, and conduct detailed geologic analyses of the site to establish the age of the artifacts more precisely. Their work had just begun.

By the time the researchers went public with their discovery, describing it in 2015 in *Nature*, they had excavated 19 stone tools from a 140-square-foot area. And they had correlated the position of the sediment layer that held the tools to layers of rock with known ages, including a 3.31-million-year-old layer of compacted volcanic ash called the Toroto Tuff and a magnetically reversed layer from a time, 3.33 million years ago, when the earth's magnetic poles switched places. They had also located the source of the raw material for the tools—a 3.33-million-year-old layer of beach-containing cobbles of volcanic basalt and phonolite, along with fish and crocodile fossils that show just how much higher lake levels were back then as compared with today. Together these clues indicated that the tools dated to a stunning 3.3 million years ago—700,000 years older than the Gona tools and half a million years older than the earliest fossil of *Homo*.

The artifacts have little in common with Oldowan tools. They are far larger, with some flakes the size of a human hand. And experiments indicate that they were knapped using different techniques. Oldowan knappers favored a freehand style, striking a hammerstone held in one hand against a core held in the other, Harmand explains. The Lomekwi knappers, in contrast, would either bang a core they held in both hands against an anvil lying on the ground or place a core on the anvil and hit it with a hammerstone. The methods and finished products demonstrate an understanding of the fracture mechanics of stone but show considerably less dexterity and planning than are evident in tools from Gona and Lokalalei. The researchers had found their pre-Oldowan stone-tool tradition. They call it the Lomekwian. Not everyone is convinced that the Lomekwi tools are as old as the discovery team claims. Some skeptics contend that the team has not proved that the artifacts originated from the sediments dated to 3.3 million years ago. Discoveries made this field season, including the knapping debris, as well as a handful of new tools recovered during excavation, may help allay those concerns. But even researchers who accept the age and the argument that the rocks were shaped by hominins are grappling with what the find means. First, who made the tools? To date, the team has not recovered any hominin remains from the site, apart from a single, enigmatic tooth. The age and geographical location of the tools suggest three possibilities: *K. platyops*, the only hominin species known to have inhabited western Turkana at the time; *A. afarensis*, the species found in association with the cut-marked animal bones from Dikika; and *Australopithecus deyiremeda*, a species that was recently named, based on a partial jawbone found in Ethiopia. Either *K. platyops* or *A. afarensis* would be surprising because both those species had a brain about the size of a chimp's—not the enlarged brain researchers thought the first toolmaker would have. (*A. deyiremeda*'s brain size is unknown.)

Small brain size is not the only anatomical trait that experts did not expect to see in an ancient knapper. Paleoanthropologists thought that tool use arose after our ancestors had abandoned life in the trees to become committed terrestrial bipeds. In this scenario, only after their hands had been freed from the demands of climbing could hominins evolve the hand shape needed to make stone tools. Yet studies of *A. afarensis*, the only one of these three species for which bones below the head have been found, indicate that although it was a capable biped on the ground, it retained some traits that would have allowed it to climb trees for food or safety. Just how important was the shift away from life in the trees to life on the ground in the emergence of stone-tool technology?

The Lomekwi 3 tools are also forcing scientists to reconsider why hominins invented stone tools to begin with. Reconstruction of the paleo environment of the greater Lomekwi area 3.3 million years ago indicates that it was wooded, not the savanna experts thought had forged Homo's stone-working skills.

Perhaps the biggest question: why are the Lomekwi 3 tools so isolated in time? If stone-tool manufacture was the game changing development that experts have always thought it to be, why did it not catch on as soon as it first appeared and initiate the feedback loop that expanded the brain?

Recent studies may help explain how a hominin more primitive than Homo could have come to make stone tools. It turns out that some of the differences in cognitive ability between hominins and other primates may not be as great as previously thought.

Observations of our closest primate cousins, for example, hint that even though they do not manufacture stone tools in the wild, they possess many of the cognitive abilities needed to do so. David Braun of George Washington University and Susana Carvalho of Oxford have found that in Bossou, Guinea, wild chimps that use stones to crack open nuts understand the physical properties of different rocks. The researchers shipped assorted stones from Kenya to Bossou and made them available to the chimps for their nut-cracking activities. Despite not having prior experience with these kinds of rock, the chimps consistently selected the ones with the best qualities for the job. And experiments with captive bonobos carried out by Nicholas Toth of the Stone Age Institute in Bloomington, Indiana, and his colleagues have shown that they can be trained to make sharp flakes and use them to cut rope. "I have no doubt that our apes could replicate what [Harmand and her team] have at Lomekwi, given the right raw material," Toth asserts. Even inventing stone tools in the first place may not have required special genius. Last fall Tomos Proffitt of Oxford and his colleagues reported that they had observed wild capuchin monkeys in Brazil's Serra da Capivara National Park unintentionally making sharp stone flakes that look for all the world like Oldowan tools. Quartzite cobbles abound in the monkeys' environment, and they will often pick up one cobble and bash it against another embedded in the ground that serves as an anvil. All the bashing dislodges sharp flakes that have the hallmarks of intentionally produced stone tools, including the scoop like shape that arises from what is known as conchoidal fracturing. The monkeys ignore the flakes, however. Instead they seem to be pulverizing the quartz to eat it—they pause between strikes to lick the resulting dust from the anvil. Perhaps early hominins invented their stone flakes by accident, too, or found naturally sharp stones in their environment, and only later, once they found a good use for them, began fashioning them on purpose.

The possibility that the Lomekwi toolmakers had hands that were at once capable of knapping and climbing in trees does not seem so improbable either, once one considers what our primate cousins can manage. The modern human hand, with its short, straight fingers and long, opposable thumb, is purpose-built for power, precision, and dexterity—traits we exploit every time we swing a hammer, turn a key, or send a text. Yet as the observations of chimps, bonobos, and capuchins show, other primates with hands built for grasping tree branches can be surprisingly dexterous. The hands of partially arboreal hominins could have been similarly clever.

In fact, recent studies of the fossilized hand bones of three small-brained hominin species from South Africa—*Australopithecus africanus*, *Australopithecus sediba*, and *Homo naledi*—show evidence for exactly this combination of activities. All three species have curved fingers—a trait associated with climbing. Yet in other respects, their hands look like those of toolmakers. Tracy Kivell and Matt Skinner, both at the University of Kent in England, examined the internal structure of the hand bones, which reflects the loading forces sustained in life and found a pattern consistent with that seen in hominins known to have made and used stone tools and different from the internal structure of the hand bones of chimps. "Being a good climber and a dexterous toolmaker are not mutually exclusive," Kivell says. A variety of hand shapes can make and use stone tools, she explains. The changes in the human hand eventually underwent just optimized it for the job. Friday is choma night for the Lomekwi team—roasted goat will be served for dinner. Nick Taylor of Stony Brook, a droll Brit, is taking advantage of the menu to try to figure out what purpose the Lomekwi stone tools served. This morning one of the local Turkana shepherds brought the purchased animal for slaughter. This afternoon, as the sun begins its descent and meal preparations begin, Taylor asks camp kitchen manager Alfred "Kole" Koki to try to process the carcass with replicas of the Lomekwi tools. Koki, an experienced butcher, doubts they will work. But he gamely takes a two-inch-long flake and starts slicing. He manages to skin most of the animal and carves some of the meat with the sharp-edged rocks, discarding them as they become dull, before reclaiming his steel knife to finish the job. Taylor observes how Koki instinctively holds each flake and how long it retains its edge before Koki requests a new one. Taylor keeps the used replica flakes, so that later he and his colleagues can compare their damaged edges with those of the real flakes. He will also collect some of the bones to study what kind of cut marks the carving might have left on them. And he will try using the tools to cut plant materials, including wood and tubers. In addition, Taylor is looking for any residues on the Lomekwi tools that might provide clues to what they were processing.

For whatever reason the Lomekwi hominins made stone tools, their tradition does not appear to have stuck. Nearly 700,000 years separates their implements from the next oldest tools at Gona. Perhaps hominins did indeed have a stone-tool culture spanning that time, and archaeologists have just not found it yet. But maybe the Lomekwi stone-working was just a flash in the pan, unrelated to the Oldowan technology that followed. Even the Oldowan record is patchy and variable, showing different tool styles at different times and places, without much continuity among them. As Roche puts it, "There is not one Oldowan but Oldowans."

This pattern suggests to many archaeologists that populations in multiple lineages of hominins and possibly other primates may have experimented with stone-tool production independently, only to have their inventions fizzle out, unbequeathed to the next generation. "We used to think that once you have toolmaking, we're off to the races," observes Dietrich Stout of Emory University. But maybe with these early populations, he says, technology was not important to their adaptation, so it simply faded away.

Around 2 million years ago, however, something changed. The tools from this period start to look as though they were manufactured according to the same rules. By around 1.7 million years ago, a more sophisticated technology arises: the Acheulean. Known for its hand ax, the Swiss Army knife of the Paleolithic, the Acheulean tradition spread across Africa and into other parts of the Old World.

Braun thinks the shift has to do with improved information transmission. Chimps appear to have what he calls low-fidelity transmission of behavior based on observational learning. It works pretty well for simple tasks: by the end of his team's six week-long experiment with the Bossou chimps, the entire community was using the rocks the same way. The activity seemed to spread by means of a recycling behavior in which one individual, typically a juvenile, would watch another, usually an adult, use a certain type of rock to crack nuts, after which the youngster would try to use the adult's tool set to achieve the same ends.

Modern humans, in contrast, actively teach others how to do complex things—from baking a cake to flying a plane—which is a high-fidelity form of transmission. Perhaps, Braun suggests, the variability seen in the Lomekwi tools and in those of the early Oldowan is the result of lower-fidelity transmission, and the standardization of the later Oldowan and the more sophisticated Acheulean signals the development of a more effective means of sharing knowledge, one that allowed humans to ratchet up their technological complexity. As ancient as the tools from Lomekwi 3 are, the team suspects that even older ones are out there, awaiting discovery. One day, while the rest of the team is excavating, Lewis, Lokorodi, and Xavier Boës, a geologist at the French National Institute for Preventive Archaeological Research, set out to look for them. They head for an area known to have sediments older than those at Lomekwi 3, speeding up the laga in a cloud of dust. They are taking the same branch they meant to take on that day five years ago when they lost their way and discovered Lomekwi 3.

When they reach their destination, they fan out, eyes trained on the ground, scanning for signs of human handiwork in a sea of rocks baked red by the sun. Before long, Lokorodi spies cobbles bearing scoop-shaped scars. In theory, they could be more than 3.5 million years old. But the team will have to follow the same painstaking procedures it carried out at Lomekwi 3. The researchers will have to determine whether the rocks have been shaped by humans and, if so, figure out which stratigraphic level they eroded from, pinpoint the age of that level and then find more of them undisturbed in the ground. Lewis photographs the rocks and notes their location for possible survey in the future. The team will also explore a promising area about three miles from Lomekwi 3 that has sediments dating to more than 4 million years ago.

Figuring out what technology came before and after Lomekwi 3 and getting a clearer picture of how the environment was shifting will be critical to elucidating the correlations among dietary change, tools, and the origins of Homo. The links are all the same, but everything happened earlier," Lewis offers. "The pieces have exploded, but that doesn't mean they won't reassemble."

"We know quite a lot now but not enough," Roche says of the discoveries in western Turkana. "This is only the beginning."

Critical Thinking

1. How does human tool use differ from that of other creatures?
2. What has been the conventional wisdom with regard to our early, direct ancestors' tool use and how has it been overturned?
3. What does the Acheulean tradition suggest about a shift in how humans came to transmit information about tool-making?

Internet References

Hartford Institute for Religion Research
Hirr.hartsem.edu/ency/Anthropology.htm
Harvard Department of Anthropology
https://anthropology.fas.harvard.edu/research/religion
Society for the Anthropology of Religion
Sar.americananthro.org/

Article Prepared by: Elvio Angeloni

The Quiet Rise of the First Toolmaker

CATHERINE BRAHIC

Learning Outcomes

After reading this article, you will be able to:

- Describe the rise of tool-making among the *australopithecines* in terms of the stones themselves as well as the fossil evidence.
- Discuss the differences in grip between apes and humans and how this helps us interpret the origins of tool-making.

Move over *Homo habilis,* you're being dethroned. It seems our "handy" ancestor wasn't the first to use stone tools. In fact, the ape-like *Australopithecus* may have figured out how to handle them before modern humans evolved. One of the first hints of this came in 2010, when German researchers working in Ethiopia discovered markings on two animal bones that were about 3.4 million years old. The cut marks had been made with a sharp stone, and the bones were at a site frequented by Lucy's species, *Australopithecus afarensis* (see timeline).

But that study, led by Shannon McPherron of the Max Planck Institute for Evolutionary Anthropology in Leipzig, Germany, was controversial. The bones were 800,000 years older than the oldest uncontested stone tools, and at the time few thought that *australopithecines* had been tool users. Plus, McPherron hadn't found the tool itself.

The problem, says McPherron, is that if we just go on tools that have been found, we must conclude that one day somebody made a beautifully flaked Oldowan hand axe, one of the oldest tools known, completely out of the blue. That is unlikely.

Now Matthew Skinner at the University of Kent, UK, and his colleagues have taken a different approach to dating tool use: looking at the hands that held them. Specifically, they looked at metacarpal bones—the five bones in the palm of the hand that articulate the fingers. Because the bone ends are made of soft, spongy bone tissue, they are shaped over a lifetime of use and moulded by what a hand does.

A chimp, for instance, spends a lot of time swinging from branches and knuckle-walking, which exerts a great deal of force on the joints in its hands. Skinner and his colleagues predicted how this should shape the soft bone in ape hands, then looked at modern ape bones, finding their predictions were right.

Modern human metacarpals look different because we use our hands differently. Most of our activities involve some kind of pinching—think of how you hold a pen. This precision squeeze between thumb and fingers is uniquely human and a legacy from our flint-wielding ancestors.

When Skinner's team looked at the metacarpals of early human species and *Neanderthals*—who also used stone flakes for tasks like scraping and butchering—they found bone ends that were shaped like modern human bones, and unlike ape bones.

Finally, they looked at metacarpals from four individuals of our ancestor *Australopithecus africanus,* which are up to 2.8 million years old. They revealed those individuals had been tree swingers but had also spent a lot of energy pinching small objects, suggesting they were indeed early tool users (*Science,* doi.org/znm).

"This study is really interesting because it shows how the hand was actually used, and that's consistent with stone tool use," says McPherron.

The similarities between *A. africanus* and human bones are relatively convincing, says John Hawks of the University of Wisconsin-Madison. "The best explanation is that the difference reflects some powerful thumb-to-finger gripping," he says.

Whether that grip was used to maneuver delicate flakes of flint remains to be seen. It's possible *A. africanus* used other types of tools, like bones or pieces of wood. Or they might have been using their precision grips to get at food, such as peeling tough skins off fruit—a task that chimps tend to do with their teeth.

But the study does suggest that 3 million years ago—400,000 years before the oldest known hand axes—*A. africanus* was already starting to use its hands differently [that] its ancestors. They were more dexterous and more precise. Whether or not their hands were already wrapped around flints, they were at least laying the foundations for their descendants to do so.

Tool-making Timeline

3.4 million years ago

Where: Dikika, Ethiopia

Species: *Australopithecus afarensis*

Evidence: Marks on animal bones suggest two types of tools: a stone with a sharp edge that was used to cut and scrape, and a blunt tool that was used to crack the bones open and extract their marrow. But this is controversial as no one has found stone tools this old—yet.

2.8–2 million years ago

Where: South Africa

Species: *Australopithecus africanus*

Evidence: The shape of soft bone tissue in hand fossils suggests their owners had a tool-user's grip (see main story). Still no tools found.

2.6–2.5 million years ago

Where: Gona, Ethiopia

Species: Unknown

Evidence: The oldest undisputed stone tools are typical "Oldowan" style: hammerstones that were used to crack hard objects, and stones that have been knapped to produce a sharp edge.

2.5 million years ago

Where: Bouri, Ethiopia

Species: Unknown, possibly *Australopithecus garhi*

Evidence: Cut marks and hammerstone fractures on animal bones suggest ancient humans were scraping and breaking them using stones.

Critical Thinking

1. What is the evidence for tool-making with respect to the stones themselves as well as the fossil bones?
2. Describe the differences in the hands between apes and humans and explain how this helps us understand the origins of tool-making.

Internet References

Fossil Hominids FAQ
www.talkorigins.org/faqs/homs

Institute of Human Origins
https://iho.asu.edu/

Smithsonian National Museum of Natural History
http://humanorigins.si.edu

Article   Prepared by: Elvio Angeloni

The First Cookout

KATE WONG

Learning Outcomes

After reading this article, you will be able to:

- Discuss Richard Wrangham's theory as to how cooking food made us human.

- Discuss the implications of Richard Wrangham's theory for how we should eat today and why.

With our supersized brains and shrunken teeth and guts, we humans are bizarre primates. Richard Wrangham of Harvard University has long argued that these and other peculiar traits of our kind arose as humans turned to cooking to improve food quality—making it softer and easier to digest and thus a richer source of energy. Humans, unlike any other animal, cannot survive on raw food in the wild, he observes. "We need to have our food cooked."

Based on the anatomy of our fossil forebears, Wrangham thinks that *Homo erectus* had mastered cooking with fire by 1.8 million years ago. Critics have countered that he lacks evidence to support the claim that cooking enhances digestibility and that the oldest known traces of fire are nowhere near as old as his hypothesis predicts. New findings, Wrangham says, lend support to his ideas.

Scientific American: How did you come up with the cooking hypothesis?

Wrangham: I think of two strands. One is that I was trying to figure out what was responsible for the evolution of the human body form, and I was sensitive to the fact that humans everywhere use fire. I started thinking about how long ago you would have to go back before humans did not use fire. And that suggested to me the hypothesis that they always used it because they would not have survived without it. Humans as a genus [*Homo*] are committed to sleeping on

the ground. I do not want to sleep on the ground in Africa without fire to keep the wild animals at bay.

The other strand is that I've studied chimpanzees and their feeding behavior for many years. I've eaten everything that I can get ahold of that chimpanzees eat. And I have been very much aware of the deeply unsatisfying nature of those foods because they are often quite fibrous, relatively dry, and contain little sugar, and they are often strong-tasting—in other words, really nasty. So here we are, two very closely related species with completely different dietary habits. It was an obvious hypothesis that cooking does something special for the food we find in nature. But I was astonished to discover that there was no systematic evidence showing what cooking does to the net energetic gain that we get from our foods.

For the past 14 years I've been focused on that question because to make a satisfactory claim about humans being adapted to cooked food, we have to produce some real evidence about what cooking does to food. Experiments conducted by Rachel N. Carmody of Harvard University have now given us the evidence: if we cook, we get more energy from our food.

Other researchers hold that increased access to meat allowed the teeth and gut to shrink. Why do you think cooking better explains these changes?

It's quite clear that humans began eating meat from large animals by 2.5 million years ago and have left a steady record of cut marks on bones since then. The cooking hypothesis does not deny the importance of meat eating. But there is a core difficulty with attributing changes in digestive anatomy to this shift.

Selection pressure on digestive anatomy is strongest when food is scarce. Under such conditions, animals have very little fat on them, and fat-poor meat is a very poor food because if you have more than about 30 percent protein in your diet, then your ability to get rid of ammonia fast enough is overwhelmed. Nowadays in surveys of hunters and gatherers, what you find is that during periods of food scarcity, there is always a substantial inclusion of plants. Very often it's tubers. To eat those raw, you would have to have the digestive apparatus to handle tough, fibrous, low-carbohydrate plant foods—that is, large teeth and a big gut.

So your idea is that by cooking those plant foods, our ancestors could evolve a smaller gut and teeth—and avoid overdosing on lean meat. Let's turn now to what happened when food was not so scarce and animals were good to eat. You have argued that cooking may have helped early humans eat more meat by freeing them up to hunt. What is your logic?

A primate the size of an early human would be expected to spend about half of its day chewing, as chimpanzees do. Modern humans spend less than an hour a day, whether you're American or living in various subsistence societies around the world. So you've got four or five hours a day freed by the fact that you're eating relatively soft food. In hunter-gatherer life, men tend to spend this time hunting.

That observation raises the question of how much hunting was possible until our ancestors were able to reduce the amount of time they chewed. Chimpanzees like to eat meat, but their average hunt is just 20 minutes, after which they go back to eating fruit. Hunting is risky. If you fail, then you need to be able to eat your ordinary food. If you hunt too long without success, you won't have enough time to process your usual, lower-quality fare. It seems to me that it was only after cooking enabled individuals to save time on chewing that they could increase the amount of time spent on an activity that, for all its potential benefits, might not yield any food.

You have also suggested that cooking allowed the brain to expand. How would cooking do that?

With regard to the brain, fossils indicate a fairly steady increase in cranial capacity, starting shortly before two million years ago. There are lots of ideas about why selection favored larger brains, but the question of how our ancestors could afford them has been a puzzle. The problem is that brains use a disproportionate amount of energy and can never be turned off.

I have extended the idea put forward by Leslie C. Aiello, now at the Wenner-Gren Foundation in New York City, and Peter Wheeler of Liverpool John Moores University in England that after cooking became obligatory, the increase in food quality contributed to reduced gut size. Their newly small guts were energetically cheaper, allowing calories to be diverted to the brain.

In 2012, Karina Fonseca-Azevedo and Suzana Herculano-Houzel of the Federal University of Rio de Janeiro added a new wrinkle. Their calculations showed that on a raw diet,

the number of calories needed to support a human-sized brain would require too many hours eating every day. They argued that cooking allowed our ancestors the extra energy needed to support more neurons, allowing the increase in brain size.

Cooking is not the only way to make food easier to digest. How does it compare with other methods?

Simply reducing the size of food particles and the structural integrity of food—through pounding, for example—makes it easier to digest. Carmody did a study that looked at tubers and meat as representative types of food that hunter-gatherers eat and asked how well mice fared when eating each of these foods, either raw versus cooked or whole versus pounded. She very carefully controlled the amount of food that the mice received, along with the amount of energy they expended moving around, and assessed their net energetic gain through looking at body-mass changes. She found that pounding had relatively little effect, whereas cooking led to significant increases in body weight whether the food was tubers or meat.

This is incredibly exciting because, amazingly, this is the first study that has ever been done to show that animals get more net energy out of their food when it is cooked than when it's raw. Second, it showed that even if pounding has some positive effects on energy gain, cooking has much bigger effects. [Editors' note: Wrangham was a co-author on the study, published in 2011.]

Is there any genetic evidence to support the cooking hypothesis?

There is essentially nothing published yet. But we're very aware that a really interesting question is going to be whether or not we can detect, in the human genome, evidence of selection for genes related to utilizing cooked food. They might be concerned with metabolism. They might be concerned with the immune system. They might be concerned somehow with responses to Maillard compounds, which are somewhat dangerous compounds produced by cooking. This is going to be a very exciting area in the future.

A central objection to the cooking hypothesis has been that there is no archaeological evidence of controlled fire as far back as the hypothesis predicts. Currently the oldest traces come from one-million-year-old deposits in Wonderwerk Cave in South Africa. But you have recently identified an independent line of evidence that humans tamed fire earlier than the archaeological record suggests. How does that work support your thinking?

Chimpanzees love honey, yet they eat very little of it because they get chased away by bees. African hunters and gatherers, in contrast, eat somewhere between 100 and 1,000 times as much honey as chimpanzees do because they use fire. Smoke interferes with the olfactory system of the bees, and under those conditions, the bees do not attack. The question is: How long have humans been using smoke to get honey? That's where the honeyguide comes in. The greater honeyguide is an African species of bird that is adapted to guiding humans to honey. The bird is attracted to human activity—sounds of chopping, whistling, shouting, banging, and, nowadays, motor vehicles. On finding people, the bird starts fluttering in front of them and then leads them off with a special call and waits for them to follow. Honeyguides can lead humans a kilometer or more to a tree that has honey in it. The human then uses smoke to disarm the bees and opens the hive up with an ax to extract the honey inside. The bird gains access to the hive's wax, which it eats.

It used to be thought that the bird's guiding behavior [which is innate, not learned] originated in partnership with the honey badger and that humans moved in on this arrangement later. But in the past 30 years, it has become very clear that honey badgers are rarely, if ever, led to honey by honeyguides. If there's no living species other than humans that has this symbiotic relationship with the bird, could there have been some extinct species of something that favored the honeyguide showing this behavior? Well, obviously, the most reasonable candidates are the extinct ancestors of humans. The argument points very strongly to our ancestors having used fire long enough for natural selection to enable this relationship to develop.

Claire Spottiswoode of the University of Cambridge discovered that there are two kinds of greater honeyguide females: those that lay their eggs in ground nests and those that lay in tree nests. Then she found that the two types of behavior are associated with different lineages of mitochondrial DNA [DNA that is found in the energy-producing components of cells and passed down from mother to offspring]. Based on a fairly conservative assessment of the rate of mutation, Spottiswoode and her colleagues determined that the two lineages had been separated for about three million years, [providing a minimum estimate for the age of the greater honeyguide species]. That doesn't necessarily mean that the guiding habit, which depends on humans using fire, is that old—it could be more recent—but at least it tells you that the species is old enough to allow for much evolutionary change.

If cooking was a driving force in human evolution, does this conclusion have implications for how people should eat today?

It does remind us that eating raw food is a very different proposition from eating cooked food. Because we don't think about the consequences of processing our food, we are getting a misunderstanding of the net energy gain from eating. One of the ways in which this can be quite serious is if people who are dedicated to a raw-food diet don't understand the consequences for their children. If you just say, "Well, animals eat their food raw, and humans are animals, then it should be fine for us to eat our food raw," and you bring your children up this way, you're putting them at very severe risk. We are a different species from every other. It's fine to eat raw food if you want to lose weight. But if you want to gain weight, as with a child or an adult who's too thin, then you don't want to eat a raw diet.

Critical Thinking

1. How and why does Richard Wrangham think that cooking food made us into the humans we have become?

2. How does Wrangham answer his critics?

3. How did cooking enable humans to hunt for meat?

4. How did cooking food allow for brain expansion?

5. How does cooking food compare with other methods of making food more digestible?

6. Why is the bird, the honeyguide, a clue to when humans began using fire?

7. What are the implications of Wrangham's theory for how people should eat today and why?

Internet References

Human Prehistory
http://users.hol.gr/~dilos/prehis.htm

Max Planck Institute for Evolutionary Anthropology
www.eva.mpg.de/english/index.htm

The Paleolithic Diet Page
www.paleodiet.com

KATE WONG is a senior editor at *Scientific American*.

Article   Prepared by: Elvio Angeloni

Neandertal Minds

KATE WONG

Learning Outcomes

After reading this article, you will be able to:

- Discuss the anatomical evidence that relates to similarities and differences between Neandertals and modern homo sapiens.

- Evaluate the archeological evidence that seems to show that Neandertals thought much like we do.

On a clear day in Gibraltar, looking out of Gorham's Cave, you can see the rugged northern coast of Morocco looming purple above the turquoise sea. Inside the cave, quiet prevails, save for the lapping of waves against its rocky beach. But offshore, the strait separating this southernmost tip of the Iberian Peninsula from the African continent bustles with activity. Fishing vessels troll the waters for tuna and marlin, cruise ships carry tourists gawking at Gibraltar's hulking limestone massif, and tankers ferry crude oil from the Mediterranean to points west. With its swift, nutrient-rich currents, mild climate and gateway location, the area has attracted humans for millennia.

One impressive group dwelled in the region for tens of thousands of years, weathering several ice ages here. During such times lower sea levels exposed a vast coastal plain in front of the cave, land that supported a variety of animals and plants. These individuals cleverly exploited the local bounty. They hunted large animals such as ibex and seals and small ones such as rabbits and pigeons; they fished for bream and gathered mussels and limpets from the distant shore; they harvested pine nuts from the surrounding evergreens. Sometimes they took ravens and eagles for their plumage to bedeck themselves with the beautiful black flight feathers. And they engraved their cave floor with symbols whose meaning has since been lost to time.

In all these ways, these people behaved just like our own *Homo sapiens* ancestors, who arose in Africa with the same anatomy we have today and later colonized every corner of the globe. But they were not these anatomically modern humans. They were Neandertals, our stocky, heavy-browed cousins, known to have lived in Eurasia between 350,000 and 39,000 years ago—those same Neandertals whose name has come to be synonymous in pop culture with idiocy and brutishness.

The scientific basis for that popular pejorative view has deep roots. Back in the early 1900s the discovery of the first largely complete Neandertal skeleton, from the site of La Chapelle-aux-Saints in France, gave rise to the group's image problem: deformities now known to reflect the old age of the individual were seen as signs of degeneracy and subhumanness.

Since then, the pendulum of paleoanthropological opinion has swung repeatedly between researchers who see Neandertals as cognitively inferior to *H. sapiens* and those who see them as our mental equals. Now a rash of new discoveries is fanning the debate. Some fossil and ancient DNA analyses seem to suggest that Neandertal brains were indeed different—and less capable—than those of *H. sapiens*. Yet mounting archaeological evidence indicates that Neandertals behaved in many of the same ways that their anatomically modern contemporaries did.

As scientists advance into the Neandertal mind, the mystery of why our closest relatives went extinct after reigning for hundreds of thousands of years is deepening. The race is on to solve this extinction riddle: such insight will help reveal what it was that distinguished our kind from the rest of the human family—and set anatomically modern humans on the path to becoming the enormously successful species we are today.

Bony Inklings

Paleoanthropologists have long sought clues to Neandertal cognition in the fossilized skulls they left behind. By studying casts of the interior of the braincase, researchers can reconstruct the external form of an extinct human's brain, which reveals the overall size as well as the shape of certain of its regions. But those analyses have failed to turn up much in the way of clear-cut differences between Neandertal brains and those of *H. sapiens.* (Some experts think Neandertals were just another population of *H. sapiens.* This article treats the two groups as different human species, albeit very closely related ones.) Neandertal brains were a little flatter than ours, but they were just as big—indeed, in many cases they were larger, explains paleoneurologist Ralph Holloway of Columbia University. And their frontal lobes—which govern problem solving, among other tasks—were almost identical to those of *H. sapiens,* judging from the impression they left on the inside of the braincase. That impression does not reveal the internal extent or structure of those key brain regions, however. "Endocasts are the most direct evidence of brain evolution, but they are extremely limited in terms of giving you solid information about behavior," Holloway admits.

In a widely publicized study published in 2013, Eiluned Pearce of the University of Oxford and her colleagues purportedly got around some of the limitations of endocasts and provided a way of estimating the size of internal brain areas. The team used eye-socket size as a proxy for the size of the visual cortex, which is the brain region that processes visual signals. They found that the Neandertal skulls they measured had significantly larger eye sockets than modern humans have—the better for coping with the lower light levels available in their high-latitude homes, according to one theory—and thus larger visual cortices. With more real estate dedicated to processing visual information, Neandertals would have had less neural tissue left over for other brain regions, including the ones that help us maintain extensive social networks, which can buffer against hard times, the researchers argued.

Holloway is not convinced. His own endocast work indicates that there is no way to delineate and measure the visual cortex. And Neandertal faces are larger than those of anatomically modern humans, which might explain their larger eye sockets. Moreover, people today are hugely variable in the proportion of visual cortex they have relative to other brain regions, he observes, and this anatomical variability does not appear to correspond to differences in behavior.

Other fossil analyses have yielded similarly equivocal signals about the Neandertal mind. Studies of limb asymmetry and wear marks on tools as well as on the teeth (from using them to grasp items such as animal hides during processing) indicate that Neandertals were as right-handed as we moderns are. A strong tendency toward favoring the right hand is one of the traits that distinguishes *H. sapiens* from chimpanzees and corresponds to asymmetries in the brain that are believed to be related to language—a key component of modern human behavior. Yet studies of skull shape in Neandertal specimens representing a range of developmental stages indicate that the Neandertals attained their large brain size through a different developmental pathway than that of *H. sapiens.* Although

Neandertal brains started off growing like modern brains in the womb, they diverged from the modern growth pattern after birth, during a critical window for cognitive development.

Those developmental differences may have deep evolutionary roots. An analysis of some 17 skulls dated to 430,000 years ago from the fossil site of Sima de los Huesos, in the Atapuerca Mountains in northern Spain, has shown that members of the population there, believed to have been Neandertal precursors, had smaller brains than later members of the lineage. The finding suggests that Neandertals did not inherit their large brain size from the last common ancestor of Neandertals and modern humans; instead the two species underwent a parallel brain expansion later in their evolution. Although Neandertal brains ended up approximately as large as ours, their independent evolution would have left plenty of opportunities for the emergence of brain differences apart from size, such as those affecting connectivity.

Genetic Hints

Glimpses of some of those differences have come from DNA analyses. Since the publication of a draft of the Neandertal genome in 2010, geneticists have been mining ancient DNA to see how Neandertals and *H. sapiens* compare. Intriguingly, the Neandertals turn out to have carried a very similar variant we have of a gene called FOXP2 that is thought to play a role in speech and language in humans. But other parts of the Neandertal genome appear to contrast with ours in significant ways. For one thing, Neandertals seem to have carried different versions of other genes involved in language, including CNTNAP2. Further, of the 87 genes in modern humans that differ significantly from their counterparts in Neandertals and another archaic hominin group, the Denisovans, several are involved in brain development and function.

Differences in the genetic codes of Neandertals and modern humans are not the whole story, however. The switching on and off of genes could have distinguished moderns from Neandertals, too, so that the groups differed in how robustly and under what circumstances they produced the substances encoded by their genes. Indeed, FOXP2 itself appears to have been expressed differently in Neandertals than in *H. sapiens,* even though the protein it made was the same. Scientists have begun studying gene regulation in Neandertals and other extinct humans by examining the patterns of chemical tags known as methyl groups in ancient genomes. These tags are known to influence gene activity.

But whether or not differences in DNA sequences and gene activity translate to differences in cognition is the big question.

To that end, intriguing clues have emerged from studies of people today who carry a small percentage of Neandertal DNA as a result of long-ago interbreeding between Neandertals and *H. sapiens.*

Geneticist John Blangero of the Texas Biomedical Research Institute runs a long-term study of extended families in San Antonio aimed at finding genes involved in complex diseases such as diabetes. In recent years he and his colleagues had begun looking at brain structure and function in the study participants. A biological anthropologist by training, Blangero started at one point to wonder how he could use living humans to answer such questions as what cognitive abilities Neandertals had.

A plan began to take shape. Over the course of their disease research, Blangero and his team had obtained whole-genome sequences and MRI scans of the brains of hundreds of patients. And they had developed a statistical method to gauge the effects of certain disease-linked gene variants on observable traits. Blangero realized that with the aid of their statistical tool, they could use the Neandertal genomes and his group's genetic and MRI data from living people to estimate the effects of the full complement of Neandertal genetic variants—the so-called polygeno-type—on traits related to cognition.

Their results suggest that several key brain regions were smaller in Neandertals than in modern humans, including the gray matter surface area (which helps to process information in the brain), Broca's area (which seems to be involved in language) and the amygdala (which controls emotions and motivation). The findings also indicate that Neandertals would have had less white matter, translating to reduced brain connectivity. And other traits would have compromised their ability to learn and remember words. "Neandertals were almost certainly less cognitively adept," asserts Blangero, who presented his preliminary findings at the annual meeting of the American Association of Physical Anthropologists in Calgary last April. "I'm willing to bet on that one."

Of course, without living Neandertals around today, Blangero cannot conduct cognitive assessments that would confirm or refute his inference. But there is, in theory, another way to put his hunch to the test. It would be possible, using existing technology, to study Neandertal brain cell function by genetically modifying modern human cells to have Neandertal DNA sequences, programming them to become neurons and observing the Neandertalized cells in petri dishes. Scientists could then examine the abilities of the neurons to conduct electrical impulses, to migrate to different brain regions and to produce projections (neurites) that aid in cell communication, for instance. Blangero notes that although there are ethical issues to consider where the creation of Neandertal cells is concerned, such work might actually help researchers identify genes involved in modern human brain disorders if the genetic changes compromise neuron function. Such findings could, in turn, lead to the discovery of new drug targets.

Not everyone is ready to draw conclusions about the Neandertal mind from DNA. John Hawks of the University of Wisconsin-Madison observes that Neandertals may have carried gene variants that affected their brain function but that have no counterparts in people today for comparison. He notes that if one were to predict Neandertal skin color based on the genes they share with modern humans, one would surmise that they had dark skin. Yet scientists now know Neandertals had some genes no longer in circulation that probably lightened their skin. But a bigger problem with attempting to suss out how Neandertal brains worked from their genes, Hawks says, is that for the most part researchers do not know how genes affect thought in our own kind. "We know next to nothing about Neandertal cognition from genetics because we know next to nothing about [modern] human cognition from genetics," he asserts.

Archaeological Insights

Given the limitations of the fossil anatomy and the fact that ancient DNA research is still in its infancy, many researchers say the clearest window on the Neandertal mind is the cultural record these extinct humans left behind. For a long time, that record did not paint a particularly flattering picture of our vanished cousins. Early modern Europeans left behind elegant art, complex tools and remainders of meals attesting to an ability to exploit a wide variety of animals and plants that enabled them to adapt to new environments and shifting climate. Neandertals, in contrast, seemed to lack art and other symbolic remains; their tools were comparatively simple; and they appeared to have had a foraging strategy narrowly focused on large game. Stuck in their ways, the thinking went, the Neandertals simply could not adapt to deteriorating climate conditions and competition from the invading moderns.

In the 1990s, however, archaeologists began to find evidence contradicting that scenario—namely, a handful of decorative items and advanced tools attributed to Neandertals. Ever since, researchers have been at loggerheads over whether these items are Neandertal inventions as claimed; doubt has arisen because the items date to the end of the Neandertal dynasty, by which time *H. sapiens* was in the area, too. (Anatomically modern humans appear to have reached Europe by around 44,000 to 41,500 years ago, hundreds of thousands of years after Neandertals settled there.) Some skeptics think that *H. sapiens* made the sophisticated artifacts, which later got mixed in with the Neandertal remains. Alternatively, they offer, Neandertals may have copied the ingenious moderns or stolen their goods.

But that position is becoming harder to uphold in the face of a raft of discoveries over the past few years that evince Neandertal savvy prior to the spread of anatomically modern humans throughout Europe. "There's been a real sea change. Every month brings something new and surprising that Neandertals did," observes David Frayer of the University of Kansas. "And the new evidence is always that they were more sophisticated, not hicks."

Some of the most surprising discoveries reveal aesthetics and abstract thought in Neandertal cultures that predated the arrival of *H. sapiens.* These finds include the engraving and signs of feather use from Gorham's Cave. In fact, artifacts of this nature have turned up at archaeological sites across Europe. At the Grotta di Fumane in Italy's Veneto region, archaeologists found signs of feather use and a fossil snail shell collected from at least 100 kilometers away that had been stained red, suspended on a string and worn as a pendant at least 47,600 years ago. Cueva de los Aviones and Cueva Antón in southeastern Spain have also yielded seashells bearing traces of pigment. Some seem to have served as cups for mixing and holding red, yellow and sparkly black pigments that may have been cosmetics; others bear holes indicating that they were worn as jewelry. The modified shells date to as many as 50,000 years ago.

Other Neandertal leavings indicate that their yen for decorating reaches back further still. Sites in France and Italy document a tradition of harvesting eagle talons that spans from 90,000 to 40,000 years ago. Cut marks on the bones show that the Neandertals focused their efforts on obtaining the claws, not the flesh. This finding led investigators to conclude that the Neandertals exploited the eagles for symbolic reasons—probably to adorn themselves with the impressive talons—rather than dietary ones.

Even older hints of Neandertal aesthetics come from the site of Maastricht-Belvedere in the Netherlands, where archaeologists have found small splatters of red ochre, or iron oxide, in deposits dating to between 250,000 and 200,000 years ago at minimum. The scarlet pigment had been finely ground and mixed into a liquid that then dripped onto the ground. Researchers cannot know for sure what those Neandertals were doing with the red liquid, but painting is one obvious possibility. Indeed, when red ochre turns up at early modern human sites, investigators assume that it was used for decorative purposes.

In addition to rendering a far more resplendent portrait of our much maligned cousins, these new discoveries provide crucial insights into the Neandertal mind. Archaeologists have long considered art, including body decoration, to be a key indicator of modern cognitive abilities because it means that the makers had the capacity to conceive of something in the abstract and to convey that information in symbols. Symbolic thinking underpins our ability to communicate via language—one of the defining traits of modern humans and one that is seen as critical to our success as a species. If Neandertals thought symbolically, as they appear to have done, then they probably had language, too. In fact, abstract thought may have dawned in the human lineage even before the last common ancestor of Neandertals and *H. sapiens:* in December researchers unveiled a mussel shell from Indonesia that they contend was engraved with a geometric pattern by a more primitive ancestor, *Homo erectus,* around 500,000 years ago.

Symbolic thought is not the only component of behavior believed to have helped *H. sapiens* get ahead, however. The manufacture of tools with specialized uses is another element, one that Neandertals appear to have mastered as well. In 2013, Marie Soressi of Leiden University in the Netherlands and her collaborators announced their discovery of bone tools known as lissoirs—implements that leather workers today use to render animal hides more pliable, lustrous and impermeable to the elements—at two Neandertal sites in the Dordogne region of France dating to between 53,000 and 41,000 years ago. Judging from the wear marks on the artifacts, Neandertals used them for the same purpose. The Neandertals made the lissoirs from deer ribs, shaping the end of the bone that attaches to the sternum to form a rounded tip. To wield the tool, they pressed the tip into a dry hide at an angle and pushed it across the surface repeatedly, smoothing and softening the skin.

Fresh evidence of Neandertal ingenuity has also come from the site of Abri du Maras in southern France, which sheltered Neandertals around 90,000 years ago. Microscopic analyses of stone tools from the site, conducted by Bruce Hardy of Kenyon College and his colleagues, revealed traces of all manner of activities once thought to be beyond the ken of the species. For instance, the team found remnants of twisted plant fibers that would have been used for making string or cords, which then could have been fashioned into nets, traps and bags. Traces of wood turned up as well, suggesting that the Neandertals crafted tools from that material.

Residue analysis additionally gives the lie to the notion that Neandertals were perilously picky eaters. Studies of the chemical makeup of their teeth, along with analyses of animal remains from Neandertal sites, have suggested that Neandertals relied heavily on large, dangerous prey such as mammoth and bison rather than an array of animals depending on availability, as anatomically modern humans did. The Abri du Maras Neandertals apparently exploited a veritable menagerie of creatures, including small, fast animals such as rabbits and fish—all species previously thought to be out of reach for Neandertals, with their low-tech gear.

Some scholars have argued that an ability to live partly on plant foods gave *H. sapiens* an edge over Neandertals, allowing them to reap more sustenance from the same area of land. (Subsisting on plants is trickier for humans than for other primates because our big brains demand a lot of calories, and yet our small guts are poorly suited to digesting large quantities of raw roughage—a combination that requires intimate knowledge of plant foods and how to prepare them.) But the Abri du Maras Neandertals gathered edible plants, including parsnip and burdock, as well as edible mushrooms. And they were not alone.

According to studies led by Amanda Henry of the Max Planck Institute for Evolutionary Anthropology in Leipzig, Germany, Neandertals across a broad swath of Eurasia—from

Iraq to Belgium—ate a variety of plants. Examining the tartar in Neandertal teeth and residues on stone tools, she determined that Neandertals consumed species closely related to modern wheat and barley, cooking them to make them palatable. She also found bits of starch from tubers and telltale components of date palms. The similarities to findings from early modern human sites were striking. "Any way we broke up the data, there were no significant differences between the groups," Henry remarks. "The evidence we have now does not suggest that the earliest modern humans in Eurasia were better at accessing plant foods."

A Long Farewell

If Neandertals actually behaved in ways once thought to distinguish anatomically modern humans and fuel their rise to world domination, that likeness makes their decline and eventual extinction all the more puzzling. Why did they die out while *H. sapiens* survived? One theory is that moderns had a bigger tool kit that may have boosted their foraging returns. Modern humans evolved in Africa, where their population size was larger than that of Neandertals, Henry explains. With more mouths to feed, preferred resources such as easy game would have declined, and the moderns would have had to develop new tools to obtain other kinds of food. When they brought this cutting-edge technology with them out of Africa and into Eurasia, they were able to exploit that environment more effectively than the resident Neandertals could. In other words, moderns honed their survival skills under more competitive circumstances than Neandertals had faced and thus entered Neandertal territory with an advantage over the incumbents.

Not only did the large population size of *H. sapiens* spur innovation, but it helped to keep new traditions alive rather than letting them fizzle out with the last member of a small, isolated group. The bigger, more connected membership of *H. sapiens* "increasingly provided a more efficient ratchet effect to maintain and build on knowledge compared with earlier humans, including the Neandertals," offers Chris Stringer of the Natural History Museum in London. Still, the arrival of moderns did not spell instant doom for Neandertals. The latest attempt to track their decline, carried out by Thomas Higham of Oxford and his colleagues, applied improved dating methods to pinpoint the ages of dozens of Neandertal and early modern European sites from Spain to Russia. The results indicate that the two groups shared the continent for some 2,600 to 5,400 years before the Neandertals finally disappeared, around 39,000 years ago.

That lengthy overlap would have left plenty of time for mating between the two factions. DNA analyses have found that people today who live outside Africa carry an average of at least 1.5 to 2.1 percent Neandertal DNA—a legacy from dalliances between Neandertals and anatomically modern humans tens of thousands of years ago, after the latter group began spreading out of Africa.

Maybe, some experts offer, mixing between the smaller Neandertal population and the larger modern one led to the Neandertal's eventual demise by swamping their gene pool. "There were never very many of them, there were people coming in from other areas and mixing with them, and they faded out," Frayer surmises. "The history of all living forms is that they go extinct," he adds. "That's not necessarily a sign that they were stupid, or culturally incapable, or adaptively incapable. It's just what happens."

Critical Thinking

1. In what ways did Neandertals behave just like our own *Homo sapiens* ancestors during the Paleolithic period?

2. What does the archaeological and anatomical evidence indicate with respect to the possibility that Neandertals were capable of aesthetics, abstract thought, and language?

Internet References

Fossil Hominids FAQ
   www.talkorigins.org/faqs/homs
Human Origins Institute
   http://humanorigins.si.edu/
Max Planck Institute for Evolutionary Biology
   http://wwwstaff.eva.mpg.de/~paabo/

KATE WONG is a senior editor at *Scientific American.*

Article   Prepared by: Elvio Angeloni

The Most Invasive Species of All

Many human species have inhabited the earth. But ours is the only one that colonized the entire planet. A new hypothesis explains why.

CURTIS W. MAREAN

Learning Outcomes

After reading this article, you will be able to:

- Discuss the various previous theories as to why our *H. sapiens* ancestors became the most invasive species of all.

- Discuss what a useful theory must do to explain the diaspora of *H. sapiens*.

- Discuss the author's alternate scenario for the spread of *H. sapiens*.

Sometime after 70,000 years ago our species, *Homo Sapiens, left Africa to begin* its inexorable spread across the globe. Other human species had established themselves in Europe and Asia, but only our *H. sapiens* ancestors ultimately managed to push out into all the major continents and many island chains. Theirs was no ordinary dispersal. Everywhere *H. sapiens* went, massive ecological changes followed. The archaic humans they encountered went extinct, as did vast numbers of animal species. It was, without a doubt, the most consequential migration event in the history of our planet.

Paleoanthropologists have long debated how and why modern humans alone accomplished this astonishing feat of dissemination and dominion. Some experts argue that the evolution of a larger, more sophisticated brain allowed our ancestors to push into new lands and cope with the unfamiliar challenges they faced there. Others contend that novel technology drove the expansion of our species out of Africa by allowing early modern humans to hunt prey—and dispatch enemies—with unprecedented efficiency. A third scenario holds that climate change weakened the populations of *Neanderthals* and other archaic human species that were occupying the territories outside Africa, allowing modern humans to get the upper hand and take over their turf. Yet none of these hypotheses provides a comprehensive theory that can explain the full extent of *H. sapiens*' reach. Indeed, these theories have mostly been proffered as explanations for records of *H. sapiens* activity in particular regions, such as western Europe. This piecemeal approach to studying *H. sapiens*' colonization of the earth has misled scientists. The great human diaspora was one event with several phases and therefore needs to be investigated as a single research question.

Excavations I have led at Pinnacle Point on the southern coast of South Africa over the past 16 years, combined with theoretical advances in the biological and social sciences, have recently led me to an alternative scenario for how *H. sapiens* conquered the globe. I think the diaspora occurred when a new social behavior evolved in our species: a genetically encoded penchant for cooperation with unrelated individuals. The joining of this unique proclivity to our ancestors' advanced cognitive abilities enabled them to nimbly adapt to new environments. It also fostered innovation, giving rise to a game-changing technology: advanced projectile weapons. Thus equipped, our ancestors set forth out of Africa, ready to bend the whole world to their will.

A Desire to Expand

To appreciate just how extraordinary *H. sapiens*' colonization of the planet was, we must page back some 200,000 years to the dawning of our species in Africa. For tens of thousands of years, these anatomically modern humans—people who looked like us—stayed within the confines of the mother continent. Around

100,000 years ago one group of them made a brief foray into the Middle East but was apparently unable to press onward. These humans needed an edge they did not yet have. Then, after 70,000 years ago, a small founder population broke out of Africa and began a more successful campaign into new lands. As these people expanded into Eurasia, they encountered other closely related human species: the *Neanderthals* in western Europe and members of the recently discovered Denisovan lineage in Asia. Shortly after the moderns invaded, the archaics went extinct, although some of their DNA persists in people today as a result of occasional interbreeding between the groups.

Once modern humans made it to the shores of Southeast Asia, they faced a seemingly limitless and landless sea. Yet they pushed on, undaunted. Like us, these people could envision and desire new lands to explore and conquer, so they built ocean-worthy vessels and set out across the sea, reaching Australia's shores by at least 45,000 years ago. The first human species to enter this part of the world, *H. sapiens* quickly filled the continent, sprinting across it with spear-throwers and fire. Many of the largest of the strange marsupials that had long ruled the land down under went extinct. By about 40,000 years ago the trailblazers found and crossed a land bridge to Tasmania, although the unforgiving waters of the southernmost oceans denied them passage to Antarctica.

On the other side of the equator, a population of *H. sapiens* traveling northeast penetrated Siberia and radiated across the lands encircling the North Pole. Land ice and sea ice stymied their entry into the Americas for a time. Exactly when they finally crossed into the New World is a matter of fierce scientific debate, but researchers agree that by around 14,000 years ago they broke these barriers and swept into a continent whose wildlife had never seen human hunters before. Within just a few thousand years they reached southernmost South America, leaving a mass extinction of the New World's great Ice Age beasts, such as mastodons and giant sloths, in their wake. Madagascar and many Pacific islands remained free of humans for another 10,000 years, but in a final push, mariners discovered and colonized nearly all these locales. Like the other places in which *H. sapiens* established itself, these islands suffered the hard hand of human occupation, with ecosystems burned, species exterminated and environments reshaped to our predecessors' purposes. Human colonization of Antarctica, for its part, was left for the industrial age.

Team Players

So how did *H. Sapiens* do it? How, after tens of thousands of years of confinement to the continent of their origin, did our ancestors finally break out and take over not just the regions that previous human species had colonized but the entire world?

A useful theory for this diaspora must do two things: First, it must explain why the process commenced when it did and not before. Second, it must provide a mechanism for rapid dispersal across land and sea, which would have required the ability to adapt readily to new environments and to displace any archaic humans found in them. I propose that the emergence of traits that made us, on one hand, peerless collaborators and, on the other, ruthless competitors best explains *H. sapiens'* sudden rise to world domination. Modern humans had this unstoppable attribute; the *Neanderthals* and our other extinct cousins did not. I think it was the last major addition to the suite of characteristics that constitute what anthropologist Kim Hill of Arizona State University has called "human uniqueness."

We modern humans cooperate to an extraordinary degree. We engage in highly complex coordinated group activities with people who are not kin to us and who may even be complete strangers. Imagine, in a scenario suggested by anthropologist Sarah Blaffer Hrdy of the University of California, Davis, in her 2009 book *Mothers and Others,* a couple of hundred chimps lining up, getting on a plane, sitting for hours extremely passively and then exiting like robots on cue. It would be unthinkable—they would battle one another nonstop. But our cooperative nature cuts both ways. The same species that leaps to the defense of a persecuted stranger will also team up with unrelated individuals to wage war on another group and show no mercy to the competition. Many of my colleagues and I think that this proclivity for collaboration—what I call hyperprosociality—is not a learned tendency but instead a genetically encoded trait found only in *H. sapiens.* Some other animals may show glimmers of it, but what modern humans possess is different in kind.

The question of how we came to have this genetic predisposition toward our extreme brand of cooperation is a tricky one. But mathematical modeling of social evolution has yielded some valuable clues. Sam Bowles, an economist at the Santa Fe Institute, has shown that an optimal condition under which genetically encoded hyperprosociality can propagate is, paradoxically, when groups are in conflict. Groups that have higher numbers of prosocial people will work together more effectively and thus outcompete others and pass their genes for this behavior to the next generation, resulting in the spread of hyperprosociality. Work by biologist Pete Richerson of UC Davis and anthropologist Rob Boyd of Arizona State additionally indicates that such behavior spreads best when it begins in a subpopulation and competition between groups is intense and when overall population sizes are small, like the original population of *H. sapiens* in Africa from which all modern-day people are descended.

Hunter-gatherers tend to live in bands of about 25 individuals, marry outside the group and cluster into "tribes" tied together by mate exchange, gifting, and common language and traditions. They also sometimes fight other tribes. They take great risks in doing so, however, which raises the question of what triggers this willingness to engage in risky combat. Insights into when it pays to fight have come from the classic "economic defendability" theory advanced in 1964 by Jerram Brown, now at the University at Albany, to explain variation in aggressiveness among birds. Brown argued that individuals act aggressively to attain certain goals that will maximize their survival and reproduction. Natural selection will favor fighting when it facilitates these goals. One major goal of all organisms is to secure a food supply, so if food can be defended, then it follows that aggressive behavior in its defense should be selected for. If the food cannot be defended or is too costly to patrol, then aggressive behavior is counterproductive.

In a classic paper published in 1978, Rada Dyson-Hudson and Eric Alden Smith, both then at Cornell University, applied economic defendability to humans living in small societies. Their work showed that resource defense makes sense when resources are dense and predictable. I would add that the resources in question must be crucial to the organism—no organism will defend a resource it does not need. This principle still holds today: ethnic groups and nation-states fight viciously over dense, predictable and valued resources such as oil, water and productive agricultural land. An implication of this territoriality theory is that the environments that would have fostered intergroup conflict, and thus the cooperative behaviors that would have enabled such fighting, were not universal in early *H sapiens'* world. They were restricted to those locales where high-quality resources were dense and predictable. In Africa, terrestrial resources are, for the most part, sparse and unpredictable, which explains why most of the hunter-gatherers there who have been studied invest little time and energy in defending boundaries. But there are exceptions to this rule. Certain coastal areas have very rich, dense and predictable foods in the form of shellfish beds. And the ethnographic and archaeological records of hunter-gatherer warfare worldwide show that the highest levels of conflict have occurred among groups who used coastal resources, such as those in coastal Pacific North America.

When did humans first adopt dense and predictable resources as a cornerstone of their diet? For millions of years our ancient ancestors foraged for terrestrial plants and animals, as well as some inland aquatic foods on occasion. All these comestibles occur at low densities, and most are unpredictable. For this reason, our predecessors lived in highly dispersed groups that were constantly traveling in search of their next meal. But as human cognition grew increasingly complex, one population figured out how to make a living on the coast by eating shellfish. My team's excavations at the Pinnacle Point sites indicate that this shift began by 160,000 years ago on the southern shores of Africa. There, for the first time in the history of humankind,

people started targeting a dense, predictable and highly valued resource—a development that would lead to major social change.

Genetic and archaeological evidence suggests that *H. sapiens* underwent a population decline shortly after it originated, thanks to a global cooling phase that lasted from around 195,000 to 125,000 years ago. Seaside environments provided a dietary refuge for *H. sapiens* during the harsh glacial cycles that made edible plants and animals hard to find in inland ecosystems and were thus crucial to the survival of our species. These marine coastal resources also provided a reason for war. Recent experiments on the southern coast of Africa, led by Jan De Vynck of Nelson Mandela Metropolitan University in South Africa, show that shellfish beds can be extremely productive, yielding up to 4,500 calories per hour of foraging. My hypothesis, in essence, is that coastal foods were a dense, predictable and valuable food resource. As such, they triggered high levels of territoriality among humans, and that territoriality led to intergroup conflict. This regular fighting between groups provided conditions that selected for prosocial behaviors within groups—working together to defend the shellfish beds and thereby maintain exclusive access to this precious resource—which subsequently spread throughout the population.

Weapon of War

With the ability to operate in groups of unrelated individuals, *H. sapiens* was well on its way to becoming an unstoppable force. But, I surmise, it needed a new technology—projectile weaponry—to reach its full potential for conquest. This invention was a long time in the making. Technologies are additive: they build on prior experiments and knowledge and become increasingly complex. The development of projectile weapons would have followed the same trajectory, most likely evolving from stabbing stick, to hand-cast spear, to leverage-assisted casting spear (atlatl), to bow and arrow, and finally to all the wildly inventive ways contemporary humans have come up with to launch deadly objects.

With each new iteration, the technology became more lethal. Simple wood spears with shaved points tend to produce a puncture wound, but such an injury has limited impact because it does not bleed the animal quickly. Tipping the spear with a sharpened stone increases the trauma of the wound. This elaboration requires several connected technologies; however, one must be able to shape a tool into a point that will penetrate an animal and shape a base that can be attached to a spear. It also requires some type of connecting technology to secure the stone point to the wood shaft—either glue or a tying material, sometimes both. Jayne Wilkins, now at the University of Cape Town in South Africa, and her colleagues have shown that stone tools from a site in South Africa called Kathu Pan 1 were used as spearpoints some 500,000 years ago. The antiquity of the Kathu Pan 1 find implies that it is the handiwork of the last common ancestor of *Neanderthals* and modern humans, and later remains from 200,000 years ago show that, as one might expect, both descendant species made these kinds of tools, too. This shared technology means that, for a time, there was a balance of power between *Neanderthals* and early *H. sapiens*. But that situation was about to change. Experts agree that the appearance of miniaturized stone tools in the archaeological record signals the advent of true projectile technology, for which lightness and ballistics are crucial. Such tools are too small to wield by hand. Instead they must have been mounted in slots grooved into bone or wood to create weapons capable of being launched at high speed and long distance. The oldest known examples of this so-called microlithic technology come from none other than Pinnacle Point. There, in a rock shelter known simply as PP5-6, my team found a long record of human occupation. Using a technique called optically stimulated luminescence dating, geochronologist Zenobia Jacobs of the University of Wollongong in Australia determined that the archaeological sequence in PP5-6 spans the time from 90,000 to 50,000 years ago. The oldest microlithic tools at the site date to around 71,000 years ago. The timing hints that climate change may have precipitated the invention of this new technology. Before 71,000 years ago, the inhabitants of PP5-6 were making large stone points and blades from a type of rock called quartzite. Back then, as team member Erich Fisher of Arizona State has shown, the coastline was close to Pinnacle Point. And reconstructions of the climate and environment by Mira Bar-Matthews of the Geological Survey of Israel and Kerstin Braun, now a postdoctoral researcher at Arizona State, indicate that conditions were similar to the ones that prevail in the area today, with strong winter rains and shrubby vegetation. But around 74,000 years ago the world's climate began shifting to glacial conditions. The sea level dropped, exposing a coastal plain; summer rains increased, resulting in the spread of highly nutritious grasses and woodlands dominated by acacia trees. We think a large migration ecosystem in which grazing animals traveled east in the summer and west in the winter, tracking the rainfall and hence the fresh grass, developed on the formerly submerged coast.

Exactly why the denizens of PP5-6 began making small, light armaments after the climate shifted is unclear. But perhaps it was to pick off animals as they migrated across the new plain. Whatever the reason, the people there developed an ingenious means of making their tiny tools: turning to a new raw material—a rock called silcrete—they heated it with fire to make it easier to shape into small, sharp points. Only with the shift in climate that occurred could these early modern humans have had access to a sufficiently steady supply of firewood from the spreading acacia

trees to make the manufacture of these heat-treated microlithic tools into an enduring tradition.

We do not yet know what kind of projectile technology these microliths were used for. My colleague Marlize Lombard of the University of Johannesburg in South Africa has studied somewhat later examples from other sites and argues that they represent the origin of the bow and arrow, given that damage patterns on them resemble those seen on known arrow tips. I am not totally convinced, because her study did not test the damage created by atlatls. Whether at Pinnacle Point or elsewhere, I think the simpler atlatl preceded the more complex bow and arrow.

I also suspect that like recent hunter-gatherers in Africa, whose lives were documented in ethnographic accounts, early *H. sapiens* would have discovered the effectiveness of poison and used it to increase the killing power of projectiles. The final killing moments of a spear hunt are chaos—pounding heart, heaving lungs, dust and blood, and the stink of sweat and urine. Danger abounds. An animal run to ground, fallen to its knees through exhaustion and blood loss, has one last trick: instinct screams for the beast to lurch to its feet one final time, close the gap and bury its horns in your guts. The short lives and broken bodies of *Neanderthals* indicate that they suffered the consequences of hunting large animals at close range with handheld spears. Now consider the advantages of a projectile launched from afar and tipped with poison that paralyzes that animal, allowing the hunter to walk up and end the chase with little threat. This weapon was a breakthrough innovation.

Force of Nature

With the joining of projectile weapons to hyperprosocial behavior, a spectacular new kind of creature was born, one whose members formed teams that each operated as a single, indomitable predator. No prey—or human foe—was safe. Availed of this potent combination of traits, six men speaking six languages can put back to oar and pull in unison, riding 10-meter swells so the harpooner can rise to the prow at the headsman's order and fling lethal iron into the heaving body of a leviathan, an animal that should see humans as nothing more than minnows. In the same way, a tribe of 500 people dispersed in 20 networked bands can field a small army to exact retribution on a neighboring tribe for a territorial incursion. The emergence of this strange brew of killer and cooperator may well explain why, when glacial conditions returned between 74,000 and 60,000 years ago, once again rendering large swathes of Africa inhospitable, modern human populations did not contract as they had before. In fact, they expanded in South Africa, flourishing with a wide diversity of advanced tools. The difference was that this time modern humans were equipped to respond to any environmental crisis with flexible social connections and technology. They became the alpha predators on land and, eventually, sea. This ability to master any environment was the key that finally opened the door out of Africa and into the rest of the world.

Archaic human groups that could not join together and hurl weapons did not stand a chance against this new breed. Scientists have long debated why our cousins the *Neanderthals* went extinct. I think the most disturbing explanation is also the most likely one: *Neanderthals* were perceived as a competitor and threat, and invading modern humans exterminated them. It is what they evolved to do.

Sometimes I think about how that fateful encounter between modern humans and *Neanderthals* played out. I imagine the boasting tales *Neanderthals* might have told around their campfires of titanic battles against impossibly huge cave bears and mammoths, fought under the gray skies of glacial Europe, barefoot on ice slick with the blood of prey and brother. Then, one day, the tradition took a dark turn; the regaling turned fearful. *Neanderthals* raconteurs spoke of new people coming into the land—fast, clever people who hurled their spears impossible distances, with dreadful accuracy. These strangers even came at night in large groups, slaughtering men and children and taking the women.

The sad story of those first victims of modern human ingenuity and cooperation, the *Neanderthals*, helps to explain why horrific acts of genocide and xenocide crop up in the world today. When resources and land get sparse, we designate those who do not look or speak like us as "the others," and then we use those differences to justify exterminating or expelling them to eliminate competition. Science has revealed the stimuli that trigger our hardwired proclivities to classify people as "other" and treat them horrifically. But just because *H. sapiens* evolved to react to scarcity in this ruthless way does not mean we are locked into this response. Culture can override even the strongest biological instincts. I hope that recognition of why we instinctively turn on one another in lean times will allow us to rise above our malevolent urges and heed one of our most important cultural directives: "Never again."

Critical Thinking

1. What have been the previous theories set forth to explain the world-wide spread of modern *H. sapiens* and why have they not been sufficient, according to the author? Describe, in general, the author's alternate scenario.

2. Where did anatomically modern humans evolve and what advantages did they have that allowed them to spread across the globe?

3. Why were archaic human groups at a disadvantage compared to anatomically modern humans?

Internet References

Fossil Hominids FAQ
www.talkorigins.org/faqs/homs

Archeurope: Prehistoric Archaeology
http://www.archeurope.com/

Smithsonian National Museum of Natural History
http://humanorigins.si.edu

Curtis W. Marean is a professor at the School of Human Evolution and Social Change at Arizona State University and associate director of the university's Institute of Human Origins. Marean is also an honorary professor at Nelson Mandela Metropolitan University in South Africa. He is particularly interested in the origins of modern humans and the occupation of coastal ecosystems. His research is funded by the National Science Foundation and the Hyde Family Foundations.

Article   Prepared by: Elvio Angeloni

From Wolf to Dog

Scientists are racing to solve the enduring mystery of how a large, dangerous carnivore evolved into our best friend.

VIRGINIA MORELL

Learning Outcomes

After reading this article, you will be able to:

- Discuss the differences between dogs and wolves that seem to be the result of dog domestication.

- Discuss the difficulty in identifying the time and place of dog domestication.

- Discuss the evidence for dog domestication during the hunter-gatherer era.

- Identify the physical characteristics that distinguish domesticated dogs from wolves.

When you have cared for dogs and wild wolves from the time they are little more than a week old and have bottle-fed and nurtured them day and night, you are wise to their differences. Since 2008 Zsófia Virányi, an ethologist at the Wolf Science Center in Austria, and her colleagues have been raising the two species to figure out what makes a dog a dog—and a wolf a wolf. At the center, the researchers oversee and study four packs of wolves and four packs of dogs, containing anywhere from two to six animals each. They have trained the wolves and dogs to follow basic commands, to walk on leashes and to use their nose to tap the screen of a computer monitor so that they can take cognition tests. Yet despite having lived and worked with the scientists for seven years, the wolves retain an independence of mind and behavior that is most undoglike.

"You can leave a piece of meat on a table and tell one of our dogs, 'No!' and he will not take it," Virányi says. "But the wolves ignore you. They'll look you in the eye and grab the meat"—a disconcerting assertiveness that she has experienced on more than one occasion. And when this happens, she wonders yet again how the wolf ever became the domesticated dog. "You can't have an animal—a large carnivore—living with you and behaving like that," she says. "You want an animal that's like a dog; one that accepts 'No!'"

Dogs' understanding of the absolute no may be connected to the structure of their packs, which are not egalitarian like those of the wolves but dictatorial, the center's researchers have discovered. Wolves can eat together, Virányi notes. Even if a dominant wolf flashes its teeth and growls at a subordinate, the lower-ranked member does not move away. The same is not true in dog packs, however. "Subordinate dogs will rarely eat at the same time as the dominant one," she observes. "They don't even try." Their studies also suggest that rather than expecting to cooperate on tasks with humans, dogs simply want to be told what to do.

How the independent-minded, egalitarian wolf changed into the obedient, waiting-for-orders dog and what role ancient humans played in achieving this feat baffle Virányi: "I try to imagine how they did it, and I really can't."

Virányi is not alone in her bafflement. Although researchers have successfully determined the time, location, and ancestry of nearly every other domesticated species, from sheep to cattle to chickens to guinea pigs, they continue to debate these questions for our best friend, *Canis familiaris*. Scientists also know why humans developed these other domesticated animals—to have food close at hand—but they do not know what inspired us to allow a large, wild carnivore into the family homestead. Yet dogs were the first domesticated species, a status that makes the mystery of their origin that much more perplexing.

As inscrutable as the mystery is, scientists are piecing it together. In the past few years they have made several break-throughs. They can now say with confidence that contrary to received wisdom, dogs are not descended from the gray wolf species that persists today across much of the Northern Hemisphere, from Alaska to Siberia to Saudi Arabia, but from an unknown and extinct wolf. They are also certain that this domestication event took place while humans were still hunter-gatherers and not after they became agriculturalists, as some investigators had proposed.

At what time and in what location wolves became dogs and whether it was only a one-time event are questions that a large research team, composed of once competing scientists, has just started to tackle. The researchers are visiting museums, universities, and other institutions around the world to study collections of canine fossils and bones, and they are readying genetic samples from ancient and modern dogs and wolves for the most comprehensive comparison to date. When they are finished, they will be very close to knowing when and where—if not exactly how—wolves first began down the path toward becoming our trusted companions. Answers to these questions will complement the growing body of evidence for how humans and dogs influenced one another after that relationship was first forged.

Mixed Signals

When modern humans arrived in Europe perhaps 45,000 years ago, they encountered the gray wolf and other types of wolves, including the megafaunal wolf, which pursued large game such as mammoths. By that time wolves had already proved themselves among the most successful and adaptable species in the canid family, having spread across Eurasia to Japan and into the Middle East and North America. They were not confined to a single habitat type but flourished in tundra, steppelands, deserts, forests, coastal regions, and the high altitude of the Tibetan Plateau. And they competed with the newly arrived humans for the same prey—mammoths, deer, aurochs, woolly rhinoceroses, antelopes, and horses. In spite of this competition, one type of wolf, perhaps a descendant of a megafaunal wolf, apparently began living close to people. For many years scientists concurred on the basis of small portions of the genome that this species was the modern gray wolf (*Canis lupus*) and that this canid alone gave rise to dogs.

But last January geneticists discovered that this long-held "fact" was wrong. Repeated interbreeding between gray wolves and dogs, which share 99.9 percent of their DNA, had produced misleading signals in the earlier studies. Such consorting between the two species continues today: wolves with black coats received the gene for that color from a dog; shepherd dogs in Georgia's Caucasus Mountains mate so often with the local wolves that hybrid ancestors are found in both species'

populations, and between 2 and 3 percent of the sampled animals are first-generation hybrids. (Building on the admixture theme, in June researchers writing in *Current Biology* reported on the sequencing of DNA from a 35,000-year-old wolf fossil from Siberia. This species appears to have contributed DNA to high-latitude dogs such as huskies through ancient interbreeding.)

Analyzing whole genomes of living dogs and wolves, last January's study revealed that today's Fidos are not the descendants of modern gray wolves. Instead the two species are sister taxa, descended from an unknown ancestor that has since gone extinct. "It was such a long-standing view that the gray wolf we know today was around for hundreds of thousands of years and that dogs derived from them," says Robert Wayne, an evolutionary geneticist at the University of California, Los Angeles. "We're very surprised that they're not." Wayne led the first genetic studies proposing the ancestor–descendant relationship between the two species and more recently was one of the 30 co-authors of the latest study, published in *PLOS Genetics*, that debunked that notion.

More surprises may come from renewed efforts to nail down the timing and location of dog domestication. Previous studies left a confusing trail. The first analysis, carried out in 1997, focused on the genetic differences between dogs and gray wolves and concluded that dogs may have been domesticated some 135,000 years ago. A later study by some members of the same group indicated that dogs originated in the Middle East. But another analysis, which examined the DNA of 1,500 modern dogs that was published in 2009, argued that dogs were first domesticated in southern China less than 16,300 years ago. Then, in 2013, a team of scientists compared the mitochondrial genomes of ancient European and American dogs and wolves with their modern counterparts. It concluded that dogs originated in Europe between 32,000 and 19,000 years ago.

Evolutionary biologist Greger Larson of the University of Oxford, who is co-leading the recently launched multidisciplinary dog-domestication project, says the previous studies, while important, have shortcomings. He faults the 1997 and 2009 studies for relying solely on DNA from modern dogs and the last one for its geographically limited samples. "You can't solve this problem by using modern animals alone as windows to the past," Larson says. The studies of modern dog DNA are not sufficiently informative, he explains, because people have moved and interbred dogs around the world numerous times, blurring their genetic heritage. Any regional signatures that might have helped identify where they were domesticated has long since been lost.

To further muddy the picture, "wolves have a ridiculously broad distribution across the world," Larson explains. In contrast, he points out, the ancestors of most other domesticated species, such as sheep and chickens, had much smaller geographical ranges, making it far easier to trace their origins.

Larson suspects that several geographically disparate populations of the ancestral wolf species may have contributed to the making of today's dog. It would not be the first time such a thing happened: Larson has shown that pigs were domesticated twice—once in the Near East and once in Europe. Intriguingly, enigmatic fossils from Belgium, the Czech Republic, and southwestern Siberia that date to between 36,000 and 33,000 years ago and exhibit a mix of wolf and dog features hint at the possibility of at least three independent instances of domestication attempts from an ancestral wolf. But the anatomical characteristics of these fossils alone cannot answer the question of where dogs came from.

To solve the dog-domestication puzzle, Larson and his collaborators are using two key techniques employed in the pig study: they are undertaking a more thorough analysis of thousands of modern and ancient samples of dog and wolf DNA from individuals across the globe and are using a fairly new technique for measuring bones. Called geometric morphometrics, this method enables scientists to quantify certain traits, such as the curves of a skull, and so better compare the bones of individuals. Previously researchers relied primarily on the length of a canid's snout and the size of the canine teeth to distinguish dogs from wolves. Dogs' snouts are generally shorter, their canines are smaller, and their teeth are on the whole more crowded than those of wolves. The new method should identify other, perhaps more telling differences. Together these techniques should yield a far more detailed picture of dog domestication than any other approach has to date.

Close Encounters

Although the when and where of dog domestication remain open questions, scientists now have a general idea of which kind of human society was the first to establish a close relationship with dogs. Perhaps not surprisingly, this question, too, has generated debate over the years. Some investigators have argued that settled agriculturalists had that distinction. After all, the other domesticated animal species all entered the human realm after people started farming and putting down roots. But other researchers credited earlier hunter-gatherers with being the first to have dogs. Wayne says that his team's latest DNA study has at last ended this part of the debate. "The domestication of the dog occurred prior to the agricultural revolution," he asserts. "It happened when people were still hunter-gatherers," sometime between 32,00 and 18,800 years ago. (Agriculture is thought to have begun in a big way roughly 12,000 years ago in the Middle East.)

And that finding leads back to the questions Virányi and most everyone who owns and loves a dog has: How did these hunter-gatherers do it? Or did they? What if the first dogs—which, it is important to remember, would have at first been more wolf than dog—showed up on their own?

The genus *Canis* goes back about 7 million years, and although some members of that group, such as jackals and the Ethiopian wolf, lived in Africa, the birthplace of humanity, there is no evidence that the earliest humans tried to domesticate any of these species. Only after modern humans spread out from Africa and into Europe 45,000 years ago did the wolf-dog-human triad begin to form.

Hints about the evolving relationship between canids and early modern humans have come from the paleontological and archaeological records. Take the canid remains unearthed between 1894 and 1930 at Předmostí, a roughly 27,000-year-old settlement in the Bečva Valley in what is now the Czech Republic. The ancient people who lived and died there are known to us as the Gravettians, after a site with similar cultural artifacts in La Gravette, France. The Czech Gravettians were mammoth hunters, killing more than 1,000 of the great creatures at this one site alone. They ate the behemoths' meat, used their shoulder blades to cover human remains and decorated their tusks with engravings. They also killed wolves. Canids are the most abundant type of mammal at the site after mammoths, and their remains include seven complete skulls. But some of the canid skulls do not look exactly like those of wolves. Three in particular stand out, says Mietje Germonpré, a paleontologist at the Royal Belgian Institute of Natural Sciences in Brussels. Compared with the wolf skulls found at Předmostí, the three unusual ones "have shorter snouts, broader braincases and crowded teeth," she notes.

These kinds of anatomical changes are the first signs of domestication, Germonpré and others say. Similar changes are found in the skulls of the silver foxes that are the focus of a famous, long-running experiment at Novosibirsk State University in Russia. Since 1959, researchers there have selected the foxes for tameness and bred them. Over the generations their coats have become spotted, their ears floppy, their tails curly, their snouts shorter and wider—even though the scientists have been selecting only for behavior. Similar changes are seen in other domesticated species, including rats and mink. Investigators have yet to explain why docile animals are consistently altered in these ways. They do know that the tame silver foxes have smaller adrenal glands and much lower levels of adrenaline than their wild counterparts.

Last year other scientists came up with a testable hypothesis: tame animals may have fewer or defective neural crest cells. These embryonic cells play a key role in the development of the teeth, jaws, ears and pigment-producing cells—as well as the nervous system, including the fight-or-flight response. If they are right, then all those cute domestic traits—spotted coats, curly tails, floppy ears—are a side effect of domestication.

Germonpré suspects that the apparent domestication at Předmostí was a dead-end event; she doubts that these animals are related to today's dogs. Nevertheless, to Germonpré, "they are dogs—Paleolithic dogs." She says these early dogs probably looked very much like today's huskies, although they would have been larger, about the size of a German shepherd. Germonpré calls the Předmostí specimens "dogs" because of what she interprets as some type of relationship between the canids and the Gravettians. For instance, a dog's lower jaw was found near a child's skeleton, according to the diary of the original excavator.

The dogs were also included in rituals in ways that other species were not. In one case, a Gravettian tucked what is most likely a piece of mammoth bone between the front teeth of one of the dog skulls after the animal died and arranged its jaws so that they clamped together on the bone. Germonpré suspects that an ancient mammoth hunter placed the bone there as part of a ritual related to hunting, or to help sustain in death an animal the hunter revered, or to enable the dog to assist a human in the afterlife. "You see this kind of thing in the ethnographic record," she says, citing, as one example, a Chukchi ceremony in Siberia for a deceased woman in the early 20th century. A reindeer was sacrificed and its stomach placed in the mouth of a dead dog's head, which was then positioned to protect the woman on her death journey.

Many researchers imagine that these early people set about making the wolf into the dog to help us hunt big game. In her book *The Invaders*, published by Harvard University Press earlier this year, anthropologist Pat Shipman argues that the first dogs (or wolf-dogs, as she calls them) were like a new and superior technology and helped the mammoth-hunting modern humans outcompete the *Neanderthals*. But she, Wayne, Larson and others think that wolves joined forces with humans on their own; that the canny, adaptable canids identified us as a new ecological niche they could exploit. The alternative scenario—people brazenly raiding wolf dens to steal pups young enough for taming—would have been a dangerous undertaking. And raising wolves in camps with young children would have presented another serious risk.

"We didn't do [domestication] deliberately; not at first," Larson surmises. Instead wolves most likely started following people for the same reason that ants trail into our kitchens—"to take advantage of a nutritional resource, our trash." Over time, some of these camp-following wolves increasingly lost their fear of people—and vice versa—and a mutually beneficial relationship developed. Wolf-dogs would sniff out prey for us, and we would share the resulting meat with them. (Circumstantial evidence for this scenario comes from the silver fox experiment. By selecting foxes that were less fearful of humans, the researchers at Novosibirsk eventually developed a silver fox

that runs to greet people. Most silver foxes in captivity hide in the back of their cage.)

There is just one problem with this imagined event, at least at Předmostí: Germonpré's early dogs were not eating mammoth meat even though that is what the humans were dining on; isotopic analysis of the Paleolithic dogs' bones indicates that they were eating reindeer, which was not a favored food of the people who inhabited the site. The Předmostí dogs also had broken teeth and severe facial injuries, many of which had healed. "Those could be signs of fighting with other dogs," Germonpré says, "or of being hit with sticks." She pictures the human-dog bond developing via the mammoth hunters' canid rituals. In this scenario, the hunter-gatherers brought pups to their camps, perhaps after killing the adult wolves, just as many modern nomadic peoples bring baby or young animals to their settlements. The mammoth bones at Předmostí show no signs of being gnawed by canids, which suggests they were not free to roam and scavenge people's scraps. Rather humans probably tied the canids up, fed them what appears to have been second-rate food, given that the humans were not eating it, and even bred them—all to ensure a ready supply of victims for their ritualistic sacrifices.

Breeding wolves in captivity would lead to the anatomical changes that Germonpré has documented in the Předmostí dogs and could even produce a less fearful and independent animal as seen in the Novosibirsk silver foxes.

Confined, beaten, fed a restricted diet, the dogs at Předmostí would likely have understood the meaning of "No!" There is no evidence at Předmostí or other comparably old sites where dog remains have been uncovered that the ancient hunter-gatherers there regarded the canines as their friends, companions, or hunting pals, Germonpré observes. "That relationship came later."

Shifting Fortunes

If Germonpré is right, then dog domestication may have begun quite early and under circumstances that were not favorable for the dogs. Not every scientist agrees that Germonpré's dogs are dogs, however. Some prefer the wolf-dog designation or simply "wolf" because their taxonomic status is not clear either from their morphology or genetics. (Larson expects to resolve this question over the course of his mega project.)

The earliest undisputed dog on record, a 14,000-year-old specimen from a site called Bonn-Oberkassel in Germany, tells a very different story of dog domestication, evincing a much more affectionate bond between humans and canines. In the early 1900s archaeologists excavating the site found the dog's skeleton interred in a grave with the remains of a man about 50 years old and a woman about 20 to 25. When researchers see such associations, they know they are looking at a fully domesticated animal—one that is treasured and regarded so highly that it is given a burial as if it, too, were a member of its human family.

The Bonn-Oberkassel dog is not the only ancient hound to have received such honors. In Israel, at Ain Mallaha, a hunter-gatherer site dating to 12,000 years ago in the upper Jordan Valley, archaeologists discovered what is perhaps the most famous dog-human burial. The skeleton of an elderly person lies curled on its right side, its left arm stretched out under the head, with the hand resting gently on a puppy. The dog was about four to five months old and was placed there, archaeologists think, to be a companion to the deceased. Unlike the Předmostí dogs, this puppy was not battered; its remains were arranged lovingly with someone who may have cared for it.

Although such touching dog-human scenes are rare during this period, dog burials are not. And after about 10,000 years ago, the practice of entombing dogs increased. No other animal species is so consistently included in human mortuary rituals. People had come to see dogs in a different light, and this shift in attitude had a profound effect on dogs' evolution. Perhaps during this period dogs acquired their human social skills, such as abilities to read our facial expressions, understand our pointing gestures, and gaze into our eyes (which increases oxytocin—the love hormone—in both dog and owner). "Dog burials happen after hunting moves away from the open plains and into dense forests," says Angela Perri, a zooarchaeologist at the Max Planck Institute for Evolutionary Anthropology in Leipzig, Germany, and a specialist on these burials. "Dogs in open environments might be good for helping you transport meat from killed mammoths but wouldn't necessarily help you hunt them," she says, noting that elephant hunters do not use dogs. "But dogs are excellent for hunting smaller game, such as deer and boar," that live in forests. Beginning at least 15,000 years ago and probably somewhat earlier, Perri says, hunter-gatherers in Europe, Asia, and the Americas began depending on their dogs' hunting skills for survival. Researchers cannot trace a direct genetic line from those animals to our pet pooches; nevertheless, they say, these animals were unquestionably dogs. "Good hunting dogs can find fresh tracks, and guide the hunters to the prey, and hold them at bay," says Perri, who has joined traditional hunters and their dogs in Japan and the U.S. "When people start using dogs for hunting, you see a switch in how they view them, and you start finding dog burials across the world." Such burials are not rituals or sacrifices, she emphasizes. "These are burials of admiration, where the dogs are interred with ocher, stone points and blades—male tools of hunting."

One of the most elaborate dog burials comes from Skateholm, Sweden, and is dated to about 7,000 years ago. Several dogs were found interred in the same area with dozens of humans. One was particularly celebrated and given the finest treatment there of anyone, human or dog. "The dog was laid on its side, flint chips were scattered at its waist, and red deer antlers and a carved stone hammer were placed with it, and it was sprinkled with red ocher," Perri says. There is no indication of why this dog was so revered, but she suspects it must have been an excellent hunter and that its human owner mourned its death. "You see this relationship among hunters and their dogs today and in the ethnographic record," Perri observes, noting that Tasmanian hunter-gatherers in the late nineteenth century were quoted as saying, "Our dogs are more important than our children. Without them, we couldn't hunt; we wouldn't survive."

Early dogs provided other important services, too. The first known attempt at the kind of intentional selection that has shaped the evolution of *C. familiaris* comes from a site in Denmark dating to 8,000 years ago. The ancient hunter-gatherers there had three sizes of dogs, possibly bred for certain tasks. "I didn't expect to see something like dog breeds," Perri says, "but they had small, medium and large dogs." It is not clear what they used the small dogs for, but the medium-sized animals had the build of hunting dogs, and the larger ones, which were the size of Greenland sled dogs (about 70 pounds), most likely transported and hauled goods. With their warning barks, all the dogs would have served as camp sentinels, too.

The dog's status plunged when people developed farming. In early agricultural settlements, dog burials are rare. "The difference is so strong," Perri says. "When people are living as hunter-gatherers, there are tons of dog burials." But as agriculture spreads, the burials end. "Dogs are no longer as useful." That fall from grace, though, did not doom them to extinction—far from it. In many places, they began to turn up on the dinner table, providing a new reason to keep dogs around.

Not all agricultural cultures consigned Fido to the menu, however. Among those groups that tended livestock, dogs were sometimes bred for herding. Those that proved their worth could still end up pampered in the afterlife. In 2006 archaeologists discovered 80 mummified dogs buried in graves next to their human owners at a 1,000-year-old cemetery near Lima, Peru. The dogs had protected the Chiribaya people's llamas and, in return for their service, were well treated in life and death. Nearly 30 of the dogs were wrapped in finely woven llama-wool blankets, and llama and fish bones were set close to their mouth. The region's arid climate mummified the dogs' remains, preserving their fur and tissue. Unwrapped, the mummies resemble the small street dogs that roam Lima today, looking for a human to take them in and tell them what—and what not—to do. (That resemblance notwithstanding, the Chiribaya herding dogs are not related to Lima's modern-day mutts. Nor is there any evidence to support claims linking any of the breeds of antiquity anywhere to the modern, standard breeds of the American Kennel Club.)

Although the Chiribaya dogs and other dog burials in the Americas hail from the wrong place and time to represent the earliest stages of domestication, Larson and his colleagues are happily measuring their bones and sampling their DNA. That is because these early North American dogs descended from ancient European or Asian dogs; their bones and genes will help the scientists determine how many dog-domestication events occurred and where they took place. Thus far, in their attempt to study as many ancient canids as possible, the researchers have analyzed upward of 3,000 wolves, dogs, and other specimens that do not readily fall into either box. More than 50 scientists worldwide are helping with the effort. They expect to have a paper ready on their initial findings by this summer. Will we then finally know where and when the dog became domesticated? "I expect we'll be very close to an answer," Larson says. But we still won't know exactly how some long-lost type of wolf managed to become a creature that respects "No."

Critical Thinking

1. How do dogs differ from wolves anatomically and behaviorally?
2. When were dogs domesticated and why?
3. Discuss the "human social skills" of dogs.
4. How has the relationship between dogs and humans changed over time and why?

Internet References

Breeding Business
https://breedingbusiness.com/origin-and-evolution-of-the-domestic-dog/

Duke Canine Cognition Center
https://evolutionaryanthropology.duke.edu/research/dogs/research

VIRGINIA MORELL is a science writer based in Oregon. She covers evolution and animal behavior for *Science* and *National Geographic*, among other publications. Her latest book is *Animal Wise* (Crown, 2013).

Unit 5

UNIT

Prepared by: Elvio Angeloni

Late Hominid Evolution

The most important aspect of human evolution is also the most difficult to decipher from the fossil evidence: our development as sentient, social beings, capable of communicating by means of language.

We detect hints of incipient humanity in the form of crudely chipped tools, the telltale signs of a home base, or the artistic achievements of ornaments and cave art. Yet none of these indicators of a distinctly hominid way of life can provide us with the nuances of the everyday lives of these creatures, their social relations, or their supernatural beliefs, if any. Most of what remains is the rubble of bones and stones from which we interpret what we can of their lifestyle, thought processes, and ability to communicate.

It is understandable, then, that some questions regarding our most recent ancestors have yet to be fully answered. Did we derive entirely from people who represented a second wave of migration out of Africa and who replaced the archaic members of species (i.e., the remnants of a much earlier migration) according to the "replacement hypothesis"? Or did our modern *Homo sapiens* ancestors mate with archaic sapiens, as proposed in the "multiregional theory"? Recent evidence seems to say the answer is not as clear-cut as either side of the controversy would have it—that there was certainly some replacement and that there was also some degree of admixture. Did modern *Homo sapiens* truly usher in an "Upper Paleolithic Revolution," involving art, mortuary rituals, personal adornments, and more complex food-getting technologies and strategies? Or did such innovations come about on a piecemeal basis, scattered in time and place depending upon the needs of the people, including the archaic members of our species? Evidence suggests the latter.

Beyond the anatomical and technological adaptations, questions have arisen as to how our hominid forebears organized themselves socially and whether modern-day human behavior is inherited as a legacy of our evolutionary past or is a learned product of contemporary circumstances. Attempts to address these questions have given rise to the technique referred to as the "ethnographic analogy." This is a method whereby anthropologists use "ethnographies," or field studies, of modern-day hunters and gatherers whose lives we take to be the best approximations we have to what life might have been like for our ancestors. Granted, these contemporary foragers have been living under conditions of environmental and social change just as industrial peoples have. Nevertheless, it seems that, at least in some aspects of their lives, they have not changed as much as we have. So, if we are to make any enlightened assessments of prehistoric behavior patterns, we are better off looking at them than at ourselves.

As if to show that controversial interpretations of the evidence are not limited to the earlier hominid period, we can also see how long-held beliefs about recent human evolution are being shattered. Hominid migrations are being revised by new evidence coming from newly discovered fossils, artifacts, and even DNA.

For some scientists, these recent revelations fit quite comfortably with previously held positions; for others it seems that reputations, as well as theories, are at stake. How it all shakes out may cause some temporary discomfort for some, but in the long run, a better understanding of our evolutionary past will benefit all of us.

Article Prepared by: Elvio Angeloni

Ancient DNA

The Lure and Limitations of a Coded Past.

BRIDGET ALEX

Learning Outcomes

After reading this article, you will be able to:

- Discuss the importance of "archaeogenetics."
- Discuss some of the important findings of "paleogenetics.

In 1984, geneticists recovered 229 base pairs of genetic code from a quagga, a subspecies of zebra extinct since the late 1800s. The achievement proved DNA could survive in dead things and spurred a new field of science: paleogenetics. Today, technological advances allow scientists to read billions of letters from the genomes of ancient humans and other organisms, transforming our view of history and evolution.

The genetic record is "like a lost library . . . and we're just starting to learn the language of all those books that we have uncovered," says Johannes Krause, director of archaeogenetics at the Max Planck Institute for the Science of Human History in Jena, Germany.

For anthropologists, ancient human DNA (aDNA) provides insights that could not be gleaned from fossils or artifacts. It's already settled some major debates, including whether modern humans interacted with Neanderthals. Ancient genomes show definitively that our ancestors not only met but also mated with Neanderthals—multiple times—between 40,000 and 100,000 years ago.

In 2015, aDNA confirmed that Kennewick Man, an 8,000-year-old skeleton found in Washington state in 1996, was genetically closest to Native Americans. The revelation ended a 20-year legal battle and allowed tribes to rebury the bones. Ancient DNA has also brought surprises. In 2010, the genome of a pinky bone from Siberia revealed the existence of Denisovans, a previously unknown type of human that lived around the time of Neanderthals. Denisovan aDNA also shows they interbred with the ancestors of some living humans, contributing genes beneficial in cold environments and at high altitudes.

A decade ago, these discoveries were not possible; geneticists could only read short stretches of ancient genomes. Consequently, studies focused either on particular genes or on narrow portions of DNA: the male Y-chromosome or maternally inherited code called mitochondrial DNA. These short sequences do not reflect an individual's complete ancestry. For that, researchers need DNA from across the full genome. Obtaining it from living humans is not difficult, but it's a formidable challenge to extract and sequence genome-wide aDNA, which can degrade into fragments, undergo chemical reactions that change its code, and be contaminated by modern DNA.

With the recent development of specialized methods for genome-wide analysis of aDNA, "the power of archaeogenetics has really been unleashed," says Krause.

Now encompassing a half-million years and hundreds of individuals, ancient DNA studies are revising our understanding of major events, such as the origins and spread of agriculture. Because aDNA can be used to track the evolution of diseases and human resistance to them over time, it's also valuable to medical research. And researchers are already working on identifying the genes unique to modern humans—at the most basic level, what unites and defines our species.

Decoding aDNA 101

1. Extraction: In a sterile lab, bones and other surviving tissues are cleaned, crushed into powder, and dissolved with chemicals that isolate short DNA strands.
2. DNA soup: Despite cleaning, the extract is a soup of DNA from the sample and contaminated material, mostly microbes from soil where the remains were

buried. Researchers add molecular tags that will later work like barcodes, selectively binding to DNA to inventory and find particular sequences.

3. Copies: To read the DNA quickly and accurately, computers must analyze millions of copies simultaneously. Geneticists make these copies by heating double-stranded DNA, causing it to separate; enzymes then build new double strands from each half. Repeating the procedure makes two strands into four, then four into eight, and so forth, until millions of strands have identical DNA code and tags. Because human genomes are over 99 percent identical, researchers often selectively copy only the parts that differ.

4. Sequencing: In the final round of copying, geneticists chemically color the different nucleotide bases—better known by their letters A, T, C, and G. Computers then read the code based on the order in which the colors appear, analyzing all the identical strands with matching tags at the same time to weed out any errors.

5. Authentication: Researchers use a number of clues to discard contaminants in the ancient code: for example, aDNA strands are usually shorter than 100 letters, with predictable degradation patterns.

6. Alignment: The short strands that have been read need to be arranged into their proper positions across the full genome. Software lines them up based on overlapping stretches of code and comparisons with previously sequenced reference genomes.

Take It to the Limit

Don't get your hopes up for dino DNA. Studies conducted in the 1990s, reporting genetic code from fossils over 50 million years old, have since been rejected as cases of contamination. Most aDNA has come from samples younger than 50,000 years and from cold climates.

Although paleogenetics is advancing technologically, it will always be limited by preservation: researchers can't extract DNA from specimens that no longer have any.

When organisms die, their DNA decomposes. How long this takes depends on factors like temperature, burial conditions, and the number of microbes making a meal of it. Calculations predict that in the optimal conditions—very cold ones—DNA could survive around 1 million years. To date, the title for oldest complete genome belongs to a horse unearthed from frozen ground in Yukon, Canada, and dated to be 560,000–780,000 years old. The oldest DNA from a member of our *Homo* genus is a fragment of genetic code from 430,000-year-old Neanderthal ancestors found in Spain's Sima de los Huesos cave, which stays at a cool 50°F.

Geneticists are starting to have success in warmer places, which is a priority because most of human evolution occurred

in Africa. Recently, they discovered that DNA preserves best—with up to 100 times higher recovery rates—in the petrous bone. Samples of this tiny, dense part of the skull from places such as the Middle East have yielded a DNA that's up to 12,000 years old.

Ancient DNA Atlas

The first big discoveries in paleogenetics came from chance specimens with well-preserved aDNA. Researchers learned whatever they could from the available sequences. With today's aDNA capture methods, geneticists can analyze hundreds of ancient genomes to answer specific questions. The emerging genetic history spans the globe from 430,000 years ago to today, representing both individuals and entire populations.

Earliest American Genome

- (Montana 12,600 years ago) In 2014, researchers recovered the genome of Anzick-1, an infant buried with Clovis tools, artifacts from the first widespread culture in the Americas. The results confirm that Native Americans mostly descend from Siberians who migrated several thousand years before Anzick lived.
- Seal Tuberculosis (Peru 1,000 years ago) Tuberculosis in the Americas is thought to have arrived with European colonists, although earlier indigenous skeletons show signs of the disease. A 2014 study found tuberculosis bacteria DNA in 1,000-year-old Peruvian bones; in a surprise twist, it was not the European strain, but one likely contracted from seals.
- Before the Black Death (Eurasia 3,000–5,000 years ago) In 2015, geneticists discovered aDNA from plague-causing *Yersina pestis* bacteria in the teeth of Bronze Age Eurasians, revealing that less-contagious strains infected people millennia before historically documented pandemics. The bubonic types responsible for the medieval Black Death and recent outbreaks emerged about 3,000 years ago from a mutation that made *Y. pestis* flea-borne.
- Oldest *Homo* DNA (Spain 430,000 years ago) Researchers in 2016 salvaged about 50,000 base pairs of genetic code from fossils excavated

years before in the Sima de los Huesos cave. The aDNA confirms what many archaeologists have long believed: the Sima hominins were Neanderthal ancestors.

- Ice Age Immigrants (Eurasia 7,000–45,000 years ago) aDNA from 51 individuals reveals the earliest modern humans to reach Europe went extinct; those arriving in subsequent waves, starting 37,000 years ago, left descendants who remain to this day. There may also have been a migration of Near Easterners into Europe roughly 14,000 years ago, detected for the first time by aDNA analysis in 2016.

- Denisova Cave (Altai Mountains 50,000–100,000 years ago) Samples of aDNA from one finger fragment and three teeth found in Siberia revealed Denisovans, a newly discovered type of extinct human. The same site also yielded a toe bone, which produced the highest-quality Neanderthal genome sequenced so far.

- Neanderthal Great- . . . Grandson (Romania 40,000 years ago) Oase 1, the jawbone of a modern human found in 2002, contained over 99 percent contaminant DNA. But in 2015, researchers sequenced enough authentic code to show that the man had a Neanderthal ancestor a mere four to six generations back.

- First Farmers (Middle East and Europe 3,000–14,000 years ago) Analyses of hundreds of genomes show how early Middle Eastern farmers spread to Europe, mixed with hunter-gatherers and adapted to agricultural diets, including through a lactase gene mutation that allowed people to drink milk after childhood.

Critical Thinking

1. What is "archaeogenetics" and why is it important?
2. What have been some of the most important findings using ancient DNA?
3. What are the best circumstances for retrieving ancient DNA?

Internet References

genomeweb
https://www.genomeweb.com/

International Society of Genetic Geneology
https://isogg.org/wiki/List_of_forensic_and_ancient_DNA_laboratories

Max Planck Institute for Molecular Genetics
https://www.molgen.mpg.de/2168/en

Article   Prepared by: Elvio Angeloni

Human Hybrids

MICHAEL F. HAMMER

Learning Outcomes

After reading this article, you will be able to:

- Discuss the ways in which DNA technology has clarified the debate between the various models for human origins.

- Discuss the evidence for positive selection of archaic genes in modern populations.

I t is hard to imagine today, but for most of humankind's evolutionary history, multiple humanlike species shared the earth. As recently as 40,000 years ago, *Homo sapiens* lived alongside several kindred forms, including the *Neandertals* and tiny *Homo floresiensis*. For decades scientists have debated exactly how *H. sapiens* originated and came to be the last human species standing. Thanks in large part to genetic studies in the 1980s, one theory emerged as the clear front runner. In this view, anatomically modern humans arose in Africa and spread out across the rest of the Old World, completely replacing the existing archaic groups. Exactly how this novel form became the last human species on the earth is mysterious. Perhaps the invaders killed off the natives they encountered, or outcompeted the strangers on their own turf, or simply reproduced at a higher rate. However it happened, the newcomers seemed to have eliminated their competitors without interbreeding with them.

This recent African replacement model, as it is known, has essentially served as the modern human origins paradigm for the past 25 years. Yet mounting evidence indicates that it is wrong. Recent advances in DNA sequencing technology have enabled researchers to dramatically scale-up data collection from living people and from extinct species. Analyses of these data with increasingly sophisticated computational tools indicate that the story of our family history is not as simple as most experts thought. It turns out that people today carry DNA inherited from *Neandertals* and other archaic humans, revealing that early *H. sapiens* mated with these other species and produced fertile offspring who were able to hand this genetic legacy down through thousands of generations. In addition to upsetting the conventional wisdom about our origins, the discoveries are driving new inquiries into how extensive the interbreeding was, which geographical areas it occurred in and whether modern humans show signs of benefiting from any of the genetic contributions from our prehistoric cousins.

Mysterious Origins

To fully appreciate the effect of these recent genetic findings on scientists' understanding of human evolution, we must look back to the 1980s, when the debate over the rise of *H. sapiens* was heating up. Examining the fossil data, paleoanthropologists agreed that an earlier member of our genus, *Homo erectus*, arose in Africa some two million years ago and began spreading out of that continent and into other regions of the Old World shortly thereafter. Yet they disagreed over how the ancestors of *H. sapiens* transitioned from that archaic form to our modern one, with its rounded braincase and delicately built skeleton—features that appear in the fossil record at around 195,000 years ago.

Proponents of the so-called multiregional evolution model, developed by Milford H. Wolpoff of the University of Michigan and his colleagues, argued that the transformation occurred gradually among archaic populations wherever they lived throughout Africa, Eurasia, and Oceania because of a combination of migration and mating that allowed beneficial modern traits to spread among all these populations. In this scenario, although all modern humans shared particular physical features by the end of this transition, some regionally distinctive features inherited from archaic ancestors persisted, perhaps because these traits helped populations to adapt to their local environments. A variant of multiregional evolution put forward by Fred Smith, now at Illinois State University, called the Assimilation model, acknowledges a greater contribution of modern traits by populations from Africa.

In contrast, champions of the replacement model (also known as the Out of Africa model, among other names), including Christopher Stringer of the Natural History Museum in London, contended that anatomically modern humans arose as a distinct species in a single place—sub-Saharan Africa—and went on to completely replace all archaic humans everywhere without interbreeding with them. A looser version of this theory—the Hybridization model proposed by Günter Bräuer of the University of Hamburg in Germany—allows for the occasional production of hybrids between these modern humans and the archaic groups they met up with as they pushed into new lands.

With only the fossil evidence to go on, the debate seemed locked in a stalemate. Genetics changed that situation. With the advent of DNA technology, scientists developed methods for piecing together the past by analyzing genetic variation in contemporary human populations and using it to reconstruct evolutionary trees for individual genes. By studying a gene tree, researchers could infer when and where the last common ancestor of all the variants of a given gene existed, thus yielding insights into the population of origin for the ancestral sequence.

In a landmark study published in 1987, Allan C. Wilson of the University of California, Berkeley, and his colleagues reported that the evolutionary tree for the DNA found in mitochondria—the energy-producing components of cells—traced back to a female ancestor who lived in an African population around 200,000 years ago. (Mitochondrial DNA, or mtDNA, is passed down from mother to child and treated as a single gene in ancestry studies.) These findings fit the expectations of the replacement model, as did subsequent studies of small sections of nuclear DNA, including the paternally inherited Y chromosome.

Further genetic support for the replacement model came a decade later, when Svante Pääbo, now at the Max Planck Institute for Evolutionary Anthropology in Leipzig, Germany, and his colleagues succeeded in extracting and analyzing a fragment of mtDNA from Neandertal bones. The study found that the Neandertal mtDNA sequences were distinct from those of contemporary humans and that there was no sign of interbreeding between them—a result that subsequent studies of mtDNA from additional Neandertal specimens confirmed.

To many researchers, these ancient mtDNA findings put the nail in the coffin of the multiregional evolution and assimilation models. Others, however, maintained that their reasoning suffered from a fundamental problem. The absence of a signal for interbreeding in any single independent region of the genome, such as in mtDNA, does not necessarily mean that other regions of the genome also lack signs of interbreeding. Further, any particular region of the genome that is tested could lack signs of interbreeding even if interbreeding did occur because DNA from other species (introgressed DNA) that provided no survival advantage to *H. sapiens* would tend to disappear from the gene pool over time by chance.

The best way to approach the question of whether *H. sapiens* interbred with archaic species, such as the *Neandertals,* is thus to compare many regions of their genomes or, ideally, their entire genomes. Yet even before such data became available for archaic humans, some early genetic studies of modern human DNA bucked the majority trend and found data contrary to the replacement model. One clear example came from a 2005 study led by Daniel Garrigan, then a postdoctoral researcher in my laboratory. Garrigan looked at DNA sequences from a nonfunctional region of the X chromosome known as RRM2P4. Analyses of its reconstructed tree pointed to an origin for the sequence, not in Africa but in East Asia around 1.5 million years ago, implying that the DNA came from an archaic Asian species that intermixed with the *H. sapiens* originally from Africa. Similarly, that same year our lab discovered variation in another nonfunctional region of the X chromosome, Xp21.1, with a gene tree showing two divergent branches that had probably been evolving in complete isolation from one another for around a million years. One of these branches was presumably introduced into anatomically modern populations by an archaic African species. The RRM2P4 and Xp21.1 evidence thus hinted that anatomically modern humans mated with archaic humans from Asia and Africa, respectively, rather than simply replacing them without interbreeding.

Our Archaic DNA

More recently, advances in sequencing technology have enabled scientists to quickly sequence entire nuclear genomes—including those of extinct humans, such as *Neandertals.* In 2010, Pääbo's group reported that it had reconstructed the better part of a *Neandertal* genome, based on DNA from several *Neandertal* fossils from Croatia. Contrary to the team's expectations, the work revealed that *Neandertals* made a small but significant contribution to the modern human gene pool: non-Africans today exhibit a 1 to 4 percent *Neandertal* contribution to their genomes on average. To explain this result, the researchers proposed that interbreeding between *Neandertals* and the ancestors of all non-Africans probably occurred during the limited period when these two groups overlapped in the Middle East, perhaps 80,000 to 50,000 years ago.

Hot on the heels of the *Neandertal* genome announcement, Pääbo's team revealed an even more startling discovery. The researchers had obtained an mtDNA sequence from a piece of an approximately 40,000-year-old finger bone found in Denisova Cave in the Altai Mountains in Siberia. Although researchers could not determine from the anatomy of the bone what species it represented, the genome sequence showed that this individual belonged to a population that was slightly more closely related to *Neandertals* than it or *Neandertals* were to our species. Further, after comparing the Denisovan sequence with its counterpart in modern populations, the team found a significant amount of DNA from a Denisovan-like population—a contribution of 1 to 6 percent—in Melanesians, Aboriginal Australians, Polynesians, and some related groups in the western Pacific but not in Africans or Eurasians.

To explain this increasingly complex pattern of DNA sharing, the researchers proposed that interbreeding with various archaic forms had occurred at two different times: first, when anatomically modern humans initially migrated out of Africa and mated with *Neandertals* and, later, when the descendants of these initial migrants made their way to Southeast Asia and encountered Denisovan-like humans. The doubly mixed ancestors of present-day groups such as Melanesians then reached Oceania around 45,000 years ago, and a second wave of anatomically modern humans migrated to East Asia without interbreeding with Denisovan-like ancestors.

Although discussion of interbreeding in human evolution typically focuses on mating between anatomically modern humans and *Neandertals* in Europe or other archaic forms in Asia, the greatest opportunity for interspecies coupling would have been in Africa, where anatomically modern humans and various archaic forms coexisted for much longer than they did anywhere else. Unfortunately, the tropical environments of the African rain forest do not favor the preservation of DNA in ancient remains. Without an African ancient DNA sequence to reference, geneticists are currently limited to scouring the genomes of modern-day Africans for signs of archaic admixture.

To that end, my team at the University of Arizona, in collaboration with Jeffrey D. Wall of the University of California, San Francisco, gathered sequence data from 61 regions of the genome in a sample of three sub-Saharan African populations. Using computer-based simulations to test various evolutionary scenarios, we concluded in a 2011 report that these populations received a 2 percent contribution of genetic material from an extinct human population. This group would have split off from the ancestors of anatomically modern humans some 700,000 years ago and interbred with moderns around 35,000 years ago in Central Africa.

Another genetic hint of archaic admixture in Africa has come from a study of an unusual Y chromosome sequence obtained from an African-American man living in South Carolina whose DNA was submitted to a direct-to-consumer genetic testing company for analysis. His particular variant had never been seen before. Comparing his Y sequence against those of other humans, as well as chimpanzees, my team determined

that his sequence represents a previously unknown Y chromosome lineage that branched off the Y chromosome tree more than 300,000 years ago. We then searched a database of nearly 6,000 African Y chromosomes and identified 11 matches—all of which came from men who lived in a very small area of western Cameroon. The finding, published in March in the *American Journal of Human Genetics*, indicates that the last common ancestor of all modern Y chromosome variants is 70 percent older than previously thought. The presence of this very ancient lineage in contemporary people is a possible sign of interbreeding between *H. sapiens* and an unknown archaic species in western Central Africa.

Recently, the fossil record, too, has yielded support for the possibility of interbreeding within Africa. Just after the publication of our results in 2011, a group of paleontologists working at the Iwo Eleru site in Nigeria reanalyzed remains that exhibit cranial features intermediate between those of archaic and modern humans and determined that they date to just 13,000 years ago—long after anatomically modern *H. sapiens* had debuted. These results, along with similar findings from the Ishango site in the Democratic Republic of the Congo, suggest that the evolution of anatomical modernity in Africa may have been more complicated than any of the leading models for modern human origins have envisioned. Either archaic humans lived alongside modern ones in the recent past, or populations with both modern and archaic features interbred over millennia.

Beneficial Contributions?

Although the analyses of *Neandertal* and Denisovan DNA provide increasing evidence that archaic humans contributed to our genetic heritage, many aspects of this interbreeding remain unresolved. Current estimates of the percentage of our genome that was contributed by *Neandertals* and Denisovan-like humans are based on a method that does not provide much information about how and when mixing occurred. To learn more, researchers need to improve their understanding of exactly which stretches of the genome came from archaic humans and which archaic species contributed what. During his dissertation work in my lab, Fernando L. Mendez took steps toward doing exactly that. He found strong evidence that some contemporary non-Africans carry a stretch of chromosome 12 containing the gene STAT2 (which is involved in the body's first line of defense against viral pathogens) that came from *Neandertals*.

Detailed studies of DNA regions inherited from archaic ancestors will also help tackle the question of whether acquiring these genetic variants conferred an adaptive advantage to early *H. sapiens*. Indeed, STAT2 provides a fascinating example of an apparently advantageous archaic variant entering the modern human gene pool. Approximately 10 percent of people from Eurasia and Oceania carry the *Neandertal*-like variant of STAT2. Interestingly, it occurs at a roughly 10-fold higher frequency in Melanesia than in East Asia. Analysis suggests that this DNA segment rose to high frequency through positive natural selection (that is, because it aided reproductive success or survival) rather than merely by chance, implying that it benefited the anatomically modern populations of Melanesia.

Similarly, a *Neandertal*-like section of the so-called human leukocyte antigen (HLA) region of the genome appears to have risen to relatively high frequency in Eurasian populations as a result of positive natural selection related to its role in fighting pathogens. Perhaps we should not be surprised to find archaic contributions containing genes that function to increase immunity. It is easy to imagine that the acquisition of a gene variant that is adapted to fending off pathogens in non-African environments would immediately benefit human ancestors as they expanded from Africa into new habitats.

In light of the accumulating evidence for interbreeding between anatomically modern *H. sapiens* and archaic humans both inside Africa and beyond its confines, the replacement model is no longer tenable. Modern and archaic species of *Homo* were able to produce viable hybrid offspring. Thus, archaic forms could go extinct while still leaving behind their genetic footprints in the modern human genome. That said, the genomes of people today seem to derive mostly from African ancestors—contributions from archaic Eurasians are smaller than either the multiregional evolution or assimilation models predict.

A number of researchers now favor Bräuer's hybridization model, which holds that mating between *H. sapiens* and archaic species was limited to a few isolated instances. I agree that such interbreeding appears to have been rare after modern humans began spreading out of Africa, but I think there is more to the story than that. Given the complexity of the African fossil record, which indicates that a variety of transitional human groups, with a mosaic of archaic and modern features, lived over an extensive geographic area from Morocco to South Africa between roughly 200,000 and 35,000 years ago, I favor a model that involves interspecies mating during the archaic-to-modern transition. Sometimes called African multiregional evolution, this scenario allows for the possibility that some of the traits that make us anatomically modern were inherited from transitional forms before they went extinct. To my mind, African multiregional evolution, in combination with Bräuer's hybridization model, best explains genetic and fossil data to date.

Before scientists can assess this model for modern human origins fully, we will need to better understand which genes code for anatomically modern traits and decipher their evolutionary history. Further analysis of both archaic and modern genomes should aid researchers in pinpointing when and where mixing occurred—and whether the archaic genes that entered the modern human gene pool benefited the populations that acquired them. This information will help us evaluate the hypothesis that interbreeding with archaic populations that were well adapted to their local environments lent traits to *H. sapiens* that spurred its rise to global preeminence. The sharing of genes through occasional interspecies mating is one way that evolutionary novelties arise in many species of animals and plants, so it should not be surprising if the same process occurred in our own past.

Many loose ends remain. Yet one thing is clear: the roots of modern humans trace back to not just a single ancestral population in Africa but to populations throughout the Old World. Although archaic humans have often been seen as rivals of modern humans, scientists now must seriously consider the possibility that they were the secret of *H. sapiens'* success.

Critical Thinking

1. Compare and contrast the African replacement model for modern human origins with the multiregional evolution model, the assimilation model, and the hybridization model.

2. Discuss the ways in which DNA technology originally supported the replacement model and the "fundamental problem" with it cited by some researchers.

3. How have more recent DNA studies indicated some interbreeding between anatomically modern humans and archaic humans?

4. How has the fossil evidence yielded support for the possibility of interbreeding within Africa?

5. What evidence is there for positive selection of archaic genes in modern populations?

6. What does the DNA evidence seem to be saying about the various models, according to the author?

Internet References

Human Prehistory
http://users.hol.gr/~dilos/prehis.htm
Max Planck Institute for Evolutionary Anthropology
www.eva.mpg.de/english/index.htm

MICHAEL F. HAMMER is a population geneticist at the University of Arizona. He studies patterns of genetic variation in modern-day populations to gain insights into the evolutionary origins of *Homo sapiens*.

Article

Prepared by: Elvio Angeloni

Dawn of a Continent

Perhaps the rumours of strange newcomers were true after all. Certainly the slender stone blade in front of the young *Neanderthal* had been fashioned by someone with skills that surpassed any he had seen before. The snap of a twig broke his reverie. He spun round, and found himself face to face with two men every bit as strange and exotic as the tool they had evidently returned to claim. Their skins were unusually dark, their eyes the colour of the sky.

COLIN BARRAS

Learning Outcomes

After reading this article, you will be able to:

- Discuss the genetic and archaeological evidence for *Homo sapiens* migration into Europe in terms of physical appearance, way of life, and culture in general.

- Explain the relationship between the Neolithic way of life and violence.

- Discuss the social and cultural traits apparently brought into Europe by the "Yamnaya" people and their significance for understanding modern European culture.

It was possibly curiosity or wonder that the young *Neanderthal* felt during his first encounter with our species. Arguably, it should have been fear: a chance meeting like this could easily have happened about 45,000 years ago in a forest somewhere between Poland and England. When it did, it would have marked the dawn of a new human conquest.

Until that point, Europe had been the exclusive playground of *Neanderthals. Homo sapiens*, meanwhile, had left Africa, marched across Arabia into East and Southeast Asia, sailed to Australia. One group was on its way to Siberia, the Bering Strait, and the promise of a New World. But what of Europe?

Not too long ago, that story appeared beguilingly simple. Our species arrived 45,000 years ago from the Middle East, outcompeted the *Neanderthals*, and that was that. Now, an explosion of studies is using fragments of DNA pulled out of ancient bones to probe Europe's genetic make-up. Together they tell a more

detailed, colourful tale: that forest encounter marked just the first of three waves of *Homo sapiens* that shaped the continent. Each came with its own skills and traits. Together they would lay the foundations for a new civilisation. Our distant ancestors first settled in Europe at least 1.2 million years ago. By 200,000 years ago, they had become *Neanderthals*. We know from their DNA that at least some of them had pale skin and red hair. They lived in caves, had basic stone tools, and hunted and fished along European shorelines. Some probably wore forms of decoration: shell necklaces and maybe even face paint. The last surviving *Neanderthal* tribes might even have etched and painted simple signs onto the rocks of the Iberian peninsula.

All told, they were a relatively sophisticated bunch but no match for a group of dark-skinned hunter-gatherers who arrived from the Middle East around 45,000 years ago. The jury is still out on whether the newcomers killed, outwitted, or simply outnumbered the *Neanderthals,* but by 39,000 years ago, our cousin species was history.

The newcomers flourished in Europe's forests, hunting the woolly rhinoceros, bison, and the like that lived there. Long before farmers tamed cows and sheep, these early Europeans made friends with wolves. Like the *Neanderthals,* some of them lived at the mouths of caves—sometimes the very same caves—which they lit and heated with roaring fires. Like them, they ate berries, nuts, fish, and game.

We are all too willing to dismiss the hunter-gatherers as "short, brutish and nasty", says Vincent Gaffney at the University of Bradford, UK. "We are fundamentally farmers, and so we tend to think of farming as an amazing step forward," he says. In fact, there was something subtly different going on in the minds of early hunter-gatherers: they had artistic sensibilities, expressed in vast murals and using musical instruments like bone flutes and bullroarers. Surviving murals tell us about the large game they hunted. Perhaps most significantly, they show that the people were keen observers of the world they lived in, and capable of abstract thought.

Nor were they all, strictly-speaking, "cavemen". Some hunter-gatherers erected rudimentary buildings. Archaeologists are studying a vast site at Star Carr in northern England, where there is evidence of a house-like structure and timber platforms on the marshy lakeside that date back to around 8500 years ago. And in 2013, in a field in north-east Scotland, Gaffney and his colleagues found a 10,000-year-old hunter-gatherer monument: an arc of 12 pits facing the point on the horizon where the sun rises on the winter solstice. Residues inside one pit suggest it held a wooden pole.

The monument was some early form of "time reckoner" that tracked the lunar months, says Gaffney. He stops short of calling it a proto-scientific instrument, but it does seem to have been used to observe and measure the natural world, perhaps even to predict when migratory animals like salmon would return. Gaffney suspects the knowledge of how the monument worked was carefully controlled, perhaps by a ruling elite. "Then, as now," he says, "knowledge was power." It is thought that a similar monument existed at Stonehenge, millennia before the stones were erected.

The New Wave

If this fresh archaeological evidence shows that hunter-gatherers were more modern than we once thought, new genetic research restates just how different they looked: for example, one hunter-gatherer who lived in Spain 7000 years ago—a good 35,000 years after their kind first arrived in Europe—had dark skin and pale blue eyes (*Nature*, vol 507, p 225). A group unearthed near Motala in Sweden had pale skin, blue eyes, and possibly even blonde hair, but they seem to have been an exception: 8000-year-old hunter-gatherers unearthed in Luxembourg and in Hungary shared the same traits as the Spanish male. "They probably had similar [skin] tones to current North Africans," says Carles Lalueza-Fox at Pompeu Fabra University in Barcelona, Spain, who sequenced the DNA of the Spanish individual.

The dark skin is surprising given that humans living at higher latitudes typically evolve pale skins so they can absorb more UV rays and make vitamin D. But on the whole, pale skin does not appear to have swept through Europe until much later, with the arrival of a new wave of conquerors.

Last year, a genetic study revealed that modern Europeans still carry traces of the early hunter-gatherers in their DNA.

It also found signs of other long-lost ancestors. By comparing DNA from 7000- and 8000-year-old bones from Germany, Luxembourg, and Sweden with the genomes of 2345 modern Europeans, Iosif Lazaridis of Harvard Medical School and his colleagues found that most living Europeans can trace their ancestry to not one but three ancestral populations (*Nature*, vol 513, p 409). The second group was strikingly different [than] the first. For 30,000 years, the hunter-gatherers had Europe largely to themselves. Then about 9000 years ago, Neolithic farmers arrived from the Middle East and began spreading through south and central Europe. They brought their understanding of how to collect and sow seeds, as well as the staples of modern European diets. "The basic livestock of Europe today, with the exception of things like chicken, arrived then," says Peter Bogucki of Princeton University. He had long suspected that early farmers consumed dairy products too, and was proven right in 2012 when he discovered that 7500-year-old ceramic sieves from Poland bear the chemical residues of cheese-making.

With farming came a more sedentary and recognisably modern lifestyle. Villages became a much more common fixture. Some archaeological sites have distinct rows of houses. "In Central Europe, folks lived in settlements based around longhouses," says Bogucki. "Those were the largest buildings in the world in the sixth millennium BC." It was around this time that the artisan was born. "From the distribution of buildings in Neolithic villages, it's evident you are getting some forms of craft specialisation, although not necessarily full-time professionals," says James Mallory at Queen's University Belfast, UK.

Changing Skin Colour

Early farmers looked more like modern Europeans too. DNA pulled from the bones of a 7000-year-old early farmer unearthed in Germany shows she had pale skin, dark hair, and brown eyes. More recently, Lazaridis and his colleague Iain Mathieson led an analysis of DNA from 83 people who lived in Europe within the last 8000 years. It shows that one of the two genes responsible for the ancient farmer's pale skin swept through Europe very soon after farmers arrived in the region. Today, many northern Europeans carry a mix of DNA from hunter-gatherers and early farmers, which suggests that at some point the two groups began interbreeding. As farming took over, a way of life that had existed in Europe for tens of thousands of years slowly faded and the continent took a giant step towards its modern identity.

Genetic analyses show that farming brought a population boom and, undoubtedly, conflict. Violence wasn't absent from Europe before the farmers showed up, of course, but there is disturbing evidence of organised killing on a massive scale once they arrived on the scene. The Talheim Death Pit in Germany is a particularly grisly example. It contains the 7000-year-old remains of 34 early farmers—men, women and children—all apparently hastily buried in a chaotic fashion. "There are holes in the skulls with the same lozenge shape as Neolithic axes," says Bogucki. "It was farmer-on-farmer violence."

"The amount of stress any group would experience probably went through the roof," he says. "The Neolithic is really predicated on a sense of property rights and ownership. This triggers all sorts of other things." A settled lifestyle made it harder to relocate if conflicts arose between neighbouring tribes, so they would often be resolved with mass violence. But, fundamentally, life in early Neolithic Europe was still relatively insular. The final, missing ingredient, the one that would truly lay the flagstones for a European civilisation, was still a few thousand years off.

Archaeologists have long debated the existence of another great prehistoric migration into Europe—one that brought in a mysterious group from the Eurasian steppe. The Yamnaya, so the argument went, founded some of the late Neolithic and Copper Age cultures, including the vast Corded Ware culture—named after its distinctive style of pottery—that stretched from the Netherlands to central Russia. "The weight of archaeological opinion has been against the idea," says David Anthony at Hartwick College in Oneonta, New York.

That might be about to change. Lazaridis's 2014 study of ancient DNA offered the first compelling evidence that a third ancient population did shape the modern European gene pool, and that it originated in northern Eurasia. With the curious exception of the blond hunter-gatherers from Sweden, Lazaridis found no signs of this population in the genes of early farmers or hunter-gatherers. So the people carrying the genes must have become common in Europe some time after most farmers arrived.

Now, two separate studies—one led by Lazaridis and Wolfgang Haak of the Australian Centre for Ancient DNA in Adelaide, the other by Eske Willerslev of the University of Copenhagen in Denmark—link the arrival of these genes to a massive Yamnaya migration into Europe about 4500 years ago. Haak and Lazaridis found that 75 percent of the genetic markers of skeletons associated with Corded Ware artefacts unearthed in Germany could be traced to Yamnaya bones previously unearthed in Russia (*Nature*, vol 522, p 207).

"That changes things dramatically," says Anthony, who also contributed to the paper. The genetic evidence provides tantalising evidence that there really was a massive influx of Yamnaya people into Europe around 4500 years ago—just as Anthony and a few archaeologists have long argued.

In appearance, the Yamnaya might not have been too different from the early farmers—light-skinned and probably with dark eyes—although there is evidence to suggest they may have been taller. It is the social and cultural traits they brought to Europe that are most significant.

The Yamnaya were cattle herders. Up until about 5500 years ago, their settlements clung to the river valleys of the Eurasian steppe—the only place where they had easy access to the water they and their livestock needed. The invention of a single, revolutionary technology changed everything. We know from linguistic studies that the Yamnaya rode horses and, crucially, had fully embraced the freedom that came with the wheel.

With wagons, they could take water and food wherever they wanted, and the archaeological record shows they began to occupy vast territories. Natalia Shishlina at the State Historical Museum in Moscow, Russia, has also found evidence for this increasingly nomadic existence. Her archaeological research shows that Yamnaya groups moved their large herds from season to season so they always had fresh pastures to feed on.

Anthony suspects that the change led to fundamental shifts in how Yamnaya society was structured, before they left the steppes. Groups roamed into each other's territories, so a political framework emerged that obliged tribal leaders to offer wanderers safe passage and protection.

There is, of course, no archaeological evidence for this new political framework, especially given that the Yamnaya didn't keep written records. "It's quite difficult to tell much about developments in social organisation from the archaeological point of view," says Shishlina. Anthony finds supports for his idea in the work of linguist Don Ringe of the University of Pennsylvania in Philadelphia, who has shown that Yamnaya vocabulary contains words for "hospitality", "feast" and "patron".

If Anthony is correct, then it's easy to imagine that the Yamnaya brought this new political framework with them as they ventured west, although why the European farmers and remaining pockets of hunter-gatherers adopted it is a puzzle. Anthony speculates that it would have brought them under the legal protection of the powerful newcomers: "like a protection racket", he says. Scholars will no doubt continue to speculate about how Yamnaya and early European cultures clashed and interacted. But in one respect at least, the arrival of the Yamnaya had a clear and profound effect on Europe. The language they spoke, Proto-Indo-European is the common ancestor of all modern European languages.

Some say the genetic evidence still needs to be backed up. "Invariably you're working with very small population samples, and you can have no idea how the picture will look in the long run," says Mallory. Martin Furholt at the University of Kiel, Germany, agrees. He says there is so much regional variation in Corded Ware artefacts that it's clear the culture was not a homogeneous entity with a single origin. "It is not very helpful to produce these stereotypic, oversimplified narratives of mass migrations or invasions," says Furholt.

If Corded Ware skeletons further west do show the same genetic pattern as those so far analysed in Germany, the case for a mass migration that brought in new languages and new ideas becomes stronger. We might not have to wait long to find out. Mallory is aware of several studies in the pipeline that explore the genetics of the western Corded Ware people.

When it comes to understanding the origin of European culture, there's another reason for looking at the Yamnaya. The very foundation of Rome may be steeped in their traditions. According to studies of Indo-European mythology, young Yamnaya men would go off in warlike groups, raping and pillaging for a few years, then return to their village and settle down into respectability as adults. Those cults were mythologically associated with wolves and dogs, like youths forming wild hunting packs, and the youths are said to have worn dog or wolf skins during their initiation.

Anthony has found a site in Russia where the Yamnaya killed wolves and dogs in midwinter. He says it's easy to imagine groups sacrificing and consuming the animals as a way to symbolically become wolves or dogs themselves. Bodies in Yamnaya graves on the western steppes frequently have pendants of dog canine teeth around their necks. Anthony says that all this offers solid archaeological evidence for the youthful "wolf packs" of Indo-European legends—and sees a link to the myth of the foundation of Rome.

"You've got two boys, Romulus and Remus and a wolf that more or less gives birth to them," he says. "And the earliest legends of the foundation of Rome are connected with a large group of homeless young men who were given shelter by Romulus. But they then wanted wives, so they invited in a neighbouring tribe and stole all their women. You can see that whole set of early legends as being connected possibly with the foundation of Rome by youthful war bands."

It's a seductive idea, and if true a very satisfying conclusion to the series of dots linking Europe's remote prehistory to the early days of modern Western civilisation.

Critical Thinking

1. What is the genetic and archaeological evidence for three separate *Homo sapiens* waves of migration into Europe beginning around 40,000 years ago?
2. What is the relationship between the Neolithic way of life and violence in Europe as shown by the archaeological evidence?
3. Who were the "Yamnaya" people and why are their cultural innovations important for understanding modern European cultures and language?

Internet References

European Association of Archaeologists
http://www.e-a-a.org/
Society for Historical Archaeology
www.sha.org

COLIN BARRAS is a writer based near Ann Arbor in Michigan, US.

Article Prepared by: Elvio Angeloni

The Awakening

The discovery of the world's oldest representational paintings in remote caves in Indonesia has scholars rethinking the origins of art—and of humanity.

Jo Marchant

Learning Outcomes

After reading this article, you will be able to:

- Discuss the significance of the representational art being found in the caves of Sulawesi, Indonesia with respect to their age and the intellect that they represent.

- Describe the standard explanations of European cave art and why the Sulawesi cave art challenges those views.

- Explain how the caves of Sulawesi show us for the first time a link between the buried evidence and the cave art.

- Explain why the animals represented are "good to think" and why the hand stencils convey a message that is distinctly human.

I struggle to keep my footing on a narrow ridge of earth snaking between flooded fields of rice. The stalks, almost ready to harvest, ripple in the breeze, giving the valley the appearance of a shimmering green sea. In the distance, steep limestone hills rise from the ground, perhaps 400 feet tall, the remains of an ancient coral reef. Rivers have eroded the landscape over millions of years, leaving behind a flat plain interrupted by these bizarre towers, called karsts, which are full of holes, channels, and interconnecting caves carved by water seeping through the rock.

We're on the island of Sulawesi, in Indonesia, an hour's drive north of the bustling port of Makassar. We approach the nearest karst undeterred by a group of large black macaques that screech at us from trees high on the cliff and climb a bamboo ladder through ferns to a cave called Leang Timpuseng. Inside, the usual sounds of everyday life here—cows, roosters, passing

motorbikes—are barely audible through the insistent chirping of insects and birds. The cave is cramped and awkward, and rocks crowd into the space, giving the feeling that it might close up at any moment. But its modest appearance can't diminish my excitement: I know this place is host to something magical, something I've traveled nearly 8,000 miles to see.

Scattered on the walls are stencils, human hands outlined against a background of red paint. Though faded, they are stark and evocative, a thrilling message from the distant past. My companion, Maxime Aubert, directs me to a narrow semicircular alcove, like the apse of a cathedral, and I crane my neck to a spot near the ceiling a few feet above my head. Just visible on darkened grayish rock is a seemingly abstract pattern of red lines.

Then my eyes focus and the lines coalesce into a figure, an animal with a large, bulbous body, stick legs, and a diminutive head: a babirusa, or pig-deer, once common in these valleys. Aubert points out its neatly sketched features in admiration. "Look, there's a line to represent the ground," he says. "There are no tusks—it's female. And there's a curly tail at the back."

This ghostly babirusa has been known to locals for decades, but it wasn't until Aubert, a geochemist and archaeologist, used a technique he developed to date the painting that its importance was revealed. He found that it is staggeringly ancient: at least 35,400 years old. That likely makes it the oldest-known example of figurative art anywhere in the world—the world's very first picture.

It's among more than a dozen other dated cave paintings on Sulawesi that now rival the earliest cave art in Spain and France, long believed to be the oldest on earth.

The findings made headlines around the world when Aubert and his colleagues announced them in late 2014, and the implications are revolutionary. They smash our most common ideas about the origins of art and force us to embrace a far richer picture of how and where our species first awoke.

Hidden away in a damp cave on the "other" side of the world, this curly-tailed creature is our closest link yet to the moment when the human mind, with its unique capacity for imagination and symbolism, switched on.

Who were the first "people," who saw and interpreted the world as we do? Studies of genes and fossils agree that *Homo sapiens* evolved in Africa 200,000 years ago. But although these earliest humans looked like us, it's not clear they thought like us.

Intellectual breakthroughs in human evolution such as tool-making were mastered by other hominin species more than a million years ago. What sets us apart is our ability to think and plan for the future, and to remember and learn from the past—what theorists of early human cognition call "higher order consciousness."

Such sophisticated thinking was a huge competitive advantage, helping us to cooperate, survive in harsh environments, and colonize new lands. It also opened the door to imaginary realms, spirit worlds, and a host of intellectual and emotional connections that infused our lives with meaning beyond the basic impulse to survive. And because it enabled symbolic thinking—our ability to let one thing stand for another—it allowed people to make visual representations of things that they could remember and imagine. "We couldn't conceive of art, or conceive of the value of art, until we had higher order consciousness," says Benjamin Smith, a rock art scholar at the University of Western Australia. In that sense, ancient art is a marker for this cognitive shift: Find early paintings, particularly figurative representations like animals, and you've found evidence for the modern human mind.

Until Aubert went to Sulawesi, the oldest dated art was firmly in Europe. The spectacular lions and rhinos of Chauvet Cave, in southeastern France, are commonly thought to be around 30,000 to 32,000 years old, and mammoth-ivory figurines found in Germany correspond to roughly the same time. Representational pictures or sculptures don't appear elsewhere until thousands of years afterward. So it has long been assumed that sophisticated abstract thinking, perhaps unlocked by a lucky genetic mutation, emerged in Europe shortly after modern humans arrived there about 40,000 years ago. Once Europeans started to paint, their skills, and their human genius, must have then spread around the world.

But experts now challenge that standard view. Archaeologists in South Africa have found that the pigment ocher was used in caves 164,000 years ago. They have also unearthed deliberately pierced shells with marks suggesting they were strung like jewelry, as well as chunks of ocher, one engraved with a zig-zag design—hinting that the capacity for art was present long before humans left Africa. Still, the evidence is frustratingly indirect. Perhaps the ocher wasn't for painting but for mosquito repellent. And the engravings could have been one-offs, doodles with no symbolic meaning, says Wil Roebroeks, an expert in the archaeology of early humans, of Leiden University in the Netherlands. Other extinct hominin species have left similarly inconclusive artifacts.

By contrast, the gorgeous animal cave paintings in Europe represent a consistent tradition. The seeds of artistic creativity may have been sown earlier, but many scholars celebrate Europe as the place where it burst, full-fledged, into view. Before Chauvet and El Castillo, the famous art-filled cave in northern Spain, "we don't have anything that smacks of figurative art," says Roebroeks. "But from that point on," he continues, "you have the full human package. Humans were more or less comparable to you and me."

Yet the lack of older paintings may not reflect the true history of rock art so much as the fact that they can be very difficult to date. Radiocarbon dating, the kind used to determine the age of the charcoal paintings at Chauvet, is based on the decay of the radioactive isotope carbon-14 and works only on organic remains. It's no good for studying inorganic pigments like ocher, a form of iron oxide used frequently in ancient cave paintings.

This is where Aubert comes in. Instead of analyzing pigment from the paintings directly, he wanted to date the rock they sat on, by measuring radioactive uranium, which is present in many rocks in trace amounts. Uranium decays into thorium at a known rate, so comparing the ratio of these two elements in a sample reveals its age; the greater the proportion of thorium, the older the sample. The technique, known as uranium series dating, was used to determine that zircon crystals from Western Australia were more than 4 billion years old, proving Earth's minimum age. But it can also date newer limestone formations, including stalactites and stalagmites, known collectively as speleothems, which form in caves as water seeps or flows through soluble bedrock.

Aubert, who grew up in Levis, Canada, and says he has been interested in archaeology and rock art since childhood, thought to date rock formations at a minute scale directly above and below ancient paintings, to work out their minimum and maximum age. To do this would require analyzing almost impossibly thin layers cut from a cave wall-less than a millimeter thick. Then a PhD student at the Australian National University in Canberra, Aubert had access to a state-of-the-art spectrometer, and he started to experiment with the machine, to see if he could accurately date such tiny samples.

Within a few years, Adam Brumm, an archaeologist at the University of Wollongong, where Aubert had received a postdoctoral fellowship—today they are both based at Griffith

University—started digging in caves in Sulawesi. Brumm was working with the late Mike Morwood, co-discoverer of the diminutive hominin *Homo floresiensis,* which once lived on the nearby Indonesian island of Flores. The evolutionary origins of this so-called "hobbit" remain a mystery, but, to have reached Flores from mainland Southeast Asia, its ancestors must have passed through Sulawesi. Brumm hoped to find them.

As they worked, Brumm and his Indonesian colleagues were struck by the hand stencils and animal images that surrounded them. The standard view was that Neolithic farmers or other Stone Age people made the markings no more than 5,000 years ago—such markings on relatively exposed rock in a tropical environment, it was thought, couldn't have lasted longer than that without eroding away. But the archaeological evidence showed that modern humans had arrived on Sulawesi at least 35,000 years ago. Could some of the paintings be older? "We were drinking palm wine in the evenings, talking about the rock art and how we might date it," Brumm recalls. And it dawned on him: Aubert's new method seemed perfect.

After that, Brumm looked for paintings partly obscured by speleothems every chance he got. "One day off, I visited Leang Jarie," he says. Leang Jarie means "Cave of Fingers," named for the dozens of stencils decorating its walls. Like Leang Timpuseng, it is covered by small growths of white minerals formed by the evaporation of seeping or dripping water, which are nicknamed "cave popcorn." "I walked in and bang, I saw these things. The whole ceiling was covered with popcorn, and I could see bits of hand stencils in between," recalls Brumm. As soon as he got home, he told Aubert to come to Sulawesi.

Aubert spent a week the next summer touring the region by motorbike. He took samples from five paintings partly covered by popcorn, each time using a diamond-tipped drill to cut a small square out of the rock, about 1.5 centimeters across and a few millimeters deep.

Back in Australia, he spent weeks painstakingly grinding the rock samples into thin layers before separating out the uranium and thorium in each one. "You collect the powder, then remove another layer, then collect the powder," Aubert says. "You're trying to get as close as possible to the paint layer." Then he drove from Wollongong to Canberra to analyze his samples using the mass spectrometer, sleeping in his van outside the lab so he could work as many hours as possible, to minimize the number of days he needed on the expensive machine. Unable to get funding for the project, he had to pay for his flight to Sulawesi—and for the analysis—himself. "I was totally broke," he says.

The very first age Aubert calculated was for a hand stencil from the Cave of Fingers. "I thought, Oh, shit,'" he says. "So I calculated it again." Then he called Brumm.

"I couldn't make sense of what he was saying," Brumm recalls. "He blurted out, '35,000!' I was stunned. I said, are you sure? I had the feeling immediately that this was going to be big."

The caves we visit in Sulawesi are astonishing in their variety. They range from small rock shelters to huge caverns inhabited by venomous spiders and large bats. Everywhere there is evidence of how water has formed and changed these spaces. The rock is bubbling and dynamic, often glistening wet. It erupts into shapes resembling skulls, jellyfish, waterfalls and chandeliers. As well as familiar stalactites and stalagmites, there are columns, curtains, steps and terraces—and popcorn everywhere. It grows like barnacles on the ceilings and walls.

We're joined by Muhammad Ramli, an archaeologist at the Center for the Preservation of Archaeological Heritage, in Makassar. Ramli knows the art in these caves intimately. The first one he visited, as a student in 1981, was a small site called Leang Kassi. He remembers it well, he says, not least because while staying overnight in the cave he was captured by local villagers who thought he was a headhunter. Ramli is now a portly but energetic 55-year-old with a wide-brimmed explorer's hat and a collection of T-shirts with messages like "Save our heritage" and "Keep calm and visit museums." He has cataloged more than 120 rock art sites in this region, and has established a system of gates and guards to protect the caves from damage and graffiti.

Almost all of the markings he shows me, in ocher and charcoal, appear in relatively exposed areas, lit by the sun. And they were apparently made by all members of the community. At one site, I climb a fig tree into a small, high chamber and am rewarded by the outline of a hand so small it could belong to my 2-year-old son. At another, hands are lined up in two horizontal tracks, all with fingers pointing to the left. Elsewhere there are hands with slender, pointed digits possibly created by overlapping one stencil with another; with painted palm lines; and with fingers that are bent or missing.

There's still a tradition on Sulawesi of mixing rice powder with water to make a handprint on the central pillar of a new house, Ramli explains, to protect against evil spirits. "It's a symbol of strength," he says. "Maybe the prehistoric man thought like that too." And on the nearby island of Papua, he says, some people express their grief when a loved one dies by cutting off a finger. Perhaps, he suggests, the stencils with missing fingers indicate that this practice too has ancient origins.

Paul Taçon, an expert in rock art at Griffith University, notes that the hand stencils are similar to designs created until recently in northern Australia. Aboriginal Australian elders he has interviewed explain that their stencils are intended to express connection to a particular place, to say: "I was here.

This is my home." The Sulawesi hand stencils "were probably made for similar reasons," he says. Taçon believes that once the leap to rock art was made, a new cognitive path—the ability to retain complex information over time—had been set. "That was a major change," he says.

There are two main phases of artwork in these caves. A series of black charcoal drawings—geometric shapes and stick figures including animals such as roosters and dogs, which were introduced to Sulawesi in the last few thousand years—haven't been dated but presumably could not have been made before the arrival of these species.

Alongside these are red (and occasionally purplish-black) paintings that look very different: hand stencils and animals, including the babirusa in Leang Timpuseng, and other species endemic to this island, such as the warty pig. These are the paintings dated by Aubert and his colleagues, whose paper, published in *Nature* in October 2014, ultimately included more than 50 dates from 14 paintings. Most ancient of all was a hand stencil (right beside the record-breaking babirusa) with a minimum age of 39,900 years—making it the oldest-known stencil anywhere, and just 900 years shy of the world's oldest-known cave painting of any kind, a simple red disk at El Castillo. The youngest stencil was dated to no more than 27,200 years ago, showing that this artistic tradition lasted largely unchanged on Sulawesi for at least 13 millennia.

The findings obliterated what we thought we knew about the birth of human creativity. At a minimum, they proved once and for all that art did not arise in Europe. By the time the shapes of hands and horses began to adorn the caves of France and Spain, people here were already decorating their own walls. But if Europeans didn't invent these art forms, who did?

On that, experts are divided. Taçon doesn't rule out the possibility that art might have arisen independently in different parts of the world after modern humans left Africa. He points out that although hand stencils are common in Europe, Asia, and Australia, they are rarely seen in Africa at any time. "When you venture to new lands, there are all kinds of challenges relating to the new environment," he says. You have to find your way around, and deal with strange plants, predators, and prey. Perhaps people in Africa were already decorating their bodies, or making quick drawings in the ground. But with rock markings, the migrants could signpost unfamiliar landscapes and stamp their identity onto new territories.

Yet there are thought-provoking similarities between the earliest Sulawesian and European figurative art—the animal paintings are detailed and naturalistic, with skillfully drawn lines to give the impression of a babirusa's fur or, in Europe, the mane of a bucking horse. Taçon believes that the technical parallels "suggest that painting naturalistic animals is part of a shared hunter-gatherer practice rather than a tradition of any particular culture." In other words, there may be something about such a lifestyle that provoked a common practice, rather than its arising from a single group.

But Smith, of the University of Western Australia, argues that the similarities—ocher use, hand stenciling and lifelike animals—can't be coincidental. He thinks these techniques must have arisen in Africa before the waves of migrations off the continent began. It's a view in common with many experts. "My bet would be that this was in the rucksack of the first colonizers," adds Wil Roebroeks, of Leiden University.

The eminent French prehistorian Jean Clottes believes that techniques such as stenciling may well have developed separately in different groups, including those who eventually settled on Sulawesi. One of the world's most respected authorities on cave art, Clottes led research on Chauvet Cave that helped to fuel the idea of a European "human revolution." "Why shouldn't they make hand stencils if they wanted to?" he asks, when I reach him at his home in Foix, France. "People reinvent things all the time." But although he is eager to see Aubert's results replicated by other researchers, he feels that what many suspected from the pierced shells and carved ocher chunks found in Africa is now all but inescapable: Far from being a late development, the sparks of artistic creativity can be traced back to our earliest ancestors on that continent. Wherever you find modern humans, he believes, you'll find art.

In a cavern known locally as Mountain-Tunnel Cave, buckets, a wheelbarrow and countless bags of clay surround a neatly dug trench, five meters long by three meters deep, where Adam Brumm is overseeing a dig that is revealing how the island's early artists lived.

People arrived on Sulawesi as part of a wave of migration from east Africa that started around 60,000 years ago, likely traveling across the Red Sea and the Arabian Peninsula to present-day India, Southeast Asia, and Borneo, which at the time was part of the mainland. To reach Sulawesi, which has always been an island, they would have needed boats or rafts to cross a minimum of 60 miles of ocean. Although human remains from this period haven't yet been found on Sulawesi, the island's first inhabitants are thought to have been closely related to the first people to colonize Australia around 50,000 years ago. "They probably looked broadly similar to Aboriginal or Papuan people today," says Brumm.

Brumm and his team have unearthed evidence of fire-building, hearths, and precisely crafted stone tools, which may have been used to make weapons for hunting. Yet while the inhabitants of this cave sometimes hunted large animals such as wild boar, the archaeological remains show that they mostly ate freshwater shellfish and an animal known as the Sulawesi bear cuscus—a slow-moving tree-dwelling marsupial with a long, prehensile tail.

The French anthropologist Claude Lévi-Strauss famously argued in 1962 that primitive peoples chose to identify with and represent animals not because they were "good to eat" but because they were "good to think." For ice age European cave painters, horses, rhinos, mammoths, and lions were less important as dinner than as inspiration. Ancient Sulawesians, it seems, were likewise moved to depict larger, more daunting and impressive animals than the ones they frequently ate.

The hunt is now on for even older paintings that might take us ever closer to the moment of our species' awakening. Aubert is collecting samples of limestone from painted caves elsewhere in Asia, including in Borneo, along the route that migrants would have taken to Sulawesi. And he and Smith are also independently working to develop new techniques to study other types of caves, including sandstone sites common in Australia and Africa. Sandstone doesn't form cave popcorn, but the rock forms a "silica skin" that can be dated.

Smith, working with colleagues at several institutions, is just getting the first results from an analysis of paintings and engravings in the Kimberley, an area in northwestern Australia reached by modern humans at least 50,000 years ago. "The expectation is that we may see some very exciting early dates," Smith says. "It wouldn't surprise me at all if pretty quickly we get a whole mass of dates that are earlier than in Europe." And scholars now talk excitedly about the prospect of analyzing cave paintings in Africa. "99.9 percent of rock art is undated," says Smith, citing, as an example, ocher representations of crocodiles and hippos found in the Sahara, often on sandstone and granite. "The conventional date on those would be 15,000 to 20,000 years old," he says. "But there's no reason they couldn't be older."

As the origins of art extend backward, we'll have to revise our often localized ideas of what prompted such aesthetic expression in the first place. It has previously been suggested that Europe's harsh northern climate necessitated strong social bonds, which in turn nudged the development of language and art. Or that competition with *Neanderthals,* present in Europe until around 25,000 years ago, pushed modern humans to express their identity by painting on cave walls—ancient hominin flag-planting. "Those arguments fall away," says Smith, "because that wasn't where it happened."

Clottes has championed the theory that in Europe, where art was hidden deep inside dark chambers, the main function of cave paintings was to communicate with the spirit world. Smith is likewise convinced that in Africa, spiritual beliefs drove the very first art. He cites Rhino Cave in Botswana, where archaeologists have found that 65,000 to 70,000 years ago people sacrificed carefully made spearheads by burning or smashing them in front of a large rock panel carved with hundreds of circular holes. "We can be sure that in instances like that, they believed in some sort of spiritual force," says Smith. "And they believed that art, and ritual in relation to art, could affect those spiritual forces for their own benefit. They're not just doing it to create pretty pictures. They're doing it because they're communicating with the spirits of the land."

In Mountain-Tunnel Cave, which has hand stencils and abundant traces of paint on the walls, Brumm is now also finding the early artists' materials. In strata dated to around the same time as nearby stencils, he says, "there's a major spike in ocher." So far, his team has found stone tools with ocher smeared over the edges and golf ball-size ocher chunks with scrape marks. There are also scattered fragments, probably dropped and splashed when the artists ground up their ocher before mixing it with water—enough, in fact, that this entire slice of earth is stained cherry red.

Brumm says this layer of habitation stretches back at least 28,000 years, and he is in the process of analyzing older layers, using radiocarbon dating for the organic remains and uranium series dating of horizontal stalagmites that run through the sediment.

He calls this "a crucial opportunity." For the first time in this part of the world, he says, "we're linking the buried evidence with the rock art." What that evidence shows is that on this island, at least, cave art wasn't always an occasional activity carried out in remote, sacred spaces. If religious belief played a part, it was entwined with everyday life. In the middle of this cave floor, the first Sulawesians sat together around the fire to cook, eat, make tools—and to mix paint.

In a small hidden valley Aubert, Ramli, and I walk across fields of rice in the early morning. Dragonflies glitter in the sun. At the far edge, we climb a set of steps high up a cliff to a breathtaking view and a cavernous entrance hall inhabited by swallows.

In a low chamber inside, pigs amble across the ceiling. Two appear to be mating—unique for cave art, Ramli points out. Another, with a swollen belly, might be pregnant. He speculates that this is a story of regeneration, the stuff of myth.

Past the pigs, a passageway leads to a deeper chamber where, at head height, there is a panel of well-preserved stencils including the forearms, which look as if they are reaching right out of the wall. Rock art is "one of the most intimate archives of the past," Aubert once told me. "It instills a sense of wonder. We want to know: Who made it? Why?" The animal paintings are technically impressive, but for me the stencils inspire the strongest emotional connection. Forty thousand years later, standing here in the torchlight feels like witnessing a spark or a birth, a sign of something new in the universe. Outlined by splattered paint, fingers spread wide, the marks look insistent and alive.

Whatever was meant by these stencils, there can be no stronger message in viewing them: We are human. We are here. I raise my own hand to meet one, fingers hovering an inch above the ancient outline. It fits perfectly.

Critical Thinking

1. How does the cave art of Sulawesi, Indonesia represent several archaeological breakthroughs?
2. How does such art challenge the standard explanations for similar European cave art?
3. How have new dating methods provided the very first link between the buried evidence and cave art?
4. What is meant by the claim that the animals depicted in Paleolithic cave art are "good to think?"
5. Why are the Paleolithic hand stencils representative of a uniquely human emotional message and cognitive awareness?

Internet References

Bradshaw Foundation
   http://www.bradshawfoundation.com/france/

For additional information/images please search the following term: Sulawesi cave art

Article Prepared by: Elvio Angeloni

The Story in the Stones

DAVID ROBSON

Learning Outcomes

After reading this article, you will be able to:

- Discuss the evidence for when our ancestors became uniquely human.
- Discuss the relationship between toolmaking, language, and cognitive skills in general in the development of our species.
- Explain how "working memory" fostered creativity and innovation in humans.

Sparks fly as stone meets stone and shards of rock ricochet off the furniture around me. Each strike makes me flinch, but Bruce Bradley is the picture of cool concentration as he chips away at his axe head. It is, after all, a skill he has been honing since before he can remember. "I was a natural born flint-knapper. Laugh at that if you want, but I've got video to prove it." As a baby, he says, he was often seen banging two rocks together in his parents' garden. Then, when his family moved to Arizona, he developed his talents by copying the Native American arrowheads scattered across the desert.

Decades later, Bradley makes stone tools spanning the breadth of human history. His workshop at the University of Exeter, UK, is full of this handiwork. Piles of rocks line the walls, and to one side a deerskin with a dark stain hangs on a wooden frame. It was butchered using some of his team's hand-made tools, he tells me. "We've got a freezer out there full of dead parts—you could eat them if you wanted."

My interests lie elsewhere. The stone tools on the table in front of me are not just useful, they tell the story of our journey from simple ape to thinking human. Previous attempts to trace the history of the mind have relied on speculation as much as hard evidence but, over the past three years, Bradley's Learning to be Human project has taken a more precise approach to looking inside the heads of the people who made these tools. Combining findings about stone-tool construction with neuroscience, psychology and archaeology, we can now estimate the origins of distinctly human mental abilities, such as when we first began to order our thoughts and actions, when our visual imagination blossomed, when we started to think about the past and future, and when we first played make-believe. There are even hints about the emergence of our capacity for patience, shame and suspicion—and the nature of our ancestors' dreams.

People have long sought a "secret ingredient" unique to human intelligence that could explain our extraordinary cognitive abilities. Most recently, the spotlight has fallen on size—the idea that a big brain is the key. However, it is becoming increasingly clear that there is no secret ingredient. Instead, our peculiar way of thinking results from a reorganisation of the different brain regions, as much as from their expansion (see "Size Isn't Everything"). What's more, this began long before we diverged from chimps, around six million years ago. Indeed, comparable but more modest changes can be seen in many of our nearest relatives. "In a way we're just an extreme great ape," says Jeroen Smaers at Stony Brook University, New York, who last year compared the brain evolution of 17 species of primates.

So what accelerated this evolution in our ancestral line beyond what was happening in other apes—and how did this give rise to new ways of thinking? Only by re-examining the archaeological record can we map out that path. And that's why I am in Bradley's workshop.

He pauses in his work to show me three stone tools. The first and crudest of them is a jagged rock that signals perhaps the first landmark moment in that journey. Aside from walking on two legs, our earlier ancestors were distinctly ape-like, and like chimps and other primates, they probably had limited tool use, picking pebbles off the ground to crush nuts. But things changed about 2.6 million years ago, with *Australopithecus garhi*. Rather than just using nature as they found it around them, they began to modify it, wielding one stone to chip the end off another and using the resulting sharp edge to butcher meat.

The idea of using one tool to create a more useful implement is itself a conceptual leap. But just as important is Bradley's discovery that it takes a dexterity and motor control not seen in other apes to create the jagged Oldowan-style tool in front of me. This includes coordinating your limbs so that one hand is doing a different job from the other. "You need one hand for support, one for striking," says Nada Khreisheh, Bradley's colleague— movements that chimps struggle to master even with training. If such bodily control seems like more of a hop than a leap, consider all the new opportunities it opened up—including the creation of better tools—that would reward increased intelligence, accelerating our evolution compared with the other apes. "I'm willing to bet there would be no consciousness on this planet if we didn't have flakable rocks," says Bradley.

Even with that trigger, our ancestors were slow to progress. Things didn't begin to take off until *Homo erectus,* about a million years later. *H. erectus* is significant for many reasons. As well as having broadly similar bodies to modern humans, they lived in bigger social groups than their predecessors. Successful communal living requires cooperation and the ability to detect and punish cheats who try to get something for nothing. According to Eva Jablonka at Tel Aviv University in Israel, those challenges may have spurred the evolution of complex emotions such as shame and embarrassment, which would help individuals toe the party line. "We became emotionally modern before we became cognitively modern," she says. But what really marks out the thinking of *H. erectus* is encapsulated in the second tool of the three in front of me, an exquisite leaf-shaped object known as an Acheulean hand axe.

Better by Design

We do not know what inspired this revolutionary design—it may even have come in a dream. The first attempts, which date from around 1.5 million years ago, were fairly crude, but over the following one million years Acheulean axes became thinner and more symmetrical as they began to embody a more systematic style of working. Bradley's demonstrations show that to achieve the more sophisticated designs, you need to prepare the surface of the rock—working away smaller chips to create an angle before striking off the larger, flatter flakes. "They take a lot more planning and understanding of force," he says as he chips away at his own rock. Breaking down a goal into a series of smaller actions in this way shows the beginnings of hierarchical thinking. Chunking and sequencing our actions seems so central to the way we operate today whether we are making a cup of tea or running a bath—that it's almost impossible to

imagine our minds working in any other way. But the refined Acheulean axes offer some of the first signs that our ancestors were beginning to develop the ability to organise their thoughts in these more complicated ways.

This innovation in axe design has been linked to another milestone in human cognition: language. It is such a complex system, dependent on many different thought processes, that its origins are sometimes described as evolution's biggest mystery, but there is some evidence suggesting that tool making could have been a catalyst. Bradley's collaborator, Dietrich Stout at Emory University in Atlanta, Georgia, points out that articulate vocalization requires precise movement of the lips and tongue. Chimps and other primates are unable to achieve these, but in our ancestors tool-making drove, the development of the brain areas involved in motor control that could later be co-opted for speech. Stout also notes that the sequential thinking needed to create the leaf-shaped hand axes is similar to the thinking that allows us to understand and construct sentences.

To test the theory, Stout used brain scans to try to pick apart the cognitive skills used in each type of tool making. As predicted, they show that people making replicas of the Oldowan tools have greatest activity in areas associated with the motor control needed to speak, while brain activity in those making the Late Acheulean tools shows an overlap with that normally associated with linguistic grammar. That includes the inferior frontal gyrus along the bottom of the frontal lobe—an area that expanded rapidly in the human line compared with other apes.

Language is, arguably, our only unique feature, and its emergence set us on a road that led away from every other animal. Unfortunately, this turning point in our journey is virtually invisible in the archaeological record: Bradley can show me no tools that definitively signify the first words. But there are hints that our ancestors had begun speaking by the time of *Homo heidelbergensis,* thought to have evolved from *H. erectus* at least 600,000 years ago.

Homo heidelbergensis was certainly more human in other respects. Its brain, at about 1200 cubic centimetres, was just a shade smaller than ours, providing a cognitive power that is evident in the variety of tools it used, including refined hand axes, cleavers, and spearheads. To envisage an amorphous lump of rock transformed into these different shapes and styles would have required good spatial cognition, perhaps signalling the birth of the visual imagination. *H. heidelbergensis* also revisited certain places again and again, sometimes scattering hand axes across the ground. Some read this apparently inexplicable waste of good handiwork as an early attempt to signpost sites of significance. That is skirting close to the mindset needed for symbolism. Crucially, *H. heidelbergensis* also possessed refinements in its vocal anatomy. For instance, traces in bones indicate that they had more nerves linking the brain and tongue than their predecessors, and their voice boxes seem to lack a balloon-like appendage that constrains vocalizations in other apes. Both of these changes would be needed to produce eloquent sounds.

Whenever it emerged, language brought a whole new set of mental challenges. "When I tell you a story, I can frighten you very easily," says Jablonka. "And you have to control this fear." It's easy to take that ability for granted, but chimps fail to make a good distinction between symbols and real things—they go wild when they see a picture of a banana, for instance. In a similar way, our ancestors may have struggled at first to understand the mental images conjured up by language. To deal with their immediate visceral reactions, Jablonka says, they must have developed greater control over their emotions—and they would have learned to be more sceptical and suspicious of others in the process. They also needed a better verbal memory, so that they could remember what others had told them, to differentiate it from what happened in their own lives. Out of that emerged the ability "to tell my own story, the autobiography", she says. If Jablonka is right, language contributed to our sense of self.

Beautifully Crafted

Our ancestors were probably still navigating these difficulties as the human mind approached the last stretch of its journey. To demonstrate this final mental leap, Bradley draws my attention to the third object on the table in front of us. The beautiful Levallois tool is carved from shiny black stone. With dimples lining its edge, it looks a little like an oyster shell. Bradley tells me the tool is little more use for cutting and scraping meat than the cruder hand-axes—its value was probably aesthetic, rather than practical. To make it, a base stone had to be fashioned into a circle before the "lid" was removed with one strike. That craftsmanship takes great skill and patience, as Bradley and Khreisheh's modern apprentices discovered. "People like making hand axes," says Khreisheh, "but they hate making Levallois tools." Since the process comprises many different stages, and the apprentices often need specific instruction, the mind that originally created this tool was probably capable of advanced hierarchical thinking and complex communication for tuition. These intricate objects first appear at least 300,000 years ago, but although they are found among the remains of our own species, they are most commonly associated with the Neanderthals.

Levallois tools provide some of the best evidence that Neanderthals shared much of the cognitive toolkit possessed by humans living at the same time. And herein lies the mystery. "Whatever the Neanderthals' cognitive leap was, it stopped; it didn't continue," says Bradley. So why did we develop more ambitious inventions and rich artistic cultures, while they hit a

dead end? Answer that question, and you get a glimpse of the final stage in the evolution of the human mind.

Some think the solution is child's play literally. Since our ancestors first diverged from the other primates, childhood has continued to get longer, giving the brain more time to develop outside the womb. From the remains of bones and teeth, it seems that early human children took longer to develop than Neanderthal ones. Child psychologist Alison Gopnik at the University of California, Berkeley, argues that the extra time spent playing may have helped them develop "counter-factual thinking"—the ability to consider how things might be, not just how they are. That allowed them to imagine the environment in more creative ways, giving them greater control over their surroundings, she says. As a result, they could do things that might not have occurred to earlier humans, like inventing new tools and building shelters.

Frederick Coolidge and Thomas Wynn at the University of Colorado in Colorado Springs see a more dramatic trigger. They argue that our last cognitive leap was down to a chance mutation that increased our ability to hold several ideas in mind and manipulate them. Even in modern humans, this "working memory" is limited to about seven items. However, a small increase would have had huge consequences. An improved ability to remember what had just been said would have increased the sophistication of conversation, allowing more complex grammar with many different clauses. That means you can think and plan more hypothetically, using "what if" and "if, then" statements, for instance.

Working memory is also associated with creativity and innovation because it allows you to mentally explore different solutions to a problem. Wynn and Coolidge also point to research suggesting that enhanced working memory could have improved our long-term memory and future planning because it provides a bigger mental "blackboard" on which we can assemble the details of our past experiences and draw on them to work out the best way to proceed with the task ahead.

A Recipe for Success

This hypothesis has been strengthened in recent years by a wave of circumstantial evidence. For example, Lyn Wadley at the University of the Witwatersrand in Johannesburg, South Africa, has looked at the steps involved in making glues used to stick spearheads to poles. Earlier humans had simple adhesives such as plant gum, but she has found that in Sibudu cave, South Africa, about 70,000 years ago, they began to cook up the tree sap with red ochre and beeswax to produce a superior glue that doesn't break on impact or dissolve in water.

When Wadley tried to replicate the complex recipes, she found that she had to pay attention to many different factors, including the temperature of the fire, the moisture, and different proportions of ingredients depending on the quality of the tree gum. "It took a lot of coordination to ensure success," she says. That's only possible with an enhanced working memory to keep all the different elements in mind at once.

Further clues come from the food these people ate. Around this time, early modern humans began to hunt small game, such as small deer species and rodents. Former army survival expert Klint Janulis, now at the University of Oxford, tried the methods they used and found he needed to place 10 to 15 traps to capture enough food to make it worthwhile. "Within a couple of hours you can set enough traps to feed yourself, and maybe another person, for a day," he says. But that requires forethought, and keeping track of their locations needs just the kind of advanced cognition that Wynn and Coolidge suggest.

The timing of these advances at 70,000 years ago is particularly significant because they come just after the eruption of the Toba supervolcano in Indonesia, which plunged the world into a mini ice age and caused a human population crash in Africa. Any beneficial mutations within the small remaining population could spread quickly, leaving a permanent mark on their descendants. "All extant humans are ancestors of those 2000 or so humans," says Coolidge. If he and Wynn are right, then the explosion at Toba marked the beginning of the home stretch to modern thinking. Armed with this slightly superior thinking, we left Africa and took over the globe, while the Neanderthals and our other evolutionary cousins became extinct.

Of course, our journey isn't over and it is tempting to speculate how the human mind will evolve in the future. Wynn wonders if we will see further changes in working memory. "It's variable within populations," he says. "We suspect it may still be under evolutionary change." And it is possible that advances in technology could substantially change the mental challenges we face, just as stone tools did in the past. Claims that the internet is making us stupid have so far proven to be unfounded but the way we interact with one another is certainly changing and so are the mental skills associated with success.

Bradley is more interested in the past than the future. The air is now thick with flint dust as he hands me the finished axe. There are still many questions left to answer, he says, as we try to fill in the gaps between the known landmarks of cognitive evolution. "From our point of view it's just scratching the surface of what could be done." But he has already achieved one of his goals—he wanted to teach a new generation of flint-knappers the skills he has been refining since childhood.

There's also a chance that his handiwork will find a place next to the artifacts he so admires. The Smithsonian Institution in Washington DC, he says, is interested in collecting his life's work to demonstrate the progression of a modern day flint-knapper. "My body could even be a permanent exhibit there

too, when I shift off this mortal coil," he jokes. It would be a fitting place of rest for the "natural born knapper" who has spent his life trying to understand how we learned to be human.

Sweet Dreams

Until about two million years ago, human ancestors probably settled for the night in trees. Some psychologists have proposed that the sensation of falling that we sometimes feel when we drop off is a remnant of an early warning system that stopped us descending so deeply into sleep that we ended up on the forest floor. Dozing on branches is likely to have ended with *Homo erectus*. "At 6 feet and 140 pounds, it was way too tall and heavy," says Frederick Coolidge at the University of Colorado in Colorado Springs. Instead, *H. erectus* slept on the ground, and this, Coolidge suggests, resulted in a great leap in cognition.

A more peaceful night's slumbers, without the constant risk of falling from a branch, would have allowed *H. erectus* to spend longer in rapid-eye-movement sleep and slow wave sleep, says Coolidge. These stages are known to be crucial for the consolidation of memories and associative thinking and that's not all. "It probably allowed many more creative dreams," he says. These could have had an impact on waking life.

Coolidge even speculates that the idea of the leaf-shaped Acheulean hand axe—a complex tool that signals a new way of thinking—might have come to a *H. erectus* knapper in one of those dreams.

Size Isn't Everything

Human intelligence has more to do with the organization of brain regions than it does with overall size. Tools may have played a key role in shaping parts of this complex organ.

Prefrontal Cortex
Self-control, introspection, social cognition

Lots of signal-transmitting "white matter" reflects this area's role in combining data from the senses and the rest of the brain. That could help with precise tool-making actions and with the insight needed for complex social relationships.

Frontostriatal System
Incremental learning of skills

As our ancestors evolved, there was a rapid increase in the size of this area relative to other brain regions. This would have improved their capacity for learning, allowing for the production of more complex tools.

Cerebellum

Sequential thinking

High connectivity between here and the frontal motor areas enables fine control of movement. This area may have grown as the tool-making and language skills of our ancestors developed.

2.6 Million Years Ago

Oldowan Tools Australopithecus garhi

* Dexterity * Motor control * Modification of nature

1.6 Million Years Ago

Acheulean Tools Homo erectus

* Hierarchical thinking * Planning * Complex emotions

600,000 Years Ago

Axes, Cleavers, Spears Homo heidelbergensis

* Language * Sense of self * Visual imagination * Emotional control * Symbolism

200,000 Years Ago

Homo sapiens

* Awareness of past and future * Creativity * Hypothetical thinking * Improved memory

300,000 Years Ago

Levallois Tools Neanderthals

* Advanced hierarchical thinking * Tuition * Patience

Critical Thinking

1. Discuss the various lines of evidence that indicate when and how our ancestors became uniquely human.
2. Discuss the stone tools that serve as landmarks in our ancestors' journey to become human and the specific cognitive skills enabled by such tools.
3. How are various language skills associated with the development of tools during human evolutionary development?
4. How might children play a role in "counter-factual thinking" and why would this be important?
5. How would the improvement of "working memory" foster creativity and innovation?

Internet References

Human Prehistory
   http://users.hol.gr/~dilos/prehis.htm
Max Planck Institute for Evolutionary Anthropology
   www.eva.mpg.de/english/index.htm

DAVID ROBSON is a features editor at *New Scientist.*

Article   Prepared by: Elvio Angeloni

The Birth of Childhood

Unlike other apes, humans depend on their parents for a long period after weaning. But when—and why—did our long childhood evolve?

ANN GIBBONS

Learning Outcomes

After reading this article, you will be able to:

- Explain why humans have such an extended period of childhood.

- Discuss the fossil evidence extension of childhood in the human evolutionary line.

Mel was just 3.5 years old when his mother died of pneumonia in 1987 in Tanzania. He had still been nursing and had no siblings, so his prospects were grim. He begged weakly for meat, and although adults gave him scraps, only a 12-year-old named Spindle shared his food regularly, protected him, and let him sleep with him at night. When Spindle took off for a month, another adolescent, Pax, came to Mel's rescue, giving him fruit and a place to sleep until Spindle returned. Mel survived to age 10.

Fortunately for Mel, he was an orphan chimpanzee living in the Gombe Stream National Park rather than a small child living in the slums of a big city. With only sporadic care from older children, a 3-year-old human orphan would not have survived.

Mel's story illustrates the uniqueness of one facet of human life: Unlike our close cousins the chimpanzees, we have a prolonged period of development after weaning, when children depend on their parents to feed them, until at least age 6 or 7. Street children from Kathmandu to Rio de Janeiro do not survive on their own unless they are at least 6. "There's no society where children can feed themselves after weaning," says anthropologist Kristen Hawkes of the University of Utah in Salt Lake City. By contrast, "chimpanzees don't have childhoods. They are independent soon after weaning," says

anthropologist Barry Bogin of Loughborough University in Leicestershire, U.K.

Humans are also the only animals that stretch out the teenage years, having a final growth spurt and delaying reproduction until about 6 years after puberty. On average, women's first babies arrive at age 19, with a worldwide peak of first babies at age 22.5. This lengthy period of development—comprised of infancy, juvenile years, and adolescence—is a hallmark of the human condition; researchers have known since the 1930s that we take twice as long as chimpanzees to reach adulthood. Even though we are only a bit bigger than chimpanzees, we mature and reproduce a decade later and live 2 to 3 decades longer, says Bogin.

Given that we are unique among mammals, researchers have been probing how this pattern of growth evolved. They have long scrutinized the few, fragile skulls and skeletons of ancient children and have now developed an arsenal of tools to better gauge how childhood has changed over the past 3 million years. Researchers are scanning skulls and teeth of every known juvenile with electron microscopes, micro-computed tomography scans, or powerful synchrotron x-rays and applying state-of-the-art methods to create three-dimensional virtual reconstructions of the skulls of infants and the pelvises of mothers. They're analyzing life histories in traditional cultures to help understand the advantages of the human condition. In addition, some new fossils are appearing. . . . Researchers report the first nearly complete pelvis of a female *Homo erectus,* which offers clues to the prenatal growth of this key human species.

All of this is creating some surprises. One direct human ancestor, whose skeleton looks much like our own, turns out to have grown up much faster than we do. The life histories of our closest evolutionary cousins, the Neandertals, remain controversial, but some researchers suspect that they may have had

Childhood Stages

	Age at Weaning (Years)	Age at Eruption of First Molar (Years)	Female Age at First Breeding (Years) (Estimated by 3rd Molar Eruption in Fossils)	Average Maximum Life Span (Years)
Chimpanzees, *Pan troglodytes*	4.0	4.0	11.5	45
Lucy, *Australopithecus afarensis*	4.0?	4.0?	11.5	45
Homo erectus	?	4.5	14.5 (est.)	60? (est.)
Modern humans, *Homo sapiens*	2.5	6.0	19.3	70

Milestones. Key events show that modern humans live slower and die later than our ancestors did.

the longest childhoods of all. The new lines of evidence are helping researchers close in on the time when childhood began to lengthen. "Evidence suggests that much of what makes our life history unique took shape during the evolution of the genus *Homo* and not before," says anthropologist Holly Smith of the University of Michigan, Ann Arbor.

Live Fast, Die Young

Back in 1925, Australian anatomist Raymond Dart announced the discovery of that rarest of rare specimens, the skull of an early hominin child. Dart estimated that the australopithecine he called the Taung baby had been about 6 years old when it died about 2 million years ago, because its first permanent molar had erupted. As modern parents know, the first of the baby teeth fall out and the first permanent molars appear at about age 6. Dart assumed that early hominins—the group made up of humans and our ancestors but not other apes—matured on much the same schedule as we do, an assumption held for 60 years. Growing up slowly was seen as a defining character of the human lineage.

Then in 1984, anatomists Christopher Dean and Timothy Bromage tested a new method to calculate the chronological ages of fossil children in a lab at University College London (UCL). Just as botanists add up tree rings to calculate the age of a tree, they counted microscopic lines on the surface of teeth that are laid down weekly as humans grow. The pair counted the lines on teeth of australopithecine children about as mature as the Taung child and were confounded: These hominin children were only about 3.5 years old rather than 6. They seemed to be closer to the chimpanzee pattern, in which the first permanent molar erupts at about age 3.5. "We concluded that [the australopithecines] were more like living great apes in their pace of development than modern humans," says Dean.

Their report in *Nature* in 1985 shook the field and focused researchers on the key questions of when and why our ancestors adopted the risky strategy of delaying reproduction. Many

other slow-growing, large-bodied animals, such as rhinos, elephants, and chimpanzees, are now threatened with extinction, in part because they delay reproduction so long that their offspring risk dying before they replace themselves. Humans are the latest to begin reproducing, yet we seem immune from those risks, given that there are 6.6 billion of us on the planet. "When did we escape those constraints? When did we extend our childhood?" asks biological anthropologist Steven Leigh of the University of Illinois, Urbana-Champaign.

The Taung baby and the other australopithecine children, including the relatively recent discovery of a stunning fossil of a 3-year-old *Australopithecus afarensis* girl from Dikika, Ethiopia, show that it happened after the australopithecines. So researchers have zeroed in on early *Homo*, which appeared in Africa about 2 million years ago.

Unfortunately, there are only a few jaw bits of early *Homo* infants and young children to nail down their ages. Most of what we know comes from a single skeleton, a *H. erectus* boy who died about 1.6 million years ago near Lake Turkana, Kenya. *H. erectus* was among the first human ancestors to share many key elements of the modern human body plan, with a brain considerably larger than that of earlier hominins. And unlike the petite australopithecines, this Turkana youth was big: He weighed 50 kilograms, stood 163 centimeters tall, and looked like he was 13 years old, based on modern human standards. Yet two independent tooth studies suggested ages from 8 or 9 to 10.5 years old.

Now a fresh look at the skeleton concludes that, despite the boy's size, he was closer to 8 years old when he died. Dean and Smith make this case in a paper in press in an edited volume, *The First Humans: Origin of the Genus* Homo. The skeleton and tooth microstructure of the boy and new data on other members of his species suggest that he attained more of his adult height and mass earlier than modern human children do. Today, "you won't find an 8-year-old boy with body weight, height, and skeletal age that are so much older," says Dean.

He and Smith concluded that the boy did not experience a "long, slow period of growth" after he was weaned but grew up earlier, more like a chimpanzee. They estimate the species' age at first reproduction at about 14.5, based on the eruption of its third molar, which in both humans and chimpanzees erupts at about the age they first reproduce. This 8-year-old Turkana Boy was probably more independent than a 13-year-old modern human, the researchers say, suggesting that *H. erectus* families were quite different from ours and did not stay together as long.

The new, remarkably complete female pelvis, however, suggests that life history changes had begun in *H. erectus.* Researchers led by Sileshi Semaw of the Stone Age Institute at Indiana University, Bloomington, found the pelvis in the badlands of Gona, Ethiopia. They present a chain of inference that leads from pelvis, to brain size, to life history strategy.

They assume that the nearly complete pelvis belongs to *H. erectus,* because other *H. erectus* fossils were found nearby and because it resembles fragmentary pelvises for the species. Lead author Scott Simpson of Case Western Reserve University in Cleveland, Ohio, paints a vivid picture of a short female with wide hips and an "obstetrically capacious" pelvic opening that could have birthed babies with brain sizes of up to 315 milliliters. That's 30% to 50% of the adult brain size for this species and larger than previously predicted based on a reconstruction of the Turkana Boy's incomplete pelvis. However, the new estimate does match with newborn brain size predicted by the size of adult brains in *H. erectus,* says Jeremy DeSilva of Worcester State College in Massachusetts, who made such calculations online in September in the *Journal of Human Evolution.*

The wide pelvis suggests *H. erectus* got a head start on its brain development, putting on extra gray matter in utero rather than later in childhood. That's similar to living people, whose brains grow rapidly before birth, says Simpson. But if *H. erectus*'s fetal growth approached that of modern humans, it built proportionately more of its brain before birth, because its brain never became as massive as our own.

Thus, *H. erectus* grew its brain before birth like a modern human, while during childhood it grew up faster like an ape. With a brain developing early, *H. erectus* toddlers may have spent less time as helpless children than modern humans do, says paleoanthropologist Alan Walker of Pennsylvania State University in State College. This suggests *H. erectus* children were neither chimplike nor humanlike but perhaps somewhere in between: "Early *H. erectus* possessed a life history unlike any species living today," write Dean and Smith. "If you look at its morphology, it fits in our genus, *Homo,*" says Smith. "But in terms of life history, they fit with australopithecines."

Live Slow, Die Old?

If *H. erectus* was just beginning to slow down its life history, when did humans take the last steps, to our current late-maturing life plan? Three juvenile fossil members of *H. antecessor,* who died 800,000 years ago in Atapuerca, Spain, offer tantalizing clues. An initial study in 1999, based on rough estimates of tooth eruption, found that this species matured like a modern human, says José María Bermúdez de Castro of the Museo Nacional de Ciencias Naturales in Madrid. Detailed studies of tooth microstructure are eagerly awaited to confirm this.

In the meantime, another recent study has shown that childhood was fully extended by the time the first members of our species, *H. sapiens,* appeared in northern Africa about 200,000 years ago. In 2007, researchers examined the daily, internal tooth lines of a *H. sapiens* child who lived 160,000 years ago in Jebel Irhoud, Morocco. They used x-rays from a powerful particle accelerator in Grenoble, France (*Science,* 7 December 2007, p. 1546), to study the teeth without destroying them and found that the 8-year-old Jebel Irhoud child had grown as slowly as a modern 8-year-old, according to Harvard University paleoanthropologist Tanya Smith, who coled the study.

That analysis narrowed the window of time when humans evolved the last extension of our childhood to between 800,000 years ago and 200,000 years ago. To constrain it still further, Tanya Smith and her colleagues recently trained their x-ray vision on our closest relatives: the extinct Neandertals, who shared their last ancestor with us about 500,000 years ago. First, the researchers sliced a molar of a Belgian Neandertal that was at the same stage of dental development as the 8-year-old Jebel Irhoud child and counted its internal growth lines. They found that it had reached the same dental milestones more rapidly and proposed that Neandertals grew up faster than we do. That suggests that a fully extended childhood evolved only in our species, in the past 200,000 years.

But Tanya Smith's results conflict with earlier studies by Dean and colleagues who also sliced Neandertal teeth and found that they had formed slowly, like those of modern humans. The case is not closed: Smith and paleontologist Paul Tafforeau of the European Synchrotron Radiation Facility in Grenoble, France, spent weeks last year imaging juvenile Neandertals and early members of *H. sapiens,* and they expect to publish within a year.

Meanwhile, new data with implications for Neandertal growth rates are coming in from other sources. The brain sizes of a Neandertal newborn and two infants show that they were at the upper end of the size range for modern humans, suggesting that their brains grew faster than ours after birth, according to virtual reconstructions by Christoph Zollikofer and anthropologist Marcia Ponce de León of the University of Zurich (*Science,* 12 September, p. 1429).

Those rapidly growing brains don't necessarily imply a rapid life history, warn Zollikofer and Ponce de León. They argue that because Neandertals' brains were more massive, they did not complete brain growth earlier than modern humans even though they grew at a faster rate. "They have to get those bigger brains somehow," says Holly Smith. For now, Neandertals' life history remains controversial.

Why Wait?

If childhood began to change in *H. erectus* and continued to get longer in our own species and possibly Neandertals, then the next question is why. What advantage did our ancestors gain from delaying reproduction so long? Many researchers agree that childhood allows us to learn from others, in order to improve our survival skills and prepare us to be better parents. Historically, researchers have also argued that humans need a long childhood to allow enough time for our larger brain to mature.

But in fact, a big brain doesn't directly cause the extension of childhood, because the brain is built relatively early. "Everyone speaks about slow human development, but the human brain develops very fast," says Zollikofer. It doubles in size in the first year of life and achieves 95% of its adult size by the age of 5 (although white matter grows at least to age 18). "We get our brains done; then, we sit around for much longer than other species before we reproduce," says Leigh. "It's almost like humans are building the outside, getting the scaffolding of the house up early, and then filling in after that."

However, there's a less direct connection between brains and life history: Big brains are so metabolically expensive that primates must postpone the age of reproduction in order to build them, according to a paper last year in the *Journal of Human Evolution* (*Science*, 15 June 2007, p. 1560). "The high metabolic costs of rapid brain growth require delayed maturation so that mothers can bear the metabolic burdens associated with high brain growth," says Leigh. "Fast brain growth tells us that maturation is late."

That's why Ponce de León and Zollikofer think that the Neandertals' rapid brain growth implies late, rather than early, maturation: Neandertal mothers must have been large and strong—and by implication, relatively old—to support infants with such big, fast-growing brains. Indeed, say the Zurich pair, Neandertals may have had even longer childhoods than we do now. Childhood, like brain size, may have reached its zenith in Neandertals and early *H. sapiens*. As our brains got smaller over the past 50,000 years, we might have begun reproducing slightly earlier than Neandertals.

To explore such questions, recent interdisciplinary studies are teasing out the reproductive advantages of waiting to become parents. Many analyses cite an influential life history model by evolutionary biologist Eric Charnov of the University of New Mexico, Albuquerque. The model shows that it pays to have babies early if parents face a high risk of death. Conversely, mammals that face a lower risk of dying benefit if they wait to reproduce, because older mothers can grow bigger, stronger bodies that grow bigger babies, who are more likely to survive. "The driving force of a prolonged life history schedule is almost certainly a reduction in mortality rates that allows growth and life span to extend and allows for reproduction to extend further into adulthood in a more spread-out manner," says Dean.

Researchers such as Loughborough's Bogin have applied Charnov's model to modern humans, proposing that delaying reproduction creates higher quality human mothers. Indeed, humans start having babies 8 years later than chimpanzees, and both species stop by about age 45 to 50. But once human mothers begin, they more than make up for their delayed start, pushing out babies on average 3.4 years apart in traditional forager societies without birth control, compared with 5.9 years for wild chimpanzees, says Bogin. This rapid-fire reproduction produces more babies for human hunter-gatherers, who have peak fertility rates of 0.31 babies per given year compared with 0.22 for chimpanzees. And human mothers who start even later than age 19 have more surviving babies. For example, in the 1950s, the Anabaptist Hutterites of North America, who eschewed birth control, had their first babies on average at age 22 and then bore children every 2 years. They produced an amazing nine children per mother, says Bogin, who has studied the group.

Such fecundity, however, requires a village or at least an extended family with fathers and grandmothers around to help provision and care for the young. That's something that other primates cannot provide consistently, if at all, says Hawkes (*Science*, 25 April 1997, p. 535). She proposed that grandmothers' provisioning allows mothers to wean early and have babies more closely together, a vivid example of the way humans use social connections to overcome biological constraints—and allow mothers to have more babies than they could raise on their own. "Late maturation works well for humans because culture lets us escape the constraints other primates have," says Leigh.

The key is to find out when our ancestors were weaned, says Holly Smith. Younger weaning implies that mothers had enough social support to feed weaned children and space babies more closely. "Weaning tells us when *Homo* species start stacking their young," says Smith. Indeed, Dean and Louise Humphrey of the Natural History Museum in London are testing a method that detects the chemical signature of weaning in human teeth. Humans may be slow starters, but our social safety net has allowed us to stack our babies closely together—and so win the reproductive sweepstakes, leaving chimpanzees, and the extinct Neandertals, far behind.

Critical Thinking

1. How does the case of Mel illustrate the contrast between chimpanzee and human childhood?

2. How do humans contrast with chimpanzees in terms of maturation and reproduction?

3. How were Dean and Bromage able to recalculate the age of the Taung child? What key questions did this cause researchers to focus upon?

4. What can be said about the Turkana boy and why? What is the estimate of this species' first reproduction? How would *H. erectus* families been different from ours?

5. What does the wide *H. erectus* pelvis suggest about its brain development and its life history?

6. What is the evidence as to when our ancestors took the last steps to our current late-maturing life plan?

7. Why does similar evidence for Neanderthals continue to be ambiguous?

8. What are the possible advantages to a long childhood? Why is the idea of allowing for brain growth not a likely explanation?

9. What is the advantage to postponing the age of reproduction?

10. Under what circumstance does it pay to have babies early? What is the benefit of having babies later? How do humans compare favorably with chimpanzees in this regard? Why does such fecundity require a village?

11. What would the time of weaning tell us about our ancestors?

Internet References

Humanorigins.si.edu

http://humanorigins.si.edu/research

This website deals with evidence for the evolution of human characteristics.

American Anthropological Association Children and Childhood Interest Group

http://aaacig.usu.edu

Article   Prepared by: Elvio Angeloni

The Evolution of Grandparents

Senior citizens may have been the secret of our species' success.

RACHEL CASPARI

Learning Outcomes

After reading this article, you will be able to:

- Discuss the evidence for increased longevity in the human evolutionary line.

- Discuss the importance of longevity with respect to the human lifespan.

During the summer of 1963, when I was six years old, my family traveled from our home in Philadelphia to Los Angeles to visit my maternal relatives. I already knew my grandmother well: she helped my mother care for my twin brothers, who were only 18 months my junior, and me. When she was not with us, my grandmother lived with her mother, whom I met that summer for the first time. I come from a long-lived family. My grandmother was born in 1895, and her mother in the 1860s; both lived almost 100 years. We stayed with the two matriarchs for several weeks. Through their stories, I learned about my roots and where I belonged in a social network spanning four generations. Their reminiscences personally connected me to life at the end of the Civil War and the Reconstruction era and to the challenges my ancestors faced and the ways they persevered.

My story is not unique. Elders play critical roles in human societies around the globe, conveying wisdom and providing social and economic support for the families of their children and larger kin groups. In our modern era, people routinely live long enough to become grandparents. But this was not always the case. When did grandparents become prevalent, and how did their ubiquity affect human evolution?

Research my colleagues and I have been conducting indicates that grandparent-aged individuals became common relatively recently in human prehistory and that this change came

at about the same time as cultural shifts toward distinctly modern behaviors—including a dependence on sophisticated symbol-based communication of the kind that underpins art and language. These findings suggest that living to an older age had profound effects on the population sizes, social interactions and genetics of early modern human groups and may explain why they were more successful than archaic humans, such as the Neandertals.

Live Fast, Die Young

The first step in figuring out when grandparents became a fixture in society is assessing the typical age breakdown of past populations—what percent were children, adults of childbearing age and parents of those younger adults? Reconstructing the demography of ancient populations is tricky business, however. For one thing, whole populations are never preserved in the fossil record. Rather paleontologists tend to recover fragments of individuals. For another, early humans did not necessarily mature at the same rate as modern humans. In fact, maturation rates differ even among contemporary human populations. But a handful of sites have yielded high enough numbers of human fossils in the same layers of sediment that scientists can confidently assess the age at death of the remains—which is key to understanding the makeup of a prehistoric group.

A rock-shelter located in the town of Krapina in Croatia, about 40 kilometers northwest of the city of Zagreb, is one such site. More than a century ago Croatian paleontologist Dragutin Gorjanović-Kramberger excavated and described the fragmentary remains of perhaps as many as 70 Neandertal individuals there, most of which came from a layer dated to about 130,000 years ago. The large number of fossils found close to one another, the apparently rapid accumulation of the sediments at the site and the fact that some of the remains share distinctive, genetically determined features all indicate that the Krapina bones approximate the remains of a single population of Neandertals. As often happens in the fossil record, the best-preserved remains at Krapina are teeth because the high mineral content of teeth protects them from degradation. Fortunately, teeth are also one of the best skeletal elements for determining age at death, which is achieved by analyzing surface wear and age-related changes in their internal structure.

In 1979, before I began my research into the evolution of grandparents, Milford H. Wolpoff of the University of Michigan at Ann Arbor published a paper, based on dental remains, that assessed how old the Krapina Neandertals were when they died. Molar teeth erupt sequentially. Using one of the fastest eruption schedules observed in modern-day humans as a guide, Wolpoff estimated that the first, second and third molars of Neandertals erupted at ages that rounded to six, 12 and 15, respectively. Wear from chewing accumulates at a steady pace over an individual's lifetime, so when the second molar emerges, the first already has six years of wear on it, and when the third emerges, the second has three years of wear on it.

Working backward, one can infer, for instance, that a first molar with 15 years of wear on it belonged to a 21-year-old Neandertal, a second molar with 15 years of wear on it belonged to a 27-year-old and a third molar with 15 years of wear on it belonged to a 30-year-old. (These estimates have an uncertainty of plus or minus one year.) This wear-based seriation method for determining age at death, adapted from a technique developed by dental researcher A.E.W. Miles in 1963, works best on samples with large numbers of juveniles, which Krapina has in abundance. The method loses accuracy when applied to the teeth of elderly individuals, whose tooth crowns can be too worn to evaluate reliably and in some cases may even be totally eroded.

Wolpoff's work indicated that the Krapina Neandertals died young. In 2005, a few years after I began researching the evolution of longevity, I decided to take another look at this sample using a novel approach. I wanted to make sure that we were not missing older individuals as a result of the inherent limitations of wear-based seriation. Working with Jakov Radovčić of the Croatian Natural History Museum in Zagreb, Steven A. Goldstein, Jeffrey A. Meganck and Dana L. Begun, all at Michigan, and undergraduate students from Central Michigan University, I developed a new nondestructive method—using high-resolution three-dimensional microcomputed tomography (μCT)—to reassess how old the Krapina individuals were when they died. Specifically, we looked at the degree of development of a type of tissue within the tooth called secondary dentin; the volume of secondary dentin increases with age and provides a way to assess how old an individual was at death when the tooth crown is too worn to be a good indicator.

Our initial findings, supplemented with scans provided by the Max Planck Institute for Evolutionary Anthropology in Leipzig, corroborated Wolpoff's results and validated the wear-based seriation method: the Krapina Neandertals had remarkably high mortality rates; no one survived past age 30. (This is not to say that Neandertals across the board never lived beyond 30. A few individuals from sites other than Krapina were around 40 when they died.)

By today's standards, the Krapina death pattern is unimaginable. After all, for most people age 30 is the prime of life. And hunter-gatherers lived beyond 30 in the recent past. Yet the Krapina Neandertals are not unique among early humans. The few other human fossil localities with large numbers of individuals preserved, such as the approximately 600,000-year-old Sima de los Huesos site in Atapuerca, Spain, show similar patterns. The Sima de los Huesos people had very high levels of juvenile and young adult mortality, with no one surviving past 35 and very few living even that long. It is possible that catastrophic events or the particular conditions under which the remains became fossilized somehow selected against the preservation of older individuals at these sites. But the broad surveys of the human fossil record—including the material from these unusually rich sites and other sites containing fewer individuals—that my colleagues and I have conducted indicate that dying young was the rule, not the exception. To paraphrase words attributed to British philosopher Thomas Hobbes, prehistoric life really was nasty, brutish and short.

Rise of the Grandparents

This new μCT approach has the potential to provide a high-resolution picture of the ages of older individuals in other fossil human populations. But a few years ago, before we hit on this technique, Sang-Hee Lee of the University of California, Riverside, and I were ready to start looking for evidence of changes in longevity over the course of human evolution. We turned to the best approach available at the time: wear-based seriation.

We faced a daunting challenge, though. Most human fossils do not come from sites, such as Krapina, that preserve so many individuals that the remains can be considered reflective of their larger populations. And the smaller the number of contemporaneous individuals found at a site, the more difficult it is to reliably estimate how old members were when they died because of the statistical uncertainties associated with small samples.

But we realized that we could get at the question of when grandparents started becoming common in another way. Instead of asking how long individuals lived, we asked how many of them lived to be old. That is, rather than focusing on absolute ages, we calculated relative ages and asked what proportion of adults survived to the age at which one could first become a grandparent. Our objective was to evaluate changes over evolutionary time in the ratio of older to younger adults—the so-called OY ratio. Among primates, including humans up until very recently, the third molar erupts at about the same time that an individual becomes an adult and reaches reproductive age. Based on data from Neandertals and contemporary hunter-gatherer populations, we inferred that fossil humans got their third molars and had their first child at around age 15. And we considered double that age to mark the beginning of grandparenthood—just as some women today can potentially give birth at age 15 and those women can become grandmothers when their own children reach age 15 and reproduce.

For our purposes, then, any archaic individual judged to be 30 years old or more qualified as an older adult—one old enough to have become a grandparent. But the beauty of the OY ratio approach is that regardless of whether maturation occurred at 10, 15 or 20 years, the number of older and younger individuals in a sample would be unaffected because the start of older adulthood would change accordingly. And because we were only looking to place the fossils in these two broad categories, we could include large numbers of smaller fossil samples in our analysis without worrying about uncertainties in absolute ages.

We calculated the OY ratios for four large aggregates of fossil samples totaling 768 individuals spanning a period of three million years. One aggregate comprised later australopithecines—those primitive relatives of "Lucy," who lived in East Africa and South Africa from three million to 1.5 million years ago. Another aggregate consisted of early members of our genus, *Homo*, from around the globe who lived between two million and 500,000 years ago. The third group was the European Neandertals from 130,000 to 30,000 years ago. And the last consisted of modern Europeans from the early Upper Paleolithic period, who lived between about 30,000 and 20,000 years ago and left behind sophisticated cultural remains.

Although we expected to find increases in longevity over time, we were unprepared for how striking our results would turn out to be. We observed a small trend of increased longevity over time among all samples, but the difference between earlier humans and the modern humans of the Upper Paleolithic was a dramatic fivefold increase in the OY ratio. Thus, for every 10 young adult Neandertals who died between the ages of 15 and 30, there were only four older adults who survived past age 30; in contrast, for every 10 young adults in the European Upper Paleolithic death distribution, there were 20 potential grandparents. Wondering whether the higher numbers of burials at Upper Paleolithic sites might account for the high number of older adults in that sample, we re-analyzed our Upper Paleolithic sample, using only those remains that had not been buried. But we got similar results. The conclusion was inescapable: adult survivorship soared very late in human evolution.

Biology or Culture?

Now that Lee and I had established that the number of potential grandparents surged at some point in the evolution of anatomically modern humans, we had another question on our hands: What was it that brought about this change? There were two possibilities. Either longevity was one of the constellations of genetically controlled traits that biologically distinguished anatomically modern humans from their predecessors, or it did not come along with the emergence of modern anatomy and was instead the result of a later shift in behavior. Anatomically modern humans did not burst onto the evolutionary scene making the art and advanced weaponry that define Upper Paleolithic culture. They originated long before those Upper Paleolithic Europeans, more than 100,000 years ago, and for most of that time they and their anatomically archaic contemporaries the Neandertals used the same, simpler Middle Paleolithic technology. (Members of both groups appear to have dabbled in making art and sophisticated weapons before the Upper Paleolithic, but these traditions were ephemeral compared with the ubiquitous and enduring ones that characterize that later period.) Although our study indicated that a large increase in grandparents was unique to anatomically modern humans, it alone could not distinguish between the biological explanation and the cultural one, because the modern humans we looked at were both anatomically and behaviorally modern. Could we trace longevity back to earlier anatomically modern humans who were not yet behaviorally modern?

To address this question, Lee and I analyzed Middle Paleolithic humans from sites in western Asia dating to between about 110,000 and 40,000 years ago. Our sample included both Neandertals and modern humans, all associated with the same comparatively simple artifacts. This approach allowed us to compare the OY ratios of two biologically distinct groups (many scholars consider them to be separate species) who lived in the same region and had the same cultural complexity. We found that the Neandertals and modern humans from western Asia had statistically identical OY ratios, ruling out the possibility that a biological shift accounted for the increase in adult survivorship seen in Upper Paleolithic Europeans. Both western Asian groups had roughly even proportions of older and younger adults, putting their OY ratios between those of the Neandertals and early modern humans from Europe.

Compared with European Neandertals, a much larger proportion of western Asian Neandertals (and modern humans) lived to be grandparents. This is not unexpected—the more temperate environment of western Asia would have been far easier to survive in than the harsh ecological conditions of Ice Age Europe. Yet if the more temperate environment of western Asia accounts for the elevated adult survivorship seen in the

Middle Paleolithic populations there, the longevity of Upper Paleolithic Europeans is even more impressive. Despite living in much harsher conditions, the Upper Paleolithic Europeans had an OY ratio more than double that of the Middle Paleolithic modern humans.

Senior Moments

We do not know exactly what those Upper Paleolithic Europeans started doing culturally that allowed so many more of them to live to older age. But there can be no doubt that this increased adult survivorship itself had far-reaching effects. As Kristen Hawkes of the University of Utah, Hillard Kaplan of the University of New Mexico and others have shown in their studies of several modern-day hunter-gatherer groups, grandparents routinely contribute economic and social resources to their descendants, increasing both the number of offspring their children can have and the survivorship of their grandchildren. Grandparents also reinforce complex social connections—like my grandmother did in telling stories of ancestors that linked me to other relatives in my generation. Such information is the foundation on which human social organization is built.

Elders transmit other kinds of cultural knowledge, too—from environmental (what kinds of plants are poisonous or where to find water during times of drought, for example) to technological (how to weave a basket or knap a stone knife, perhaps). Studies led by Pontus Strimling of Stockholm University have shown that repetition is a critical factor in the transmission of the rules and traditions of one's culture. Multigenerational families have more members to hammer home important lessons. Thus, longevity presumably fostered the intergenerational accumulation and transfer of information that encouraged the formation of intricate kinship systems and other social networks that allow us to help and be helped when the going gets tough.

Increases in longevity would also have translated into increases in population size by adding an age group that was not there in the past and that was still fertile. And large populations are major drivers of new behaviors. In 2009 Adam Powell of University College London and his colleagues published a paper in *Science* showing that population density figures importantly in the maintenance of cultural complexity. They and many other researchers argue that larger populations promoted the development of extensive trade networks, complex systems of cooperation, and material expressions of individual and group identity (jewelry, body paint, and so on). Viewed in that light, the hallmark features of the Upper Paleolithic—the explosive increase in the use of symbols, for instance, or the incorporation of exotic materials in tool manufacture—look as

though they might well have been consequences of swelling population size.

Growing population size would have affected our forebears another way, too: by accelerating the pace of evolution. As John Hawks of the University of Wisconsin-Madison has emphasized, more people mean more mutations and opportunities for advantageous mutations to sweep through populations as their members reproduce. This trend may have had an even more striking effect on recent humans than on Upper Paleolithic ones, compounding the dramatic population growth that accompanied the domestication of plants 10,000 years ago. In their 2009 book *The 10,000 Year Explosion,* Gregory Cochran and Henry Harpending, both at the University of Utah, describe multiple gene variants—from those influencing skin color to those that determine tolerance of cow milk—that arose and spread swiftly over the past 10,000 years, thanks to the ever larger numbers of breeding individuals.

The relation between adult survivorship and the emergence of sophisticated new cultural traditions, starting with those of the Upper Paleolithic, was almost certainly a positive feedback process. Initially a by-product of some sort of cultural change, longevity became a prerequisite for the unique and complex behaviors that signal modernity. These innovations in turn promoted the importance and survivorship of older adults, which led to the population expansions that had such profound cultural and genetic effects on our predecessors. Older and wiser, indeed.

Critical Thinking

1. What are the critical roles played by elders around the world?

2. When did grandparent-aged individuals become common in human prehistory? What do these findings suggest?

3. Why is reconstructing the demography of ancient populations a tricky business? Why were sites such as Krapina useful in this regard?

4. How was Wolpoff able to estimate the ages of death at Krapina?

5. Describe the high mortality rates among the Neandertals at Krapina. How does this compare to today's standards? What indications are there that dying young was the rule?

6. Why did the author use the OY (older to younger adults) ratio?

7. What four aggregates of fossil samples were used?

8. What were the results?

9. What were the two possible explanations for increased longevity? Why was it important to know if longevity could be traced back to the early anatomically modern humans?

10. What was found in comparing Middle Paleolithic Neandertals with modern humans in western Asia? What was the

significance of this find? How did western Asian Neandertals compare to the European Neandertals?

11. Why was the longevity of the Upper Paleolithic Europeans impressive?

12. Discuss the far-reaching effects that increased adult survivorship must have had on humanity.

Internet References

American Anthropological Association Children and Childhood Interest Group
http://aaacig.usu.edus

Humanorigins.si.edu
http://humanorigins.si.edu/research

Article   Prepared by: Elvio Angeloni

A Bigger, Better Brain

Observations of chimpanzees and dolphins strengthen the notion that humanlike intelligence may not be uniquely human.

MADDALENA BEARZI AND CRAIG STANFORD

Learning Outcomes

After reading this article, you will be able to:

- Discuss and explain the similarities between the brains of chimpanzees and dolphins.

- Why is a big, sophisticated brain an advantage in life?

When the orange sun rises in the east of Gombe National Park in Tanzania, it takes time to cross the mountain ridge above and warm the forest below. There, a party of chimpanzees is waking up. One by one they roll over, look up at the morning sky and slowly revive themselves. Each sits sleepily on the branch supporting his or her nest, peeing quietly onto the ground many meters below. Every tree has an ape or two, and one towering Chrysophyllum tree holds several nests. In minutes, the silent band descends to sit like boulders on the hillside.

Then, as if on cue, one of the older males gets up and begins walking from the sleeping area, heading north. Several males follow, but two walk instead to the west toward a lake. A mother and her infant embark southward, alone. A couple of young males stay put; later they will travel to the east, up into the rugged hills. What started out at dawn as a nesting party of 26 chimpanzees fragments into at least five separate parties of one to eight chimpanzees each, all venturing into a day of multiple decisions and complicated social encounters.

At the opposite side of the world, dawn begins to light up the coast of the Yucatan Peninsula in Mexico. Like clockwork, a group of dolphins passes the fisherman's rickety wharf at this time. Gordo, a chubby male bottlenose with a clear, deep notch halfway down his dorsal fin, is the first to appear in the morning mist. He makes his way slowly westward along the shoreline; the rest of the gang, a football field behind, follows. As the sun brightens, one dark grey body after another passes the pier. They are 14: a female with her calf and 12 others. Twenty or so meters past the wharf, they cluster together next to a colorful string of moored pangas. Some dive, others mill about at the surface.

A few at a time, the dolphins explore the sandy bottom with no sign of hurry while another group of dolphins leisurely joins them from the opposite direction. They are now 23 with a couple of calves next to their mothers, all tightly grouped in a murky patch of water that likely hides a fishy meal. Suddenly, the circle unwinds in two lively threads: Five animals move steadily back toward the wharf in a monklike procession; the others disappear quickly to the west. The sun is already high on the horizon. What seemed for a moment to be a singular and cohesive group has reshuffled and divided, ready for the complex tasks and interactions that will make up their day.

Chimpanzees and dolphins look completely different. One resembles people, more or less. The other has the body of a cruise missile. One has hands that can skillfully manipulate a tool, delicately groom a partner or converse in sign language. The other has no hands at all. Chimpanzees swing through the trees of African forests. Dolphins dive deep in oceans. These mammals, about as closely related as mice and elephants, haven't had a common ancestor for nearly 100 million years. It takes dissection to see how their organs and limbs share common features.

One of us (Maddalena) is a marine mammalogist who has studied bottlenose and other dolphin species for nearly 20 years in Santa Monica Bay, near Los Angeles, and other parts of the world. The other (Craig) is a primatologist who has observed chimpanzees and gorillas in Africa for more than 15 years. As unlikely as it might seem, we find more parallel behavioral traits in these species than we do in more closely related animals. What's even more compelling is that many of these distinctive traits are also found in humans—an observation that may have implications for the origin of human intelligence.

Humanlike intelligence may not be a quality that could only have emerged from our own recent evolutionary lineage. Instead convergent evolution could have played a role. Evidence for this argument is not yet irrefutable but it is increasing. And it all starts with one unusual quality shared by humans, chimpanzees and dolphins: the large size of their brains. The various dolphin species, the four great apes and Homo sapiens possess brains that are the cognitive crowning glory of Earth's millions of species.

A Rare Intelligence

Of all the species on our planet, only a handful has possessed a high degree of intellect: apes and humans (including many extinct forms of both), dolphins, whales, and some others, such as elephants. The brains of an ape and a dolphin differ in their external morphology and neuroanatomical organization, in particular their cortical cytoarchitecture, which in dolphins has less cellular differentiation. Despite these differences, primate (including human) and dolphin brains share important similarities. For one, the brains of dolphins and apes increased in size and complexity over their evolutionary history. Both possess a high encephalization quotient (EQ) due to their unusually large brain-to-body-size ratios. EQ is the ratio of an animal's actual brain size to its expected brain size based on measurements of other animals its size. In both dolphins and apes, the neocortex is also more elaborately developed compared to that of other animals. Also distinctive is the neocortical gyrification, or folding of the cerebral cortex—which in dolphins surpasses that of any primate—and the presence of spindleshaped neurons, called Von Economo neurons, which have been linked in people to social fluency and the ability to sense what others think. Only recently were those neurons found in bottlenose dolphins.

But why is a big, sophisticated brain an advantage in life? Dinosaurs had puny brains but flourished for hundreds of millions of years. Intelligence is an adaptation, but not necessarily the only or even the most effective one. What works best for a given organism depends on its environmental context. Some creatures have changed precious little over many millions of years. Other lineages, such as primates and cetaceans, have undergone dramatic changes and a mushrooming of brain size in just a few million years. Natural selection has acted to favor intelligence when it conferred survival and reproductive benefits and when it complemented traits that were genetically hard-wired.

Brain power has allowed dolphins and apes to possess communication and social skills so complex that we are only now beginning to understand how they work. Unlike most animals, apes and dolphins live in fluid societies and engage in relationships that require accurate memories of who is a friend and who owes whom a favor. The social alliances they become a part of can change as their needs change. Great apes possess an intellect often referred to as Machiavellian. They remember favors owed and debts incurred and they operate in a "service economy" of behavior exchange. Male chimpanzees form paramilitary patrol parties and hunting parties. They also shift alliances in accordance with their self-interest. They may work with one group to manipulate a female for sexual access and with another to overthrow an alpha male. We used to think that some of these alliances were based entirely on kinship. Anthony Goldberg and Richard Wrangham showed some years ago, however, that such coalitions are not necessarily based on genetic relatedness.

Some dolphins also form coalitions of males in order to sexually coerce females. As was very recently observed by David Lusseau of the University of Aberdeen in Scotland, these groupings can also cooperate to overthrow other male coalitions. The alliances allow for highly complex behavioral "agreements" between males of the same school who cooperate in pairs and triplets to sequester females likely to be in estrus. In other contexts, dolphins can also practice deceit and deception, practices that require a theory of mind—the ability to perceive mental states in oneself and in others. Stan Kuczaj of the University of Southern Mississippi and his colleagues observed intentional deception in Kelly, a female dolphin kept in captivity. Kelly had been trained—along with her tank-mates—to retrieve objects from the pool in exchange for fish. After all the other dolphins had finished with their retrieval chores and gone their own way, Kelly appeared at the surface with some objects of unknown origin in the hope of gaining more fish. After searching the pool, Kelly's trainer discovered a secret cache of "toys" that the dolphin had astutely concealed under a drain cover. Day after day, she had collected objects inadvertently dropped into the pool by tourists, to be used for barter with her trainers for fish. On closer observation, it also became clear that Kelly was extremely careful not to add or remove objects from her cache when other dolphins were present.

Great apes also seem to be skilled at deceiving one another. In Tanzania, one of us (Craig) once watched a low-ranking male chimpanzee named Beethoven use deception to mate with a female despite the presence of the alpha male called Wilkie. As a party of chimpanzees sat in a forest clearing, Beethoven made a charging display through the middle of the group, his hair standing on end and his arched posture indicating bravado. As a low-ranking male, this was taken by the alpha Wilkie as an act of insubordination. As Beethoven charged past Wilkie and into dense thickets, Wilkie pursued and launched into his own display, dragging branches, drumming tree trunks with his feet and generally trying to be maximally impressive. With Wilkie absorbed in his display of dominance, Beethoven furtively made his way back to the clearing and mated with an eagerly awaiting female.

Intelligence Opens the Toolbox

Our understanding of how chimpanzees and dolphins apply their intelligence to tool use is expanding as well. Jane Goodall and others showed decades ago that chimpanzees use sticks to harvest insects. A 2007 report by primatologist Jill Pruetz taught us more: She and her colleagues, working in Senegal, observed a chimpanzee use a stick it had peeled to a tapered end as a weapon to hunt another mammal, something once only seen in humans. The chimpanzee jabbed the stick into tree cavities until it found a bushbaby, a squirrel-sized primate, which the stick extracted. Although not exactly a spear, the stick was evidence that the chimpanzee had foreseen a problem in immobilizing and extracting its intended prey and had devised a solution.

Dolphins do not have hands to use tools, but wild Indian Ocean bottlenose dolphin females are the first "tool-using cetacean" ever documented. Marine biologist Rachel Smolker and colleagues in the early 1980s observed these animals carrying a large cone-shaped sponge on the tip of their elongated beaks, or rostra, like a mask. These "nose mittens" were used for protection against stinging organisms or sand abrasion, or to extract prey from the sea floor. In a 2005 publication, Michael Kriitzen of the University of Zurich and his colleagues, using mitochondrial DNA analyses, concluded that "sponging" was socially transmitted vertically within a single matrilineal group, from mother sponge-carriers to their female offspring.

Knowing how to use a tool is not the fundamental adaptation that a large brain provides. Instead, a large brain conveys the ability to learn and to imitate another's behavior to appropriate its benefits. Tools allow chimpanzees to harvest protein, fat and carbohydrates that would be otherwise unavailable. The added nutrition can help a gestating or lactating female through an otherwise lean time of year, and enhance her reproductive output over the course of her long life. The ability to respond to rapidly changing dynamics in the social group, such as when males form coalitions to control females, is not limited to higher primates and dolphins, but it certainly typifies many species among them. In each case, these skills require years of learning. But the payoff is a potential reproductive windfall.

For many years the study of chimpanzee technological culture consisted mostly of anecdotes, which are fascinating but not always convincing. But when chimpanzee researchers obtained enough long-term data that they were able to analyze cultural traditions from a range of field sites, they found unequivocal evidence for a systematic pattern of these traditions. Using tool use and other cultural data from the seven longest-running field studies in Africa, Andrew Whiten of the University of St. Andrews and his colleagues in 1999 found at least 39 behaviors that could be attributable to the influence of learned traditions. This number may seem rather limited compared with the myriad examples of such behavior in our species, where almost everything is learned at some level. But compared with other nonhuman animals, it is a long list. The logical conclusion here is that animals that live by their wits, as it were, tend to be like chimpanzees and us—big-brained and with a long period of growth and maturation during which key life skills can be acquired by watching one's elders and peers.

We can ask how and why certain cultural traditions, whether technological or social behavior, arise and spread. Biological evolution occurs primarily via natural selection and is preserved through the transfer of genetic material from one generation to the next. It is also an inefficient process, because of the time required for genes to pass to the next generation, and because each reproductive act requires (in all higher animals) the reshuffling of genes from mother and father. Cultural "evolution" does not require the massive shuffling of the genetic deck that can slow the rate of change to a glacial pace. If a cultural trait confers on its user higher odds of survival and enhanced reproduction, then it has a good chance of being passed on. Even though the tool-use innovation, for example, has no genetic basis, the tradition of its use, once established, should spread, to the reproductive benefit of the inventor. Thus an entirely nongenetic feature could have a long-term effect on the species. Only a few groups of animals on this planet exhibit cultural traits. Higher primates certainly are cultural animals. Cetaceans also exhibit elements of culture. A good example of social learning in dolphins is the vertical cultural transmission of foraging and feeding specializations and vocal dialects. John Ford, for instance, reported what he calls "interpod call mimicry" in the wild, showing that killer whales are capable of vocal learning.

Language Building Blocks

Scientists disagree about whether dolphins have language capabilities but evidence persists that they may, depending on how one defines it. In one of the best-known cases, Louis Herman and his colleagues at the Kewalo Basin Marine Mammal Lab in Honolulu in the 1980s devised two artificial languages to teach to bottlenose dolphins at their facility. Neither language approximated human conversation, but both were based on a set of grammatical rules. One was computer-generated and included high-pitched words. The other was a sign language conveyed by trainers' arm and hand signals.

In an underwater classroom, two animals, Ake and Phoenix, were taught a series of sentences, including some commands describing how to take a Frisbee through a particular hoop or to swim under another dolphin. The dolphins also displayed the ability to recognize meaningless phrases. When a trainer occasionally said something that didn't make sense in the created languages, for instance, Ake ignored the command.

Evidence that apes can acquire and use language, including sign language, has grown over decades. Perhaps the most persuasive evidence of language capability in nonhuman apes comes from primatologist Sue Savage-Rumbaugh, who for 30 years was affiliated with Georgia State University's Language Research Center. Kanzi, a male bonobo she worked with, learned to communicate by touching symbols on a lexicon board and understand some spoken English. Savage-Rumbaugh estimated he could produce 300 words himself and could understand more than 1,000 when spoken.

Work by Savage-Rumbaugh and many other researchers has conclusively settled at least two arguments over ape language. First, she demonstrated that apes understand and employ the concept of reference, using words as symbols to represent things in their environment. Second, they can spontaneously use and combine these words to make requests, give information and comment on the world around them. If there is a difference between what Kanzi comprehends and what a human toddler understands, scientists have not yet discovered it.

Evidence also exists that dolphins and chimpanzees can recognize themselves as individuals. Chimpanzees, gorillas, bonobos and orangutans not only recognize themselves in mirrors but also are able to understand that paint blotches they observe in mirrors during experiments were placed on their bodies. The same holds true for bottlenose dolphins. These experiments do not prove that the animals are self-aware in human terms. But they do provide evidence that these animals exhibit cognition, as does their behavior in the wild.

Large brains likely also help these animals succeed in foraging. Both chimpanzees and dolphins feed on widely scattered, temporarily available food. Many species of dolphins chase schools of fish; chimpanzees chase the fleeting appearances of ripe fruits in tree crowns. These two dietary specialties keep them moving all day long, in search of the next school, the next patch. Predicting where and when to search is one challenge. Chimpanzees have the spatial memory of forest rangers. They monitor particular fruit trees in the weeks leading up to the ripening of a crop and return to the right spot day after day until the bounty is gone. Dolphins have a taller order; they have to know where to locate rapidly moving fish schools without such

obvious landmarks as trees, streams and mountains. For this they have sonar, a wonderfully evolved system that humans only relatively recently were able to replicate for their own uses. But in addition to their purely sensory adaptations, dolphins put their intelligence (and memory) to good use to find fish.

Chimpanzees mostly eat fruit but, like dolphins, they do hunt. And their hunting is social. They will attack groups of monkeys they encounter during their rambles in search of fruit in African forests. The chase, capture and kill are heart stopping, often gruesome, and always illustrative of the chimpanzees' social nature. To a lion, the zebra it is chasing may be only a meal, but to a chimpanzee the chance to kill and share prey is not only nutritional, but socially significant as well. The monkeys and pigs and antelopes the chimpanzees capture sometimes become pawns in the social dynamics of the group. Researchers in a range of studies across Africa have shown that males use meat to negotiate new alliances, rub salt in the wounds of old rivals and secure status that a chimpanzee without prey cannot. Adult and adolescent males do most of the hunting, making about 90 percent of the kills recorded at Gombe. Females also hunt but more often receive a share of meat from the male who either captured the meat or stole it from the captor. Although lone chimpanzees, both male and female, sometimes hunt by themselves, most hunts are social.

For many dolphin species, hunting is also a social affair. Dolphins are efficient predators who use both agility and braininess to achieve success. Killer whales, the largest dolphins, display one of the most cooperative hunting practices. Feeding at the top of the food chain, transient killer whales prey on small marine mammals such as seals lying on beaches or slabs of ice, and scientists have observed coordinated and intentional stranding by killer whales in the waters of Patagonia. On occasion, the killing of a pinniped represents a learning lesson for the calf, which will use the same technique throughout its life. In groups, they also attack whales much larger than themselves without any sign of fear or hesitation and with a high degree of predatory success.

Being such accomplished ocean hunters makes dolphins a valuable asset for other ocean dwellers in search of a meal. In the coastal waters of Los Angeles, one of us (Maddalena) frequently observes sea lions in proximity to dolphins during feeding and foraging activities. Two predatory species travel and feed together, with no evident hostility or competition. Sea lions capitalize on the superior food-finding ability of echolocating common dolphins to find their own prey. The diverse hunting strategies employed by dolphin and ape societies are an excellent gauge of their social complexity, and another example of how brain complexity, social complexity and ecological complexity are all linked.

Familiar Yet Threatened

These growing insights into the intelligence of great apes and dolphins are emerging as these animals become increasingly threatened worldwide. As we reach farther and farther into tropical forests in search of timber, farmland and spaces for human dwellings, we disrupt the apes' terrestrial habitat. The ongoing hunting of these animals is also taking a toll. And as we continue to use the oceans as our dumping ground, we threaten dolphins' habitat. The incidental catching of nontarget species in commercial fishing activity, known as bycatch, is just one of the major problems facing these animals today. Many conservationists believe that a century from now, great apes will survive only in a few carefully protected sanctuaries or in captivity. Dolphin populations are much less visible than those of great apes but the threats to them are also insidious. Today, several dolphin species are either critically endangered, endangered, threatened or of unknown status.

As scientists who have spent many years studying dolphins and apes in the wild, we believe that our research must incorporate respect and a sense of stewardship for the animals we study. We have both reached the same conclusion: Without conservation and protection of these species and the ecosystems in which they live, they will not survive to see the next century. Sadly, this projection comes just as we are beginning to better understand their complex abilities and social interactions.

Bibliography

Bearzi, M., and C. B. Stanford. 2008. *Beautiful Minds: The Parallel Lives of Great Apes and Dolphins.* Cambridge: Harvard University Press.

Butti, C, C. C. Sherwood, A. Y. Hakeem, J. M. Allman, and P. R. Hof. 2009. Total number and volume of Von Economo neurons in the cerebral cortex of cetaceans. *The Journal of Comparative Neurology, Research in Systems Neuroscience* 515:243–259.

Goldberg, T. L., and R. W. Wrangham. 1997. Genetic correlates of social behaviour in wild chimpanzees: Evidence from mitochondrial DNA. *Animal Behaviour* 54:559–570.

Kriitzen, M., J. Mann, M. R. Heithaus, R. C. Connor, L. Bejder, and W. B. Sherwin. 2005. Cultural transmission of tool use in bottlenose dolphins. Proceedings of the National Academy of Sciences of the U.S.A. 105:8939–8943.

Lusseau, D. 2007. Why are male social relationships complex in the Doubtful Sound bottlenose dolphin population? *PLoS ONE* 2(4):e348.

Marino, L. 2002. Convergence of complex cognitive abilities in cetaceans and primates. *Brain, Behavior and Evolution* 59:21–32.

Marino, L. 1996. What can dolphins tell us about primate evolution? *Evolutionary Anthropology* 5:73–110.

Marino, L. et al. 2007. Cetaceans have complex brains for complex cognition. *PLoS Biology* 139:966–972.

Pruetz, J. D., and P. Bertolani. 2007. Savanna chimpanzees, *Pan troglodytes verus,* hunt with tools. *Current Biology* 17:1–6.

Reiss, D., B. McCowan, and L. Marino. 1997. Communicative and other cognitive characteristics of bottlenose dolphins. *Trends in Cognitive Sciences* 1:123–156.

Reiss, D., and L. Marino. 2001. Mirror self-recognition in the bottlenose dolphin: A case of cognitive convergence. Proceedings of the National Academy of Sciences 98:5937–5942.

Smolker, R., A. Richards, R. Connor, J. Mann, and P. Berggren. 1997. Sponge carrying by dolphins (*Delphindea, Tursiops sp.*) A foraging specialization involving tool use? *Ethology* 103:454–465.

Stanford, C. 2007. *Apes of the Impenetrable Forest.* Upper Saddle River, NJ: Prentice Hall (Primate Field Studies Series).

Whiten, A., J. Goodall, W. C. McGrew, T. Nishida, V. Reynolds, Y. Sugiyama, C. E. G. Tutin, R. W. Wrangham, and C. Boesch. 1999. Cultures in chimpanzees. *Nature* 399:682–685.

Critical Thinking

1. What are some of the important similarities shared by primate and dolphin brains?

2. Why is a big, sophisticated brain an advantage in the social lives of both dolphins and chimpanzees?

3. How do chimpanzees and dolphins each apply their intelligence to tool use?

4. What are the other, more fundamental advantages of having a large brain?

5. What have long-term studies revealed about tool use and how it is acquired?

6. Why is "cultural evolution" rather than natural selection a more effective way of transferring technological or social behavior?

7. How do the authors assess the language ability and cognition among chimpanzees and dolphins?

8. How have large brains helped both chimpanzees and dolphins in foraging for food?

Internet References

Humanorigins.si.edu
http://humanorigins.si.edu/research

Journal of Human Evolution
www.journals.elsevier.com/journal-of-human-evolution

Society for Neuroscience
www.sfn.org/public-outreach/brainfacts-dot-org

MADDALENA BEARZI is president and cofounder of the Ocean Conservation Society and a nature and travel journalist. She received her PhD in biology at the University of California, Los Angeles, and has studied dolphins and whales in California and other parts of the world for more than 20 years. CRAIG STANFORD is a professor of anthropology and biological sciences at the University of Southern California and codirector of its Jane Goodall Research Center. He received his PhD in anthropology from the University of California, Berkeley, and has conducted field research on great apes in Africa for more than 15 years.

Article

Prepared by: Elvio Angeloni

What Are Big Brains For? Or, How Culture Stole Our Guts

JOSEPH HEINRICH

Learning Outcomes

After reading this article, you will be able to:

- Discuss the relationship between our big brains and the anatomical adjustments required for giving birth.

- Discuss the importance of the differences in myelination between humans and chimpanzees.

- Relate the uniquely human patterns of growth and maturation to the hunting way of life.

- Describe and explain the "externalization" of food digestion in humans and how this has changed our anatomy.

- Explain the ways in which tools have made us "fat wimps."

- Explain our ability to "endurance run" and how water containers enabled this to happen.

- Describe and explain the uniquely human thermoregulatory adaptations.

Compared to those of other animals, our brains are big, dense, and groovy. While we don't have the biggest brains in the natural world—whales and elephants beat us—we do have the most cortical interconnections and the highest degree of cortical folding. Cortical folding produces that "crumpled wad of paper" (groovy) appearance that particularly characterizes human brains. But that's just the beginning of our oddities. Our brains evolved from the size of a chimpanzee's, at roughly 350 cm³, to 1350 cm³ in about 5 million years. Most of that expansion, from about 500 cm³ upward, took place only in about the last 2 million years. That's fast in genetic evolutionary terms.

This expansion was finally halted about 200,000 years ago, probably by the challenges of giving birth to babies with increasingly bulbous heads. In most species, the birth canal is larger than the newborn's head, but not in humans. Infant skulls have to remain unfused in order to squeeze through the birth canal in a manner that isn't seen in other species. It seems our brains only ceased expanding because we hit the stops set by our primate body plan; if babies heads got any bigger, they wouldn't be able to squeeze out of mom at birth. Along the way, natural selection came up with numerous tricks to circumvent this big-headed baby problem, including intense cortical folding, high-density interconnections (which permit our brains to hold more information without getting bigger) and a rapid post birth expansion. Specifically, newborn human brains continue expanding at the faster pre-birth gestational rate for the first year, eventually tripling in size. By contrast, newborn primate brains grow more slowly after birth, eventually only doubling in size.

After this initial growth spurt, our brains continue adding more connections for holding and processing information (new glial cells, axons, and synapses) over the next three decades of life and even beyond, especially in the neocortex. Consider our white matter and, specifically, the process of myelination. As vertebrate brains mature, their white matter increases as the (axonal) connections among neurons are gradually "burned in" and wrapped in a performance-enhancing coating of fat called myelin. This process of myelination makes brain regions more efficient, but less plastic and thus less susceptible to learning. To see how human brains are different, we can compare our myelination with that of our closest relatives, chimpanzees. . . . [T]he cerebral cortex . . . shows the fraction of myelination (as a percentage of the adult level) during three different developmental periods: (1) infancy, (2) childhood (called the "juvenile period" in primates), and (3) adolescence and young adulthood. Infant chimpanzees arrive in the world with 15% of their cortex already myelinized, whereas humans start with only 1.6% myelinized. For the neocortex, which has evolved more recently and is massive in humans, the percentages are 20% and 0%, respectively. During adolescence and young adulthood, humans still have only 65% of their eventual myelination complete, whereas chimpanzees are almost done, at 96%. These data suggest that, unlike chimpanzees, we continue substantial "wiring-up" into our third decade of life.

Human brain development is related to another unusual feature of our species, our extended childhoods and the emergence of that memorable period called adolescence. Compared to other primates, our gestational and infancy periods (birth to weaning) have shortened while our childhoods have extended and a uniquely human period of adolescence has emerged, prior to full maturity. Childhood is a period of intensive cultural learning, including playing and the practicing of adult roles and skills, during which time our brains reach nearly their adult size while our bodies remain small. Adolescence begins at sexual maturity, after which a growth spurt ensues. During this time, we engage in apprenticeships, as we hone the most complex of adult skills and areas of knowledge, as well as build relationships with peers and look for mates.

The emergence of adolescence and young adulthood has likely been crucial over our evolutionary history, since in hunting and gathering populations, hunters do not produce enough calories to even feed themselves (let alone others) until around age 18 and won't reach their peak productivity until their late thirties. Interestingly, while hunters reach their peak strength and speed in their twenties, individual hunting success does not peak until around age 40, because success depends more on know-how and refined skills than on physical prowess. By contrast, chimpanzees—who also hunt and gather—can obtain enough calories to sustain themselves immediately after infancy ends, around age 5. Consistent with our long period of wiring-up, this pattern and contrast with chimpanzees reveals the degree to which we humans are dependent on learning for our survival as foragers.

Our unusually big brains, with their slow neurological and behavioral development but rapid evolutionary expansion, is precisely what you'd expect if cumulative cultural evolution had become the driving selection pressure in the evolution of our species. Once cumulative cultural evolution began to produce cultural adaptations, like cooking and spears, individuals whose genes have endowed them with the brains and developmental processes that permit them to most effectively acquire, store, and organize cultural information will be the most likely to survive, find mates, and leave progeny. As each generation gets brains that are a little bigger and a little better at cultural

learning, the body of adaptive know-how will rapidly expand to fill any available brain space. This process will shape the development of our brains, by keeping them maximally plastic and "programmed to receive," and our bodies, by keeping them small (and calorically inexpensive) until we've learned enough to survive. This culture-gene coevolutionary interaction creates an autocatalytic process such that no matter how big our brains get, there will always be much more cultural information in the world than any one of us can learn in a lifetime. The better our brains get at cultural learning, the faster adaptive cultural information accumulates, and the greater the pressure on brains to acquire and store this information.

This view also explains three puzzling facts about human infants. First, compared to other species, babies are altricial, meaning that they are weak, undermuscled, fat, and uncoordinated (sorry, babies, but it's true). By contrast, some mammals exit the womb ready to walk, and even primates rapidly figure out how to hang onto mom. Meanwhile, above the neck, human babies' brains are developmentally advanced at birth compared to those of other animals, having passed more of the mammalian neurological landmarks than other species. Fetuses are already acquiring aspects of language in the womb, babies arrive ready to engage in cultural learning. Before they can walk, feed themselves, or safely defecate, infants are selectively learning from others and can read others' intentions in order to copy their goals. Third, despite being otherwise developmentally and cognitively advanced, babies' brains arrive highly plastic (unmyelinized) and continue to expand at their gestational rate. In short, while being otherwise nearly helpless, babies and toddlers are sophisticated cultural learning machines.

Food Processing Externalizes Digestion

Compared to other primates, humans have an unusual digestive system. Starting at the top, our mouths, gapes, lips, and teeth are oddly small, and our lip muscles are weak. Our mouths are the size of a squirrel monkey's, a species that weighs less than three pounds. Chimpanzees can open their mouths twice as wide as we can and hold substantial amounts of food compressed between their lips and large teeth. We also have puny jaw muscles that reach up only to just below our ears. Other primates' jaw muscles stretch to the tops of their heads, where they sometimes even latch onto a bony central ridge. Our stomachs are small, having only a third of the surface area that we'd expect for a primate of our size, and our colons are too short, being only 60% of their expected mass. Our bodies are also poor at detoxifying wild foods. Overall, our guts—stomachs, small intestines, and colons—are much smaller than they ought to be for our overall body size. Compared to other primates, we lack a substantial amount of digestive power all the way down the line, from our mouth's (in) ability to breakdown food to our colon's capacity to process fiber. Interestingly, our small intestines are about the size they should be, an exception that we'll account for below.

How can culture explain this strange physiological patterning in humans?

The answer is that our bodies, and in this case our digestive systems, have coevolved with culturally transmitted know-how related to food processing. People in every society process food using techniques that have accumulated over generations, including cooking, drying, pounding, grinding, leaching, chopping, marinating, smoking, and scraping. Of these, the oldest are probably chopping, scraping, and pounding with stone tools. Chopping, scraping, and pounding meat can go a long way, because they tenderize by slicing, dicing, and crushing the muscle fibers, partially replacing some of the functions of teeth, mouths, and jaws. Similarly, marinades initiate the chemical breakdown of foods. Acidic marinades, such as that used for the coastal South American dish ceviche, begin literally breaking down meat proteins before they reach your mouth, mimicking the approach taken by your stomach acid. Leaching is one of a host of techniques that hunter-gatherers have long used to process food and remove toxins.

Of all these techniques, cooking is probably the most important piece of cultural know-how that has shaped our digestive system. The primatologist Richard Wrangham has persuasively argued that cooking (and therefore fire) has played a crucial role in human evolution. Richard and his collaborators laid out how cooking, if done properly, does an immense amount of digestion for us. It softens and prepares both meat and plant foods for digestion. The right amount of heating tenderizes, detoxifies, and breaks down fibrous tubers and other plant foods. Heating also breaks down the proteins in meat, dramatically reducing the work for our stomach acid. Consequently, by contrast with meat-eating carnivores (e.g., lions), we do not often retain meat in our stomachs for hours, because it typically arrives partially digested by pounding, scraping, marinating, and cooking.

While all this food processing reduces the digestive workload of our mouths, stomachs, and colons, it does not alter the need to actually absorb the nutrients, which is why our small intestines are about the right size for a primate of our stature.

What is often underemphasized in this account is that food-processing techniques are primarily products of cultural evolution. Cooking, for example, is not something we instinctually know how to do, or even can easily figure out. If you don't believe me, go outside and make a fire without using any modern technology. Rub two sticks together, make a fire drill, find

naturally occurring flint or quartz, etc. Put that big brain to work. Maybe some fire instincts designed by natural selection to solve this recurrent dilemma of our ancestral environments will kick in and guide you.

. . .

No luck? Unless you've had training—that is, received cultural transmission—it's very unlikely you were successful. Our bodies have been shaped by fire and cooking, but we have to learn from others how to make fire and cook. Making fire is so "unnatural" and technically difficult that some foraging populations have actually lost the ability to make fire. These include the Andaman Islanders (off the coast of Malaysia), Sirionó (Amazonia), Northern Aché, and perhaps Tasmanians. Now, to be clear, these populations couldn't have survived without fire; they retained fire but lost the ability to start new fires on demand. When one band's fire was inadvertently extinguished, say during a fierce storm, they had to head off to locate another band whose fire had not gone out (hopefully). However, living in small and widely scattered groups in frosty Paleolithic Europe, the fires of our bigger-brained *Neanderthal* cousins probably sometimes went out and weren't to be reignited for thousands of years.

It's likely that our species' reliance on fire began with the control of fire, perhaps obtained from naturally occurring sources. Nevertheless, just capturing, sustaining, and controlling fire requires some know-how. Keeping a fire going may sound easy, but you have to keep it going all the time, during rainstorms, high winds, and long journeys across rivers and through swamps. I learned something about this while living in the Peruvian Amazon among an indigenous group called the Matsigenka. After transporting what looked like a dead, charred log to her distant garden, I saw a Matsigenka woman breathe life back into a hidden ember using a combination of dried moss, which she brought with her, and thermal reflection from other logs. I was also embarrassed when another young Matsigenka woman, with the requisite infant slung at her side, stopped by my house in the village to rearrange my cooking fire. Her adjustments increased the heat, created a convenient spot for my pot, reduced the smoke (and my choking), and eliminated much of the need for my constant tending.

Cooking is also difficult to learn through individual trial-and-error experience. For cooking to provide a digestive aid, it has to be done right. Bad cooking can actually make food harder to digest and increase its toxins. And what constitutes effective cooking depends on the type of food. With meat, doing the most obvious thing (to me) of placing pieces right in the flames can lead to a hard, charred outside and a raw interior—exactly what you don't want. Consequently, small-scale societies have complex repertoires of food-processing techniques that are specific to the food in question. For example, the best cooking technique for some foods involves wrapping them in leaves and burying them in the fire's ash for a long time (how long?). Meanwhile, many hunters eat the liver of their kill raw, on the spot. Livers, it turns out, are energy rich, soft, and delicious when eaten raw—except for those species in which eating the liver can be deadly (do you know which those are?). Inuit hunters don't eat polar bear livers raw because they believe such livers are toxic (and they are correct, according to laboratory research on the question). The rest of the kill is typically butchered, sometimes pounded, possibly dried, and then cooked—though different parts of the kill are cooked in different ways.

The impact of this culturally transmitted know-how about fire and cooking has had such an impact on our species' genetic evolution that we are now, essentially, addicted to cooked food. Wrangham reviewed the literature on the ability of humans to survive by eating only raw foods. His review includes historical cases in which people had to survive without cooking, as well as studies of modern fads, such as the raw foods movement. The long and short of all this is that it's very difficult to survive for months without cooking. Raw-foodists are thin and often feel hungry. Their body fat drops so low that women often stop menstruating or menstruate only irregularly. This occurs despite the supermarket availability of a vast range of raw foods, the use of powerful processing technologies like blenders, and the consumption of some preprocessed foods. The upshot is that human foraging populations could never survive without cooking; meanwhile, apes do just fine without cooking, though they do love cooked foods.

Our species' increasing dependence on fire and cooking over our evolutionary history may have also shaped our cultural learning psychology in ways that facilitated the acquisition of know-how about fire making. This is a kind of content bias in our cultural learning. The UCLA anthropologist, Dan Fessler, argues that during middle childhood (ages six to nine), humans go through a phase in which we are strongly attracted to learning about fire, by both observing others and manipulating it ourselves. In small-scale societies, where children are free to engage this curiosity, adolescents have both mastered fire and lost any further attraction to it. Interestingly, Fessler also argues that modern societies are unusual because so many children never get to satisfy their curiosity, so their fascination with fire stretches into the teen years and early adulthood.

The influence of socially learned food-processing techniques on our genetic evolution probably occurred very gradually, perhaps beginning with the earliest stone tools. Such tools had likely begun to emerge by at least 3 million years ago and were probably used for processing meat—pounding, chopping, slicing, and dicing. Drying meat or soaking plant foods may have emerged at any time, and probably repeatedly. By the emergence of the genus *Homo*, it's plausible that cooking began to

be used sporadically but with increasing frequency, especially where large fibrous tubers or meat were relatively abundant.

Our repertoire of food-processing methods altered the genetic selection pressures on our digestive system by gradually supplanting some of its functions with cultural substitutes. Techniques such as cooking actually increase the energy available from foods and make them easier to digest and detoxify. This effect allowed natural selection to save substantial amounts of energy by reducing our gut tissue, the second most expensive tissue in our bodies (next to brain tissue), and our susceptibility to various diseases associated with gut tissue. The energy savings from the externalization of digestive functions by cultural evolution became one component in a suite of adjustments that permitted our species to build and run bigger and bigger brains.

How Tools Made Us Fat Wimps

Responding to posters that read "Wanted, athletic men to earn $ 5 per second by holding 85-pound ape's shoulders to the floor," beefy linebacker types would line up at Noell's Ark Gorilla Show, part of a circus that traveled up and down the eastern seaboard of the United States from the 1940s to the 1970s. Inspired to impress the crowds at this star attraction, no man in thirty years ever lasted more than five seconds pinning down a juvenile chimpanzee. Moreover, the chimpanzees had to be seriously handicapped, as they wore "silence of the lambs" masks to prevent them from using their preferred weapon, their large canine teeth. Later, the show's apes were forced to wear large gloves because a chimp named Snookie had rammed his thumbs up an opponent's nose, tearing the man's nostrils apart. The organizers of Noell's Ark Gorilla Show were wise to use young chimps, because a full-grown male chimpanzee (150 lbs.) is quite capable of breaking a man's back. The authorities did finally put an end to this spectacle, but it wasn't clear whether they were concerned about the young apes or the brawny wrestlers who voluntarily entered the ring with them.

How did we become such wimps?

It was culture. As cumulative cultural evolution generated increasingly effective tools and weapons, like blades, spears, axes, snares, spear-throwers, poisons, and clothing, natural selection responded to the changed environment generated by these cultural products by shaping our genes to make us weak. Manufactured from wood, flint, obsidian, bone, antler, and ivory, effective tools and weapons can replace big molars for breaking down seeds or fibrous plants and big canines, strong muscles, and dense bones for fighting and hunting.

To understand this, realize that big brains are energy hogs. Our brains use between a fifth and a quarter of the energy we take in each day, while the brains of other primates use between 8% and 10%. Other mammals use only 3% to 5%. Even worse, unlike muscles, you can't shut down a brain to save energy; it takes almost as much energy to sustain a resting brain as it does an active one. Our cultural knowledge about the natural world combined with our tools, including our food-processing techniques, allowed our ancestors to obtain a high-energy diet with much less time and effort than other species. This was crucial for brain expansion in our lineage. However, since brains need a constant supply of energy, periods of food scarcity—such as those initiated by floods, droughts, injuries, and disease—pose a serious threat to humans. To deal with this threat, natural selection needed to trim our body's energy budget and create a storehouse for times of scarcity. The emergence of tools and weapons allowed natural selection to trade expensive tissues for fat, which is cheaper to maintain and provides an energy-storage system crucial for sustaining big brains through periods of scarcity. This is why infants, who devote 85% of their energy to brain building, are so fat—they need the energy buffer to sustain neurological development and optimize cultural learning.

So, if you are challenged to wrestle a chimpanzee, I recommend that you decline and instead suggest a contest based on (1) threading a needle (a sewing contest?), (2) fast-ball pitching, or (3) long-distance running. While natural selection traded strength for fat, increasingly complex tools and techniques drove another key genetic change: the human neocortex sends corticospinal connections deeper into the motor neurons, spinal cord, and brain stem than in other mammals. It is the depth of these connections—in part—that facilitates our fine dexterity for learned motor patterns (recall the plasticity of the neocortex mentioned above). In particular, these motor neurons directly innervate our hands, allowing us to thread a needle or throw accurately, as well as our tongues, jaws, and vocal cords, facilitating speech. Improved motor control was favored once cumulative cultural evolution began delivering more and finer tools. Such tools also created genetic evolutionary pressures that shaped the anatomy of our hands, giving us wider fingertips, more muscular thumbs, and a "precision grip." Cultural evolution may also have produced packages for throwing, including techniques, artifacts (wooden spears and throwing clubs), and strategies, suitable for using projectiles in hunting, scavenging, raiding, or community policing. The emergence of these, along with the ability to learn to practice throwing by observing others, may have fostered some of the anatomical specializations in our shoulders and wrist, while at the same time explaining why many children are so keenly interested in throwing.

Alongside these anatomical changes, our species' long history with complex tools has also likely shaped our learning psychology. We are cognitively primed to categorize "artifacts" (e.g., tools and weapons) as separate from all other things in the world, like rocks and animals. Unlike plants, animals, and other nonliving things like water, we think about function when we think about artifacts. For example, when young children ask about artifacts they ask "What's it for" or "What does it do?" instead of "What kind is it?" which is their initial query when seeing a novel plant or animal. This specialized thinking about artifacts, as opposed to thinking about other nonliving things, requires, first, that there be some complex artifacts with nonobvious, or causally opaque, functions in the world that one needs to learn about.

How Water Containers and Tracking Made Us Endurance Runners

Traditional hunters throughout the world have shown that we humans can run down antelopes, giraffes, deer, steenboks, zebras, waterbucks, and wildebeests. These pursuits often take three or more hours, but eventually the prey animal drops over, either from fatigue or heat exhaustion. With the exception of domesticated horses, which we have artificially selected for endurance, our species' main competition for the mammalian endurance champion comes from some of the social carnivores, like African wild dogs, wolves, and hyenas, that also engage in persistence hunting and habitually run 6 to 13 miles (10 to 20 km) per day.

To beat these species, we only need to turn up the heat, literally, because these carnivores are much more susceptible to warmer temperatures than we are. In the tropics, dogs and hyenas can only hunt at dawn and dusk, when it's cooler. So, if you want to race your dog, plan a 25-kilometer race on a hot summer day. He'll conk out. And the hotter it is, the more you'll beat him by. Chimpanzees aren't even in our league in this domain.

Comparisons of human anatomy and physiology with those of other mammals, including both living primates and hominins (our ancestor species and extinct relatives), reveal that natural selection has likely been at work shaping our bodies for serious distance running for over a million years. We have a full suite of specialized distance running adaptations, from toe to head. Here's a sampling:

- Our feet, unlike other apes, possess springy arches that store energy and absorb the shock of repeated impacts. This is provided that we learn proper form, and avoid landing on our heels.
- Our comparatively longer legs possess extended springlike tendons, including the crucial Achilles, that connect to short muscle fibers. This setup generates efficient power and provides us with the ability to increase speed by taking longer, energy-saving, strides.
- Unlike animals built for speed, which possess mostly fast-twitch muscle fibers, frequent distance running can

shift the balance in our legs upward from 50% slow-twitch muscle fibers to as high as 80%, yielding much greater aerobic capacity.

- The joints in our lower body are all reinforced to withstand the stresses of endurance running.
- To stabilize our trunk while running, our species sports a distinctively enlarged gluteus maximus, along with substantial muscles—the erector spinae—that run up our backbone.
- Coupled with our notably broad shoulders and short forearms, arm swinging creates a compensatory torque that balances us while running. And unlike other primates, the musculature in our upper back allows our head to twist independently from our torso.
- The nuchal ligament, connecting our heads and shoulders, secures and balances our skulls and brains against running-related shocks. Other running animals also have a nuchal ligament, but other primates do not.

Perhaps most impressive of all are our thermoregulatory adaptations—we are certainly the sweatiest species. Mammals must maintain their body temperature in a relatively narrow range, from roughly 36°C (96.8°F) to 38°C (100°F). The lethal core temperature of most mammals ranges from 42°C (107.6°F) to 44°C (111.2°F). Since running can generate a tenfold increase in heating, the inability of most mammals to run long distances arises from their inability to manage this heat buildup.

To overcome this adaptive challenge, natural selection favored the (1) nearly complete loss of hair, (2) proliferation of eccrine sweat glands, and (3) emergence of a "head-cooling" system. The idea here is that sweat coats and cools the skin through evaporation, which is fostered by the airflow generated by running. To appreciate what happened, note that sweat glands come in two varieties, apocrine and eccrine. At puberty, apocrine glands start producing a viscous pheromone-containing secretion, which is often processed by bacteria to create a strong aroma. These glands are confined to our armpits, nipples, and groin (guess what they are for?). By contrast, eccrine glands, which secrete clear salty water and some other electrolytes, can be found all over our bodies and are much more numerous on us than on other primates. The highest densities of these glands occur in the scalp and feet, the two locations most in need of cooling during running. Measured over body surfaces, no other animal can sweat faster than we do. Moreover, our eccrine glands are "smart glands," because they contain nerves that may permit centralized control from the brain (in other animals sweating is controlled locally). It was these innervated eccrine glands, and not the apocrine glands, that proliferated to cover our bodies during human evolution.

Because brains are particularly susceptible to overheating, natural selection also engineered a special brain cooling system in our ancestors. This system involves a network of veins that run near the surface of the skull, where they are first cooled by the ample sweat glands on the face and head. They then flow into the sinus cavities, where they absorb heat from the arteries responsible for transporting blood to the brain. This cooling system may be why humans, unlike so many mammals, can sustain core temperatures above the 44°C (111.2°F) limit.

At this point, you might be thinking that all these features of our bodies are clearly adaptive, so why would I think that it was cultural evolution that created the conditions that led to the evolution of our species' running adaptations. To get at this point, let's look at three aspects of this adaptive design more closely. First, really putting our endurance abilities into action, where they give us the biggest survival advantage, requires running for hours in the heat of the day in the tropics. When our evaporative cooling system kicks into overdrive, a prime athlete will begin sweating out 1 to 2 liters per hour, with 3 liters being well within our bodies' capacity. This system can run, and keep us running, for many hours provided it doesn't run short of a critical ingredient—water. So, where's the genetically evolved water storage system or tank?

Horses, which as I mentioned can compete with us for distance, do have the ability to store large amounts of water. By contrast, not only are humans unable to consume and store large amounts of water, but we are actually relatively poor hydrators compared to other animals. While a donkey can drink 20 liters in 3 minutes, we top out at 2 liters in 10 minutes (camels do 100 liters in the same time). How can this crucial element be missing from our thermoregulatory system? Is our otherwise elegant running design fatally flawed?

The answer is that cultural evolution supplied water containers and water-finding know-how. Among ethnographically known foraging populations, hunters carry water in gourds, skins, and ostrich eggs. Such containers are used in conjunction with detailed, local, culturally transmitted knowledge about where and how to locate water. In the Kalahari Desert of southern Africa, foragers use ostrich eggs as canteens (water containers), which keep the water refreshingly cool, or occasionally use the stomach sacs of small antelopes. They also use long reed straws to suck water from hollow tree trunks, where it collects, and they can readily locate water-bearing roots by spotting certain dry wispy vines. In Australia, hunter-gatherers created water containers using a technique that involved turning small mammals "inside-out". Like the Kalahari foragers, they also used surface signs to locate hidden underground water sources. These techniques are nonobvious: recall that Burke and Wills became trapped along Coopers Creek for want of such know-how.

This reasoning suggests that the evolution of our fancy sweat-based thermoregulatory systems could take off only after cultural evolution generated the know-how for making water containers and locating water sources in diverse environments. The suite of adaptations that make us stunning endurance runners is actually part of a coevolutionary package into which culture delivered a critical ingredient, water.

Supplied with water, any good marathoner probably has the endurance to chase down a zebra, antelope, or steenbok. However, there's more to persistence hunting than endurance, a lot more. Endurance hunters need to be able to recognize specific target prey and then track that specific individual over long distances. Almost any animal we might want to pursue is much faster than we are in a sprint and will immediately disappear into the distance. To exploit our endurance edge, we need to be able to track a specific individual for several hours, by identifying and reading their spoor and anticipating their actions. The ability to distinguish the target, say a zebra, from other zebras is crucial since many herd animals have a defensive strategy in which they circle back to their herd and try to disappear by blending back into the group. If you can't selectively target the one you've been chasing—the tired one—then you could end up chasing a fresh zebra (a disaster). Thus, persistence hunters must be able to track and identify individuals.

Although many species engage in some form of tracking, no other animal tracks the way we do. Studies of tracking among modern hunter-gatherers reveal that it is an arena of intensive cultural knowledge that is acquired through a kind of apprenticeship, as adolescents and young men watch the best hunters in their group interpret and discuss spoor. From the spoor, skilled trackers can deduce an individual's age, sex, physical condition, speed, and fatigue level, as well as the time of day it passed by. Such feats are accomplished, in part, by knowledge of particular species' habits, feeding preferences, social organization, and daily patterns.

A number of culturally transmitted tricks further aid persistence hunters. The most interesting of these bits of strategy highlights the subtle, adaptive edge that culture-gene coevolution has isolated and exploited. This is a little complicated, so stay with me.

Many four-legged animals are saddled with a design disadvantage. Game animals thermoregulate by panting, like a dog. If they need to release more heat, they pant faster. This works fine unless they are running. When they run, the impact of their forelimbs compresses their chest cavities in a manner that makes breathing during compressions inefficient. This means that, ignoring oxygen and thermoregulation requirements, running quadrupeds should breathe only once per locomotor cycle. But since the need for oxygen goes up linearly with speed, they will be breathing too frequently at some speeds and not frequently enough at other speeds. Consequently, a running quadruped must pick a speed that (1) demands only one breath per cycle but (2) supplies enough oxygen for his muscle-speed demands (lest fatigue set in), and (3) delivers enough panting to prevent a meltdown (heat stroke), which depends on factors unrelated to speed, such as the temperature and breeze. The outcome of these constraints is that quadrupeds have a discrete set of optimal—or preferred—speed settings (like the gears on a stick-shift car) for different styles of locomotion (e.g., walking, trotting, and galloping). If they deviate from these preferred settings, they operate less efficiently.

Humans lack these restrictions because (1) our lungs do not compress when we stride (we're bipedal) so (2) our breathing rates can vary independent of our speed, and (3) our thermoregulation is managed by our fancy sweating system, so the need to pant does not constrain our breathing. Because of this, within our range of aerobic running speeds (not sprinting), energy use doesn't vary too much. That means we can change speeds within this range without paying much of a penalty. As a result, a skilled endurance hunter can strategically vary his speed in order to force his prey to run inefficiently. If his prey picks an initial speed to escape that is just faster than the hunter's, the hunter can speed up. This forces the prey to shift to a much faster speed, which will cause rapid overheating. The animal's only alternative is to run inefficiently, at a slower speed, which will exhaust his muscles more quickly. The consequence is that hunters force their prey into a series of sprints and rests that eventually result in heat stroke. The overheated prey collapses and is easily dispatched. Tarahumara, Paiute, and Navajo hunters report that they then simply strangle the collapsed deer or pronghorn antelope.

Persistence hunters can also take advantage of a wide range of other tricks that increase their edge. In the Kalahari, where this aspect has been most studied, hunters tend to pursue game during midday, when temperatures are hottest, between 39°C (102°F) and 42°C (107.6°F). They adjust their prey choice depending on the seasonally varying health status of their target species, pursuing duiker, steenbok, and gemsbok in the rainy season and zebra and wildebeest in the dry season. They hunt in the morning after a bright full moon (no clouds) because many species will be tired after remaining active on well-lit nights. When chasing a herd, hunters watch for "dropouts" since these will be the weakest members. Nonhuman predators tend to follow the herd, not the loners, since they rely on scent, not sight and spoor. Perhaps not surprisingly, foragers can spot heat stroke in other people and know how to treat it, as they did with one anthropologist who tried to keep up with the locals (an occupational hazard).

Finally, to achieve a running form that maximizes both performance and freedom from injury, humans need to rely on some cultural learning, on top of much individual practice. The evolutionary biologist and anatomist Dan Lieberman has studied long-distance barefoot and minimally shod running in communities around the globe. When he asks runners of all ages how they learned to run, they never say they "just knew how." Instead, they often name or point to an older, highly skilled, and more prestigious member of their group or community and say they just watch him and do what he does. We are such a cultural species that we've come to rely on learning from others even to figure out how to run in ways that best harness our anatomical adaptations.

The genetic evolution of our big brains, long childhoods, short colons, small stomachs, flexible nuchal ligaments, long legs, arched feet, dexterous hands, lightweight bones, and fat laden bodies was driven by cumulative cultural evolution—by the growing pool of information available in the minds of other people.

Critical Thinking

1. What have been the human anatomical adjustments for giving birth to large-brained babies?

2. What is "myelination" and why is there a uniquely human pattern of growth in humans?
3. How are human maturation patterns uniquely human and why?
4. Explain the "externalization" of food digestion as a uniquely human quality and describe the ways in which it has changed our anatomy.
5. Why have tools made us "fat wimps?"
6. Why did our ancestors become endurance runners and how did water containers enable this to happen?
7. Describe and explain the uniquely human thermoregulatory adaptations.

Internet References

Evolutionary Demography Group
http://blogs.lshtm.ac.uk/evolutionarydemography/

Evolutionary Demography Society
http://www.evodemos.org/

Fossil Hominids FAQ
www.talkorigins.org/faqs/homs

Institute of Human Origins
https://iho.asu.edu/

Unit 6

UNIT

Prepared by: Elvio Angeloni

Human Diversity

The field of biological anthropology has come a long way since the days when one of its primary concerns was the classification of human beings according to racial type. Although human diversity is still a matter of major interest in terms of how and why we differ from one another, most anthropologists have concluded that human beings cannot be sorted into sharply distinct entities called "races." Without denying the fact of human variation throughout the world, the prevailing view today is that the differences between us exist along geographical gradients, as differences in degree, rather than in terms of the separate and discrete entities as were perceived in the past.

One of the old ways of looking at human "races" was that each such group was a subspecies of humans that, if left reproductively isolated long enough, would eventually evolve into separate species. While this concept of subspecies, or racial varieties within a species, would seem to apply to some living creatures (such as the dog and wolf or the horse and zebra) and might even be relevant to hominid diversification in the past, the current consensus is that it does not apply today, at least not within the human species.

A more recent attempt to salvage the idea of human races has been to perceive them not so much as reproductively isolated entities, but as many clusters of gene frequencies, separable only by the fact that the proportions of traits (such as skin color, hair form, etc.) differ in each artificially constructed group. Some scientists, such as those who work in the area of forensic physical anthropology, appreciate the practical value of this approach. In a similar manner, our ability to reconstruct human prehistory is dependent upon an understanding of human variation.

Lest anyone think that anthropologists are "in denial" regarding the existence of human races and are merely expressing an anthropological version of political correctness, it should be pointed out that serious, scholarly attempts to classify people in terms of precise, biological units have been going on now for 200 years, and, so far, nothing of scientific value has come of them.

Complicating the matter is the fact that there are actually two concepts of race: the strictly biological one, as described above, and the more popular cultural one, which has been around since time immemorial. These two perspectives have resulted not only in fuzzy thinking about racial biology, but they have led to confusion as to which traits are truly biological in origin and which ones are environmentally and socially influenced. This confusion has infected the way we think about people and, therefore, the way we treat each other in the social arena.

What we should recognize, claim most anthropologists, is that, despite the superficial physical and biological differences between us, when it comes to intelligence, all human beings are basically the same. The degrees of variation within our species may be accounted for by the subtle, and changing, selective forces experienced as one moves from one geographical area to another. However, no matter what the environmental pressures have been, the same intellectual demands have been made upon all of us. This is not to say, of course, that we do not vary from each other as individuals. Rather, what is being said is that when we look at these artificially created groups of people called "races," we find a varying range of intellectual skills within each group. Indeed, even when we look at traits other than intelligence, we find much greater variation within each group than we find between such groups.

It is time, therefore, to put the idea of human "races" to rest, at least as far as science is concerned. If such notions remain in the realm of social discourse, then so be it. That is where the problems associated with notions of race have to be resolved anyway. As one anthropologist, Jonathan Marks, has put it: "You may group humans into a small number of races if you want to, but you are denied biology as a support for it."

Article   Prepared by: Elvio Angeloni

Skin Deep

Throughout the world, human skin color has evolved to be dark enough to prevent sunlight from destroying the nutrient folate but light enough to foster the production of vitamin D.

NINA G. JABLONSKI AND GEORGE CHAPLIN

Learning Outcomes

After reading this article, you will be able to:

- Discuss the general loss of body hair during human evolution.

- Explain why skin color varies among humans

Among primates, only humans have a mostly naked skin that comes in different colors. Geographers and anthropologists have long recognized that the distribution of skin colors among indigenous populations is not random: darker peoples tend to be found nearer the equator, lighter ones closer to the poles. For years, the prevailing theory has been that darker skins evolved to protect against skin cancer. But a series of discoveries has led us to construct a new framework for understanding the evolutionary basis of variations in human skin color. Recent epidemiological and physiological evidence suggests to us that the worldwide pattern of human skin color is the product of natural selection acting to regulate the effects of the sun's ultraviolet (UV) radiation on key nutrients crucial to reproductive success.

From Hirsute to Hairless

The evolution of skin pigmentation is linked with that of hairlessness, and to comprehend both these stories, we need to page back in human history. Human beings have been evolving as an independent lineage of apes since at least seven million years ago, when our immediate ancestors diverged from those of our closest relatives, chimpanzees. Because chimpanzees have changed less over time than humans have, they can provide an idea of what human anatomy and physiology must have been like. Chimpanzees' skin is light in color and is covered by hair over most of their bodies. Young animals have pink faces, hands, and feet and become freckled or dark in these areas only as they are exposed to sun with age. The earliest humans almost certainly had a light skin covered with hair. Presumably hair loss occurred first, then skin color changed. But that leads to the question, When did we lose our hair?

The skeletons of ancient humans—such as the well-known skeleton of Lucy, which dates to about 3.2 million years ago—give us a good idea of the build and the way of life of our ancestors. The daily activities of Lucy and other hominids that lived before about three million years ago appear to have been similar to those of primates living on the open savannas of Africa today. They probably spent much of their day foraging for food over three to four miles before retiring to the safety of trees to sleep.

By 1.6 million years ago, however, we see evidence that this pattern had begun to change dramatically. The famous skeleton of Turkana Boy—which belonged to the species *Homo ergaster*—is that of a long-legged, striding biped that probably walked long distances. These more active early humans faced the problem of staying cool and protecting their brains from overheating. Peter Wheeler of John Moores University in Liverpool, England, has shown that this was accomplished through an increase in the number of sweat glands on the surface of the body and a reduction in the covering of body hair. Once rid of most of their hair, early members of the genus *Homo* then encountered the challenge of protecting their skin from the damaging effects of sunlight, especially UV rays.

Built-In Sunscreen

In chimpanzees, the skin on the hairless parts of the body contains cells called melanocytes that are capable of synthesizing the dark-brown pigment melanin in response to exposure to UV radiation. When humans became mostly hairless, the ability of the skin to produce melanin assumed new importance. Melanin is nature's sunscreen: it is a large organic molecule that Overview/Skin Color Evolution serves the dual purpose of physically and chemically filtering the harmful effects of UV radiation; it absorbs UV rays, causing them to lose energy, and it neutralizes harmful chemicals called free radicals that form in the skin after damage by UV radiation.

Overview/Skin Color Evolution

- After losing their hair as an adaptation for keeping cool, early hominids gained pigmented skins. Scientists initially thought that such pigmentation arose to protect against skin-cancer-causing ultra-violet [UV] radiation.
- Skin cancers tend to arise after reproductive age, however. An alternative theory suggests that dark skin might have evolved primarily to protect against the breakdown of folate, a nutrient essential for fertility and for fetal development.
- Skin that is too dark blocks the sunlight necessary for catalyzing the production of vitamin D, which is crucial for maternal and fetal bones. Accordingly, humans have evolved to be light enough to make sufficient vitamin B yet dark enough to protect their stores of folate.
- As a result of recent human migrations, many people now live in areas that receive more [or less] UV radiation than is appropriate for their skin color.

Anthropologists and biologists have generally reasoned that high concentrations of melanin arose in the skin of peoples in tropical areas because it protected them against skin cancer. James E. Cleaver of the University of California at San Francisco, for instance, has shown that people with the disease xeroderma pigmentosum, in which melanocytes are destroyed by exposure to the sun, suffer from significantly higher than normal rates of squamous and basal cell carcinomas, which are usually easily treated. Malignant melanomas are more frequently fatal, but they are rare (representing 4 percent of skin cancer diagnoses) and tend to strike only light-skinned people. But all skin cancers typically arise later in life, in most cases after the first reproductive years, so they could not have exerted enough evolutionary pressure for skin protection alone to account for darker skin colors. Accordingly, we began to ask what role melanin might play in human evolution.

The Folate Connection

In 1991 one of US (Jablonski) ran across what turned out to be a critical paper published in 1978 by Richard F. Branda and John W. Eaton, now at the University of Vermont and the University of Louisville, respectively. These investigators showed that light-skinned people who had been exposed to simulated strong sunlight had abnormally low levels of the essential B vitamin folate in their blood. The scientists also observed that subjecting human blood serum to the same conditions resulted in a 50-percent loss of folate content within one hour.

The significance of these findings to reproduction—and hence evolution—became clear when we learned of research being conducted on a major class of birth defects by our colleagues at the University of Western Australia. There Fiona J. Stanley and Carol Bower had established by the late 1980s that folate deficiency in pregnant women is related to an increased risk of neural tube defects such as spina bifida, in which the arches of the spinal vertebrae fail to close around the spinal cord. Many research groups throughout the world have since confirmed this correlation, and efforts to supplement foods with folate and to educate women about the importance of the nutrient have become widespread.

We discovered soon afterward that folate is important not only in preventing neural tube defects but also in a host of other processes. Because folate is essential for the synthesis of DNA in dividing cells, anything that involves rapid cell proliferation, such as spermatogenesis (the production of sperm cells), requires folate. Male rats and mice with chemically induced folate deficiency have impaired spermatogenesis and are infertile. Although no comparable studies of humans have been conducted, Wai Yee Wong and his colleagues at the University Medical Center of Nijmegen in the Netherlands have recently reported that folic acid treatment can boost the sperm counts of men with fertility problems.

Such observations led us to hypothesize that dark skin evolved to protect the body's folate stores from destruction. Our idea was supported by a report published in 1996 by Argentine pediatrician Pablo Lapunzina, who found that three young and otherwise healthy women whom he had attended gave birth to infants with neural tube defects after using sun beds to tan themselves in the early weeks of pregnancy. Our evidence about the breakdown of folate by UV radiation thus supplements what is already known about the harmful (skin-cancer-causing) effects of UV radiation on DNA.

Human Skin on the Move

The earliest members of *Homo sapiens*, or modern humans, evolved in Africa between 120,000 and 100,000 years ago and had darkly pigmented skin adapted to the conditions of

UV radiation and heat that existed near the equator. As modern humans began to venture out of the tropics, however, they encountered environments in which they received significantly less UV radiation during the year. Under these conditions their high concentrations of natural sunscreen probably proved detrimental. Dark skin contains so much melanin that very little UV radiation, and specifically very little of the shorter-wavelength UVB radiation, can penetrate the skin. Although most of the effects of UVB are harmful, the rays perform one indispensable function: initiating the formation of vitamin D in the skin. Dark-skinned people living in the tropics generally receive sufficient UV radiation during the year for UVB to penetrate the skin and allow them to make vitamin D. Outside the tropics this is not the case. The solution, across evolutionary time, has been for migrants to northern latitudes to lose skin pigmentation.

The connection between the evolution of lightly pigmented skin and vitamin D synthesis was elaborated by W. Farnsworth Loomis of Brandeis University in 1967. He established the importance of vitamin D to reproductive success because of its role in enabling calcium absorption by the intestines, which in turn makes possible the normal development of the skeleton and the maintenance of a healthy immune system. Research led by Michael Holick of the Boston University School of Medicine has, over the past 20 years, further cemented the significance of vitamin D in development and immunity. His team also showed that not all sunlight contains enough UVB to stimulate vitamin D production. In Boston, for instance, which is located at about 42 degrees north latitude, human skin cells begin to produce vitamin D only after mid-March. In the wintertime there isn't enough UVB to do the job. We realized that this was another piece of evidence essential to the skin color story.

During the course of our research in the early 1990s, we searched in vain to find sources of data on actual UV radiation levels at the earth's surface. We were rewarded in 1996, when we contacted Elizabeth Weatherhead of the Cooperative Institute for Research in Environmental Sciences at the University of Colorado at Boulder. She shared with us a database of measurements of UV radiation at the earth's surface taken by NASA's Total Ozone Mapping Spectrophotometer satellite between 1978 and 1993. We were then able to model the distribution of UV radiation on the earth and relate the satellite data to the amount of UVB necessary to produce vitamin D.

We found that the earth's surface could be divided into three vitamin D zones: one comprising the tropics, one the subtropics and temperate regions, and the last the circumpolar regions north and south of about 45 degrees latitude. In the first, the dosage of UVB throughout the year is high enough that humans have ample opportunity to synthesize vitamin D all year. In the second, at least one month during the year has insufficient UVB radiation, and in the third area not enough UVB arrives on average during the entire year to prompt vitamin D synthesis. This distribution could explain why indigenous peoples in the tropics generally have dark skin, whereas people in the subtropics and temperate regions are lighter-skinned but have the ability to tan, and those who live in regions near the poles tend to be very light skinned and burn easily.

One of the most interesting aspects of this investigation was the examination of groups that did not precisely fit the predicted skin-color pattern. An example is the Inuit people of Alaska and northern Canada. The Inuit exhibit skin color that is somewhat darker than would be predicted given the UV levels at their latitude. This is probably caused by two factors. The first is that they are relatively recent inhabitants of these climes, having migrated to North America only roughly 5,000 years ago. The second is that the traditional diet of the Inuit is extremely high in foods containing vitamin D, especially fish and marine mammals. This vitamin D-rich diet offsets the problem that they would otherwise have with vitamin D synthesis in their skin at northern latitudes and permits them to remain more darkly pigmented.

Our analysis of the potential to synthesize vitamin D allowed us to understand another trait related to human skin color: women in all populations are generally lighter-skinned than men. (Our data show that women tend to be between 3 and 4 percent lighter than men.) Scientists have often speculated on the reasons, and most have argued that the phenomenon stems from sexual selection—the preference of men for women of lighter color. We contend that although this is probably part of the story, it is not the original reason for the sexual difference. Females have significantly greater needs for calcium throughout their reproductive lives, especially during pregnancy and lactation, and must be able to make the most of the calcium contained in food. We propose, therefore, that women tend to be lighter-skinned than men to allow slightly more UVB rays to penetrate their skin and thereby increase their ability to produce vitamin D. In areas of the world that receive a large amount of UV radiation, women are indeed at the knife's edge of natural selection, needing to maximize the photoprotective function of their skin on the one hand and the ability to synthesize vitamin D on the other.

Where Culture and Biology Meet

As modern humans moved throughout the Old World about 100,000 years ago, their skin adapted to the environmental conditions that prevailed in different regions. The skin color of the indigenous people of Africa has had the longest time to adapt because anatomically modern humans first evolved there. The skin-color changes that modern humans underwent as they moved from one continent to another—first Asia, then Austro-Melanesia, then Europe and, finally, the Americas—can be reconstructed to some extent. It is important to remember, however, that those humans had clothing and shelter to help protect them from the elements. In some places, they also had the ability to harvest foods that were extraordinarily rich in vitamin D, as in the case of the Inuit. These two factors had profound effects on the tempo and degree of skin-color evolution in human populations.

Africa is an environmentally heterogeneous continent. A number of the earliest movements of contemporary humans outside equatorial Africa were into southern Africa. The descendants of some of these early colonizers, the Khoisan (previously known as Hottentots), are still found in southern Africa and have significantly lighter skin than indigenous equatorial Africans do—a clear adaptation to the lower levels of UV radiation that prevail at the southern extremity of the continent.

Interestingly, however, human skin color in southern Africa is not uniform. Populations of Bantu-language speakers who live in southern Africa today are far darker than the Khoisan. We know from the history of this region that Bantu speakers migrated into this region recently—probably within the past 1,000 years—from parts of West Africa near the equator. The skin-color difference between the Khoisan and Bantu speakers such as the Zulu indicates that the length of time that a group has inhabited a particular region is important in understanding why they have the color they do.

Cultural behaviors have probably also strongly influenced the evolution of skin color in recent human history. This effect can be seen in the indigenous peoples who live on the eastern and western banks of the Red Sea. The tribes on the western side, which speak so-called Nilo-Hamitic languages, are thought to have inhabited this region for as long as 6,000 years. These individuals are distinguished by very darkly pigmented skin and long, thin bodies with long limbs, which are excellent biological adaptations for dissipating heat and intense UV radiation. In contrast, modern agricultural and pastoral groups on the eastern bank of the Red Sea, on the Arabian Peninsula, have lived there for only about 2,000 years. These earliest Arab people, of European origin, have adapted to very similar environmental conditions by almost exclusively cultural means—wearing heavy protective clothing and devising portable shade in the form of tents. (Without such clothing, one would have expected their skin to have begun to darken.) Generally speaking, the more recently a group has migrated into an area, the more extensive its cultural, as opposed to biological, adaptations to the area will be.

Perils of Recent Migrations

Despite great improvements in overall human health in the past century, some diseases have appeared or reemerged in populations that had previously been little affected by them. One of these is skin cancer, especially basal and squamous cell carcinomas, among light-skinned peoples. Another is rickets, brought about by severe vitamin D deficiency, in dark-skinned peoples. Why are we seeing these conditions?

As people move from an area with one pattern of UV radiation to another region, biological and cultural adaptations have not been able to keep pace. The light-skinned people of northern European origin who bask in the sun of Florida or northern Australia increasingly pay the price in the form of premature aging of the skin and skin cancers, not to mention the unknown cost in human life of folate depletion. Conversely, a number of dark-skinned people of southern Asian and African origin now living in the northern U.K., northern Europe or the northeastern U.S. suffer from a lack of UV radiation and vitamin D, an insidious problem that manifests itself in high rates of rickets and other diseases related to vitamin D deficiency.

The ability of skin color to adapt over long periods to the various environments to which humans have moved reflects the importance of skin color to our survival. But its unstable nature also makes it one of the least useful characteristics in determining the evolutionary relations between human groups. Early Western scientists used skin color improperly to delineate human races, but the beauty of science is that it can and does correct itself. Our current knowledge of the evolution of human skin indicates that variations in skin color, like most of our physical attributes, can be explained by adaptation to the environment through natural selection. We look ahead to the day when the vestiges of old scientific mistakes will be erased and replaced by a better understanding of human origins and diversity. Our variation in skin color should be celebrated as one of the most visible manifestations of our evolution as a species.

More to Explore

The Evolution of Human Skin Coloration. Nina G. Jablonski and George Chaplin in *Journal of Human Evolution,* vol. 39, no. 1, pages 57–106; July 1, 2000. An abstract of the article is available online at www.idealibrary.com/links/doi/10.1006/jhev.2000.0403.

Why Skin Comes in Colors. Blake Edgar in *California Wild,* vol. 53, no. 1, pages 6–7; Winter 2000. The article is also available at www.calacademy.org/calwild/winter2000/html/horizons.html.

The Biology of Skin Color: Black and White. Gina Kirchweger in *Discover,* vol. 22, no. 2, pages 32–33; February 2001. The article is also available at www.discover.com/feb_01/featbiology.html.

Critical Thinking

1. Why did our ancestors lose most of their body hair? What was the resulting challenge?

2. What is the function of melanin?

3. What is the relationship between light skin, exposure to the sun, and skin cancer? Why is this insufficient to explain darker skin colors?

4. Discuss the evidence that relates skin color to folate deficiency.

5. How do the authors describe the earliest member of *Homo sapiens,* or modern humans in this context? Why would skin color become lighter as people moved out of the tropics? How is vitamin D production important to health?

6. Discuss the three vitamin D zones on the earth's surface and how they help to explain skin color variations.

7. Why don't the Inuit precisely fit the predicted skin color pattern?

8. Why do women tend to be lighter skinned than men?

9. What two factors have had profound effects on the tempo and degree of skin color evolution in human populations? Give some examples.

10. Discuss the "perils of recent migrations" and the examples cited.

11. Why is skin color unreliable as a means to delineate human races?

12. Why should we celebrate our variation in skin color?

Internet References

Ethnic and Racial Studies
www.tandfonline.com/rers

Journal of Human Evolution
www.journals.elsevier.com/journal-of-human-evolution

NINA G. JABLONSKI and **GEORGE CHAPLIN** work at the California Academy of Sciences in San Francisco, where Jablonski is Irvine Chair and curator of anthropology and Chaplin is a research associate in the department of anthropology. Jablonski's research centers on the evolutionary adaptations of monkeys, apes and humans. She is particularly interested in how primates have responded to changes over time in the global environment. Chaplin is a private geographic information systems consultant who specializes in describing and analyzing geographic trends in biodiversity. In 2001 he was awarded the Student of the Year prize by the Association of Geographic Information in London for his master's thesis on the environmental correlates of skin color.

Article   Prepared by: Elvio Angeloni

How Real Is Race?

Using Anthropology to Make Sense of Human Diversity

Race is not a scientifically valid biological category, and yet it remains important as a socially constructed category. Once educators grasp this concept, they can use the suggestions and resources the authors offer here to help their students make sense of race.

CAROL MUKHOPADHYAY AND ROSEMARY C. HENZE

Learning Outcomes

After reading this article, you will be able to:

- Discuss whether the human species can be subdivided into racial categories and support your position.

- Explain how and why the concept of race developed.

- Discuss both the positive and negative aspects of racial classification.

S urely we've all heard people say there is only one race—the human race. We've also heard and seen overwhelming evidence that would seem to contradict this view. After all, the U.S. Census divides us into groups based on race, and there are certainly observable physical differences among people—skin color, nose and eye shape, body type, hair color and texture, and so on. In the world of education, the message of racial differences as biological "facts" is reinforced when we are told that we should understand specific learning styles and behavior patterns of black, Asian, Native American, white, and Latino children and when books such as *The Bell Curve* make pseudoscientific claims about race and learning.[1]

How can educators make sense of these conflicting messages about race? And why should they bother? Whether we think of all human beings as one race, or as four or five distinct races, or as hundreds of races, does anything really change?

If we accept that the concept of race is fundamentally flawed, does that mean that young African Americans are less likely to be followed by security guards in department stores? Are people going to stop thinking of Asians as the "model" minority? Will racism become a thing of the past?

Many educators understandably would like to have clear information to help them teach students about human biological variability. While multicultural education materials are now widely available, they rarely address basic questions about why we look different from one another and what these biological differences do (and do not) mean. Multicultural education emphasizes respecting differences and finding ways to include all students, especially those who have been historically marginalized. Multicultural education has helped us to understand racism and has provided a rich body of literature on antiracist teaching strategies, and this has been all to the good. But it has not helped us understand the two concepts of race: the biological one and the social one.

In this article, we explain what anthropologists mean when they say that "races don't exist" (in other words, when they reject the concept of race as a scientifically valid biological category) and why they argue instead that "race" is a socially constructed category. We'll also discuss why this is such an important understanding and what it means for educators and students who face the social reality of race and racism every day. And finally, we'll offer some suggestions and resources for teachers who want to include teaching about race in their classes.

Why Race Isn't Biologically Real

For the past several decades, biological anthropologists have been arguing that races don't really exist, or, more precisely, that the concept of race has no validity as a biological category. What exactly does this mean?

First, anthropologists are unraveling a deeply embedded ideology, a long-standing European and American racial world view.[2] Historically, the idea of race emerged in Europe in the 17th and 18th centuries, coinciding with the growth of colonialism and the transatlantic slave trade. Attempts were made to classify humans into "natural," geographically distinct "races," hierarchically ordered by their closeness to God's original forms. Europeans were, not surprisingly, at the top, with the most perfect form represented by a female skull from the Caucasus Mountains, near the purported location of Noah's ark and the origin of humans. Hence the origins of the racial term "Caucasian" or "Caucasoid" for those of European ancestry.[3]

In the late 19th century, anthropologists sought to reconstruct human prehistory and trace the evolution of human cultural institutions. Physical and cultural evolution were seen as moving in tandem; "advances" in human mental capacity were thought to be responsible for human cultural inventions, such as marriage, family, law, and agriculture. If cultural "evolution" was propelled by biological evolution, according to this logic, the more "advanced" cultures must be more biologically and intellectually evolved. Physical indicators of evolutionary rank, such as skull size, were sought in order to classify and rank human groups along an evolutionary path from more "primitive" to more "advanced" races.

Nineteenth-century European scientists disagreed on when the "races" began. Theologians had long argued that there was "one human origin," Adam and Eve, and that certain races subsequently "degenerated" (predictably, the non-Europeans). Some evolutionary scientists, however, began to argue for multiple origins, with distinct races evolving in different places and times. By the beginning of the 20th century, European and American science viewed races as natural, long-standing divisions of the human species, evolving at different rates biologically and hence culturally. By such logic was racial inequality naturalized and legitimized.

When contemporary scientists, including anthropologists, assert that races are not scientifically valid, they are rejecting at least three fundamental premises of this old racial ideology: 1) the archaic subspecies concept, 2) the divisibility of contemporary humans into scientifically valid biological groupings, and 3) the link between racial traits and social, cultural, and political status.

1. *There were no distinct, archaic human subspecies.* The first premise anthropologists reject is that humans were originally divided, by nature or God, into a small set of biologically distinct, fixed species, subspecies, or races. Anthropologists now know conclusively, from fossil and DNA evidence, that contemporary humans are one variable species, with our roots in Africa, which moved out of Africa into a wide range of environments around the world, producing hundreds, perhaps thousands, of culturally and genetically distinct populations. Local populations, through natural selection as well as random genetic mutation, acquired some distinctive genetic traits, such as shovel-shaped incisor teeth, hairy ears, or red hair. Adaptation to human cultural inventions—such as agriculture, which creates concentrations of water that allow malaria-carrying mosquitoes to breed—also produced higher frequencies of sickle-cell genes (related to malaria resistance) in human populations in some parts of Africa, India, Arabia, and the Mediterranean.[4] At the same time, continuous migration and intermating between local populations prevented us from branching off into distinct subspecies or species and instead created a richer and more variable gene pool, producing new combinations and permutations of the human genome.

Human prehistory and history, then, are a continuing story of fusion and fission, of a myriad of populations, emerging and shifting over time and space, sometimes isolated temporarily, then fusing and producing new formations. There have been thousands and thousands of groups throughout human history, marrying in and, more often, out; they have disappeared and reemerged in new forms over time.

In short, there are no "basic" or "ancient" races; there are no stable, "natural," permanent, or even long-standing groupings called races. There have never have been any "pure" races. All human populations are historically specific mixtures of the human gene pool. This is human evolution, and we see these same processes at work in the 19th and 20th centuries and today. "Races" are ephemeral—here today, gone tomorrow.

2. *Contemporary humans are not divisible into biological races.* When anthropologists say races aren't biologically real, they also reject the idea that *modern* humans can be divided into scientifically valid, biologically distinct groupings or races. For races to be real as biological categories, the classification must be based on objective, consistent, and reliable biological criteria. The classification system must also have predictive value that will make it useful in research.

Scientists have demonstrated that both the concept of race and racial criteria are subjective, arbitrary, and inconsistently applied.[5] U.S. racial categories, such as the ones used in the Census, aren't valid in part because the biological attributes used to define races and create racial classifications rely on only a few visible, superficial, genetic traits—such as skin color and hair texture—and ignore the remaining preponderance of human variation. Alternative, equally visible racial classifications could be constructed using such criteria as hair color, eye color, height, weight, ear shape, or hairiness. However, there are less visible genetic traits that have far greater biological significance. For example, there are at least 13 genetic factors related to hemoglobin, the protein that helps carry oxygen to tissues, and there is also significant variation in the ABO, RH, and other blood systems. We could create racial classifications based on genetic factors that affect susceptibility to diabetes or to certain kinds of breast cancer or to the ability to digest milk. In sum, given the variety of possible biologically based traits for classifying human beings, the criteria used in U.S. racial categorizations are highly arbitrary and subjective. Our discussion here focuses on the U.S. concept of race. While racial concepts are no doubt similar in Canada and Europe, this is not true in other parts of the Americas.[6]

The number of potential biologically based racial groupings is enormous. Not only are there millions of genetic traits, but most genetic traits—even culturally salient but superficial traits such as skin color, hair texture, eye shape, and eye color—do not cluster together. Darker skin can cluster with straight hair as well as with very curly hair or with hairy or nonhairy bodies; paler skin can cluster with straight or curly hair or with black or blond hair or with lighter to darker eyes. Each trait could produce a different racial classification. For example, if one used height as a criterion rather than skin pigmentation, then the Northern Afghan population would be in the same racial category as the Swedes and the Tutsi of Rwanda. There are huge numbers of genetically influenced traits, visible and non-visible, which could be used to classify humans into biologically distinct groups. There is no "natural" classification—no co-occurring clusters of racial traits. There are just alternatives, with different implications and uses.

Racial classifications are also unscientific because they are unreliable and unstable over time. Individuals cannot reliably be "raced," partly because the criteria are so subjective and unscientific. Robert Hahn, a medical anthropologist, found that 37% of babies described as Native American on their birth certificates ended up in a different racial category on their death certificates.[7] Racial identifications by forensic anthropologists, long touted as accurate, have been shown to be disturbingly unreliable, even in relatively ethnically homogeneous areas, such as Missouri and Ohio.[8] Forensic evidence from such urban areas as San Jose, California, or New York City is even more problematic.

Racial categories used by the U.S. Census Bureau have changed over time. In 1900, races included "mulatto, quadroon, or octoroon" in addition to "black." Southern Europeans and Jews were deemed to be separate races before World War II. Asian Indians ("Hindus") were initially categorized as "Caucasoid"—except for voting rights. The number and definitions of races in the most recent U.S. Census reflect the instability—and hence unreliability—of the concept of race.

And U.S. racial classifications simply don't work in much of the rest of the world. Brazil is a classic, often-studied example, but they also don't work in South Asia, an area that includes over one-fifth of the world's population.

Historical and contemporary European and American racial categories are huge, biologically diverse macro-categories. Members of the same racial group tend to be similar in a few genetic ways that are often biologically irrelevant. Moreover, the genetic variability found within each racial grouping is far greater than the genetic similarity. Africa, by itself, is home to distinct populations whose average height ranges from less than five feet (the Mbuti) to over six feet (the Tutsi). Estimates suggest that contemporary racial variation accounts for less than 7% of all human genetic variation.[9] U.S. races, then, are not biologically distinct or biologically meaningful, scientifically based groupings of the human species.

3. *Race as biology has no scientific value.* An additional critique of the concept of race is that racial categories, as defined biologically, are not very useful in understanding other phenomena, whether biological or cultural.

There is no substantial evidence that race, as a biological category, and "racial" characteristics, such as skin color, hair texture, and eye shape, are causally linked to behavior, to capacities, to individual and group accomplishments, to cultural institutions, or to propensities to engage in any specific activities. In the area of academic achievement, the focus on race as biology can lead researchers to ignore underlying nonbiological causal factors. One classic study found that controlling for socioeconomic and other environmental variables eliminated purported "racial" differences in I.Q. scores and academic achievement between African American, Mexican American, and European American students.[10]

Health professionals have also critiqued the concept of race. Alan Goodman and others have shown that race does not help physicians with diagnosis, prevention, or treatment of medical diseases.[11] Racial categories and a false ideology of race as "biology" encourage both doctors and their patients to view medical conditions as necessarily genetic, ignoring possible environmental sources. Hypertension, infant birthweights, osteoporosis, ovarian cysts—all traditionally viewed as "racial" (i.e., genetically based)—now seem to reflect environmental rather than racially linked genetic factors. The Centers for Disease Control concluded in 1993 that most associations between race and disease have no genetic or biological basis and that the concept of "race" is therefore not useful in public health.

As a result of recent evolution and constant interbreeding between groups of humans, two individuals from different "races" are just as likely to be more similar to one another genetically than two individuals from the same "race." This being so, race-as-biology has no predictive value.

If Not Race, Then What?

Classifications are usually created for some purpose. Alan Goodman and other biological anthropologists suggest that investigators focus on using traits relevant to the problem at hand. For example, if a particular blood factor puts an individual at risk for a disease, then classify individuals on that basis for that purpose.

Some suggest using the term "population" or "breeding population" to refer to the multitude of small, often geographically localized, groups that have developed high frequencies of one or more somewhat distinctive biological traits (e.g., shovel-shaped incisors) in response to biological, historical, and cultural factors. But others point out that there could be thousands of such groups, depending on the classifying criteria used, and that the groups would be merging and recombining over time and space. Moreover, the variability "captured" would reflect only a fraction of the variability in the human species.

Most anthropologists now use the concept of "clines" to help understand how genetic traits are distributed.[12] New data indicate that biological traits, such as blood type or skin color, are distributed in geographic gradations or "clines"; that is, the frequency of a trait varies continuously over a geographic area. For example, the genes for type B blood increase in frequency in an east-to-west direction (reflecting, in part, the travels of Genghis Khan and his army). In contrast, skin pigmentation grades from north to south, with increasing pigmentation as one gets closer to the equator. The frequency of the gene for sickle cell decreases from West Africa moving northeast.

Virtually all traits have distinct geographic distributions. Genes controlling skin color, body size and shape (head, limbs, lips, fingers, nose, ears), hairiness, and blood type are each distributed in different patterns over geographic space. Once again, for biological races to exist, these traits would have to co-vary, but they don't. Instead, biological traits produce a nearly infinite number of potential races. This is why anthropologists conclude that there are no scientifically distinguishable biological races—only thousands of clines!

So What Is Race Then?

We hope we have made the point that the concept of separate, biologically distinct human races is not scientifically defensible. Unfortunately, racial ideology, by focusing on a few physical attributes, traps us into a discourse about race as biology rather than race as a cultural construction. The concept of race is a cultural invention, a culturally and historically specific way of thinking about, categorizing, and treating human beings.[13] It is about social divisions within society, about social categories and identities, about power and privilege. It has been and remains a particular type of ideology for legitimizing social inequality between groups with different ancestries, national origins, and histories. Indeed, the concept of race is also a major system of social identity, affecting one's own self-perception and how one is perceived and treated by others.

But race does have a biological component, one that can trick us into thinking that races are scientifically valid, biological subdivisions of the human species. As noted earlier, geographically localized populations—as a result of adaptation, migration, and chance—tend to have some characteristic physical traits. While these may be traits that characterize an entire population, such as hairy ears, it is more accurate to talk about the relative frequency of a particular trait, such as blood type O, in one population as compared to another, or the relative amount of pigmentation of individuals in a population, relative to other populations. Some traits, such as skin color, reflect climatic conditions; others, such as eye color and shape, probably reflect random, historical processes and migration patterns. The U.S. was peopled by populations from geographically distinct regions of the world—voluntary immigrants, forced African slaves, and indigenous American groups. Therefore, dominant northwestern European ethnic groups, such as the English and Germans, were able to exploit certain visually salient biological traits, especially skin color, as markers of race.

The effectiveness of these physical traits as markers of one's race depended, of course, on their being preserved in future generations. So dominant cultural groups created elaborate social and physical barriers to mating, reproduction, and marriage that crossed racial lines. The most explicit were the so-called anti-miscegenation laws, which outlawed sex between members of different races, whether married or not. These laws were not declared unconstitutional by the U.S. Supreme Court until the 1967 case of *Loving v. Virginia*.[14] Another vehicle was the cultural definition of kinship, whereby children of interracial (often forced) matings acquired the racial status of their lower-ranking parent; this was the so-called one-drop rule or hypo-descent. Especially during the time of slavery, the lower-ranking parent was generally the mother, and thus the long-standing European cultural tradition of affiliating socially "legitimate" children with the father's kinship group was effectively reversed.

In contrast, there have been fewer social or legal barriers in the U.S. to mating and marriage between Italians, British, Germans, Swedes, and others of European ancestry. Consequently, the physical and cultural characteristics of European regional populations are less evident in the U.S. With intermarriage, distinct European identities were submerged in the culturally relevant macroracial category of "white"—more accurately, European American.

Thus even the biological dimension of contemporary racial groupings is the result of sociocultural processes. That is, humans as cultural beings first gave social significance to some physical differences between groups and then tried to perpetu-ate these "racial markers" by preventing social and physical intercourse between members of the groups. Although the dom-inant racial ideology was about maintaining racial "purity," the issue was not about biology; it was about maintaining social, political, and economic privilege.[15]

Why Is This Understanding Important for Educators?

We hope we've convinced you that race isn't biologically "real" and that race in the U.S. and elsewhere is a historical, social, and cultural creation. But so what? What is the significance of this way of viewing race for teachers, students, and society?

1. *The potential for change.* First, it is important to under-stand that, while races are biological fictions, they are social realities. Race may not be "real" in a biological sense, but it surely is "real" socially, politically, economically, and psycho-logically. Race and racism profoundly structure who we are, how we are treated, how we treat others, and our access to resources and rights.

Perhaps the most important message educators can take from the foregoing discussion is that race, racial classifications, racial stratification, and other forms of racism, including racial ideology, rather than being part of our biology, are part of our culture. Like other cultural forms, both the concept of race and our racial classifications are part of a system we have created. This means that we have the ability to change the system, to transform it, and even to totally eradicate it. Educators, in their role as transmitters of official culture, are particularly well poised to be active change agents in such a transformation.

But how, you may well ask, can teachers or anybody else make people stop classifying by race? And are there any good reasons to do so? These familiar categories—black, white, Asian, Native American, and so on—seem so embedded in U.S. society. They seem so "natural." Of course, that's how culture works. It seems "natural" to think of chicken, but not rats, as food. But, as we have shown above, the labels and underlying constructs that we use to talk about human diversity are unsta-ble, depending on particular social, political, and historical con-texts. Individuals in positions of authority, of course, have the ability to change them institutionally. But ordinary people also have the ability to change how they classify and label people in their everyday lives.

Several questions arise at this point. Do we as educators consciously want to change our way of conceptualizing and discussing human biological variation? What makes the "race as biology" assumption so dangerous? Are we going to con-tinue to classify people by race, even while recognizing that it is a social construct? What vested interests do people have

in holding onto—or rejecting—racial categories? How can we become more sophisticated in our understanding of how systems of classification work while also becoming more criti-cal of our own ways of classifying people? Are there alterna-tive ways of thinking about, classifying, and labeling human beings that might be more empowering for students, teachers, and community members? By eliminating or changing labels, will we change the power structures that perpetuate privilege and entitlement? Moving beyond race as biology forces us to confront these and other issues.

2. *The dangers of using racial classifications.* Categories and classifications are not intrinsically good or bad. Peo-ple have always grouped others in ways that were important within a given society. However, the myth of race as biology is dangerous because it conflates physical attributes, such as skin color, with unrelated qualities, such as intelligence. Racial labels delude people into thinking that race predicts such other outcomes and behaviors as achievement in sports, music, or school; rates of employment; pregnancies outside marriage; or drug use. Race was historically equated with intelligence and, on that basis, was used to justify slavery and educational discrimination; it later provided the rationale that supported the genocide of Jews, blacks, Gypsies, and other "inferior" races under Hitler. So using racial categories brings along this history, like unwanted baggage.

Macroracial categories are dangerous in that the categories oversimplify and mask complex human differences. Saying that someone is Asian tells us virtually nothing concrete, but it brings with it a host of stereotypes, such as "model minority," "quiet," "good at math," "inscrutable," and so on. Yet the Asian label includes a wide range of groups, such as Koreans, Filipinos, and Vietnamese, with distinct histories and languages. The same is true for "white," a term that homogenizes the multiple nationali-ties, languages, and cultures that constitute Europe. The label "African American" ignores the enormous linguistic, physical, and cultural diversity of the peoples of Africa. The term "black" conflates people of African descent who were brought to the U.S. as slaves with recent immigrants from Africa and the Carib-bean. These macroracial labels oversimplify and reduce human diversity to four or five giant groups. Apart from being bad science, these categories don't predict anything helpful—yet they have acquired a life of their own.

Macroracial categories, such as those used in the U.S. Census and other institutional data-collection efforts, force people to use labels that may not represent their own self-identity or clas-sifying system. They must either select an existing category or select "other"—by definition, a kind of nonidentity. The impos-sibility, until recently, of selecting more than one ethnic/racial category implicitly stigmatizes multiracial individuals. And the term "mixed" wrongly implies that there are such things as "pure" races, an ideology with no basis in science. The recent expansion of the number of U.S. Census categories still cannot accommodate the diversity of the U.S. population, which includes people whose ancestry ranges from Egypt, Brazil, Sri Lanka, Ghana, and the Dominican Republic to Iceland and Korea.

3. *How macroracial categories have served people in positive ways.* Having noted some negative aspects, it is equally important to discuss how macroracial categories also serve society. Recall that labels are not intrinsically "good" or "bad." It depends on what people do with them. During the 1960s, the U.S. civil rights movement helped bring about consciousness and pride in being African American. This consciousness— known by terms such as ethnic pride and black power—united people who had been the victims of racism and oppression. From that consciousness sprang such educational interventions as black and Chicano history classes, ethnic studies departments, Afrocentric schools, and other efforts to empower young people. The movement to engender pride in and knowledge of one's ancestry has had a powerful impact. Many individuals are deeply attached to these racial labels as part of a positive identity. As one community activist put it, "Why should I give up being a race? I like being a race."

Racial classification can also have positive impact by allowing educators to monitor how equitably our institutions are serving the public. Racial categories are used by schools to disaggregate data on student outcomes, including achievement, attendance, discipline, course placements, college attendance rates, and other areas of school and student performance. These data are then used to examine whether certain groups of students are disproportionately represented in any outcome areas. For example, a school might discover that the percentage of Latino students who receive some type of disciplinary intervention is higher than that for other school populations. The school can then consider what it can do to change this outcome. Teachers might ask, Is there something about the way Latino students are treated in the school that leads to higher disciplinary referral rates? What other factors might be involved?

The racial classifications that educators use to monitor student outcome data reflect our society's social construction of race. As such, the categories represent groups that have been historically disenfranchised, oppressed, or marginalized. Without data disaggregated by race, gender, and other categories, it would be difficult to identify problems stemming from race-based institutional and societal factors that privilege certain groups, such as the widespread U.S. practice of tracking by so-called ability. Without data broken out according to racial, gender, and ethnic categories, schools would not be able to assess the positive impact intervention programs have had on different groups of students.

4. *Shifting the conversation from biology to culture.* One function of the myth of race as biology has been to distract us from the underlying causes of social inequality in the United States. Dismantling the myth of race as biology means that we must now shift our focus to analyzing the social, economic, political, and historical conditions that breed and serve to perpetuate social inequality. For educators, this means helping students to recognize and understand socioeconomic stratification, who benefits and who is harmed by racial discrimination, and how we as individuals and institutional agents can act to dismantle ideologies, institutions, and practices that harm young people.

There is another, more profound implication of the impermanence of race. Culture, acting collectively, and humans, acting individually, can make races disappear. That is, we can mate and marry across populations, thus destroying the racial "markers" that have been used to facilitate categorization and differential treatment of people of different ancestry and social rank. An understanding of human biological variation reveals the positive, indeed essential, role that intermating and intermarriage have played in human evolution and human adaptation. Rather than "mongrelizing" a "pure species," mating between different populations enriches the genetic pool. It is society, rather than nature—and socially and economically stratified societies, for the most part—that restricts social and sexual intercourse and severely penalizes those who mate across racial and other socially created lines.

Suggestions and Resources for Educators

Anthropological knowledge about race informs us about what race is and is not, but it cannot guide educational decision making. The underlying goal of social justice can help educators in making policy decisions, such as whether to use racial and ethnic categories to monitor educational outcomes. As long as we continue to see racially based disparities in young peoples' school achievement, then we must monitor and investigate the social conditions that produce these disparities. We must be careful, however, to avoid "biologizing" the classification; that is, we must avoid assuming genetic explanations for racial differences in behaviors and educational outcomes or even diseases.

As we pursue a more socially just world, educators should also continue to support young people's quest for knowledge about the history and struggles of their own people, as well as those of other groups, so that students in the future will not be able to point to their textbooks and say, "My people are not included in the curriculum." In the process, we can encourage both curiosity about and respect for human diversity, and we can emphasize the importance that historical and social context plays in creating social inequality. We can also encourage comparative studies of racial and other forms of social stratification, further challenging the notion that there is a biological explanation for oppression and inequality. In short, students will understand that there is no biological explanation for a group's historical position as either oppressed—or oppressor. We can encourage these studies to point out variations and fine distinctions within human racial groupings.

In addition to viewing the treatment of race and racial categories through a social-justice lens, we would apply another criterion that we call "depth of knowledge." We believe that it is important to challenge and inspire young people by exposing them to the best of our current knowledge in the sciences, social sciences, and other disciplines. Until now, most students in our education system have not been exposed to systematic, scientifically based teaching about race and human biological variation. One reason is that many social studies teachers may think they lack sufficient background in genetics and human biology. At the same time, many biology teachers may feel uncomfortable teaching about race as a social construct. The null move for teachers seems to be to say that we should all be "color blind." However, this does not help educate students about human diversity, both biological and social. In rare cases when students have the opportunity to engage in studies of race, ethnicity, culture, and ways to end racism, they are both interested and intellectually challenged.[16] One high school teacher who teaches students about race said he wants to dispel the notion that teaching about diversity is "touchy feely." "We don't just want to touch diversity; we want to approach it academically. . . . We feel we have a definite discipline."[17]

Rather than shield students and ourselves from current scientific knowledge about race, including its contradictions and controversies, we submit that educators should be providing opportunities for students to learn what anthropologists, geneticists, and other scientists, including social scientists, have to say about human biological variation and the issue of race. Particularly in middle schools, high schools, and beyond, students should be involved in inquiry projects and social action projects, in critical examination of the labels we currently use, and in analysis of the reasons for and against using them in particular contexts. Rather than tell students that they should or should not use racial labels (except for slurs), educators should be creating projects in which students explore together the range of possible ways of classifying people and the implications and political significance of alternative approaches in different contexts.

We would like to conclude by offering readers some ideas for student inquiry and by suggesting some resources that can serve to get teachers in all subject areas started on the quest to learn about human biological variation and ways to teach about it.

1. *Ideas for student inquiry.* Here are some examples of how teachers might engage students in critically examining the social, historical, and cultural construction of racial categories.

- Have students create and employ alternative "racial" classification schemes using as many observable and nonobservable physical differences as they can think of (e.g., foot size, height, ear shape, eyebrow shape, waist/shoulder ratio, hairiness). What do the groups look like? What does this tell us about macroracial classifications based on skin pigmentation and other surface features?
- Show students U.S. Census forms from 1870, 1950, and 2000, and ask them to place themselves in the most appropriate category.[18] Or show a photograph of a person of multiple ethnic ancestry and ask students to place this person in one of the categories from these three censuses. Ask them why they think the census form has changed over time and what that says about the meaning of "race."
- Ask immigrant students to investigate the racial/ethnic categories used in their country of origin and to reflect on how well they mesh with the U.S. categories. For example, have students from Mexico taken on an identity as Latino or Hispanic? And what does it mean for them to become part of a larger "macro" race in the U.S.?[19]
- Ask students how they feel when someone asks them to "represent their race." For example, how do students who identify themselves as African Americans feel when someone asks, "How do African Americans feel about this issue?" or "What's the African American perspective on this?"
- Discuss "reverse discrimination." When did this term come into use and why? Who is being discriminated against when discrimination is reversed?
- Discuss "political correctness." Where did this term come from? Who uses it and for what purposes? And why did it emerge?

2. *Resources for teachers.* The following examples will give readers a place to start in compiling resources available for teaching about race.

- Two major anthropological associations have produced highly readable position statements on the topic of race and human biological variation. First, the American Anthropological Association website features both the AAA position and a summary of testimony given in conjunction with the debates on the 2000 census categories. Second, the official statement of the American Association of Physical Anthropologists has appeared in that organization's journal.[20]

- The American Anthropological Association is making a special effort to disseminate understandings about race and human variation to the broader public. *AnthroNotes,* designed for precollege teachers, is a superb resource that offers concrete approaches to teaching about race, human diversity, and human evolution. It is available at no charge from the Anthropology Outreach Office (anthroutreach@nmnh.si.edu). Several past issues of *AnthroNotes* treat race and ethnicity.[21] Anthropologists have produced materials for precollege teachers and teacher educators that deal with cultural diversity; some include strategies for teaching about culture and human diversity.[22] Others provide useful overviews of relevant topics.[23]

- The AAA is currently engaged in a public education initiative called Understanding Race and Human Variation, which will involve a traveling museum exhibit and a website. The Ford Foundation has contributed one million dollars to this project.

- In 1999, the AAA created a special commission called the Anthropology Education Commission (AEC) to "help achieve significant progress towards the integration of anthropological concepts, methods, and issues into pre-K through community college and adult education as a means of increasing public understanding of anthropology." The two teaching modules by Leonard Lieberman and by Lieberman and Patricia Rice, which we cited above, are available at no charge on the AEC website (www.aaanet.org/committees/commissions/aec). The AEC webpage contains extensive resources that teachers can use to teach anthropological concepts and methods, including some that address race.

Anthropologists recognize an obligation to disseminate their knowledge of human biological variation and the social construction of race to the wider public. We hope that this article and the resources we have provided will contribute to this effort.

Notes

1. Richard Herrnstein and Charles Murray, *The Bell Curve: Intelligence and Class Structure in American Life* (New York: Free Press, 1994).

2. Audrey Smedley, *Race in North America: Origin and Evolution of a Worldview* (Boulder, Colo.: Westview Press, 1998).

3. Jonathan Marks, *Human Biodiversity: Genes, Race, and History* (New York: Aldine de Gruyter, 1995).

4. Leonard Lieberman and Patricia Rice, "Races or Clines?," p. 7, available on the Anthropology Education Commission page of the American Anthropological Association website, www.aaanet.org/committees/commissions/aec—click on Teaching About Race.

5. George J. Armelagos and Alan H. Goodman, "Race, Racism, and Anthropology," in Alan H. Goodman and Thomas L. Leatherman, eds., *Building a New Biocultural Synthesis: Political-Economic Perspectives on Human Biology* (Ann Arbor: University of Michigan Press, 1998).

6. Jeffrey M. Fish, "Mixed Blood," in James Spradley and William McCurdy, eds., *Conformity and Conflict,* 11th ed. (New York: Allyn & Bacon, 2002), pp. 270–80.

7. Alan Goodman, "Bred in the Bone?," *Sciences,* vol. 37, no. 2, 1997, p. 24.

8. Ibid., p. 22.

9. Leonard Lieberman, "'Race' 1997 and 2001: A Race Odyssey," available on the Anthropology Education Commission page of the American Anthropological Association website, www.aaanet.org/committees/commissions/aec—click on Teaching About Race.

10. Jane Mercer, "Ethnic Differences in IQ Scores: What Do They Mean? (A Response to Lloyd Dunn)," *Hispanic Journal of Behavioral Sciences,* vol. 10, 1988, pp. 199–218.

11. Goodman, op. cit.

12. Lieberman and Rice, op. cit.

13. Carol Mukhopadhyay and Yolanda Moses, "Reestablishing 'Race' in Anthropological Discourse," *American Anthropologist,* vol. 99, 1997, pp. 517–33.

14. Janet Hyde and John DeLamater, *Understanding Human Sexuality,* 6th ed. (New York: McGraw-Hill, 1997).

15. Smedley, op. cit.

16. Karen Donaldson, *Through Students' Eyes: Combating Racism in United States Schools* (Westport, Conn.: Praeger, 1996); and Rosemary C. Henze, "Curricular Approaches to Developing Positive Interethnic Relations," *Journal of Negro Education,* vol. 68, 2001, pp. 529–49.

17. Henze, p. 539.

18. American Anthropological Association. (2002). Front End Evaluation of *Understanding Race and Human Variability.* Arlington, VA: American Anthropological Association.

19. Clara Rodriguez, *Changing Race: Latinos, the Census, and the History of Ethnicity in the United States* (New York: New York University Press, 2000); and Gilberto Arriaza, "The School Yard as a Stage: Missing Culture Clues in Symbolic Fighting," *Multicultural Education Journal,* Spring 2003, in press.

20. American Anthropological Association, "AAA Statement on Race," www.aaanet.org/stmts/racepp.htm; and American Association of Physical Anthropologists, "AAPA Statement on Biological Aspects of Race," *American Journal of Physical Anthropology,* vol. 101, 1996, pp. 569–70.

21. Alison S. Brooks et al., "Race and Ethnicity in America," in Ruth O. Selig and Marilyn R. London, eds., *Anthropology*

Explored: The Best of Smithsonian AnthroNotes (Washington, D.C.: Smithsonian Institution Press), pp. 315–26; E. L. Cerrini-Long, "Ethnicity in the U.S.A.: An Anthropological Model," *AnthroNotes,* vol. 15, no. 3, 1993; William L. Merrill, "Identity Transformation in Colonial Northern Mexico," *AnthroNotes,* vol. 19, no. 2, 1997, pp. 1–8; and Boyce Rensberger, "Forget the Old Labels: Here's a New Way to Look at Race," *AnthroNotes,* vol. 18, no. 1, 1996, pp. 1–7.

22. Hilda Hernandez and Carol C. Mukhopadhyay, *Integrating Multicultural Perspectives in Teacher Education: A Curriculum Resource Guide* (Chico: California State University, 1985); and Conrad P. Kottak, R. Furlow White, and Patricia Rice, eds. *The Teaching of Anthropology: Problems, Issues, and Decisions* (Mountain View, Calif.: Mayfield Publishing, 1996).

23. Faye Harrison, "The Persistent Power of 'Race' in the Cultural and Political Economy of Racism," *Annual Review of Anthropology,* vol. 24, 1995, pp. 47–74; and Ida Susser and Thomas Patterson, eds., *Cultural Diversity in the United States: A Critical Reader* (Malden, Mass.: Blackwell, 2001).

Critical Thinking

1. What physical characteristics do the authors list as being the basis for racial divisions?

2. What is the historical origin of the concept of race?

3. On what three bases do contemporary scientists criticize the traditional race concept? Explain each.

4. What are some of the "less visible genetic traits that have far greater biological significance"? How would racial classifications based on these look?

5. How have racial classifications used by the U.S. Census Bureau changed over time?

6. What does it mean to say that the genetic variation within each racial grouping is greater than the genetic similarity?

7. What evidence exists that race or racial characteristics are causally linked to behavior? What about the relationship between race and health? What were some of the traditional "racial" health problems? How are they now viewed?

8. What terms have anthropologists sought to replace "race" with? What is the meaning of each of these terms? Which term do the authors seem to prefer?

9. Why was the United States, in particular, a place where racial ideas found fertile ground? What are anti-miscegenation laws? What is "hypodescent" or the "one-drop rule"?

10. What do you think about the prospects for change? What has your experience of race been in your own educational background?

11. What are some of the dangers of racial classifications listed by the authors? What are some of the problems they mention with the terms "Asian," "African American," and "black"?

12. What are some of the positive ways "macroracial categories have served people"?

13. What is the point (as they advise) of "shifting the conversation from biology to culture"?

14. What do you think of the suggestions they make ("ideas for student inquiry") for teaching about the notion of race?

Internet References

Human Genome Project Information
www.ornl.gov/TechResources/Human_Genome/home.html

OMIM Home Page-Online Mendelian Inheritance in Man
www.ncbi.nlm.nih.gov

CAROL MUKHOPADHYAY is a professor in the Department of Anthropology, San Josè State University, San Josè, Calif., where ROSEMARY C. HENZE is an associate professor in the Department of Linguistics and Language Development. They wish to thank Gilberto Arriaza, Paul Erickson, Alan Goodman, and Yolanda Moses for their comments on this article.

Mukhopadhyay, Carol; Henze, Rosemary C. "How Real Is Race? Using Anthropology to Make Sense of Human Diversity," *Phi Delta Kappan,* May 2003. Copyright ©2003 by Phi Delta Kappan. Used with permission.

Article   Prepared by: Elvio Angeloni

Still Evolving (After All These Years)

For 30,000 years our species has been changing remarkably quickly. And we're not done yet.

JOHN HAWKS

Learning Outcomes

After reading this article, you will be able to:

- Discuss the evidence for continuing human evolution since the transition from hunting and gathering to farming.
- Discuss the "shallowness" of races in terms of recent human evolution.
- Explain the relationship between population size and recent human evolution.
- Describe the ways in which today's scientist can watch human evolution in action.

Humans are willful creatures. No other species on the planet has gained so much mastery over its own fate. We have neutralized countless threats that once killed us in the millions: we have learned to protect ourselves from the elements and predators in the wild; we have developed cures and treatments for many deadly diseases; we have transformed the small gardens of our agrarian ancestors into the vast fields of industrial agriculture; and we have dramatically increased our chances of bearing healthy children despite all the usual difficulties.

Many people argue that our technological advancement—our ability to defy and control nature—has made humans exempt from natural selection and that human evolution has effectively ceased. There is no "survival of the fittest," the argument goes, if just about everyone survives into old age. This notion is more than just a stray thought in the public consciousness. Professional scientists such as Steven Jones of University College London and respected science communicators such as David Attenborough have also declared that human evolution is over.

But it is not. We have evolved in our recent past, and we will continue to do so as long as we are around. If we take the more than seven million years since humans split from our last common ancestor with chimpanzees and convert it to a 24-hour day, the past 30,000 years would take about a mere six minutes. Yet much has unfolded during this last chapter of our evolution: vast migrations into new environments, dramatic changes in diet and a more than 1,000-fold increase in global population. All those new people added many unique mutations to the total population. The result was a pulse of rapid natural selection. Human evolution is not stopping. If anything, it is accelerating.

An Anthropological Legacy

Skeletons of ancient people have long suggested that humans evolved certain traits swiftly and recently. About 11,000 years ago, as people started to transition from hunting and gathering to farming and cooking, human anatomy changed. Ten thousand years ago, for example, people's teeth averaged more than 10 percent larger in Europe, Asia and North Africa than today. When our ancestors started to eat softer cooked foods that required less chewing, their teeth and jaws shrank, bit by bit, each generation.

Although anthropologists have known about such traits for decades, only in the past 10 years has it become clear just how new they really are. Studies of human genomes have made the recent targets of selection highly visible to us. It turns out, for example, that descendants of farmers are much more likely to have a greater production of salivary amylase, a key enzyme that breaks down starches in food. Most people alive today have several copies of the gene that codes for amylase, $AMY1$. Modern hunter-gatherers—such as the Datooga in Tanzania—tend to have far fewer copies than people whose ancestors came from farming populations, whether they live in Africa, Asia or the Americas. Getting a jump on starch processing at the point of entry seems to have been an advantage for ancient farmers wherever they adopted starchy grains.

Another dietary adaptation is one of the best-studied examples of recent human evolution: lactose tolerance. Nearly everyone in the world is born with the ability to produce the enzyme lactase, which breaks down the milk sugar lactose and makes it easier to extract energy from milk—essential for the survival of a suckling child. Most people lose this ability by adulthood. At least five different times in our recent evolutionary past, as people started to discover dairy, a genetic mutation arose to lengthen the activity of the lactase gene. Three of the mutations originated in different parts of sub-Saharan Africa, where there is a long history of cattle herding. Another one of the five genetic tweaks is common in Arabia and seems to have sprung up in ancient populations of camel and goat herders.

The fifth and most common variant of the mutation that keeps the lactase gene turned on in adulthood is found today in human populations stretching from Ireland to India, with its highest frequencies across northern Europe. The mutation originated in a single individual 7,500 years ago (give or take a few thousand years). In 2011, scientists analyzed DNA recovered from Ötzi the Iceman, who was naturally mummified about 5,500 years ago in northern Italy. He did not have the lactose-tolerance mutation, a hint that it had not yet become common in this region thousands of years after its initial origin. In following years, researchers sequenced DNA extracted from the skeletons of farmers who lived in Europe more than 5,000 years ago. None carried the lactase mutation. Yet in the same region today, the lactase-persistence mutation occurs in hundreds of millions of people—more than 75 percent of the gene pool. This is not a paradox but the mathematical expectation of natural selection. A new mutation under selection grows exponentially, taking many generations to become common enough to notice in a population. But once it becomes common, its continued growth is very rapid and ultimately dominates.

The Shallowness of Races

What is perhaps most extraordinary about our recent evolution is how many common physical features are completely new to human anatomy. The thick, straight black hair shared by most East Asians, for example, arose only within the past 30,000 years, thanks to a mutation in a gene called EDAR, which is crucial for orchestrating the early development of skin, hair, teeth and nails. That genetic variant traveled with early colonizers of the Americas, all of whom share an evolutionary past with East Asians.

In fact, the overall evolutionary history of human skin, hair and eye pigmentation is surprisingly shallow. In the earliest stages of our evolution, all our ancestors had dark skin, hair and eyes. Since this initial state, dozens of genetic changes have lightened these features to some extent. A few of these changes are ancient variations present within Africa but more common elsewhere in the world. Most are new mutations that have emerged in one population or another: a change in a gene named TYRP1, for instance, that makes certain Solomon Islanders blond; the HERC2 mutation that results in blue eyes; changes to MC1R that causes red hairs to sprout instead of black ones; and a mutation in the SLC24A5 gene that lightens skin color and that is now found in up to 95 percent of Europeans. As in the case of lactase, ancient DNA is giving clear information about the antiquity of such mutations. Blue eyes seem to have appeared in people who lived more than 9,000 years ago, but the massive change to SLC24A5 is not found in the DNA of ancient skeletons from the same time period. Skin, hair, and eye color evolved with stunning speed.

Variations in pigmentation are some of the most obvious differences between the races and, in some ways, the easiest to study. Scientists have also investigated much odder and less evident features of human anatomy. Consider the variations of earwax. Most people in the world today have sticky earwax. In contrast, many East Asians have dry, flaky earwax that does not stick together. Anthropologists have known about this variation for more than 100 years, but geneticists did not uncover the cause until recently. Dry earwax results from a relatively new mutation to a gene called ABCC11. Only 30,000 to 20,000 years old, the mutation also affects the apocrine glands, which produce sweat. If you have stinky armpits and sticky earwax, chances are you have the original version of ABCC11. If you have dry earwax and a little less need for deodorant, you probably have the newer mutation.

A few thousand years before dry earwax first appeared among East Asians, another seemingly simple mutation started saving millions of Africans from a deadly disease. A gene called DARC produces a starchy molecule on the surface of red blood cells that mops up excess immune system molecules known as chemokines from the blood. About 45,000 years ago a mutation in DARC conferred remarkable resistance to *Plasmodium vivax*, one of the two most prevalent malaria parasites infecting humans today. The vivax parasites enter red blood cells through the DARC molecule encoded by the gene, so hindering the expression of DARC keeps the pathogens at bay. The absence of DARC also increased the amount of inflammation-causing chemokines circulating in the blood, which has in turn been linked to an increase in prostate cancer rates in African-American men. Yet on the whole, the mutation was so successful that 95 percent of people living below the Sahara now have it, whereas only 5 percent of Europeans and Asians do.

The Power of Random

We are used to thinking about evolution as a process of "good" genes replacing "bad" ones, but the most recent phase of human adaptation is a testament to the power of randomness in evolution. Beneficial mutations do not automatically persist. It all depends on timing and population size.

I first learned this lesson from the late anthropologist Frank Livingstone. The beginning of my training coincided with the end of his long career, during which he investigated the genetic basis for malaria resistance. More than 3,000 years ago in Africa and India, a mutation arose in the gene coding the oxygen-transporting blood cell molecule known as hemoglobin. When people inherited two copies of this mutation—dubbed hemoglobin S—they developed sickle cell anemia, a disease in which unusually shaped blood cells clog vessels. Red cells are normally supple and flexible enough to squeeze through tiny capillaries, but the mutant blood cells were rigid and pointed into the characteristic "sickle" shape. As it turns out, changing the shape of red blood cells also thwarted the ability of the malaria parasite to infect those cells.

Another mutation that interested Livingstone was hemoglobin E. Common in Southeast Asia today, hemoglobin E confers substantial malaria resistance without the severe side effects of hemoglobin S. "Hemoglobin E seems like it would be a lot better to have than hemoglobin S," I said in class one day. "Why didn't they get E in Africa?"

"It didn't happen there," Livingstone said.

His reply stunned me. I had supposed natural selection to be the most powerful force in evolution's arsenal. Humans had lived with deadly falciparum malaria for thousands of years in Africa. Surely natural selection would have weeded out less helpful mutations and hit on the most successful one.

Livingstone went on to show how the previous existence of hemoglobin S in a population made it harder for hemoglobin E to invade. Malaria rips through a population full of only normal hemoglobin carriers, and a new mutation that provides a slight advantage can quickly become more common. Yet a population already supplied with the protective hemoglobin S mutation will have a lower mortality risk. Sickle cell carriers still face formidable risks, but hemoglobin E is less of a relative advantage in a population that already has this imperfect form of malaria resistance. Perversely, what matters is not only the luck of having the mutation but also when the mutation happens. A partial adaptation with bad side effects can win, at least over the few thousand years humans have been adapting to malaria.

Ever since humans first began battling malaria, scores of different genetic changes emerged that increased immunity to the disease, different ones in different places. Each started as a serendipitous mutation that managed to persist in a local population despite being very rare at first. Any one of those mutations was, individually, unlikely to last long enough to become established, but the huge and rapidly increasing population size of our ancestors gave them many more rolls of the dice. As human populations have spread into new parts of the world and grown larger, they have rapidly adapted to their new homes precisely because those populations were so big.

Our Evolutionary Future

Human populations continue to evolve today. Unlike the distant past, where we must infer the action of selection from its long-term effects on genes, today scientists can watch human evolution in action, often by studying trends in health and reproduction. Even as medical technology, sanitation and vaccines have greatly extended life spans, birth rates in many populations still vacillate.

In sub-Saharan Africa, women who have a certain variant of a gene called FLT1 and who are pregnant in the malarial season are slightly more likely to bear children than are pregnant women who lack the variant, because the possessors have a lower risk that the placenta will be infected by malaria parasites. We do not yet understand how this gene reduces the risk of placental malaria, but the effect is profound and measurable.

Stephen Stearns of Yale University and his colleagues have examined years of records from long-term public health studies to see which traits may correlate with reproduction rates today. During the past 60 years, relatively short and heavy women in the U.S. who have low cholesterol counts had slightly more children on average than women who have the opposite traits. Why these traits have been related to family size is not yet clear.

New public health studies on the horizon, such as U.K. Bio-bank, will be tracking the genotypes and lifetime health of hundreds of thousands of people. Such studies are being undertaken because the interactions of genes are complicated, and we need to examine thousands of outcomes to understand which genetic changes underlie human health. Tracing the ancestry of human mutations gives us a tremendous power to observe evolution over hundreds of generations but can obscure the complex interactions of environment, survival, and fertility that unfolded in the past. We see the long-term winners, such as lactase persistence, but may miss the short-term dynamics. Human populations are about to become the most intensively observed long-term experiment in evolutionary biology.

What will the future of human evolution look like? Across the past few thousand years, human evolution has taken a distinctive path in different populations yet has maintained surprising commonality. New adaptive mutations may have elbowed their way into human populations, but they have not muscled out the old versions of genes. Instead the old, "ancestral" versions of genes mostly have remained with us. Meanwhile millions of people are moving between nations every year, leading to an unprecedented rate of genetic exchanges and mixture.

With such a high rate of genetic mixing, it may seem reasonable to expect that additive traits—for example, pigmentation, where many different genes have independent effects on skin color—will become ever more blended in future human populations. Could we be looking at a human future where we are a homogeneous slurry instead of a colorful stew of variability?

The answer is no. Many of the traits that differ between human populations are not additive. Even pigmentation is hardly so simple, as is readily seen in mixed populations in the U.S., Mexico, and Brazil. Instead of a featureless mass of café-au-lait-colored clones, we are already starting to see a glorious riot of variations—dark-skinned, freckled blondes, and striking combinations of green eyes and olive skin. Each of our descendants will be a living mosaic of human history.

More to Explore

Are Human Beings Still Evolving? It Would Seem That Evolution Is Impossible Now That the Ability to Reproduce Is Essentially Universally Available. Are We Nevertheless Changing as a Species? Meredith F. Small; Ask the Experts, ScientificAmerican.com, October 21, 1999.

African Adaptation to Digesting Milk Is "Strongest Signal of Selection Ever." Nikhil Swaminathan; ScientificAmerican.com, December 11, 2006.

Did Lactose Tolerance First Evolve in Central, Rather Than Northern Europe? Lynne Peeples; ScientificAmerican.com, August 28, 2009.

From our Archives

Evolution in the Future. Henry M. Lewis, Jr.; April 1941.

The Evolution of Man. Sherwood L. Washburn; September 1978.

The Future of Human Evolution. John Rennie; From the Editors, March 2001.
scientificamerican.com/magazine/sa

In Brief

Some scientists and science communicators have claimed that humans are no longer subject to natural selection and that human evolution has effectively ceased.

In fact, humans have evolved rapidly and remarkably in the past 30,000 years. Straight, black hair, blue eyes, and lactose tolerance are all examples of relatively recent traits.

Such rapid evolution has been possible for several reasons, including the switch from hunting and gathering to agrarian-based societies, which permitted human populations to grow much larger than before. The more people reproduce within a population, the higher the chance of new advantageous mutations.

Humans will undoubtedly continue to evolve into the future. Although it may seem that we are headed toward a cosmopolitan blend of human genes, future generations will likely be striking mosaics of our entire evolutionary past.

Many Commonplace Features of human biology are relatively new. Blue eyes, straight, thick black hair, the ability to digest milk in adulthood and some mutations that lightened skin all emerged in the past 30,000 years.

Findings
The Milk Mutation

Enjoying dairy in adulthood is a privilege that emerged relatively recently in our evolutionary history. We depend on the enzyme lactase to break down lactose, the sugar found in milk, but the human body usually stops producing lactase after adolescence. In fact, most of the world's adults are lactose-intolerant. Within the past 10,000 years, however, different populations of dairy farmers independently evolved genetic mutations that kept lactase active throughout life. Scientists have identified five such mutations, but there are likely several more. Collectively, all these adaptations explain the prevalence of lactose tolerance seen around the world today.

One of the so-called lactase-persistence mutations arose around 7,500 years ago among dairy farmers in a region between Central Europe and the northern Balkans. This is the most common lactase mutation in Europe today.

Three different lactase-persistence mutations originated in sub-Saharan Africa, the most common of which spread rapidly through the region in the past 7,000 years.

The world's first daily farmers lived in the Middle East and North Africa between 10,000 and 8,000 years ago. They primarily raised sheep, goats, and cattle, but at least one lactase-persistence mutation likely sprung up among camel herders.

Critical Thinking

1. What is the evidence for continuing human evolution since our ancestors transitioned from hunting and gathering to farming?

2. What are some of the more recent evolutionary adaptations made by humans and why?

3. What is the relationship between recent increases in human populations and evolutionary change?

4. How are scientists able to watch human evolution in action even today?

Internet References

American Journal of Physical Anthropology

http://onlinelibrary.wiley.com/journal/10.1002/(ISSN)1096-8644

Journal of Human Evolution

http://www.journals.elsevier.com/journal-of-human-evolution/

National Geographic Future of Food

natgeofood.com

The Paleolithic Diet Page

www.paleodiet.com

JOHN HAWKS is an anthropologist and an expert on human evolution at the University of Wisconsin-Madison.

Unit 7

UNIT

Prepared by: Elvio Angeloni

Living with the Past

Anthropology continues to evolve as a discipline, not only with respect to the tools and techniques of the trade, but also in the application of whatever knowledge we stand to gain about ourselves. Sometimes an awareness of our biological and behavioral past may help us to better understand the present. In the context of our bodily health, for instance, it may be instructive to know that some traditional hunters, such as the Inuit of the Arctic, would gorge themselves on fat, rarely saw a vegetable and, yet, were still healthier than we are today. When assessing the symptoms of disease, such as coughing or sneezing, should we interpret them as part of the aggressive strategies evolved by microbes to induce us to spread them to other human hosts or as part of our own evolved defense mechanisms to get rid of them? Finally, in the area of genetics, we find that, while there are many deleterious genes that get weeded out of the population by means of natural selection, there are other harmful ones, such as the genes for sickle cell anemia, cystic fibrosis, and iron deficiency anemia, that may actually have a good side to them and may therefore be perpetuated in the human species in spite of their downsides.

As we reflect upon where we have been and how we came to be as we are in the evolutionary sense, the inevitable question arises as to what will happen next. This is the most difficult issue of all, because our biological future depends so much on long-range environmental trends that no one seems to be able to predict. Take, for example, the sweeping effects of ecological change upon the viruses of the world, which in turn seem to be paving the way for new waves of human epidemics. There is no better example of this problem than the recent explosion of new diseases, such as the various strains of flu, Ebola, and HIV.

As we gain a better understanding of the processes of mutation and natural selection, and their relevance to human beings,

we might even gain some control over the evolutionary direction of our species. However, the issue of what is a beneficial application of scientific knowledge becomes a subject for debate. Who will have the final word as to how these technological breakthroughs are to be employed in the future? Even with the best of intentions, how can we be certain of the long-range consequences of our actions in such a complicated field?

Knowledge in itself, of course, is neutral—its potential for good or ill being determined by those who happen to be in the position to use it. Consider, for example, that some men may be dying from a genetically caused overabundance of iron in their blood systems in a trade-off that allows some women to absorb sufficient amounts of the element to guarantee their own survival. The question of whether we should eliminate such a gene that brings about this situation would seem to depend on which sex we decide should reap the benefit.

Much of what is being discussed here is known collectively as "Darwinian medicine," which is based upon the premise that an understanding of how we humans and the microbes that afflict us have evolved in relation to each other will help us to reduce disease and alleviate suffering. This perspective is even more important today, as we have come to live in ever more crowded conditions, thus making it easier for microbes to spread. At the same time, we must remain aware that someone, at some time, may actually use the same knowledge to increase rather than reduce the misery that exists in the world.

Since it has been our conscious decision making (and not the genetically predetermined behavior that characterizes some species) that has gotten us into this situation, then it is the conscious will of our generation and future generations that will get us out of it. But, can we wait much longer for humanity to collectively come to its senses? Or is it too late already?

Article   Prepared by: Elvio Angeloni

The Perfect Plague

The next killer germ could burst from the African rain forest—or from your family pet.

JARED DIAMOND AND NATHAN WOLFE

Learning Outcomes

After reading this article, you will be able to:

- Determine whether the concept of natural selection has any relevance to the treatment of disease and defend your answer.
- Describe the modern conditions for human pandemic diseases.

Shortly after one of us (Jared Diamond) boarded a flight from Hong Kong back to Los Angeles, the passenger in the next seat sneezed. She sneezed again—and again— and then she began coughing. Finally she gagged, pulled out the vomit bag from the seat back in front of her, threw up into the bag, stood up, squeezed past, and lurched to the toilet at the front of the plane. The woman was obviously miserable, but sympathy for her pain was not what I felt. Instead I was frightened and asked the flight attendant to move me to a seat as far from her as possible.

All I could think of was another sick person, a man from Guangdong province in southern China, who spent the night of February 21, 2003, at the Metropole Hotel in Hong Kong, an upscale establishment with a swimming pool, fitness center, restaurants, a bar, and all kinds of areas where visitors could socialize and connect. The man stayed a single night in room 911. Unfortunately for him and for many other people, he had picked up severe acute respiratory syndrome, or SARS—perhaps directly from an infected bat or from a small, arboreal mammal called a civet, common in one of Guangdong's famous "wet markets" that sell wild animals for food, or else from a person or chain of people ultimately infected from one of those animal sources.

In the course of his brief stay, the man initiated a SARS "super spreader" event that led to at least 16 more SARS cases among the hotel's guests and visitors and then to hundreds of other cases throughout Asia, Europe, and North America as those guests and visitors continued on their travels—just as my neighbor was now traveling to L.A. The infectiousness of room 911's guest can be gauged from the fact that three months later, the carpet right outside the door and near the hotel elevator yielded genetic evidence of the SARS virus, presumably spewed out in his own sneezing, coughing, or vomiting.

I didn't end up with SARS, but my experience drives home the terrifying prospect of a novel, unstoppable infectious disease. Globalization, changing climate, and the threat of drug resistance have conspired to set the stage for that perfect microbial storm: a situation in which an emerging pathogen—another HIV or smallpox, perhaps—might burst on the scene and kill millions before we can respond.

Pathogen Paradox

To grasp the risk, we first must understand why *any* microbe would evolve to sicken or kill us. In evolutionary terms, how does destroying its host help a microbe to survive?

Think of your body as a potential "habitat" for tiny microbes, just as a forest provides a habitat for bigger creatures like birds and squirrels. The species living in the forests of our bodies include lice, worms, bacteria, viruses, and amoebas. Many of those denizens are benign and cause us no harm. But some microbes seem to go out of their way to make us sick—either mildly sick, as in the case of the common cold, or else sick to the point of killing us, as in the case of smallpox.

Killer microbes have long posed a paradox for evolutionary biologists. Why would a microbe evolve to devastate the very habitat on which it depends? By analogy, you might reason that there should be no squirrels that destroy the forest they live in, because such a species would quickly go extinct.

The answer stems from the fact that in order to survive over the long haul, any microbe restricted to humans must be able to spread from one victim to the next. There is a simple mathematical requirement here: On average, the germ must infect at least one new victim for every old one who either dies or recovers and purges himself of the microbe. If the average number of new victims per old drops to fewer than one, then the spread of the microbe is doomed.

A microbe can't walk or fly from one host to the next. Instead it must resort to a range of nefarious tricks. What from our point of view is simply a disease symptom can, from the bug's perspective, be an all-important means of enlisting our help to move around. Common microbe tricks are to make us cough or sneeze, suffer from diarrhea, or develop open sores on our skin. Respectively, these symptoms spread the microbe into our exhaled breath, into the local water supply via our feces, and onto the skin of those who touch us, explaining why a microbe might want to induce unpleasant symptoms in its victims.

Evolutionary biologists reason that keeping us alive and pumping out new microbes would be an excellent strategy for such a bug, which might therefore evolve to be less, not more, virulent over time. An example comes from the history of syphilis. When it first appeared in Europe in 1495, it caused severe and painful symptoms within a few months, but by 1546 it had begun evolving into the slowly progressing disease that we know today.

Yet if keeping us alive is strategically sound, why do some pathogens go so far as to actually kill us?

Sometimes a microbe's deadly rampage through a human population stems from an accident of nature. For instance, the microbe could be comfortably adapted to some animal host that it routinely inhabits without deadly consequences, but it could be maladapted to the human environment. The microbe may rarely infect people, but when it does, it may kill the human host, who becomes a literal dead end for the virus as well.

A microbe's deadly rampage through humans might stem from an accident of nature.

But what of those killer microbes that target humans, making us their primary host? Their survival strategy, evolutionary

biologists now realize, differs from that of a disease like syphilis but works just as well. Take the cholera bacterium that gives us diarrhea or the smallpox virus that makes us develop skin sores; both of these can kill us in days to weeks. Such virulence may be evolutionary favored if, in the brief time between our becoming infected and dying, the fatal symptoms spread trillions of microbes to potential new victims. The fact that we may die is unfortunate for us but an acceptable cost for the microbe. In the world of evolution and natural selection, anything that the microbe does to us is fair—just as long as at least one new victim gets infected for each old one.

Hence the recipe for a killer disease is for the microbe to achieve a balance between two things: the probability of its killing us quickly once we become infected and its efficiency in leading our bodies to transmit the microbe to new victims.

Humanity's greatest predators can be seen only with the aid of a microscope. The virus responsible for AIDS; the SARS virus; *Vibrio cholerae* bacteria, responsible for cholera; and spores of anthrax.

Those two things are connected. The greater its efficiency in inducing lethal, bug-spreading syndromes (good for the microbe), the faster the microbe kills us (bad for the microbe). Following this logic, a pathogen may end up killing lots of people by one of two routes. In the style of HIV, it can keep the disease carrier alive for a long time, infecting new victims over the course of months or years. Or in the style of smallpox and cholera, it might kill quickly with explosive symptoms that can spread an infection to dozens of new victims within a day.

Searching for the Source

For epidemiologists hoping to stanch such outbreaks, tracking killer germs to the source is key. Do deadly pandemics arise spontaneously in human populations? Or are they "gifts" from other species, mutating and then crossing over to make us ill? Which ecosystems are spawning them, and can we catch them at the start, before they cause too much damage?

Some answers can be found in the history of yellow fever, a virus spread by mosquitoes. The cause of devastating human epidemics throughout history, yellow fever is still rife in tropical South America and Africa. Biologists now understand that yellow fever arose in tropical African monkeys, which, through the mosquito vector, infected (and continue to infect) tropical African people, some of whom unintentionally carried yellow fever with them on slave ships several hundred years ago to South America.

Mosquitoes bit the infected slaves and in turn carried the virus to South American monkeys. In due course, mosquitoes bit infected monkeys and transmitted yellow fever right back to the human population there.

In Venezuela today, the Ministry of Health keeps a lookout for the appearance of unusual numbers of dead wild monkeys, such as howler monkeys. Because the monkeys are so susceptible to yellow fever and can act as a reservoir from which the virus leaps to the human population, an explosion of monkey deaths serves as an advance warning system, signaling the need to vaccinate humans in the vicinity.

This pattern of cross-infection from animals to humans is par for the course in emerging infectious disease. In fact, the big killer diseases of history all came to us from microbes living in other species, overwhelmingly from other warm-blooded mammals and, to a lesser extent, from birds.

On reflection, this all makes sense. Each new animal host to which a microbe adapts represents a new habitat. It is easiest for a microbe to jump between closely related habitats, from an animal species with one sort of body chemistry to a closely related animal species with very similar body chemistry.

In the tropics, disease sources have included a host of wild animals, most notably the nonhuman primates. We can thank our primate cousins not just for yellow fever but also for HIV, dengue fever, hepatitis B, and vivax malaria. Other wild animal disease donors include rats, the source of the plague and typhus.

In temperate regions like the United States, meanwhile, ticks in suburban neighborhoods and domestic livestock living in proximity to humans have posed threats. Mammalian reservoirs like mice and chipmunks carry Lyme disease and tularemia; ticks transmit these diseases to humans. Cattle probably gave rise to the measles and tuberculosis. Smallpox is likely to have come from camels, biologists say, and flu from pigs and ducks.

The Next Wave

Today, with fewer people tending farms and more living in the suburbs, things have certainly changed. The principles of infectious disease are the same as they have always been, but modern conditions, including life in proximity to pets and mammal-filled woods, are exposing us to new pathogen reservoirs and new modes of transmitting disease.

One of us (Nathan Wolfe) has spent much of the last six years in the tropical African country of Cameroon, studying the kinds of interspecies jumps that such conditions might spawn. To examine the mechanisms, I worked with rural hunters who butchered wild animals for food. I collected blood samples from the hunters, from other people in their community, and from their animal prey. By testing all those samples, I identified microbes inhabiting the animal reservoirs and focused on those

that showed up in the hunters' blood, making them candidates for firing up human disease.

Three strains of influenza virus, including H5N1, better known as the avian flu virus. The influenza virus frequently mutates, creating new strains. This makes it difficult to produce vaccines and opens the door to another global influenza pandemic, such as the one that struck in 1918 and eventually killed more than 20 million people.

One evening I asked a group of hunters if they had ever cut themselves while butchering wild monkeys or apes. The response was incredulous laughter: "You don't know the answer to that?" Of course, they said. All of them had cut themselves once or more, thereby giving themselves ample opportunity to get infected from animal blood.

On reflection, I shouldn't have been surprised. I can't count all the times I have cut myself while chopping onions. The difference is that onions aren't closely related to us humans, and an onion virus has far less chance of taking hold in us than does a monkey virus.

The statistics are telling. Researchers like Mark Woolhouse, professor of infectious disease epidemiology at the University of Edinburgh in Scotland, have found at least 868 human pathogens that infect both animals and humans, although some are not as fearsome as they seem.

Overhyped microbes include anthrax (famous for the U.S. mail attacks in 2000), the Ebola and Marburg viruses (which can cause dramatic bleeding and high fever in their victims), and the prion agent of mad cow disease (otherwise known as bovine spongiform encephalopathy, or BSE), which kills people by making their nervous systems degenerate. These bugs arouse terror because they kill so many of their victims. For example, in the 2000 Ebola outbreak, which struck the Gulu district of Uganda, 53 percent of the 425 people who contracted the disease died. The case fatality rate for BSE is 100 percent.

Although spectacularly lethal, these pathogens generally kill just a few hundred people at a time and then burn themselves out. They transmit from human to human too inefficiently to spread very widely; 100 percent of a small number of victims is still a small number of fatalities.

There are many reasons why an agent leaping from animals to humans might not affect more individuals. For example, humans do not normally bite, scratch, hunt, or eat each other. This surely contributes to the rarity or nonexistence of human-to-human transmission of rabies (acquired by the bite of an infected dog or bat); cat-scratch disease (which causes skin lesions and swollen lymph nodes); tularemia (a disease, often acquired when hunting and cutting up an infected rabbit, that can cause skin ulcers, swollen lymph nodes, and fever); and

BSE (probably acquired by eating the nervous system tissue of infected cows).

Some outbreaks, once recognized, are relatively easy to control. Anthrax is treatable with antibiotics; after an initial malaria-like stage, the rapid onset and severity of Ebola and Marburg symptoms have made identification and containment straightforward.

In fact, within the last 40 years, only HIV (derived from chimpanzees) has taken off to cause a pandemic.

Back to the Future

If not anthrax or Ebola, which pathogens might spawn the next deadly pandemic in our midst?

New pandemics are most likely to be triggered by mutant strains of familiar microbe species, especially those that have caused plagues by churning out mutant strains in the past. For example, the highest known epidemic death toll in history was caused by a new strain of influenza virus that killed more than 20 million people in 1918 and 1919. Unfairly named Spanish influenza, it apparently emerged in Kansas during World War I, was carried by American troops to Europe, and then spread around the world in three waves before ebbing in outbreaks of declining virulence in the 1920s. Mutant strains of influenza or cholera remain prime candidates for another deadly outbreak. Both can persist in animal reservoirs or the environment, and both are adept at spawning new strains. Both pathogens also transmit efficiently, and it is possible that these two important diseases of the past could become important diseases of the future.

A future pandemic could also come from tuberculosis. New mutants have already arisen through the mechanism of drug resistance. And the disease lives on in the human population, especially among those with weakened immunity, including patients with HIV.

Also of concern are emerging sexually transmitted diseases, which, once introduced, may be difficult to control because it is hard to persuade humans to change sexual behavior or to abstain from sex. HIV offers a grim warning: Despite its huge global impact, the AIDS epidemic would have been far worse if the sexual transmissibility of HIV (which is actually rather modest) had equaled that of some other sexually transmitted agents, such as human papilloma virus (HPV). While the probability of HIV transmission varies with the stage of the disease and the type of sexual contact, it appears to pass from infected to uninfected individuals in less than 1 percent of acts of unprotected heterosexual intercourse, while the corresponding probability of HPV transmission is thought to be higher than 5 percent—probably much higher.

Similarly, it could be difficult to control emerging pathogens transmitted by pets, which increasingly include exotic species along with traditional domestic animals like dogs and cats. Already we are at risk of catching rabies from our dogs, toxoplasmosis and cat-scratch disease from our cats, and psittacosis from our parrots. Most people now accept the need to cull millions of farmyard animals in the face of epidemics like mad cow disease, but it is hard to imagine killing beloved puppies, bunnies, and kittens, even if those pets do turn out to offer a pathway for a dangerous new disease.

Have Plague, Will Travel

Once a killer disease has emerged, modern societies offer new ways for it to flourish and spread. Global travel, the close quarters of the urban environment, climate change, the evolution of drug-resistant microbes, and increasing numbers of the elderly or antibiotic-treated immunosuppressed could all aid the next great plague.

For example, rapid urbanization in Africa could transform yellow fever, Chikungunya fever (which causes severe joint pain and fever), and other rural African arboviruses (viruses, including yellow fever, spread by bloodsucking insects) into plagues of African cities, as has already happened with dengue hemorrhagic fever. One of us (Wolfe) theorizes that this might follow increasing demand in those cities for bush meat. Like urban people everywhere, urban Africans love to eat the foods enjoyed by their village-dwelling ancestors, and in tropical Africa this means bush meat. In that respect it's similar to the smoked fish and bagels that I eat in the United States, which give me some comforting memory of my Eastern European roots. But there's an important difference: The wild game that I see served in fancy restaurants in the capital of Cameroon is much more likely to transmit a dangerous virus to the person who hunted and butchered it, or to the cook who prepared it, or to the restaurant patron who ate the meat undercooked, than is my brunch of smoked fish and bagels.

By connecting distant places, meanwhile, globalization permits the long-distance transfer of microbes along with their insect vectors and their human victims, as evidenced not only by the spread of HIV around the world, but also by North American cases of cholera and SARS brought by infected passengers on jet flights from South America and Asia, respectively. Indeed, when a flight from Buenos Aires to Los Angeles stopped in Lima in 1992, it picked up some seafood infected with the cholera then making the rounds in Peru. As a result, dozens of passengers who arrived in Los Angeles, some of whom then changed planes and flew on to Nevada and even as far as Japan, found they had contracted cholera. Within days that single airplane spread cholera 10,000 miles around the whole rim of the Pacific Basin.

The tuberculosis bacterium, *Mycobacterium tuberculosis,* has developed a resistance to antibiotics in many regions of the world, fueling a resurgence of this disease.

Consider as well those diseases thought of as "just" tropical because they are transmitted by tropical vectors: malaria transmitted by mosquitoes, sleeping sickness spread by tsetse flies, and Chagas' disease (associated with edema, fever, and heart disease) spread by kissing bugs. How will we feel about those tropical diseases if global warming enables their vectors to spread into temperate zones? While microbe and vector movement can be difficult to detect, modeling suggests that global warming will expand the reach of malaria to higher latitudes and into tropical mountain regions.

The transmission of emerging diseases has also been enhanced by a host of modern practices and technologies. The commercial bush meat trade has introduced retroviruses into human populations. Ecotourism has exposed first-world tourists to cutaneous leishmaniasis and other third-world diseases. Underequipped rural hospitals have facilitated Ebola virus outbreaks in Africa. Air conditioners and water circulation systems have spread Legionnaires' disease. Industrial food production was responsible in Europe for the spread of BSE. And intravenous drug use and blood transfusion have both spread HIV and hepatitis B and C.

We have the potential to avert the next HIV, saving millions of lives and billions of dollars.

All this shows that disease prevention and treatment need to be supplemented by a new effort: disease forecasting. This refers to the early detection of potential pandemics at a stage when we might still be able to localize them, before they have had the opportunity to infect a high percentage of the local population and thereby spread around the world, as happened with HIV. Already one of us (Wolfe) is working through a new initiative, the Global Viral Forecasting Initiative (GVFI), to do just that. GVFI works in countries throughout the world to monitor the entry and movement of new agents before they become pandemics. By studying emerging agents at the interface between humans and animals, GVFI hopes to stop new epidemics before they explode. Monitoring for the emergence of both new sexually transmitted diseases and pet-associated diseases would be good investments.

The predictions here are admittedly educated guesses—but they are educated by some of the best science available. The time to act is now. If we don't, then we will continue to be like the cardiologists of the 1950s, waiting for their patients' heart attacks and doing little to prevent them. If we do act, we have the potential to avert the next HIV, saving millions of lives and billions of dollars. The choice seems obvious.

Critical Thinking

1. How did the author's (Jared Diamond) airline experience illustrate the possible spread of a novel, unstoppable infectious disease?
2. What must a microbe be able to do to survive if it kills its host?
3. What are some of the "microbe tricks" designed to allow it to spread from one victim to the next?
4. Under what circumstance would keeping us alive be an excellent strategy?
5. When would virulence be evolutionarily favored?
6. In what sense does a recipe for a killer disease involve a balance between two things?
7. By what two routes may a pathogen end up killing lots of people?
8. Discuss the cross-infection from animals to humans as the explanation for the big killer disease of history and why this could easily happen.
9. What are the modern conditions exposing us to new pathogen reservoirs?
10. What is a principle way in which African hunters become exposed to infectious microbes?
11. Where are new pandemics likely to come from and why?
12. How have modern societies offered new ways for killer disease to flourish and spread?
13. What is "disease forecasting" and why is it important?

Internet References

Evolution and Medicine Network
   http://evmedreview.com
The Evolution & Medicine Review
   http://evmedreview.com

Article   Prepared by: Elvio Angeloni

The Inuit Paradox

How can people who gorge on fat and rarely see a vegetable be healthier than we are?

Patricia Gadsby

Learning Outcomes

After reading this article, you will be able to:

- Describe some healthful habits we can learn by studying hunter-gatherers.

- Identify the traditional Inuit (Eskimo) practices that are important for their survival in the circumstances they live in and contrast them with the values professed by the society you live in.

Patricia Cochran, an Inupiat from Northwestern Alaska, is talking about the native foods of her childhood: "We pretty much had a subsistence way of life. Our food supply was right outside our front door. We did our hunting and foraging on the Seward Peninsula and along the Bering Sea."

"Our meat was seal and walrus, marine mammals that live in cold water and have lots of fat. We used seal oil for our cooking and as a dipping sauce for food. We had moose, caribou, and reindeer. We hunted ducks, geese, and little land birds like quail, called ptarmigan. We caught crab and lots of fish—salmon, whitefish, tomcod, pike, and char. Our fish were cooked, dried, smoked, or frozen. We ate frozen raw whitefish, sliced thin. The elders liked stinkfish, fish buried in seal bags or cans in the tundra and left to ferment. And fermented seal flipper, they liked that too."

Cochran's family also received shipments of whale meat from kin living farther north, near Barrow. Beluga was one she liked; raw muktuk, which is whale skin with its underlying blubber, she definitely did not. "To me it has a chew-on-a-tire consistency," she says, "but to many people it's a mainstay." In the short subarctic summers, the family searched for roots and

greens and, best of all from a child's point of view, wild blueberries, crowberries, or salmonberries, which her aunts would mix with whipped fat to make a special treat called *akutuq*—in colloquial English, Eskimo ice cream.

Now Cochran directs the Alaska Native Science Commission, which promotes research on native cultures and the health and environmental issues that affect them. She sits at her keyboard in Anchorage, a bustling city offering fare from Taco Bell to French cuisine. But at home Cochran keeps a freezer filled with fish, seal, walrus, reindeer, and whale meat, sent by her family up north, and she and her husband fish and go berry picking—"sometimes a challenge in Anchorage," she adds, laughing. "I eat fifty-fifty," she explains, half traditional, half regular American.

No one, not even residents of the northernmost villages on Earth, eats an entirely traditional northern diet anymore. Even the groups we came to know as Eskimo—which include the Inupiat and the Yupiks of Alaska, the Canadian Inuit and Inuvialuit, Inuit Greenlanders, and the Siberian Yupiks—have probably seen more changes in their diet in a lifetime than their ancestors did over thousands of years. The closer people live to towns and the more access they have to stores and cash-paying jobs, the more likely they are to have westernized their eating. And with westernization, at least on the North American continent, comes processed foods and cheap carbohydrates—Crisco, Tang, soda, cookies, chips, pizza, fries. "The young and urbanized," says Harriet Kuhnlein, director of the Centre for Indigenous Peoples' Nutrition and Environment at McGill University in Montreal, "are increasingly into fast food." So much so that type 2 diabetes, obesity, and other diseases of Western civilization are becoming causes for concern there too.

Today, when diet books top the best-seller list and nobody seems sure of what to eat to stay healthy, it's surprising to learn how well the Eskimo did on a high-protein, high-fat diet. Shaped by glacial temperatures, stark landscapes, and protracted winters, the traditional Eskimo diet had little in the way of plant food, no agricultural or dairy products, and was unusually low in carbohydrates. Mostly people subsisted on what they hunted and fished. Inland dwellers took advantage of caribou feeding on tundra mosses, lichens, and plants too tough for humans to stomach (though predigested vegetation in the animals' paunches became dinner as well). Coastal people exploited the sea. The main nutritional challenge was avoiding starvation in late winter if primary meat sources became too scarce or lean.

These foods hardly make up the "balanced" diet most of us grew up with, and they look nothing like the mix of grains, fruits, vegetables, meat, eggs, and dairy we're accustomed to seeing in conventional food pyramid diagrams. How could such a diet possibly be adequate? How did people get along on little else but fat and animal protein?

The diet of the far north shows that there are no essential foods—only essential nutrients.

What the diet of the Far North illustrates, says Harold Draper, a biochemist and expert in Eskimo nutrition, is that there are no essential foods—only essential nutrients. And humans can get those nutrients from diverse and eye-opening sources.

One might, for instance, imagine gross vitamin deficiencies arising from a diet with scarcely any fruits and vegetables. What furnishes vitamin A, vital for eyes and bones? We derive much of ours from colorful plant foods, constructing it from pigmented plant precursors called carotenoids (as in carrots). But vitamin A, which is oil soluble, is also plentiful in the oils of cold-water fishes and sea mammals, as well as in the animals' livers, where fat is processed. These dietary staples also provide vitamin D, another oil-soluble vitamin needed for bones. Those of us living in temperate and tropical climates, on the other hand, usually make vitamin D indirectly by exposing skin to strong sun—hardly an option in the Arctic winter—and by consuming fortified cow's milk, to which the indigenous northern groups had little access until recent decades and often don't tolerate all that well.

As for vitamin C, the source in the Eskimo diet was long a mystery. Most animals can synthesize their own vitamin C, or ascorbic acid, in their livers, but humans are among the exceptions, along with other primates and oddballs like guinea pigs and bats. If we don't ingest enough of it, we fall apart from scurvy, a gruesome connective-tissue disease.

In the United States today we can get ample supplies from orange juice, citrus fruits, and fresh vegetables. But vitamin C oxidizes with time; getting enough from a ship's provisions was tricky for early 18th- and 19th-century voyagers to the polar regions. Scurvy—joint pain, rotting gums, leaky blood vessels, physical and mental degeneration—plagued European and U.S. expeditions even in the 20th century. However, Arctic peoples living on fresh fish and meat were free of the disease.

Impressed, the explorer Vilhjalmur Stefansson adopted an Eskimo-style diet for five years during the two Arctic expeditions he led between 1908 and 1918. "The thing to do is to find your antiscorbutics where you are," he wrote. "Pick them up as you go." In 1928, to convince skeptics, he and a young colleague spent a year on an Americanized version of the diet under medical supervision at Bellevue Hospital in New York City. The pair ate steaks, chops, organ meats like brain and liver, poultry, fish, and fat with gusto. "If you have some fresh meat in your diet every day and don't overcook it," Stefansson declared triumphantly, "there will be enough C from that source alone to prevent scurvy."

In fact, all it takes to ward off scurvy is a daily dose of 10 milligrams, says Karen Fediuk, a consulting dietitian and former graduate student of Harriet Kuhnlein's who did her master's thesis on vitamin C. (That's far less than the U.S. recommended daily allowance of 75 to 90 milligrams— 75 for women, 90 for men.) Native foods easily supply those 10 milligrams of scurvy prevention, especially when organ meats—preferably raw—are on the menu. For a study published with Kuhnlein in 2002, Fediuk compared the vitamin C content of 100-gram (3.55-ounce) samples of foods eaten by Inuit women living in the Canadian Arctic: Raw caribou liver supplied almost 24 milligrams, seal brain close to 15 milligrams, and raw kelp more than 28 milligrams. Still higher levels were found in whale skin and muktuk.

As you might guess from its antiscorbutic role, vitamin C is crucial for the synthesis of connective tissue, including the matrix of skin. "Wherever collagen's made, you can expect vitamin C," says Kuhnlein. Thick skinned, chewy, and collagen rich, raw muktuk can serve up an impressive 36 milligrams in a 100-gram piece, according to Fediuk's analyses. "Weight for weight, it's as good as orange juice," she says. Traditional Inuit practices like freezing meat and fish and frequently eating them raw, she notes, conserve vitamin C, which is easily cooked off and lost in food processing.

Hunter-gatherer diets like those eaten by these northern groups and other traditional diets based on nomadic herding or subsistence farming are among the older approaches to human eating. Some of these eating plans might seem strange to us— diets centered around milk, meat, and blood among the East African pastoralists, enthusiastic tuber eating by the

Quechua living in the High Andes, the staple use of the mongongo nut in the southern African !Kung—but all proved resourceful adaptations to particular eco-niches. No people, though, may have been forced to push the nutritional envelope further than those living at Earth's frozen extremes. The unusual makeup of the far-northern diet led Loren Cordain, a professor of evolutionary nutrition at Colorado State University at Fort Collins, to make an intriguing observation.

Four years ago, Cordain reviewed the macronutrient content (protein, carbohydrates, fat) in the diets of 229 hunter-gatherer groups listed in a series of journal articles collectively known as the Ethnographic Atlas. These are some of the oldest surviving human diets. In general, hunter-gatherers tend to eat more animal protein than we do in our standard Western diet, with its reliance on agriculture and carbohydrates derived from grains and starchy plants. Lowest of all in carbohydrate, and highest in combined fat and protein, are the diets of peoples living in the Far North, where they make up for fewer plant foods with extra fish. What's equally striking, though, says Cordain, is that these meat-and-fish diets also exhibit a natural "protein ceiling." Protein accounts for no more than 35 to 40 percent of their total calories, which suggests to him that's all the protein humans can comfortably handle.

Wild-animal fats are different from other fats. Farm animals typically have lots of highly saturated fat.

This ceiling, Cordain thinks, could be imposed by the way we process protein for energy. The simplest, fastest way to make energy is to convert carbohydrates into glucose, our body's primary fuel. But if the body is out of carbs, it can burn fat, or if necessary, break down protein. The name given to the convoluted business of making glucose from protein is gluconeogenesis. It takes place in the liver, uses a dizzying slew of enzymes, and creates nitrogen waste that has to be converted into urea and disposed of through the kidneys. On a truly traditional diet, says Draper, recalling his studies in the 1970s, Arctic people had plenty of protein but little carbohydrate, so they often relied on gluconeogenesis. Not only did they have bigger livers to handle the additional work but their urine volumes were also typically larger to get rid of the extra urea. Nonetheless, there appears to be a limit on how much protein the human liver can safely cope with: Too much overwhelms the liver's waste-disposal system, leading to protein poisoning—nausea, diarrhea, wasting, and death.

Whatever the metabolic reason for this syndrome, says John Speth, an archaeologist at the University of Michigan's Museum of Anthropology, plenty of evidence shows that hunters through the ages avoided protein excesses, discarding fat-depleted animals even when food was scarce. Early pioneers and trappers in North America encountered what looks like a similar affliction, sometimes referred to as rabbit starvation because rabbit meat is notoriously lean. Forced to subsist on fat-deficient meat, the men would gorge themselves, yet wither away. Protein can't be the sole source of energy for humans, concludes Cordain. Anyone eating a meaty diet that is low in carbohydrates must have fat as well.

Stefansson had arrived at this conclusion, too, while living among the Copper Eskimo. He recalled how he and his Eskimo companions had become quite ill after weeks of eating "caribou so skinny that there was no appreciable fat behind the eyes or in the marrow." Later he agreed to repeat the miserable experience at Bellevue Hospital, for science's sake, and for a while ate nothing but defatted meat. "The symptoms brought on at Bellevue by an incomplete meat diet [lean without fat] were exactly the same as in the Arctic . . . diarrhea and a feeling of general baffling discomfort," he wrote. He was restored with a fat fix but "had lost considerable weight." For the remainder of his year on meat, Stefansson tucked into his rations of chops and steaks with fat intact. "A normal meat diet is not a high-protein diet," he pronounced. "We were really getting three-quarters of our calories from fat." (Fat is more than twice as calorie dense as protein or carbohydrate, but even so, that's a lot of lard. A typical U.S diet provides about 35 percent of its calories from fat.)

Stefansson dropped 10 pounds on his meat-and-fat regimen and remarked on its "slenderizing" aspect, so perhaps it's no surprise he's been co-opted as a posthumous poster boy for Atkins-type diets. No discussion about diet these days can avoid Atkins. Even some researchers interviewed for this article couldn't resist referring to the Inuit way of eating as the "original Atkins." "Superficially, at a macronutrient level, the two diets certainly look similar," allows Samuel Klein, a nutrition researcher at Washington University in St. Louis, who's attempting to study how Atkins stacks up against conventional weight-loss diets. Like the Inuit diet, Atkins is low in carbohydrates and very high in fat. But numerous researchers, including Klein, point out that there are profound differences between the two diets, beginning with the type of meat and fat eaten.

Fats have been demonized in the United States, says Eric Dewailly, a professor of preventive medicine at Laval University in Quebec. But all fats are not created equal. This lies at the heart of a paradox—the Inuit paradox, if you will. In the Nunavik villages in northern Quebec, adults over 40 get almost half their calories from native foods, says Dewailly, and they don't die of heart attacks at nearly the same rates as other Canadians or Americans. Their cardiac death rate is about half of ours, he says. As someone who looks for links between diet and cardiovascular health, he's intrigued by that reduced risk. Because the traditional Inuit diet is "so restricted," he says, it's easier to study than the famously heart-healthy Mediterranean diet, with its cornucopia of vegetables, fruits, grains, herbs, spices, olive oil, and red wine.

A key difference in the typical Nunavik Inuit's diet is that more than 50 percent of the calories in Inuit native foods come from fats. Much more important, the fats come from wild animals.

Wild-animal fats are different from both farm-animal fats and processed fats, says Dewailly. Farm animals, cooped up and stuffed with agricultural grains (carbohydrates) typically have lots of solid, highly saturated fat. Much of our processed food is also riddled with solid fats, or so-called trans fats, such as the reengineered vegetable oils and shortenings cached in baked goods and snacks. "A lot of the packaged food on supermarket shelves contains them. So do commercial french fries," Dewailly adds.

Trans fats are polyunsaturated vegetable oils tricked up to make them more solid at room temperature. Manufacturers do this by hydrogenating the oils—adding extra hydrogen atoms to their molecular structures—which "twists" their shapes. Dewailly makes twisting sound less like a chemical transformation than a perversion, an act of public-health sabotage: "These man-made fats are dangerous, even worse for the heart than saturated fats." They not only lower high-density lipoprotein cholesterol (HDL, the "good" cholesterol) but they also raise low-density lipoprotein cholesterol (LDL, the "bad" cholesterol) and triglycerides, he says. In the process, trans fats set the stage for heart attacks because they lead to the increase of fatty buildup in artery walls.

Wild animals that range freely and eat what nature intended, says Dewailly, have fat that is far more healthful. Less of their fat is saturated, and more of it is in the monounsaturated form (like olive oil). What's more, cold-water fishes and sea mammals are particularly rich in polyunsaturated fats called n-3 fatty acids or omega-3 fatty acids. These fats appear to benefit the heart and vascular system. But the polyunsaturated fats in most Americans' diets are the omega-6 fatty acids supplied by vegetable oils. By contrast, whale blubber consists of 70 percent monounsaturated fat and close to 30 percent omega-3s, says Dewailly.

Dieting is the price we pay for too little exercise and too much mass-produced food.

Omega-3s evidently help raise HDL cholesterol, lower triglycerides, and are known for anticlotting effects. (Ethnographers have remarked on an Eskimo propensity for nosebleeds.) These fatty acids are believed to protect the heart from life-threatening arrhythmias that can lead to sudden cardiac death. And like a "natural aspirin," adds Dewailly, omega-3 polyunsaturated fats help put a damper on runaway inflammatory processes, which play a part in atherosclerosis, arthritis, diabetes, and other so-called diseases of civilization.

You can be sure, however, that Atkins devotees aren't routinely eating seal and whale blubber. Besides the acquired taste problem, their commerce is extremely restricted in the United States by the Marine Mammal Protection Act, says Bruce Holub, a nutritional biochemist in the department of human biology and nutritional sciences at the University of Guelph in Ontario.

"In heartland America it's probable they're not eating in an Eskimo-like way," says Gary Foster, clinical director of the Weight and Eating Disorders Program at the Pennsylvania School of Medicine. Foster, who describes himself as open-minded about Atkins, says he'd nonetheless worry if people saw the diet as a green light to eat all the butter and bacon—saturated fats—they want. Just before rumors surfaced that Robert Atkins had heart and weight problems when he died, Atkins officials themselves were stressing saturated fat should account for no more than 20 percent of dieters' calories. This seems to be a clear retreat from the diet's original don't-count-the-calories approach to bacon and butter and its happy exhortations to "plow into those prime ribs." Furthermore, 20 percent of calories from saturated fats is *double* what most nutritionists advise. Before plowing into those prime ribs, readers of a recent edition of the *Dr. Atkins' New Diet Revolution* are urged to take omega-3 pills to help protect their hearts. "If you watch carefully," says Holub wryly, "you'll see many popular U.S. diets have quietly added omega-3 pills, in the form of fish oil or flaxseed capsules, as supplements."

Needless to say, the subsistence diets of the Far North are not "dieting." Dieting is the price we pay for too little exercise and too much mass-produced food. Northern diets were a way of life in places too cold for agriculture, where food, whether hunted, fished, or foraged, could not be taken for granted. They were about keeping weight on.

This is not to say that people in the Far North were fat: Subsistence living requires exercise—hard physical work. Indeed, among the good reasons for native people to maintain their old way of eating, as far as it's possible today, is that it provides a hedge against obesity, type 2 diabetes, and heart disease. Unfortunately, no place on Earth is immune to the spreading taint of growth and development. The very well-being of the northern food chain is coming under threat from global warming, land development, and industrial pollutants in the marine environment. "I'm a pragmatist," says Cochran, whose organization is involved in pollution monitoring and disseminating food-safety information to native villages. "Global warming we don't have control over. But we can, for example, do cleanups of military sites in Alaska or of communication cables leaching lead into fish-spawning areas. We can help communities make informed food choices. A young woman of childbearing age may choose not to eat certain organ meats that concentrate contaminants. As individuals, we do have options. And eating our salmon and our seal is still a heck of a better option than pulling something processed that's full of additives off a store shelf."

Not often in our industrial society do we hear someone speak so familiarly about "our" food animals. We don't talk of "our pig" and "our beef." We've lost that creature feeling, that sense of kinship with food sources. "You're taught to think in boxes," says Cochran. "In our culture the connectivity between humans, animals, plants, the land they live on, and the air they share is ingrained in us from birth.

"You truthfully can't separate the way we get our food from the way we live," she says. "How we get our food is intrinsic to our culture. It's how we pass on our values and knowledge to the young. When you go out with your aunts and uncles to hunt or to gather, you learn to smell the air, watch the wind, understand the way the ice moves, know the land. You get to know where to pick which plant and what animal to take."

"It's part, too, of your development as a person. You share food with your community. You show respect to your elders by offering them the first catch. You give thanks to the animal that gave up its life for your sustenance. So you get all the physical activity of harvesting your own food, all the social activity of sharing and preparing it, and all the spiritual aspects as well," says Cochran. "You certainly don't get all that, do you, when you buy prepackaged food from a store."

"That's why some of us here in Anchorage are working to protect what's ours, so that others can continue to live back home in the villages," she adds. "Because if we don't take care of our food, it won't be there for us in the future. And if we lose our foods, we lose who we are." The word Inupiat means "the real people." "That's who we are," says Cochran.

Critical Thinking

1. What kinds of diseases are on the increase among the Inuit and why?

2. Discuss the traditional high-protein, high-fat diet. How does this compare with the "balanced diet" most of us grew up with? What does this mean, according to Harold Draper?

3. Discuss the contrasting sources of vitamins A, D, and C between our diet and the diet of the Inuit. What is the advantage of eating meat and fish raw?

4. What is a "protein ceiling" and why? How did hunter-gatherers cope with the problem?

5. Where do the more healthful fats (monounsaturated and omega-3 fatty acids) come from? What are their benefits?

6. Why is it that Atkins-dieters are not really eating in an "Eskimo-like way"?

7. What are the differences between the subsistence diets of the Far North and "dieting"?

8. Were people of the Far North fat? Why not? In what ways did the old way of eating protect them?

9. How is the northern food chain threatened?

10. In what sense is there a kinship with food sources in the Far North that our industrial societies does not have and why? Why is it also a part of one's development as a person?

Internet References

The Paleolithic Diet Page
www.paleodiet.com

The Institute for Intercultural Studies
www.interculturalstudies.org/main.html

Article   Prepared by: Elvio Angeloni

The Food Addiction

PAUL J. KENNY

Learning Outcomes

After reading this article, you will be able to:

- Discuss the biological basis and evolutionary context of food addiction.

- Discuss the similarities between food addiction and drug addiction.

Would a rat risk dying just to satisfy its desire for chocolate?

I recently found out that in my laboratory, we gave rats unlimited access to their standard fare as well as to a mini cafeteria full of appetizing, high-calorie foods: sausage, cheesecake, chocolate. The rats decreased their intake of the healthy but bland items and switched to eating the cafeteria food almost exclusively. They gained weight. They became obese.

We then warned the rats as they were eating—by flashing a light—that they would receive a nasty foot shock. Rats eating the bland chow would quickly stop and scramble away, but time and again the obese rats continued to devour the rich food, ignoring the warning they had been trained to fear. Their hedonic desire overruled their basic sense of self-preservation.

Our finding mirrored a previous trial by Barry Everitt of the University of Cambridge—only his rats were hooked on cocaine.

So are the fat rats addicted to food? An inability to suppress a behavior, despite the negative consequences, is common in addiction. Scientists are finding similar compulsiveness in certain people. Almost all obese individuals say they want to consume less, yet they continue to overeat even though they know that doing so can have shockingly negative health or social consequences. Studies show that overeating juices up the reward systems in our brain—so much so in some people that it overpowers the brain's ability to tell them to stop eating when they have had enough. As with alcoholics and drug addicts, the more

they eat, the more they want. Whether overeating is technically an addiction, if it stimulates the same brain circuits as drug use, in the same way, then medications that dial down the reward system could help obese people to eat less.

Suspicious Hormones

Until the early 1990s, society viewed obesity solely as a behavioral disorder: overweight individuals lacked willpower and self-control. Since then, the view has changed dramatically, in the scientific community at least.

The first change in opinion arose from pioneering work by Douglas Coleman of the Jackson Laboratory in Bar Harbor, Me., and by Jeffrey Friedman of the Rockefeller University. Experiments with two strains of mice, both genetically prone to obesity and diabetes, determined what drove the mice to overeat. The researchers discovered that one strain had a genetic defect in fat cells that secrete a hormone called leptin. Mice, like humans, normally secrete leptin after a meal to suppress appetite and prevent overeating. The obese mice had a leptin deficiency—and an insatiable appetite. Researchers later found that obesity in the second strain of mice was caused by a genetic defect in their ability to respond to leptin and regulate its actions. The findings seemed to make it clear that hormones regulate appetite and therefore body weight. A hormonal imbalance could lead to overeating; indeed, obesity runs rampant in certain human families that have a genetic deficiency in leptin.

Two observations suggest that viewing obesity as a hormone disorder is too simplistic, however. First, only a small number of obese people in the U.S. and elsewhere have a genetic deficiency in appetite-related hormones. Second, we would expect blood tests of obese people to show either a lower level of hormones that suppress appetite or a higher level of hormones that increase appetite. Yet the reverse is true. Obese individuals generally have a paradoxically high level of appetite-suppressing hormones, including leptin and insulin.

This is where the concept of food addiction comes into play. Appetite-controlling hormones affect certain pathways of neurons—feeding circuits—in the hypothalamus. They also affect systems in the brain that control feelings of reward, which makes perfect sense. If you have not eaten for many hours, you will spend a great deal of time, effort, and money to obtain food—and it will taste very good! As the old adage says, "Hunger is the best sauce."

During periods of hunger, hormones heighten the reactivity of food-related reward circuits in the brain, particularly in the striatum. The striatum contains high concentrations of endorphins—chemicals that enhance feelings of pleasure and reward.

As you eat, your stomach and gut release appetite-suppressing hormones that decrease pleasure signals that are triggered by the striatum and other components of the reward system. This process makes food seem less attractive, and you may switch your activity away from eating and toward other pursuits. Appetite-regulating hormones control feeding, in part by modulating the pleasurable experience of consuming a meal.

Yet some modern, appetizing foods—dense in fat and sugar and often visually appealing—affect reward systems strongly enough to override the appetite-suppressing hormones, thus prompting us to eat. These foods activate our reward circuits more powerfully than leptin's ability to shut them down. All of us have experienced this effect: you have just finished a big dinner and could not possibly eat another bite. Yet when the chocolate cake appears, you can miraculously "find room" for one last morsel—one that happens to be the most calorie-laden of the day.

Therein lies the rub. We have evolved an efficient brain system to help maintain a healthy and consistent body weight by signaling when it is time to eat and when it is time to stop. But highly appetizing foods can often override these signals and drive weight gain.

Our body responds to the override by elevating the blood levels of appetite-suppressing hormones such as leptin and insulin higher and higher as body weight increases; yet, the hormones become progressively less effective as the body develops tolerance to their actions. Moreover, brain-imaging studies by researchers at Brookhaven National Laboratory and the Oregon Research Institute show that the brain's reward systems in overweight individuals respond weakly to food, even to junk food. These muffled reward circuits depress mood. How does an individual overcome this funk? By eating more delectable food to gain a temporary boost, thereby perpetuating the cycle. Obese individuals may overeat just to experience the same degree of pleasure that lean individuals enjoy from less food.

Obesity, it seems, is not caused by a lack of willpower. And it is not always caused by an imbalance in hormones. In some cases at least, obesity may be caused by hedonic overeating that hijacks the brain's reward networks. Like addictive drugs, overeating creates a feedback loop in the brain's reward centers—the more you consume, the more you crave, and the harder it is for you to satisfy that craving.

But does that make hedonic eating an addiction?

Tolerance and Relapse

Drugs of abuse, such as morphine, stimulate the brain's reward systems the way food does. Yet the similarities do not end there. When morphine is injected into the striatum of rats, it triggers binge-like overeating, even in rats that have been fed to satiety. This response shows that morphine and other opiates mimic the effects of neurotransmitters (brain chemicals) such as endorphins that are naturally produced in the brain to stimulate feeding behaviors.

We might expect, then, that drugs that block the action of endorphins could reduce hedonic overeating. Recent studies have shown that endorphin blockers do lessen the activation of reward circuits in humans and rodents that are presented with appetizing food—the subjects eat less. The blockers can also reduce heroin, alcohol, and cocaine use in human drug addicts, supporting the idea that common mechanisms regulate hedonic overeating and addictive drug use. Strikingly, rats that binge on food every day display behaviors that closely resemble withdrawal, a symptom of drug addiction, after they are treated with endorphin blockers. This behavior raises the remarkable notion that hedonic overeating can induce a drug-dependence-like state.

These discoveries add credence to the idea that overeating in some circumstances may share core features of drug addiction. We see the same similarities with another basic neurotransmitter: dopamine. All known addictive drugs lead to the release of dopamine into the striatum. Dopamine is central to motivation, spurring people to seek the drug. Most experts maintain that this action drives the development of addiction, although the precise mechanisms are hotly debated. It turns out that appetizing food also stimulates the release of dopamine into the striatum, motivating people to focus on obtaining and consuming food. Imaging studies reveal that the striatum of obese individuals shows low levels of a receptor that responds to dopamine, termed the dopamine D2 receptor (D2R). The same holds true for those suffering from alcoholism or from opiate, cocaine, or meth-amphetamine addiction.

We now also know that people who are born with reduced levels of D2R are at greater genetic risk of developing obesity and drug addiction. The condition results in lower levels of activity in the brain's reward systems, suggesting that these individuals may overeat just to obtain the same level of pleasure from food as those who do not have D2R deficits. These people also tend to have trouble learning to avoid actions that have negative consequences; brain systems involved in suppressing risky yet rewarding behaviors, such as consuming high-calorie food or using drugs, may not work as effectively.

Our lab study of rats backs up this idea. The obese rats that ate the cafeteria food regardless of warnings about being shocked had reduced levels of D2R in their striatum. Our study and others demonstrate that drug use in addicted rats and hedonic eating in overweight rats persist even when the animals face negative consequences. Many obese individuals struggle so badly with their poor food choices that they will voluntarily undergo potentially dangerous procedures, such as gastric bypass surgery, to help them control their eating. Yet very often they will relapse to overeating and gain weight.

This cycle of engaging in a bad habit that gives short-term pleasure, then attempting to abstain from it and eventually relapsing, sounds disturbingly like drug addiction. Given the latest research, it seems that obesity is caused by an overpowering motivation to satisfy the reward centers—the pleasure centers—of the brain. The hormonal and metabolic disturbances in obese individuals may be a consequence of weight gain rather than a cause.

New Treatments Possible

The similarities between obesity and addiction have led certain experts to say that the two conditions should be treated in the same manner. Some of them recommended that obesity be included in the most recent update to the Diagnostic and Statistical Manual of Mental Disorders—the bible of psychiatry that provides guidelines for diagnosing mental illnesses, known as the DSM-5. This proposal sparked lively debate among neuroscientists and psychiatrists, but arbiters for the DSM-5 ultimately dropped the idea, largely to avoid labeling obese people, in essence, as mentally ill.

Caution may have been warranted because despite the parallels, obesity and addiction differ in important ways. For example, if food is addictive, then surely it must contain some unique component that drives the addiction—the nicotine of junk food, if you will. Work by Nicole Avena of the University of Florida, the late Bartley Hoebel of Princeton University and others lends some credence to the idea that particular fats or sugars may be responsible. A small study by David Ludwig of Boston Children's Hospital suggests that highly processed, quickly digested carbohydrates could trigger cravings. But research overall indicates that no one ingredient stokes addiction-like behaviors. Rather the combination of fats and sugars, together with calorie content, seems to maximize food's "hedonic impact."

Other experts, including Hisham Ziauddeen, I. Sadaf Farooqi and Paul C. Fletcher of the University of Cambridge, do not think that tolerance and withdrawal occur in obese people the way they do in drug addicts. They argue that obesity and drug addiction are fundamentally different. This view is debatable, however. If obese individuals must eat more and more to overcome reduced activation of reward networks in the brain, that sounds a lot like tolerance. And weight loss can trigger negative mood and depression, much like that experienced by former addicts who try to practice abstinence, suggesting that withdrawal may be in effect.

Other experts have argued that the entire notion of food addiction is preposterous because we are all, in a sense, addicted to food. If we were not, we would not survive.

The difference in obesity, I would suggest, is that modern high-calorie foods can overwhelm our biological feedback networks in a way that other foods cannot. During millions of years of evolution, the major concern of humans was not suppressing appetite but hunting, collecting, or growing enough food to persist during lean times. Perhaps our feeding circuits are better at motivating food intake when we are hungry than they are at suppressing food intake when we are full. It is easy to imagine that the brain would regard overeating of high-calorie food as tremendously beneficial if it is unclear when food will again be available. Perhaps this behavior is no longer adaptive and could even be counterproductive in a world where food is bountiful.

The scientists who argue against an addiction model of obesity make reasonable points, and I also fear that the term "addiction" comes loaded with unhelpful preconceptions. Still, compulsive eating and compulsive drug use seem to share obvious features, most notably an inability to control consumption. It is up to scientists to determine if these similarities are superficial or stem from common, underlying alterations in the brain. More important will be determining whether the addiction model is useful. Unless it helps us design new treatment approaches, the debate is simply an academic exercise.

For an addiction model to have value, it should make accurate predictions about treatment options, including new medications. One example comes from Arena Pharmaceuticals, which recently obtained approval from the U.S. Food and Drug Administration to market a drug called Belviq for weight loss in obese or overweight adults. The drug stimulates a brain protein called the serotonin 2C receptor, which reduces the desire to consume nicotine in lab rats.

Another drug is rimonabant, which had been approved in Europe to help curb appetite in obese individuals. The drug exploits the well-known property of cannabis to increase desire for food—the so-called munchies. Cannabis activates a brain protein called the cannabinoid receptor 1, so researchers reasoned that inhibiting that receptor would decrease desire for food. Rimonabant does exactly that. A notable side effect is its ability to decrease tobacco users' desire to smoke. In rats, the drug also decreases the desire to use alcohol, opiates and stimulants such as cocaine.

As with all potentially therapeutic drugs, however, caution is required. Rimonabant has triggered depression and thoughts of suicide in some individuals. This finding led European authorities to suspend its use and prompted U.S. officials to not approve it. Why depression emerged is still unclear. Thus, although an addiction model of obesity could yield unexpected treatments, those modalities must be thoroughly scrutinized.

Before scientists can declare that overeating is or is not an addiction, they will have to identify precisely which networks and cellular adaptations in the brain drive compulsive drug use and then determine if the same mechanisms also motivate compulsive food intake. It is possible, even likely, that addiction networks for cocaine and for food operate in different parts of the brain yet use similar mechanisms. Scientists will also have to determine if common genetic variations, such as those that affect D2R, contribute to drug addiction and obesity. Identifying such genes may reveal new targets for medications to treat both disorders.

Even if scientists prove that obesity can stem from an addiction to food, and we find that anti-addiction medications can help people lose weight, obese individuals will have to struggle with one factor that seems now to be endemic in America: they will probably be surrounded by overweight family members, friends and co-workers who are still overeating, putting them in the same difficult environment they were in before. As we know from recovering drug addicts and alcoholics, environmental cues are a major cause of craving and relapse. Western society, saturated in fat and temptation, will make it hard for any obese person to quit.

Critical Thinking

1. Discuss the evidence that food addiction is much like alcohol and drug addiction.

2. Discuss the biological basis for addiction.

3. In what respects are modern appetizing foods conducive to addiction? What evidence is there that drugs of abuse have the same effect?

4. Discuss the effects of administering drugs that block the action of endorphins in treating drug addiction as well as food addiction.

5. Discuss the evidence that shows that dopamine plays a role in both drug and food addiction?

6. What is it about the modern diet that seems to trigger addiction, in other words, what is the "nicotine of junk food?"

7. In what ways are the symptoms of drug and food addiction similar?

8. Discuss the evolutionary context of food addiction.

Internet References

Evolution and Medicine Network
http://evmedreview.com

The Paleolithic Diet Page
www.paleodiet.com

PAUL J. KENNY is an associate professor at the Scripps Research Institute in Jupiter, Fla. His laboratory investigates the mechanisms of drug addiction, obesity, and schizophrenia, as well as medications for these disorders.

Article   Prepared by: Elvio Angeloni

The Evolution of Diet

ANN GIBBONS

Learning Outcomes

After reading this article, you will be able to:

- Discuss the popularity of the caveman or Stone Age diet.
- Discuss the "stew of misconceptions" regarding the Paleo diet.
- Discuss the question as to whether or not we are still evolving.
- Discuss the effect that eating meat and, later, food processing in general have had on humans.

It's suppertime in the Amazon of lowland Bolivia, and Ana Cuata Maito is stirring a porridge of plantains and sweet manioc over afire smoldering on the dirt floor of her thatched hut, listening for the voice of her husband as he returns from the forest with his scrawny hunting dog.

With an infant girl nursing at her breast and a seven-year-old boy tugging at her sleeve, she looks spent when she tells me that she hopes her husband, Deonicio Nate, will bring home meat tonight. "The children are sad when there is no meat," Maito says through an interpreter, as she swats away mosquitoes.

Nate left before dawn on this day in January with his rifle and machete to get an early start on the two-hour trek to the old-growth forest. There he silently scanned the canopy for brown capuchin monkeys and raccoonlike coatis, while his dog sniffed the ground for the scent of pig-like peccaries or reddish brown capybaras. If he was lucky, Nate would spot one of the biggest packets of meat in the forest—tapirs, with long, prehensile snouts that rummage for buds and shoots among the damp ferns.

This evening, however, Nate emerges from the forest with no meat. At 39, he's an energetic guy who doesn't seem easily defeated—when he isn't hunting or fishing or weaving palm fronds into roof panels, he's in the woods carving a new canoe from a log. But when he finally sits down to eat his porridge from a metal bowl, he complains that it's hard to get enough meat

for his family: two wives (not uncommon in the tribe) and 12 children. Loggers are scaring away the animals. He can't fish on the river because a storm washed away his canoe.

The story is similar for each of the families I visit in Anachere, a community of about 90 members of the ancient Tsimane Indian tribe. It's the rainy season, when it's hardest to hunt or fish. More than 15,000 Tsimane live in about a hundred villages along two rivers in the Amazon Basin near the main market town of San Borja, 225 miles from La Paz. But Anachere is a two-day trip from San Borja by motorized dugout canoe, so the Tsimane living there still get most of their food from the forest, the river, or their gardens.

I'm traveling with Asher Rosinger, a doctoral candidate who's part of a team, co-led by biological anthropologist William Leonard of Northwestern University, studying the Tsimane to document what a rain forest diet looks like. They're particularly interested in how the Indians' health changes as they move away from their traditional diet and active lifestyle and begin trading forest goods for sugar, salt, rice, oil, and increasingly, dried meat and canned sardines. This is not a purely academic inquiry. What anthropologists are learning about the diets of indigenous peoples like the Tsimane could inform what the rest of us should eat.

Rosinger introduces me to a villager named José Mayer Cunay, 78, who, with his son Felipe Mayer Lero, 39, has planted a lush garden by the river over the past 30 years. José leads us down a trail past trees laden with golden papayas and mangoes, clusters of green plantains, and orbs of grapefruit that dangle from branches like earrings. Vibrant red "lobster claw" heliconia flowers and wild ginger grow like weeds among stalks of corn and sugarcane. "José's family has more fruit than anyone," says Rosinger.

Yet in the family's open-air shelter Felipe's wife, Catalina, is preparing the same bland porridge as other households. When I ask if the food in the garden can tide them over when there's little meat, Felipe shakes his head. "It's not enough to live on," he says. "I need to hunt and fish. My body doesn't want to eat just these plants."

As we look to 2050, when we'll need to feed two billion more people, the question of which diet is best has taken on new urgency. The foods we choose to eat in the coming decades will have dramatic ramifications for the planet. Simply put, a diet that revolves around meat and dairy, a way of eating that's on the rise throughout the developing world, will take a greater toll on the world's resources than one that revolves around unrefined grains, nuts, fruits, and vegetables.

Until agriculture was developed around 10,000 years ago, all humans got their food by hunting, gathering, and fishing. As farming emerged, nomadic hunter-gatherers gradually were pushed off prime farmland, and eventually they became limited to the forests of the Amazon, the arid grasslands of Africa, the remote islands of Southeast Asia, and the tundra of the Arctic. Today only a few scattered tribes of hunter-gatherers remain on the planet.

That's why scientists are intensifying efforts to learn what they can about an ancient diet and way of life before they disappear. "Hunter-gatherers are not living fossils," says Alyssa Crittenden, a nutritional anthropologist at the University of Nevada, Las Vegas, who studies the diet of Tanzania's Hadza people, some of the last true hunter-gatherers. "That being said, we have a small handful of foraging populations that remain on the planet. We are running out of time. If we want to glean any information on what a nomadic, foraging lifestyle looks like, we need to capture their diet now."

So far studies of foragers like the Tsimane, Arctic Inuit, and Hadza have found that these peoples traditionally didn't develop high blood pressure, atherosclerosis, or cardiovascular disease. "A lot of people believe there is a discordance between what we eat today and what our ancestors evolved to eat," says paleo-anthropologist Peter Ungar of the University of Arkansas. The notion that we're trapped in Stone Age bodies in a fast-food world is driving the current craze for Paleolithic diets. The popularity of these so-called caveman or Stone Age diets is based on the idea that modern humans evolved to eat the way hunter-gatherers did during the Paleolithic—the period from about 2.6 million years ago to the start of the agricultural revolution—and that our genes haven't had enough time to adapt to farmed foods.

A Stone Age diet "is the one and only diet that ideally fits our genetic makeup," writes Loren Cordain, an evolutionary nutritionist at Colorado State University in his book *The Paleo Diet: Lose Weight and Get Healthy by Eating the Foods You Were Designed to Eat.* After studying the diets of living hunter-gatherers and concluding that 73 percent of these societies derived more than half their calories from meat, Cordain came up with his own Paleo prescription: Eat plenty of lean meat and fish but not dairy products, beans, or cereal grains—foods introduced into our diet after the invention of cooking and agriculture. Paleo-diet advocates like Cordain say that if we stick to the foods our hunter-gatherer ancestors once ate, we can avoid the diseases of civilization, such as heart disease, high blood pressure, diabetes, cancer, even acne.

That sounds appealing. But is it true that we all evolved to eat a meat-centric diet? Both paleontologists studying the fossils of our ancestors and anthropologists documenting the diets of indigenous people today say the picture is a bit more complicated. The popular embrace of a Paleo diet, Ungar and others point out, is based on a stew of misconceptions.

Meat has played a starring role in the evolution of the human diet. Raymond Dart, who in 1924 discovered the first fossil of a human ancestor in Africa, popularized the image of our early ancestors hunting meat to survive on the African savanna. Writing in the 1950s, he described those humans as "carnivorous creatures, that seized living quarries by violence, battered them to death . . . slaking their ravenous thirst with the hot blood of victims and greedily devouring livid writhing flesh."

Eating meat is thought by some scientists to have been crucial to the evolution of our ancestors' larger brains about two million years ago. By starting to eat calorie-dense meat and marrow instead of the low-quality plant diet of apes, our direct ancestor, *Homo erectus,* took in enough extra energy at each meal to help fuel a bigger brain. Digesting a higher quality diet and less bulky plant fiber would have allowed these humans to have much smaller guts. The energy freed up as a result of smaller guts could be used by the greedy brain, according to Leslie Aiello, who first proposed the idea with paleoanthropologist Peter Wheeler. The brain requires 20 percent of a human's energy when resting; by comparison, an ape's brain requires only 8 percent. This means that from the time of *H. erectus,* the human body has depended on a diet of energy-dense food—especially meat.

Fast-forward a couple of million years to when the human diet took another major turn with the invention of agriculture. The domestication of grains such as sorghum, barley, wheat, corn, and rice created a plentiful and predictable food supply, allowing farmers' wives to bear babies in rapid succession—one every 2.5 years instead of one every 3.5 years for hunter-gatherers. A population explosion followed; before long, farmers outnumbered foragers.

Over the past decade anthropologists have struggled to answer key questions about this transition. Was agriculture a clear step forward for human health? Or in leaving behind our hunter-gatherer ways to grow crops and raise livestock, did we give up a healthier diet and stronger bodies in exchange for food security?

When biological anthropologist Clark Spencer Larsen of Ohio State University describes the dawn of agriculture, it's a grim picture. As the earliest farmers became dependent on crops, their diets became far less nutritionally diverse than hunter-gatherers' diets. Eating the same domesticated grain every day gave early farmers cavities and periodontal disease rarely found in hunter-gatherers, says Larsen. When farmers began domesticating animals, those cattle, sheep, and goats became sources of milk and meat but also of parasites and new infectious diseases. Farmers suffered from iron deficiency and developmental delays, and they shrank in stature.

Despite boosting population numbers, the lifestyle and diet of farmers were clearly not as healthy as the lifestyle and diet of hunter-gatherers. That farmers produced more babies, Larsen says, is simply evidence that "you don't have to be disease free to have children."

The real Paleolithic diet, though, wasn't all meat and marrow. It's true that hunter-gatherers around the world crave meat more than any other food and usually get around 30 percent of their annual calories from animals. But most also endure lean times when they eat less than a handful of meat each week. New studies suggest that more than a reliance on meat in ancient human diets fueled the brain's expansion.

Year-round observations confirm that hunter-gatherers often have dismal success as hunters. The Hadza and Kung bushmen of Africa, for example, fail to get meat more than half the time when they venture forth with bows and arrows. This suggests it was even harder for our ancestors who didn't have these weapons. "Everybody thinks you wander out into the savanna and there are antelopes everywhere, just waiting for you to bonk them on the head," says paleoanthropologist Alison Brooks of George Washington University, an expert on the Dobe Kung of Botswana. No one eats meat all that often, except in the Arctic, where Inuit and other groups traditionally got as much as 99 percent of their calories from seals, narwhals, and fish.

So how do hunter-gatherers get energy when there's no meat? It turns out that "man the hunter" is backed up by "woman the forager," who, with some help from children, provides more calories during difficult times. When meat, fruit, or honey is scarce, foragers depend on "fallback foods," says Brooks. The Hadza get almost 70 percent of their calories from plants. The Kung traditionally rely on tubers and mongongo nuts, the Aka and Baka Pygmies of the Congo River Basin on yams, the Tsimane and Yanomami Indians of the Amazon on plantains and manioc, the Australian Aboriginals on nut grass and water chestnuts.

"There's been a consistent story about hunting defining us and that meat made us human," says Amanda Henry, a paleobiologist at the Max Planck Institute for Evolutionary Anthropology in Leipzig. "Frankly, I think that misses half of the story. They want meat, sure. But what they actually live on is plant foods." What's more, she found starch granules from plants on fossil teeth and stone tools, which suggests humans may have been eating grains, as well as tubers, for at least 100,000 years—long enough to have evolved the ability to tolerate them.

The notion that we stopped evolving in the Paleolithic period simply isn't true. Our teeth, jaws, and faces have gotten smaller, and our DNA has changed since the invention of agriculture. "Are humans still evolving? Yes!" says geneticist Sarah Tishkoff of the University of Pennsylvania.

One striking piece of evidence is lactose tolerance. All humans digest mother's milk as infants, but until cattle began being domesticated 10,000 years ago, weaned children no longer needed to digest milk. As a result, they stopped making the enzyme lactase, which breaks down the lactose into simple sugars. After humans began herding cattle, it became tremendously advantageous to digest milk, and lactose tolerance evolved independently among cattle herders in Europe, the Middle East, and Africa. Groups not dependent on cattle, such as the Chinese and Thai, the Pima Indians of the American Southwest, and the Bantu of West Africa, remain lactose intolerant.

Humans also vary in their ability to extract sugars from starchy foods as they chew them, depending on how many copies of a certain gene they inherit. Populations that traditionally ate more starchy foods, such as the Hadza, have more copies of the gene than the Yakut meat-eaters of Siberia, and their saliva helps break down starches before the food reaches their stomachs.

These examples suggest a twist on "You are what you eat." More accurately, you are what your ancestors ate. There is tremendous variation in what foods humans can thrive on, depending on genetic inheritance. Traditional diets today include the vegetarian regimen of India's Jains, the meat-intensive fare of Inuit, and the fish-heavy diet of Malaysia's Bajau people. The Nochmani of the Nicobar Islands off the coast of India get by on protein from insects. "What makes us human is our ability to find a meal in virtually any environment," says the Tsimane study co-leader Leonard.

Studies suggest that indigenous groups get into trouble when they abandon their traditional diets and active lifestyles for Western living. Diabetes was virtually unknown, for instance, among the Maya of Central America until the 1950s. As they've switched to a Western diet high in sugars, the rate of diabetes has skyrocketed. Siberian nomads such as the Evenk reindeer herders and the Yakut ate diets heavy in meat, yet they had almost no heart disease until after the fall of the Soviet Union, when many settled in towns and began eating market foods. Today about half the Yakut living in villages are overweight, and almost a third have hypertension, says Leonard. And Tsimane people who eat market foods are more prone to diabetes than those who still rely on hunting and gathering.

For those of us whose ancestors were adapted to plant-based diets—and who have desk jobs—it might be best not to eat as much meat as the Yakut. Recent studies confirm older findings that although humans have eaten red meat for two million years, heavy consumption increases atherosclerosis and cancer in most populations—and the culprit isn't just saturated fat or cholesterol. Our gut bacteria digest a nutrient in meat called L-carnitine. In one mouse study, digestion of L-carnitine boosted artery-clogging plaque. Research also has shown that the human immune system attacks a sugar in red meat that's called Neu5Gc, causing inflammation that's low level in the young but that eventually could cause cancer. "Red meat is great, if you want to live to 45," says Ajit Varki of the University of California, San Diego, lead author of the Neu5Gc study.

Many paleoanthropologists say that although advocates of the modern Paleolithic diet urge us to stay away from unhealthy processed foods, the diet's heavy focus on meat doesn't replicate the diversity of foods that our ancestors ate—or take into account the active lifestyles that protected them from heart disease and diabetes. "What bothers a lot of paleoanthropologists is that we actually didn't have just one caveman diet," says Leslie Aiello, president of the Wenner-Gren Foundation for Anthropological Research in New York City. "The human diet goes back at least two million years. We had a lot of cavemen out there."

In other words, there is no one ideal human diet. Aiello and Leonard say the real hallmark of being human isn't our taste for meat but our ability to adapt to many habitats—and to be able to combine many different foods to create many healthy diets. Unfortunately the modern Western diet does not appear to be one of them.

The latest clue as to why our modern diet may be making us sick comes from Harvard primatologist Richard Wrangham, who argues that the biggest revolution in the human diet came not when we started to eat meat but when we learned to cook. Our human ancestors who began cooking sometime between 1.8 million and 400,000 years ago probably had more children who thrived, Wrangham says. Pounding and heating food "predigests" it, so our guts spend less energy breaking it down, absorb more than if the food were raw, and thus extract more fuel for our brains. "Cooking produces soft, energy-rich foods," says Wrangham. Today we can't survive on raw, unprocessed food alone, he says. We have evolved to depend upon cooked food.

To test his ideas, Wrangham and his students fed raw and cooked food to rats and mice. When I visited Wrangham's lab at Harvard, his then graduate student, Rachel Carmody, opened the door of a small refrigerator to show me plastic bags filled with meat and sweet potatoes, some raw and some cooked. Mice raised on cooked foods gained 15 to 40 percent more weight than mice raised only on raw food.

If Wrangham is right, cooking not only gave early humans the energy they needed to build bigger brains but also helped them get more calories from food so that they could gain weight. In the modern context the flip side of his hypothesis is that we may be victims of our own success. We have gotten so good at processing foods that for the first time in human evolution, many humans are getting more calories than they burn in a day. "Rough breads have given way to Twinkies, apples to apple juice," he writes. "We need to become more aware of the calorie-raising consequences of a highly processed diet."

It's this shift to processed foods, taking place all over the world, that's contributing to a rising epidemic of obesity and related diseases. If most of the world ate more local fruits and vegetables, a little meat, fish, and some whole grains (as in the highly touted Mediterranean diet), and exercised an hour a day, that would be good news for our health—and for the planet.

On my last afternoon visiting the Tsimane in Anachere, one of Deonicio Nate's daughters, Albania, 13, tells us that her father and half-brother Alberto, 16, are back from hunting and that they've got something. We follow her to the cooking hut and smell the animals before we see them—three raccoonlike coatis have been laid across the fire, fur, and all. As the fire singes the coatis' striped pelts, Albania and her sister, Emiliana, 12, scrape off fur until the animals' flesh is bare. Then they take the carcasses to a stream to clean and prepare them for roasting.

Nate's wives are cleaning two armadillos as well, preparing to cook them in a stew with shredded plantains. Nate sits by the fire, describing a good day's hunt. First he shot the armadillos as they napped by a stream. Then his dog spotted a pack of coatis and chased them, killing two as the rest darted up a tree. Alberto fired his shotgun but missed. He fired again and hit a coati. Three coatis and two armadillos were enough, so father and son packed up and headed home.

As family members enjoy the feast, I watch their little boy, Alfonso, who had been sick all week. He is dancing around the fire, happily chewing on a cooked piece of coati tail. Nate looks pleased. Tonight in Anachere, far from the diet debates, there is meat, and that is good.

Science prevented the last food crisis. Can it save us again?

Critical Thinking

1. What kinds of health problems have indigenous groups experienced when abandoning their traditional diets?

2. Why is there no one ideal human diet?

3. What was the biggest revolution in the human diet and what have been some of its consequences?

Internet References

The Future of Food
http://food.nationalgeographic.com/

Journal of Human Evolution
http://www.journals.elsevier.com/journal-of-human-evolution/

ANN GIBBONS is the author of *The First Human: The Race to Discover Our Earliest Ancestors*.

Article   Prepared by: Elvio Angeloni

The Science of Good and Evil

What Makes People Especially Giving or Cruel? Researchers Say the Way Our Brains Are Wired Can Affect How Much Empathy We Feel for Others.

YUDHIJIT BHATTACHARJEE

Learning Outcomes

After reading this article, you will be able to:

- Discuss the human tendencies toward both altruism and psychopathy in terms of our evolutionary past.

- Discuss the evidence for biological predispositions for both empathy and an "active disregard for others."

- Discuss the ways in which psychopathic behavior can be prevented or, at least, treated.

From the kitchen window of her mobile home in Auburn, Illinois, Ashley Aldridge had a clear view of the railroad crossing about a hundred yards away.

When the 19-year-old mother first saw the man in the wheelchair, she had just finished feeding lunch to her two children, aged one and three, and had moved on to washing dishes—one more in an endless string of chores. Looking up, Aldridge noticed that the wheelchair wasn't moving. It was stuck between the tracks. The man was yelling for help as a motorcycle and two cars went by without stopping.

Aldridge hurried out to ask a neighbor to watch her kids so she could go help. Then she heard the train horn and the clanging of the crossing gate as it came down, signaling that a train was on its way. She ran, barefoot, over a gravel path along the tracks. When she got to the man, the train was less than half a mile away, bearing down at about 80 miles an hour. Failing to dislodge the wheelchair, she wrapped her arms around the man's chest from behind and tried to lift him, but couldn't. As the train barreled toward them, she pulled with a mighty heave. She fell backward, yanking him out of the chair. Within seconds, the train smashed the wheelchair, carrying fragments of steel and plastic half a mile up the track.

The man Aldridge saved that afternoon in September 2015 was a complete stranger. Her unflinching determination to save him despite the threat to her own life sets her apart from many. Aldridge's heroic rescue is an example of what scientists call extreme altruism—selfless acts to help those unrelated to oneself at the risk of grave personal harm. Not surprisingly, many of these heroes—such as Roi Klein, an Israeli army major who jumped on a live grenade to save his men—work in professions in which endangering one's life to protect others is part of the job. But others are ordinary men and women—like Rick Best, Taliesin Namkai-Meche, and Micah Fletcher, who intervened to defend two young women, one wearing a hijab, from a man spewing anti-Muslim abuse at them on a commuter train in Portland, Oregon. All three were stabbed; only Fletcher survived.

Contrast these noble acts with the horrors that humans commit: murder, rape, kidnapping, torture. Consider the carnage perpetrated by the man who sprayed bullets from the 32nd floor of the Mandalay Bay hotel in Las Vegas, Nevada, in October at a country music festival. Three weeks later, officials put the casualty toll at 58 dead and 546 wounded. Or think about the chilling ruthlessness of a serial killer like Todd Kohlhepp, a real estate agent in South Carolina, who appears to have left clues about his murderous habit in bizarre online reviews for products, including a folding shovel: "keep in car for when you have to hide the bodies." In spite of how aberrant these horrors are, they occur often enough to remind us of a dark truth: humans are capable of unspeakable cruelty.

Extreme altruists and psychopaths exemplify our best and worst instincts. On one end of the moral spectrum, sacrifice, generosity, and other ennobling traits that we recognize as good and on the other end, selfishness, violence, and destructive impulses that we see as evil. At the root of both types of behaviors, researchers say, is our evolutionary past. They hypothesize that humans—and many other species, to a lesser degree—evolved the desire to help one another because cooperation within large social groups was essential to survival. But because groups had to compete for resources, the willingness to maim and possibly kill opponents was also crucial. "We are the most social species on Earth, and we are also the most violent species on Earth," says Jean Decety, a social neurologist at the University of Chicago. "We have two faces because these two faces were important to survival."

For centuries, the question of how good and evil originate and manifest in us was a matter of philosophical or religious debate. But in recent decades, researchers have made significant advances toward understanding the science of what drives good and evil. Both seem to be linked to a key emotional trait: empathy, which is an intrinsic ability of the brain to experience how another person is feeling. Researchers have found that empathy is the kindling that fires compassion in our hearts, impelling us to help others in distress. Studies also have traced violent, psychopathic, and antisocial behaviors to a lack of empathy, which appears to stem from impaired neural circuits. These new insights are laying the foundation for training regimens and treatment programs that aim to enhance the brain's empathic response.

Researchers once thought young children had no concern for the well-being of others—a logical conclusion if you've seen a toddler's tantrums. But recent findings show that babies feel empathy long before their first birthday. Maayan Davidov, a psychologist at Hebrew University of Jerusalem, and her colleagues have conducted some of these studies, analyzing the behavior of children as they witness somebody in distress—a crying child, an experimenter, or their own mother pretending to be hurt. Even before six months of age, many infants respond to such stimuli with facial expressions reflecting concern; some also exhibit caring gestures such as leaning forward and trying to communicate with the one in distress. In their first year, infants also show signs of trying to understand the suffering they're seeing. Eighteen-month-olds often translate their empathy into such positive social behavior as giving a hug or a toy to comfort a hurt child.

That's not true of all children, however. In a small minority, starting in the second year of life, researchers see what they call an "active disregard" of others. "When someone reported that someone had hurt themselves," says Carolyn Zahn-Waxler, a researcher at the University of Wisconsin–Madison, "these children would kind of laugh at them or even kind of swipe at them and say, 'You're not hurt,' or 'You should be more careful'—saying it in a tone of voice that was judgmental." Following these toddlers into adolescence, Zahn-Waxler and her colleague Soo Hyun Rhee, a psychologist at the University of Colorado Boulder, found they had a high likelihood of developing antisocial tendencies and getting into trouble.

Other studies have measured callousness and lack of emotional expression in adolescents using questions such as whether the subject feels remorseful upon doing something wrong. Those with high scores for "callous–unemotional" traits tend to have frequent and severe behavioral problems—showing extreme aggression in fights, for instance, or vandalizing property. Researchers have also found that some of these adolescents end up committing major crimes such as murder, rape, and violent robbery. Some are prone to becoming full-blown psychopaths as adults—individuals with cold, calculating hearts who wouldn't flinch while perpetrating the most horrific acts imaginable. (Most psychopaths are men.)

If the empathy deficit at the core of psychopathic behaviors can be traced all the way back to toddlerhood, does evil reside in the genes, coiled up like a serpent in the DNA, waiting to strike? The answer isn't a categorical yes or no. As it is with many illnesses, both nature and nurture have a hand. Studies of twins have established that callous–unemotional traits displayed by some young children and adolescents arise to a substantial degree from genes they inherit. Yet in a study of 561 children born to mothers with a history of antisocial behaviors, researchers found that those living with adoptive families that provided a warm and nurturing environment were far less likely to exhibit callous–unemotional traits than those with adoptive families that were not as nurturing.

Children born with genes making it more likely that they will have difficulty empathizing are often unable to get a break. "You can imagine that if you have a child who doesn't show affection in the same way as a typically developing child, doesn't show empathy, that child will evoke very different reactions in the people around them—the parents, the teachers, the peers—than a child who's more amenable, more empathetic," says Essi Viding, a research psychologist at University College London. "And many of these children, of course, reside within their biological families, so they often have this double whammy of having parents who are perhaps less well equipped for many of the parenting tasks, are less good at empathizing, less good at regulating their own emotions."

The firefighters tried desperately to save the six Philpott children from their burning house in Derby, England, in the early hours of May 11, 2012. But the heat and smoke were so intense that only one of the kids was alive when rescuers finally made their way upstairs where they had been sleeping. That boy, too, perished two days later in the hospital. The police suspected arson based on evidence that the fire had been started by pouring gasoline through the door's mail slot.

Derby residents raised money to help the children's parents—Mick and Mairead Philpott—pay for a funeral. At a news conference to thank the community, Philpott was sobbing and dabbing his eyes with a tissue that remained curiously dry. Leaving the event, he collapsed, but Derbyshire's assistant chief constable, walking behind, was struck by the unnaturalness of the behavior. Eighteen days later, the police arrested Philpott and his wife. Investigators determined that they had set fire to the house with an accomplice to frame Mick's mistress. A court found all three guilty of manslaughter.

Philpott's faking of grief and his lack of remorse are among the characteristics that define psychopaths, a category of individuals who have come to embody evil in the popular imagination. Psychopaths have utter disregard for the feelings of others, although they seem to learn to mimic emotions. "They really just have a complete inability to appreciate anything like empathy or guilt or remorse," says Kent Kiehl, a neuroscientist at the Mind Research Network and the University of New Mexico who was drawn to studying psychopathy in part because he grew up in a neighborhood that was once home to the serial killer Ted Bundy. These are people who are "just extremely different than the rest of us."

Kiehl has spent the past two decades exploring this difference by scanning the brains of prison inmates. (Nearly one in every five adult males in prison in the United States and Canada scores high in psychopathy, measured using a checklist of 20 criteria such as impulsivity and lack of remorse, compared with one of every 150 in the general male population.)

Using an MRI scanner installed inside a tractor trailer, Kiehl and his colleagues have imaged more than 4,000 prison inmates since 2007, measuring the activity in their brains as well as the size of different brain regions.

Psychopathic criminals show reduced activity in their brain's amygdala, a primary site of emotional processing, compared with nonpsychopathic inmates when recalling emotionally charged words they were shown moments earlier, such as "misery" and "frown." In a task designed to test moral decision-making, researchers ask inmates to rate the offensiveness of pictures flashed on a screen, such as a cross burning by the Ku Klux Klan or a face bloodied by a beating. Although the ratings by psychopathic offenders aren't that different from those by nonpsychopaths—they both recognize the moral violation in the pictures—psychopaths tend to show weaker activation in brain regions instrumental in moral reasoning.

Based on these and other, similar findings, Kiehl is convinced that psychopaths have impairments in a system of interconnected brain structures—including the amygdala and the orbitofrontal cortex—that help process emotions, make decisions, control impulses, and set goals. There is "basically about 5–7 percent less gray matter in those structures in individuals with high psychopathic traits compared to other inmates," Kiehl says. The psychopath appears to compensate for this deficiency by using other parts of the brain to cognitively simulate what really belongs in the realm of emotion. "That is, the psychopath must think about right and wrong while the rest of us feel it," Kiehl wrote in a paper he coauthored in 2011.

When abigail marsh, a psychologist at Georgetown University, was 19, her car skidded on a bridge after she swerved to avoid hitting a dog. The vehicle spun out of control and finally came to a stop in the fast lane, facing oncoming traffic. Marsh couldn't get the engine to start and was too afraid to get out, with cars and trucks rushing past the vehicle. A man pulled over, ran across the highway, and helped start the car. "He took an enormous risk running across the freeway. There's no possible explanation for it other than he just wanted to help," Marsh says. "How can anybody be moved to do something like that?"

Marsh kept turning that question over in her head. Not long after she began working at Georgetown, she wondered if the altruism shown by the driver on the bridge wasn't in some ways the polar opposite of psychopathy. She began looking for a group of exceptionally kind individuals to study and decided that altruistic kidney donors would make ideal subjects. These are people who've chosen to donate a kidney to a stranger, sometimes even incurring financial costs, yet receive no compensation in return.

Marsh and her colleagues brought 19 donors in from around the country for the study. The researchers showed each one a series of black-and-white photographs of facial expressions, some fearful, some angry, and others neutral, while their brains were scanned using an MRI machine to map both activity and structure.

When looking at fearful faces, donors showed a greater response in their right amygdala than a control group. Separately, the researchers found that their right amygdalas were, on average, 8 percent larger than those of the control group. Similar studies done previously on psychopathic subjects had found the opposite: the amygdalas in psychopathic brains are smaller and activated less than those in controls while reacting to frightened faces.

"Fearful expressions elicit concern and caring. If you're not responsive to that expression, you're unlikely to experience concern for other people," Marsh explains. "And altruistic kidney donors just seem to be very sensitive to other people's distress, with fear being the most acute kind of distress—maybe in part because their amygdalas are larger than average."

The majority of people in the world are neither extreme altruists nor psychopaths, and most individuals in any society do not ordinarily commit violent acts against one another. And yet, there are genocides—organized mass killings that require the complicity and passivity of large numbers of people. Time and again, social groups organized along ethnic, national, racial, and religious lines have savaged other groups. Nazi Germany's gas chambers extinguished millions of Jews, the Communist Khmer Rouge slaughtered fellow Cambodians in the killing fields, Hutu extremists in Rwanda wielding machetes slaughtered several hundred thousand Tutsis and moderate Hutus, and Islamic State terrorists massacred Iraq's Yazidis—virtually every part of the world appears to have suffered through a genocide. Events such as these provide ghastly evidence that evil can hold entire communities in its grip.

How the voice of conscience is rendered inconsequential to foot soldiers of a genocide can be partly understood through the prism of the well-known experiments conducted in the 1960s by the psychologist Stanley Milgram at Yale University. In those studies, subjects were asked to deliver electric shocks to a person in another room for failing to answer questions correctly, increasing the voltage with every wrong answer. At the prodding of a person in a lab coat who played the role of an experimenter, the subjects often dialed up the shocks to dangerously high voltage levels. The shocks weren't real, and the cries of pain heard by the subjects were prerecorded, but the subjects only found that out afterward. The studies demonstrated what Milgram described as "the extreme willingness of adults to go to almost any lengths on the command of an authority."

Gregory Stanton, a former U.S. State Department official and founder of Genocide Watch, a nonprofit that works to prevent mass murder, has identified the stages that can cause otherwise decent people to commit murder. It starts when demagogic leaders define a target group as "the other" and claim it is a threat to the interests of supporters. Discrimination follows, and soon the leaders characterize their targets as subhuman, eroding the in-group's empathy for "the other."

Next, society becomes polarized. "Those planning the genocide say, 'You are either with us or against us,'" says Stanton. This is followed by a phase of preparation, with the architects of the genocide drawing up death lists, stocking weapons, and planning how the rank and file are to execute the killings. Members of the out-group are sometimes forced to move into ghettos or concentration camps. Then the massacres begin.

Many of the perpetrators remain untouched by remorse, not because they are incapable of feeling it—as is the case with psychopathic killers—but because they find ways to rationalize the killings. James Waller, a genocide scholar at Keene State College in New Hampshire, says he got a glimpse of this "incredible capacity of the human mind to make sense of and to justify the worst of actions" when he interviewed dozens of Hutu men convicted or accused of committing atrocities during the Rwandan genocide. Some of them had hacked children, even those they personally knew, to death. Their rationale, according to Waller, was: "if I didn't do this, those children would have grown up to come back to kill me. This was something that was a necessity for my people to be safe, for my people to survive."

Our capacity to empathize and channel that into compassion may be innate, but it is not immutable. Neither is the tendency to develop psychopathic and antisocial personalities so fixed in childhood as to be unchangeable. In recent years, researchers have shown the feasibility of nipping evil in the bud as well as strengthening our positive social instincts.

The possibility of preventing violent teenage boys from hardening into lifelong criminals has been put to the test at the Mendota Juvenile Treatment Center in Wisconsin, a facility that houses serious offenders but is run more as a psychiatric unit than as a prison. The adolescents referred to the center come in with already long criminal histories—teenagers who are a threat to others. "These are folks who essentially have dropped out of the human race—they don't have any connection to anyone, and they are in a real antagonistic posture with everybody," says Michael Caldwell, a senior staff psychologist.

The center attempts to build a connection with the kids despite their aggressive and antisocial behaviors. Even when an inmate hurls feces or sprays urine at staff members—a common occurrence at many correctional institutions—the staff members keep treating the offender humanely. The kids are scored on a set of behavior rating scales every day. If they do well, they earn certain privileges the following day, such as a chance to play video games. If they score badly, say, by getting into a fight, they lose privileges. The focus is not on punishing bad behavior but on rewarding good conduct. That's different from most correctional institutions. Over time, the kids start to behave better, says Greg Van Rybroek, the center's director. Their callous–unemotional traits diminish. Their improved ability to manage their emotions and control their violent impulses seems to endure beyond the walls of Mendota. Adolescents treated in the program have committed far fewer and less violent offenses between two and six years after release than those treated elsewhere, the center's studies have found. "We don't have any magic," Van Rybroek says, "but we've actually created a system that considers the world from the youth's point of view and tries to break it down in a fair and consistent manner."

During the past decade, researchers have discovered that our social brain is plastic, even in adulthood, and that we can be trained to be more kind and generous. Tania Singer, a social neuroscientist at the Max Planck Institute for Human Cognitive and Brain Sciences in Leipzig, Germany, has pioneered studies demonstrating this.

Empathy and compassion use different networks in the brain, Singer and her colleagues found. Both can lead to positive social behavior, but the brain's empathic response to seeing another person suffer can sometimes lead to empathic distress—a negative reaction that makes the onlooker want to turn away from the sufferer to preserve his or her own sense of well-being.

To enhance compassion, which combines awareness of another's distress with the desire to alleviate it, Singer and her colleagues have tested the effects of various training exercises. A prominent exercise, derived from Buddhist traditions, involves having subjects meditate on a loved one—a parent or a child, for example—directing warmth and kindness toward that individual and gradually extending those same feelings toward acquaintances, strangers, and even enemies, in an ever widening circle of love. Singer's group has shown that subjects who trained in this form of loving-kindness meditation even for a few days had a more compassionate response—as measured by the activation of certain brain circuits—than untrained subjects, when watching short film clips of people suffering emotional distress.

In another study, Singer and her colleagues tested the effects of compassion training on helpfulness by using a computer game in which subjects guide a virtual character on a computer screen through a maze to a treasure chest, opening gates along the way. They can also choose to open gates for another character wandering about, looking for treasure. The researchers found that subjects who underwent compassion training were more helpful than those in a control group toward the other character—the equivalent of a stranger.

That we might be able to mold our brains to be more altruistic is an ennobling prospect for society. One way to bring that future closer, Singer believes, would be to include compassion training in schools. The result could be a more benevolent world, populated by people like Ashley Aldridge, in which reflexive kindness loses its extraordinariness and becomes a defining trait of humanity.

Critical Thinking

1. Why are people especially giving or cruel?
2. Is human behavior the result of biology, culture, or both? Explain.
3. What are the primary antidotes to bad behavior?

Internet References

Health Place
   https://www.healthyplace.com/personality-disorders/psychopath/psychopathic-children-psychopathic-behavior-in-children
Self-Assessment on Psychopathy
   https://www.counseling-office.com/surveys/test_psychopathy.phtml

Article   Prepared by: Elvio Angeloni

How PTSD Became a Problem Far Beyond the Battlefield

Though only 10 percent of American forces see combat, the U.S. military now has the highest rate of post-traumatic stress disorder in its history.

Sebastian Junger

Learning Outcomes

After reading this article, you will be able to:

- Explain, from an evolutionary perspective, why PTSD is exactly the response you want to have when your life is in danger.
- Explain why some people fail to overcome trauma.
- Discuss the biological and social root causes of PTSD and what that implies for a solution.

The first time I experienced what I now understand to be post-traumatic stress disorder, I was in a subway station in New York City, where I live. It was almost a year before the attacks of 9/11, and I'd just come back from two months in Afghanistan with Ahmad Shah Massoud, the leader of the Northern Alliance. I was on assignment to write a profile of Massoud, who fought a desperate resistance against the Taliban until they assassinated him two days before 9/11. At one point during my trip, we were on a frontline position that his forces had just taken over from the Taliban, and the inevitable counterattack started with an hour-long rocket barrage. All we could do was curl up in the trenches and hope. I felt deranged for days afterward, as if I'd lived through the end of the world.

By the time I got home, though, I wasn't thinking about that or any of the other horrific things we'd seen; I mentally buried all of it until one day, a few months later, when I went into the subway at rush hour to catch the C train downtown. Suddenly, I found myself backed up against a metal support column, absolutely convinced I was going to die. There were too many people on the platform, the trains were coming into the station too fast, the lights were too bright, the world was too loud. I couldn't quite explain what was wrong, but I was far more scared than I'd ever been in Afghanistan.

I stood there with my back to the column until I couldn't take it anymore, and then I sprinted for the exit and walked home. I had no idea that what I'd just experienced had anything to do with combat; I just thought I was going crazy. For the next several months, I kept having panic attacks whenever I was in a small place with too many people—airplanes, ski gondolas, crowded bars. Gradually the incidents stopped, and I didn't think about them again until I found myself talking to a woman at a picnic who worked as a psychotherapist. She asked whether I'd been affected by my war experiences, and I said no, I didn't think so. But for some reason I described my puzzling panic attack in the subway. "That's called post-traumatic stress disorder," she said. "You'll be hearing a lot more about that in the next few years."

I had classic short-term (acute) PTSD. From an evolutionary perspective, it's exactly the response you want to have when your life is in danger: you want to be vigilant, you want to react to strange noises, you want to sleep lightly and wake easily, you want to have flashbacks that remind you of the danger, and you want to be, by turns, anxious and depressed. Anxiety keeps you ready to fight, and depression keeps you from being too active and putting yourself at greater risk. This is a universal human adaptation to danger that is common to other mammals as well. It may be unpleasant, but it's preferable to getting eaten. (Because PTSD is so adaptive, many have begun leaving the word "disorder" out of the term to avoid stigmatizing a basically healthy reaction.)

Because PTSD is a natural response to danger, it's almost unavoidable in the short term and mostly self-correcting in the long term. Only about 20 percent of people exposed to trauma react with long-term (chronic) PTSD. Rape is one of the most psychologically devastating things that can happen to a person, for example—far more traumatizing than most military deployments—and, according to a 1992 study published in the *Journal of Traumatic Stress,* 94 percent of rape survivors exhibit signs of extreme trauma immediately afterward. And yet, nine months later 47 percent of rape survivors have recovered enough to resume living normal lives.

Combat is generally less traumatic than rape but harder to recover from. The reason, strangely, is that the trauma of combat is interwoven with other, positive experiences that become difficult to separate from the harm. "Treating combat veterans is different from treating rape victims, because rape victims don't have this idea that some aspects of their experience are worth retaining," says Dr. Rachel Yehuda, a professor of psychiatry and neuroscience and director of traumatic-stress studies at Mount Sinai Hospital in New York. Yehuda has studied PTSD in a wide range of people, including combat veterans and Holocaust survivors. "For most people in combat, their experiences range from the best to the worst of times," Yehuda adds. "It's the most important thing someone has ever done—especially since these people are so young when they go in—and it's probably the first time they're ever free, completely, of their societal constraints. They're going to miss being entrenched in this very important and defining world."

Oddly, one of the most traumatic events for soldiers is witnessing harm to other people—even to the enemy. In a survey done after the first Gulf War by David Marlowe, an expert in stress-related disorders working with the Department of Defense, combat veterans reported that killing an enemy soldier—or even witnessing one getting killed—was more distressing than being wounded oneself. But the very worst experience, by a significant margin, was having a friend die. In war after war, army after army, losing a buddy is considered to be the most distressing thing that can possibly happen. It serves as a trigger for psychological breakdown on the battlefield and re-adjustment difficulties after the soldier has returned home.

Terrible as such experiences are, however, roughly 80 percent of people exposed to them eventually recover, according to a 2008 study in the *Journal of Behavioral Medicine.* If one considers the extreme hardship and violence of our prehistory, it makes sense that humans are able to sustain enormous psychic damage and continue functioning; otherwise, our species would have died out long ago. "It is possible that our common generalized anxiety disorders are the evolutionary legacy of a world in which mild recurring fear was adaptive," writes anthropologist and neuroscientist Melvin Konner, in a collection called *Understanding Trauma.* "Stress is the essence of evolution by natural selection and close to the essence of life itself."

A 2007 analysis from the Institute of Medicine and the National Research Council found that, statistically, people who fail to overcome trauma tend to be people who are already burdened by psychological issues—either because they inherited them or because they suffered trauma or abuse as children. According to a 2003 study on high-risk twins and combat-related PTSD, if you fought in Vietnam and your twin brother did not—but suffers from psychiatric disorders—you are more likely to get PTSD after your deployment. If you experienced the death of a loved one, or even weren't held enough as a child, you are up to seven times more likely to develop the kinds of anxiety disorders that can contribute to PTSD, according to a 1989 study in the *British Journal of Psychiatry.* And according to statistics published in the *Journal of Consulting and Clinical Psychology* in 2000, if you have an educational deficit, if you are female, if you have a low I.Q., or if you were abused as a child, you are at an elevated risk of developing PTSD. These factors are nearly as predictive of PTSD as the severity of the trauma itself.

Suicide by combat veterans is often seen as an extreme expression of PTSD, but currently there is no statistical relationship between suicide and combat, according to a study published in April in the *Journal of the American Medical Association Psychiatry.* Combat veterans are no more likely to kill themselves than veterans who were never under fire. The much-discussed estimated figure of 22 vets a day committing suicide is deceptive: it was only in 2008, for the first time in decades, that the U.S. Army veteran suicide rate, though enormously tragic, surpassed the civilian rate in America. And even so, the majority of veterans who kill themselves are over the age of 50. Generally speaking, the more time that passes after a trauma, the less likely a suicide is to have anything to do with it, according to many studies. Among younger vets, deployment to Iraq or Afghanistan *lowers* the incidence of suicide because soldiers with obvious mental-health issues are less likely to be deployed with their units, according to an analysis published in *Annals of Epidemiology* in 2015. The most accurate predictor of post-deployment suicide, as it turns out, isn't combat or repeated deployments or losing a buddy but suicide attempts *before* deployment. The single most effective action the U.S. military could take to reduce veteran suicide would be to screen for pre-existing mental disorders.

It seems intuitively obvious that combat is connected to psychological trauma, but the relationship is a complicated one. Many soldiers go through horrific experiences but fare better than others who experienced danger only briefly, or not at all. Unmanned-drone pilots, for instance—who watch their missiles kill human beings by remote camera—have been calculated as having the same PTSD rates as pilots who fly actual combat missions in war zones, according to a 2013 analysis published in the *Medical Surveillance Monthly Report.* And even among regular infantry, danger and psychological breakdown during combat are not necessarily connected. During the 1973 Yom Kippur War, when Israel was invaded simultaneously by Egypt and Syria, rear-base troops in the Israeli military had psychological breakdowns at three times the rate of elite frontline troops, relative to their casualties. And during the air campaign of the first Gulf War, more than 80 percent of psychiatric casualties in the U.S. Army's VII Corps came from support units that took almost no incoming fire, according to a 1992 study on Army stress casualties.

Conversely, American airborne and other highly trained units in World War II had some of the lowest rates of psychiatric casualties of the entire military, relative to their number of wounded. A sense of helplessness is deeply traumatic to people, but high levels of training seem to counteract that so effectively that elite soldiers are psychologically insulated from even extreme risk. Part of the reason, it has been found, is that elite soldiers have higher-than-average levels of an amino acid called neuropeptide-Y, which acts as a chemical buffer against hormones that are secreted by the endocrine system during times of high stress. In one 1968 study, published in the *Archive of General Psychiatry,* Special Forces soldiers in Vietnam had levels of the stress hormone cortisol go down before an anticipated attack, while less experienced combatants saw their levels go up.

Shell Shock

All this is new science, however. For most of the nation's history, psychological effects of combat trauma have been variously attributed to neuroses, shell shock, or simple cowardice. When men have failed to obey orders due to trauma they have been beaten, imprisoned, "treated" with electroshock therapy, or simply shot as a warning to others. (For British troops, cowardice was a capital crime until 1930.) It was not until after the Vietnam War that the American Psychiatric Association listed combat trauma as an official diagnosis. Tens of thousands of vets were struggling with "Post-Vietnam Syndrome"—nightmares, insomnia, addiction, paranoia—and their struggle could no longer be written off to weakness or personal failings. Obviously, these problems could also affect war reporters, cops, firefighters, or anyone else subjected to trauma. In 1980, the A.P.A. finally included post-traumatic stress disorder in the third edition of the *Diagnostic and Statistical Manual of Mental Disorders.*

Thirty-five years after acknowledging the problem in its current form, the American military now has the highest PTSD rate in its history—and probably in the world. Horrific experiences are unfortunately universal, but long-term impairment from them is not, and despite billions of dollars spent on treatment, half of our Iraq and Afghanistan veterans have applied for permanent disability. Of those veterans treated, roughly a third have been diagnosed with PTSD. Since only about 10 percent of our armed forces actually see combat, the majority of vets claiming to suffer from PTSD seem to have been affected by something other than direct exposure to danger.

This is not a new phenomenon: decade after decade and war after war, American combat deaths have dropped steadily while trauma and disability claims have continued to rise. They are in an almost inverse relationship with each other. Soldiers in Vietnam suffered roughly one-quarter the casualty rate of troops in World War II, for example, but filed for disability at a rate that was nearly 50 percent higher, according to a 2013 report in the *Journal of Anxiety Disorders.* It's tempting to attribute this disparity to the toxic reception they had at home, but that doesn't seem to be the case. Today's vets claim three times the number of disabilities that Vietnam vets did despite a generally warm reception back home and a casualty rate that, thank God, is roughly one-third what it was in Vietnam. Today, most disability claims are for hearing loss, tinnitus, and PTSD—the latter two of which can be exaggerated or faked. Even the first Gulf War—which lasted only a hundred hours—produced nearly twice the disability rates of World War II. Clearly, there is a feedback loop of disability claims, compensation, and more disability claims that cannot go on forever.

Part of the problem is bureaucratic: in an effort to speed up access to benefits, in 2010 the Veterans Administration declared that soldiers no longer have to cite a specific incident—a firefight, a roadside bomb—in order to be eligible for disability compensation. He or she simply has to report being impaired in daily life. As a result, PTSD claims have reportedly risen 60 percent to 150,000 a year. Clearly, this has produced a system that is vulnerable to abuse and bureaucratic error. A recent investigation by the V.A.'s Office of Inspector General found that the higher a veteran's PTSD disability rating, the more treatment he or she tends to seek until achieving a rating of 100 percent, at which point treatment visits drop by 82 percent and many vets quit completely. In theory, the most traumatized people should be seeking more help, not less. It's hard to avoid the conclusion that some vets are getting treatment simply to raise their disability rating.

In addition to being an enormous waste of taxpayer money, such fraud, intentional or not, does real harm to the vets who truly need help. One Veterans Administration counselor I spoke with described having to physically protect someone in a PTSD support group because some other vets wanted to beat him up for faking his trauma. This counselor, who asked to remain anonymous, said that many combat veterans actively avoid the V.A. because they worry about losing their temper around patients who are milking the system. "It's the real deals—the guys who have seen the most—that this tends to bother," this counselor told me.

The majority of traumatized vets are *not* faking their symptoms, however. They return from wars that are safer than those their fathers and grandfathers fought, and yet far greater numbers of them wind up alienated and depressed. This is true even for people who didn't experience combat. In other words, the problem doesn't seem to be trauma on the battlefield so much as re-entry into society. Anthropological research from around the world shows that recovery from war is heavily influenced by the society one returns to, and there are societies that make that process relatively easy. Ethnographic studies on hunter-gatherer societies rarely turn up evidence of chronic PTSD among their warriors, for example, and oral histories of Native American warfare consistently fail to mention psychological trauma. Anthropologists and oral historians weren't expressly looking for PTSD, but the high frequency of warfare in these groups makes the scarcity of any mention of it revealing. Even the Israeli military—with mandatory national service and two generations of intermittent warfare—has by some measures a PTSD rate as low as 1 percent.

If we weed out the malingerers on the one hand and the deeply traumatized on the other, we are still left with enormous numbers of veterans who had utterly ordinary wartime experiences and yet feel dangerously alienated back home. Clinically speaking, such alienation is not the same thing as PTSD, but both seem to result from military service abroad, so it's understandable that vets and even clinicians are prone to conflating them. Either way, it makes one wonder exactly what it is about modern society that is so mortally dispiriting to come home to.

Soldier's Creed

Any discussion of PTSD and its associated sense of alienation in society must address the fact that many soldiers find themselves missing the war after it's over. That troubling fact can be found in written accounts from war after war, country after country, century after century. Awkward as it is to say, part of the trauma of war seems to be giving it up. There are ancient human behaviors in war—loyalty, inter-reliance, cooperation—that typify good soldiering and can't be easily found in modern society. This can produce a kind of nostalgia for the hard times that even civilians are susceptible to: after World War II, many Londoners claimed to miss the communal underground living that characterized life during the Blitz (despite the fact that

more than 40,000 civilians lost their lives). And the war that is missed doesn't even have to be a shooting war: "I am a survivor of the AIDS epidemic," a man wrote on the comment board of an online talk I gave about war. "Now that AIDS is no longer a death sentence, I must admit that I miss those days of extreme brotherhood . . . which led to deep emotions and understandings that are above anything I have felt since the plague years."

What all these people seem to miss isn't danger or loss, per se, but the closeness and cooperation that danger and loss often engender. Humans evolved to survive in extremely harsh environments, and our capacity for cooperation and sharing clearly helped us do that. Structurally, a band of hunter-gatherers and a platoon in combat are almost exactly the same: in each case, the group numbers between 30 and 50 individuals, they sleep in a common area, they conduct patrols, they are completely reliant on one another for support, comfort, and defense, and they share a group identity that most would risk their lives for. Personal interest is subsumed into group interest because personal survival is not possible without group survival. From an evolutionary perspective, it's not at all surprising that many soldiers respond to combat in positive ways and miss it when it's gone.

There are obvious psychological stresses on a person in a group, but there may be even greater stresses on a person in isolation. Most higher primates, including humans, are intensely social, and there are few examples of individuals surviving outside of a group. A modern soldier returning from combat goes from the kind of close-knit situation that humans evolved for into a society where most people work outside the home, children are educated by strangers, families are isolated from wider communities, personal gain almost completely eclipses collective good, and people sleep alone or with a partner. Even if he or she is in a family, that is not the same as belonging to a large, self-sufficient group that shares and experiences almost everything collectively. Whatever the technological advances of modern society—and they're nearly miraculous—the individual lifestyles that those technologies spawn may be deeply brutalizing to the human spirit.

"You'll have to be prepared to say that we are not a good society—that we are an *anti-human* society," anthropologist Sharon Abramowitz warned when I tried this theory out on her. Abramowitz was in Ivory Coast during the start of the civil war there in 2002 and experienced, firsthand, the extremely close bonds created by hardship and danger. "We are not good to each other. Our tribalism is about an extremely narrow group of people: our children, our spouse, maybe our parents. Our society is alienating, technical, cold, and mystifying. Our fundamental desire, as human beings, is to be close to others, and our society does not allow for that."

This is an old problem, and today's vets are not the first Americans to balk at coming home. A source of continual embarrassment along the American frontier—from the late 1600s until the end of the Indian Wars, in the 1890s—was a phenomenon known as "the White Indians." The term referred to white settlers who were kidnapped by Indians—or simply ran off to them—and became so enamored of that life that they refused to leave. According to many writers of the time, including Benjamin Franklin, the reverse never happened: Indians never ran off to join white society. And if a peace treaty required that a tribe give up their adopted members, these members would often have to be put under guard and returned home by force. Inevitably, many would escape to rejoin their Indian families. "Thousands of Europeans are Indians, and we have no examples of even one of those aborigines having from choice become European," wrote a French-born writer in America named Michel-Guillaume-Saint-Jean de Crèvecoeur in an essay published in 1782.

One could say that combat vets are the White Indians of today, and that they miss the war because it was, finally, an experience of human closeness that they can't easily find back home. Not the closeness of family, which is rare enough, but the closeness of community and tribe. The kind of closeness that gets endlessly venerated in Hollywood movies but only actually shows up in contemporary society when something goes wrong—when tornados obliterate towns or planes are flown into skyscrapers. Those events briefly give us a reason to act communally, and most of us do. "There is something to be said for using risk to forge social bonds," Abramowitz pointed out. "Having something to fight for, and fight through, is a good and important thing."

Certainly, the society we have created is hard on us by virtually every metric that we use to measure human happiness. This problem may disproportionately affect people, like soldiers, who are making a radical transition back home.

It is incredibly hard to measure and quantify the human experience, but some studies have found that many people in certain modern societies self-report high levels of happiness. And yet, numerous cross-cultural studies show that as affluence and urbanization rise in a given society, so do rates of depression, suicide, and schizophrenia (along with health issues such as obesity and diabetes). People in wealthy countries suffer unipolar depression at more than double the rate that they do in poor countries, according to a study by the World Health Organization, and people in countries with large income disparities—like the United States—run a much higher risk of developing mood disorders at some point in their lives. A 2006 cross-cultural study of women focusing on depression and modernization compared depression rates in rural and urban Nigeria and rural and urban North America, and found that women in rural areas of both countries were far less likely to get depressed than urban women. And urban American women—the most affluent demographic of the study—were the *most* likely to succumb to depression.

In America, the more assimilated a person is into contemporary society, the more likely he or she is to develop depression in his or her lifetime. According to a 2004 study in *The**Journal of Nervous and Mental Disease,* Mexicans born in the United States are highly assimilated into American culture and have much higher rates of depression than Mexicans born in Mexico. By contrast, Amish communities have an exceedingly low rate of reported depression because, in part, it is theorized, they have completely resisted modernization. They won't even drive cars. "The economic and marketing forces of modern society have engineered an environment promoting decisions that maximize consumption at the long-term cost of well-being," one survey of these studies, from the *Journal of Affective Disorders* in 2012, concluded. "In effect, humans have dragged a body with a long hominid history into an overfed, malnourished, sedentary, sunlight-deficient, sleep-deprived, competitive, inequitable and socially-isolating environment with dire consequences."

For more than half a million years, our recent hominid ancestors lived nomadic lives of extreme duress on the plains of East Africa, but the advent of agriculture changed that about 10,000 years ago. That is only 400 generations—not enough to adapt, genetically, to the changes in diet and society that ensued. Privately worked land and the accumulation of capital made humans less oriented toward group welfare, and the Industrial Revolution pushed society further in that direction. No one knows how the so-called Information Age will affect us, but there's a good chance that home technology and the Internet will only intensify our drift toward solipsism and alienation.

Meanwhile, many of the behaviors that had high survival value in our evolutionary past, like problem solving, cooperation, and inter-group competition, are still rewarded by bumps of dopamine and other hormones into our system. Those hormones serve to reinforce whatever behavior it was that produced those hormones in the first place. Group affiliation and cooperation were clearly adaptive because in many animals, including humans, they trigger a surge in levels of a neuropeptide called oxytocin. Not only does oxytocin create a glow of well-being in people, it promotes greater levels of trust and bonding, which unite them further still. Hominids that were rewarded with oxytocin for cooperating with one another must have out-fought, out-hunted, and out-bred the ones that didn't. Those are the hominids that modern humans are descended from.

According to one study published in *Science* in June 2010, this feedback loop of oxytocin and group loyalty creates an expectation that members will "self-sacrifice to contribute to in-group welfare." There may be no better description of a soldier's ethos than that sentence. One of the most noticeable things about life in the military is that you are virtually never alone: day after day, month after month, you are close enough to speak to, if not touch, a dozen or more people. You eat together, sleep together, laugh together, suffer together. That level of intimacy duplicates our evolutionary past very closely and must create a nearly continual oxytocin reward system.

Hero's Welcome

When soldiers return to modern society, they must go through—among other adjustments—a terrific oxytocin withdrawal. The chronic isolation of modern society begins in childhood and continues our entire lives. Infants in hunter-gatherer societies are carried by their mothers as much as 50 to 90 percent of the time, often in wraps that keep them strapped to the mother's back so that her hands are free. That roughly corresponds to carrying rates among other primates, according to primatologist and psychologist Harriet J. Smith. One can get an idea of how desperately important touch is to primates from a landmark experiment conducted in the 1950s by a psychologist and primatologist named Harry Harlow. Baby rhesus monkeys were separated from their mothers and presented with the choice of two kinds of surrogates: a cuddly mother made out of terry cloth or an uninviting mother made out of wire mesh. The wire-mesh mother, however, had a nipple that would dispense warm milk. The babies invariably took their nourishment quickly in order to rush back and cling to the terry-cloth mother, which had enough softness to provide the illusion of affection. But even that isn't enough for psychological health: in a separate experiment, more than 75 percent of female baby rhesus monkeys raised with terry-cloth mothers—as opposed to real ones—grew up to be abusive and neglectful to their own young.

In the 1970s, American mothers maintained skin-to-skin contact with their nine-month-old babies as little as 16 percent of the time, which is a level of contact that traditional societies would probably consider a form of child abuse. Also unthinkable would be the common practice of making young children sleep by themselves in their own room. In two American studies of middle-class families during the 1980s, 85 percent of young children slept alone—a figure that rose to 95 percent among families considered "well-educated." Northern European societies, including America, are the only ones in history to make very young children sleep alone in such numbers. The isolation is thought to trigger fears that make many children bond intensely with stuffed animals for reassurance. Only in Northern European societies do children go through the well-known developmental stage of bonding with stuffed animals; elsewhere, children get their sense of safety from the adults sleeping near them.

More broadly, in most human societies, almost nobody sleeps alone. Sleeping in family groups of one sort or another has been the norm throughout human history and is still commonplace in most of the world. Again, Northern European societies are among the few where people sleep alone or with a partner in a private room. When I was with American soldiers at a remote outpost in Afghanistan, we slept in narrow plywood huts where I could reach out and touch three other men from where I slept. They snored, they talked, they got up in the middle of the night to use the piss tubes, but we felt safe because we were in a group. The Taliban attacked the position regularly, and the most determined attacks often came at dawn. Another unit in a nearby valley was almost overrun and took 50 percent casualties in just such an attack. And yet I slept better surrounded by those noisy, snoring men than I ever did camping alone in the woods of New England.

Many soldiers will tell you that one of the hardest things about coming home is learning to sleep without the security of a group of heavily armed men around them. In that sense, being in a war zone with your platoon feels safer than being in an American suburb by yourself. I know a vet who felt so threatened at home that he would get up in the middle of the night to build fighting positions out of the living-room furniture. This is a radically different experience from what warriors in other societies go through, such as the Yanomami, of the Orinoco and Amazon Basins, who go to war with their entire age cohort and return to face, together, whatever the psychological consequences may be. As one anthropologist pointed out to me, trauma is usually a group experience, so trauma recovery should be a group experience as well. But in our society it's not.

"Our whole approach to mental health has been hijacked by pharmaceutical logic," I was told by Gary Barker, an anthropologist whose group, Promundo, is dedicated to understanding and preventing violence. "PTSD is a crisis of connection and disruption, not an illness that you carry within you."

This individualizing of mental health is not just an American problem, or a veteran problem; it affects everybody. A British anthropologist named Bill West told me that the extreme poverty of the 1930s and the collective trauma of the Blitz served to unify an entire generation of English people. "I link the experience of the Blitz to voting in the Labour Party in 1945, and the establishing of the National Health Service and a strong welfare state," he said. "Those policies were supported well into the 60s by all political parties. That kind of cultural cohesiveness, along with Christianity, was very helpful after the war. It's an open question whether people's problems are located in the individual. If enough people in society are sick, you have to wonder whether it isn't actually society that's sick."

Ideally, we would compare hunter-gatherer society to post-industrial society to see which one copes better with PTSD. When the Sioux, Cheyenne, and Arapaho fighters returned to their camps after annihilating Custer and his regiment at Little Bighorn, for example, were they traumatized and alienated by the experience—or did they fit right back into society? There is no way to know for sure, but less direct comparisons can still illuminate how cohesiveness affects trauma. In experiments with lab rats, for example, a subject that is traumatized—but not injured—after an attack by a larger rat usually recovers within 48 hours *unless it is kept in isolation,* according to data published in 2005 in *Neuroscience & Biobehavioral Reviews.* The ones that are kept apart from other rats are the only ones that develop long-term traumatic symptoms. And a study of risk factors for PTSD in humans closely mirrored those results. In a 2000 study in the *Journal of Consulting and Clinical Psychology,* "lack of social support" was found to be around two times more reliable at predicting who got PTSD and who didn't than the severity of the trauma itself. You could be mildly traumatized, in other words—on a par with, say, an ordinary rear-base deployment to Afghanistan—and experience long-term PTSD simply because of a lack of social support back home.

Anthropologist and psychiatrist Brandon Kohrt found a similar phenomenon in the villages of southern Nepal, where a civil war has been rumbling for years. Kohrt explained to me that there are two kinds of villages there: exclusively Hindu ones, which are extremely stratified, and mixed Buddhist/Hindu ones, which are far more open and cohesive. He said that child soldiers, both male and female, who go back to Hindu villages can remain traumatized for years, while those from mixed-religion villages tended to recover very quickly. "PTSD is a disorder of recovery, and if treatment only focuses on identifying symptoms, it pathologizes and alienates vets," according to Kohrt. "But if the focus is on family and community, it puts them in a situation of collective healing."

Israel is arguably the only modern country that retains a sufficient sense of community to mitigate the effects of combat on a mass scale. Despite decades of intermittent war, the Israel Defense Forces have a PTSD rate as low as 1 percent. Two of the foremost reasons have to do with national military service and the proximity of the combat—the war is virtually on their doorstep. "Being in the military is something that most people have done," I was told by Dr. Arieh Shalev, who has devoted the last 20 years to studying PTSD. "Those who come back from combat are reintegrated into a society where those experiences are very well understood. We did a study of 17-year-olds who had lost their father in the military, compared to those who had lost their fathers to accidents. The ones whose fathers died in combat did much better than those whose fathers hadn't."

According to Shalev, the closer the public is to the actual combat, the better the war will be understood and the less difficulty soldiers will have when they come home. The Israelis are benefiting from what could be called the shared public meaning of a war. Such public meaning—which would often occur in more communal, tribal societies—seems to help soldiers even in a fully modern society such as Israel. It is probably not generated by empty, reflexive phrases—such as "Thank you for your service"—that many Americans feel compelled to offer soldiers and vets. If anything, those comments only serve to underline the enormous chasm between military and civilian society in this country.

Another Israeli researcher, Reuven Gal, found that the perceived legitimacy of a war was more important to soldiers' general morale than was the combat readiness of the unit they were in. And that legitimacy, in turn, was a function of the war's physical distance from the homeland: "The Israeli soldiers who were abruptly mobilized and thrown into dreadful battles in the middle of Yom Kippur Day in 1973 had no doubts about the legitimacy of the war," Gal wrote in the *Journal of Applied Psychology* in 1986. "Many of those soldiers who were fighting in the Golan Heights against the flood of Syrian tanks needed only to look behind their shoulders to see their homes and remind themselves that they were fighting for their very survival."

In that sense, the Israelis are far more like the Sioux, Cheyenne, and Arapaho at Little Bighorn than they are like us. America's distance from her enemies means that her wars have generally been fought far away from her population centers, and as a result those wars have been harder to explain and justify than Israel's have been. The people who will bear the psychic cost of that ambiguity will, of course, be the soldiers.

A Bright Shining Lie

"I talked to my mom only one time from Mars," a Vietnam vet named Gregory Gomez told me about the physical and spiritual distance between his home and the war zone. Gomez is a pure-blooded Apache who grew up in West Texas. He says his grandfather was arrested and executed by Texas Rangers in 1915 because they wanted his land; they strung him from a tree limb, cut off his genitals, and stuffed them in his mouth. Consequently, Gomez felt no allegiance to the U.S. government, but he volunteered for service in Vietnam anyway. "Most of us Indian guys who went to Vietnam went because we were warriors," Gomez told me. "I did not fight for this country. I fought for Mother Earth. I wanted to experience combat. I wanted to know how I'd do."

Gomez was in a Marine Corps Force Recon unit, one of the most elite designations in the U.S. military. He was part of a four-man team that would insert by helicopter into enemy territory north of the DMZ and stay for two weeks at a time. They had no medic and no backup and didn't even dare eat C rations, because, Gomez said, they were afraid their body odor would give them away. They ate Vietnamese food and watched enemy soldiers pass just yards away in the dense jungle. "Everyone who has lived through something like that has lived through trauma, and you can never go back," he told me. "You are 17 or 18 or 19 and you just hit that wall. You become very old men."

American Indians, proportionally, have provided more soldiers to America's wars than almost any other ethnic group in this country. They are also the product of an ancient and vibrant warring culture that takes great pains to protect the warrior from society, and vice versa. Although those traditions have obviously broken down since the end of the Indian Wars, there may be something to be learned from the principles upon which they stand. When Gomez came home he essentially isolated himself for more than a decade. He didn't drink, and he lived a normal life except that occasionally he'd go to the corner store to get a soda and would wind up in Oklahoma or East Texas without any idea how he got there.

He finally started seeing a therapist at the V.A. as well as undergoing traditional Indian rituals. It was a combination that seemed to work. In the 1980s, he underwent an extremely painful ceremony called the Sun Dance. At the start of the ceremony, the dancers have wooden skewers driven through the skin of their chests. Leather thongs are tied to the skewers and then attached to the top of a tall pole at the center of the dance ground. To a steady drumbeat, the dancers move in a circle while leaning back on the leather thongs until, after many hours, the skewers finally tear free. "I dance back and I throw my arms and yell and I can see the ropes and the piercing sticks like in slow motion, flying from my chest towards the grandfather's tree," Gomez told me about the experience. "And I had this incredible feeling of euphoria and strength, like I could do anything. That's when the healing takes place. That's when life changes take place."

America is a largely de-ritualized society that obviously can't just borrow from another society to heal its psychic wounds. But the spirit of community healing and empowerment that forms the basis of these ceremonies is certainly one that might be converted to a secular modern society. The shocking disconnect for veterans isn't so much that civilians don't know what they went through—it's unrealistic to expect anyone to fully understand another person's experience—but that what they went through doesn't seem relevant back home. Given the profound alienation that afflicts modern society, when combat vets say that they want to go back to war, they may be having an entirely healthy response to the perceived emptiness of modern life.

One way to change this dynamic might be to emulate the Israelis and mandate national service (with a military or combat option). We could also emulate the Nepalese and try to have communities better integrate people of different ethnic and religious groups. Finally, we could emulate many tribal societies—including the Apache—by getting rid of parades and replacing them with some form of homecoming ceremony. An almost universal component of these ceremonies is the dramatic retelling of combat experiences to the warrior's community. We could achieve that on Veterans Day by making every town and city hall in the country available to veterans who want to speak publicly about the war. The vapid phrase "I support the troops" would then mean actually showing up at your town hall every Veterans Day to hear these people out. Some vets will be angry, some will be proud, and some will be crying so hard they can't speak. But a community ceremony like that would finally return the experience of war to our entire nation, rather than just leaving it to the people who fought.

It might also begin to reassemble a society that has been spiritually cannibalizing itself for generations. We keep wondering how to save the vets, but the real question is how to save ourselves. If we do that, the vets will be fine. If we don't, it won't matter anyway.

Critical Thinking

1. In what ways has the national discussion about violence in the United States been a matter of talk without actually doing anything about it?

2. How does the Pistorius case illustrate the origins of white fear and how it has shaped the justice system's treatment of blacks in in South Africa as well in the United States?

Internet References

Harvard University Center on the Developing Child
  http://developingchild.harvard.edu/resources/inbrief-early-childhood-mental-health/

National Institute of Mental Health
  https://www.nimh.nih.gov/health/topics/post-traumatic-stress-disorder-ptsd/index.shtml

U.S. Department of Veterans Affairs
  https://www.ptsd.va.gov/public/ptsd-overview/basics/what-is-ptsd.asp

World Psychiatry
  http://onlinelibrary.wiley.com/